Migration, Mill Work, and Portuguese Communities In New England

Migration, Mill Work, and Portuguese Communities in New England

EDITED BY
CRISTIANA BASTOS, BELA FELDMAN-BIANCO,
AND MIGUEL MONIZ

Tagus Press, University of Massachusetts Dartmouth
Dartmouth, MA

Tagus Press is the publishing arm of the Center for Portuguese Studies and Culture at the University of Massachusetts Dartmouth.

Center director: Paula Celeste Gomes Noversa

Tagus Press at the University of Massachusetts Dartmouth

European Research Council
Established by the European Commission

This book is part of the Colour of Labour project, which has received funding from the European Research Council (ERC) under the European Union's Horizon 2020 Research and Innovation Programme (Advanced Grant No. 695573).

Manufactured in the United States of America

Executive Editor: Mario Pereira
Copyedited by Sharon Brinkman
Cover design by Frank Gutbrod
Designed and typeset by Jen Jackowitz

For all inquiries, please contact:
Tagus Press Center for Portuguese Studies and Culture
University of Massachusetts Dartmouth,
285 Old Westport Road,
North Dartmouth, MA 02747–2300
(508)-999-8255, fax 508-999-9272
www.umassd.edu/portuguese-studies-center

ISBN: 978-1-951470-27-2
Library of Congress control number: 2024932164

Distributed by University of Massachusetts Press

Contents

Migration, Mill Work, and Portuguese Communities in New England

INTRODUCTION TO THE VOLUME

Beyond *Two Portuguese Communities in New England*

Place, Time, Resistance, and Change

......

CRISTIANA BASTOS AND BELA FELDMAN-BIANCO

This book has multiple roots. One of them can be traced to the year 2010, when Portuguese American scholar Frank Sousa challenged Portuguese anthropologist Cristiana Bastos to critically revisit the social monograph *Two Portuguese Communities in New England*. Sousa was at the time director of the Center for Portuguese Studies and Culture at the University of Massachusetts Dartmouth; Bastos was on a visiting appointment at the Portuguese and Brazilian Studies and Anthropology Departments at Brown University and had a research interest on the 1910s–20s period; *Two Portuguese Communities* was a 1923 book that had achieved an infamous life of its own due to some of its passages, obfuscating what might be of interest in its sociographic depictions and analyses. The challenge materialized in a semester of teaching and research as Hélio and Amélia Pedroso Professor of Portuguese Studies at UMass Dartmouth in the spring of 2013, in which Bastos investigated the contexts of production and reception of *Two Portuguese Communities*. Originally a doctoral dissertation presented at Columbia University in the then embryonic discipline of sociology, the book addressed the social variables associated to one identified public health problem, that of high infant mortality among some immigrant communities; the empirical research was conducted in the Portuguese communities of industrial Fall River (Massachusetts) and rural Portsmouth (Rhode Island). As discussed in what is now chapter 1 in this volume, *Two Portuguese Communities* had plenty of state-of-the-art statistical analysis, but it also contained some racialist commentaries that infuriated many of those who identified themselves as Portuguese in New England. Bastos's interest on the topic and its potential contribution for wider comparative frameworks on the social processes of racialization led her to include a research track on industrial New England in her project *The Colour of Labour—The Racialized Lives of Migrants,* otherwise focused on conventional plantation economies.[1]

Another root for this volume comes from New England anthropologist Miguel Moniz's personal engagement with Portuguese culture, society, and language, with a special focus on the role of Portuguese working men and women in the labor movements. His interests and engagement led him to conduct fieldwork in the Azores, to achieve fluency in the Portuguese language, and to settle for years in mainland Portugal. Along the way, Moniz entered *The Colour of Labour* team to do research and outreach in the New England track. In that context he organized the memorable conference "Migration and Mill Work," held in December 2017 in Lowell, New Bedford, Dartmouth, and Fall River, in collaboration with a large network of researchers, community representatives, and institutions—Boott Cotton Mills Museum, University of Massachusetts at Lowell, University of Massachusetts Dartmouth, Ferreira-Mendes Portuguese Archives, New Bedford Whaling Museum, Casa dos Açores da Nova Inglaterra, Fall River Town Hall, and a few others. The conference combined academic sessions, in-depth debates, public talks, community testimonies, and visits to museums and heritage sites, along with formal and informal interactions. While the vibrancy of the meetings cannot be reproduced in a printed book, this volume largely draws from the papers presented at the time and the discussions that followed.

A third root of this publication comes from the expertise of Brazilian anthropologist Bela Feldman-Bianco, who, as the visiting University Professor of Portuguese Studies at Southeastern Massachusetts University (now UMass Dartmouth), conducted ethnographic research among the Portuguese in New Bedford between 1986 and 1991, updating it in 2008 while holding the Hélio and Amélia Pedroso chair. Feldman-Bianco's engagement with the communities and with their history shaped the remarkable documentary film *Saudade* (1991); her published analytical work brought forward conceptual developments on transnationalism and on the reconfigurations of empire and diasporas, and she became an author of reference in those fields. This volume would not have been possible without her careful critical reading, commentaries and interventions, besides her own chapter on more recent transformations in New Bedford.

Finally, and above all, the roots and motivations for this book can be traced to any of its contributors' trajectories of lived experience of, and research about, the Portuguese communities in New England. The collection combines revised versions of the *Migration and Mill Work* papers and other contributions with analytical, testimonial, and artistic approaches to lives in industrial New England, including fiction and poetry, historical photographs of the work at the mills, watercolors of what is left of those mills, and contemporary photographs of the working lives that persist in what were once the factory floors.

The different chapters move along substantive depictions and analyses of what it was, while identified as Portuguese in New England, to arrive, settle, endure, work, feed families, struggle, resist, succeed; to create living arrangements, homes, gardens, spaces of sociability, festivals, churches, monuments, heritage foods, businesses, academic centers; and to live in a multilayered society under the pressures for upward mobility, the racialized tensions, the politics of assimilation, the moments of ethnic revival, the labor struggles, the resurgence of prejudice, and the intersections of class, gender, race, place, and other elements of structure and of circumstance.

While our main focus is on the lives shaped by the textile mills economy, which was the main magnet for Portuguese migration to New England, it should be noted that there had been previous routes bringing Portuguese subjects to its shores. New Bedford–based whaling fleets already in the eighteenth century and all through the nineteenth century recruited crew members in the Azores and Cape Verde islands, and occasionally also in Madeira, when stopping for water and produce.[2] With the developments in whaling techniques, journeys that used to last a few weeks turned into titanic, years-long crossings of the north and south Atlantic, Pacific, and Indian oceans. It was not uncommon for some crew members, in spite of their indenture, to jump ship in distant islands, marry local, and settle there as fishermen or agriculturalists. In Hawai'i, a small community of a few hundred Portuguese whalers and sailors and their families preceded the massive arrival of about twenty thousand Madeirans and Azoreans who came as contract workers for the sugarcane fields between 1878 and 1913.[3] Many others settled in southern California. Yet the largest portion of those wandering Portuguese seamen settled in New England, where they also moved into fishing, agriculture, and other jobs, partly paving the way for those who later came from the old country to work on a variety of things, from urban crafts to construction, commerce, and, above all, the textile mills—as will be discussed throughout the chapters of this book.

By the time the Portuguese arrived in massive numbers to the mills of New England (1890s–1920s), the labor force and the mill cities were composed of multiple strata and their composition had varied throughout the decades. The pioneer experiment of Lowell had originally relied on recruiting local young women and turning them into skilled workers. The rapid growth and expansion of the industry pushed the recruitment toward wider circles, and labor became predominantly provided by overseas migrants from Europe.[4] Many of those who crossed the north Atlantic in search of a better life in the Americas found a place in the textile mills of Lowell, Manchester, Worcester, New Bedford, Pawtucket, Fall River, and others in New England, where they earned their wages by enduring a brutal regiment of long hours, extenuating repetitive gestures, deafening noise, unbreathable atmosphere of cotton particles and heightened temperatures, and multiple hazards and machine-related injuries; they occupied the lowest positions as sweepers, spoolers, doffers and spinners before they could move up in the labor hierarchies that culminated in the positions of weavers and loom fixers. The earlier contingents came from Great Britain and Northern Europe; later, they came from Ireland, Eastern Europe, Italy, French-speaking Canada, and, since the 1890s, Portugal. In Fall River, one of Donald Taft's Two Portuguese Communities, Azoreans were, in the 1920s, the basis of the textile workforce (see chaps. 1, 4, 8, 16).

The cycle of migration into New England's frantic textile economy would radically change after the Immigration Act of 1924—and the economy itself would also be relocated to the southern states. The Immigration Act established quotas that in theory were calculated as a function of the proportion of nationalities as counted in the 1890 census—a fact that would severely limit the incoming of Portuguese migrants in the following decades. But this math involved more than percentages: it contained an ideology that hierarchized nationalities, types, "races." Those racialist hierarchies were made explicit in some of the documents that preceded the Immigration Act, such as the Dillingham Commission Report (1911) and Lothrop Stoddard's *Rising Tide of Color* (1920). Eugenicism, antisemitism, racism, and white suprematism helped define who could contribute to the nation and who should be excluded. While the dividing line between those categories shifted throughout the years, there was an underlying pseudoscience of race that hierarchized every type of human, putting Europeans above Asians and Africans and ranking European types with Nordics and Anglo-Saxons above all others, while Jews, Alpines, and Southern Europeans (which included the Portuguese) stood at the bottom. Race, racialism, and racism were at work, too, in the complex, multilayered societies of early twentieth-century industrial New England.

In its own way, the mill economy echoed the mechanism of generating social differences that were "naturalized", that is, attributed to inherent features of the "nations" or "races"—a mechanism that had its radical and most violent expression in the old plantation economy.[5] When compared to the brutal, structural, plantation-related racialism and racism, or against the wider framework of the dispossession of indigenous peoples by settler colonialism, the microscale racialism of the nineteenth and twentieth centuries targeting immigrants in the U.S. mill economy almost disappears into historical insignificance. Yet at a local level it shaped the immigrants' existences in racialized, hierarchized, and stereotyped ways, with effects in perceptions, attitudes, interiorized stigma, pay scales, immigration quotas, and other material and immaterial effects.

Analytic literature on migration to the United States in the nineteenth and early twentieth centuries shows how specific groups of migrants—Jews, Italians, Irish, French Canadians—negotiated their racialized positions at entry level and eventually achieved a place among U.S. mainstream whiteness.[6] Further comparative work on the ways those groups coexisted and competed in the context of a divided labor force would be most useful to dialogue with what has already been analyzed for the late nineteenth- and twentieth-century plantation labor in the Caribbean, Pacific, and Indian Ocean sugar islands.[7] Chapters in this volume provide a basis for that comparative analysis; *Two Portuguese Communities*, the Immigration Act of 1924, and the related eugenicist and racialist literature provide a triple door of entry into the complex history of the Portuguese in New England, their specificity regarding other Portuguese-descent communities in the Americas, their articulation with other migrant and ethnicized communities—and, ultimately into the understanding of wider trends in the racialization of labor.

It should be noted, however, that the Portuguese and Portuguese-descent communities in the 1920s New England were not a consistent, homogeneous group. Many among them had attained economic prosperity, social influence, and a standard of cultural assimilation that brought them close to mainstream whiteness. Many more had just arrived and remained at the entry levels in the mills, vulnerable to the slur of "Portagee" and its pack of prejudices evoking backwardness, inferiority, acceptance of low standards of living, poor housing, low wages—in sum, they were matter-of-factly racialized and pushed away from the ideal of whiteness that at the time shaped the politics of the nation and filtered the policies of immigration.[8]

The chapters in this volume address the actual lives that existed alongside and against those stereotypes. The first section, "Deconstructing Racialist Paradigms," combines critical readings of *Two Portuguese Communities* with detailed approaches to the early twentieth-century Portuguese communities of New Bedford, Boston, and Fall River. In chapter 1, Bastos contextualizes the scientific, political, and social environment in which Donald Taft conducted his empirical research among the Portuguese in New England and the sensitive key that triggered the angry reactions to his book. In chapter 2, Rose P. Rodrigues addresses the Portuguese in New Bedford during the transition from whaling to the textile mill economy (1870–1900); using an impressive array of primary sources and original maps, she shows the role of homeowning (via family income pooling and strategic choices) in the upward mobility of the local Portuguese. In chapter 3, Graça Índias Cordeiro analyzes the representations of the Portuguese in early twentieth century greater Boston via a 1912 report on East Boston as a zone of emergence; like in New Bedford, some local Portuguese got to own property on a relatively short time. The horizon that emerges for the Portuguese in New Bedford and East Boston contrasts with the "underdog" picture reinforced in *Two Portuguese Communities.* That picture is also challenged in Chapter 4, as Paula Celeste Gomes Noversa confronts the assumptions and stereotypes of "uprootedness" applied to the immigrant communities, follows the agency of the Portuguese in Fall River at that time—from settlement patterns to involvement on labor strikes—and discusses how the Portuguese in New England confronted the racialized hierarchies that structured the involving society.

The section "Participation in Labor Movements" further dismisses prevailing stereotypes of passive backwardness of the Portuguese by analyzing their role in strikes and other crucial labor actions. In chapter 5, Philip T. Silvia critically assesses the persistent production of such stereotypes and stigmas affecting the influxes of "new" immigrants during the local cotton mills era; as each "new" contingent of immigrants began their lives in Fall River by entering the lower and unskilled echelons of the cotton mills labor force, they were recurrently stigmatized and stereotyped by older skilled trade union leaders and (later) also by the Dillingham National Commission—as happened to French Canadians who came to Fall River in large numbers in the 1870s, and later to the Portuguese, who came since the 1890s and who all quickly learned to get involved with the labor movements of their times. Yet unlike the French Canadians and other predecessors, the newer Portuguese and Polish immigrants faced the decline of the local textile industry in the 1920s which hindered them in their efforts to gain progressive social mobility. Daniel Georgianna and Roberta Hazen Aaronson, in chapter 6, push forward the analysis by addressing the famous, six-month-long strike of '28. They dissect the complexities of the power structure, the social cleavages, and the built alliances and solidarities of that historic moment in the labor movement. Again, the understanding of a supposed disengagement with the labor movements by the "new immigrants" is dismissed with facts: many who came from Portugal had previous involvement with unionism, and those who hadn't quickly learned to join the workers struggle, even if they had to rely on family gardens for survival during the long months of strike. In chapter 7, Penn Reeve further reinforces how the Portuguese were actively involved in labor organizations and acted as leading protagonists not only in the New Bedford strike of 1928 but also later at the CIO organizing of the 1930s and 1940. Like Georgianna and Aaronson, Reeve notes that despite the defeat, the long strike added to workers' achievements of the legal rights to organize, strike, and be recognized through unionism in collective bargaining. Miguel Moniz's chapter 8 completes this section with an extended discussion on the effects of the racialist typologies on the classification and positionality of the Portuguese, the pressures for assimilation, and their place and role in the labor movements. He further engages on the complexities of the racialist readings of the diversity of identifications and regional origin of the Portuguese in New England, who came from diverse backgrounds in the archipelagoes of the Azores, Cape Verde, Madeira, and mainland Portugal.

The poem "At the Portuguese Feast," by Portuguese American literary scholar Nelson Vieira, provides the transition into the next section, "Memories of Life and Work." The following chapters combine commentaries on literary expressions and direct testimonies of lives in Fall River, New Bedford, Lowell, and Providence by Portuguese or part-Portuguese-identified subjects. In chapter 10, Carmen Ramos Villar critically examines Joseph Conforti's *Another City upon a Hill* (2013), an insider's view of life in mid-twentieth-century Fall River that is also an eloquent depiction of the rise and fall of the city's industry, its class divide, ethnicized tensions, environmental hazards, and social horizons, in dialogue with the understandings of ethnicity in the context of Fall River, of wider New England, and of the nation—ultimately an example of how the Portuguese American community has always sought outlets for its voice to be heard with respect to its ethnic experience. Chapter 11, by Kady Phelps-El Mernissi, contains the direct voices of Portuguese workers in Lowell whose accounts provide insight into how ethnic districts impacted life in the city while simultaneously fostering a new group identity—an analysis that was further explored in the exhibition "From the Atlantic Islands to Lowell." Camilo Viveiros's accounts of three life stories of migration, in chapter 12, report how the aftermath of the 1957–58 Capelinhos volcanic explosion in the Azores generated a new wave of migration into New England, one that revitalized the preexisting communities. Chapter 13, with Onésimo Almeida's short story "Adriano(s)," provides an open-ended golden coda to this section, for Adriano is the very epitome of the multiple and contradictory possibilities, roles, identities, elocutions, projects, accomplishments, and shortages that one can experience while Portuguese and American in a New England town—something which Almeida, with his unmatchable and sensitive insider's knowledge, wrote about extensively, intensively, and often ironically.

The section "The Making of an Academic Field" brings us further in time and depicts in detail the emergence of the scholarly field of Portuguese studies in New England and its relationship to the communities, the universities, the donors, the politics of language, the neighboring disciplines, and other elements that contributed to its prominence. This is not composed of chapters analyzing what became a most expressive, productive, and innovative field, crossing literary, cultural, historic, and social studies, international by definition, and prone to making bridges with Brazilian and Lusophone African studies. Nor is this an inventory of its extensive production and intensive connections. Instead, this section is an exploration of the backstage conditions, actions, politics, alliances, and personal efforts that made the field possible, using the format of interviews with two key actors in the shaping of the Portuguese studies centers in New England: Nelson Vieira, for Brown, interviewed by Bastos and Feldman-Bianco (chap. 14), and Frank Sousa, for UMass Dartmouth and, later, UMass Lowell, interviewed by Feldman-Bianco (chap. 15). Both narrators provide generous accounts interweaving each one's personal experience at the confluence of Portuguese and U.S. cultures, each one's personal growth as academics and researchers, and each one's role in the making of centers of reference in Portuguese studies—along with colleagues, community involvement, savvy strategies for persuading university hierarchies, fundraising, engagement in language teaching, articulation with other fields, politics of visibility, and emancipation.

Finally, the section "The Changing Positions of Portuguese Americans" addresses the reconfigurations of the communities into the present day and adds analytic engagement to matters of gender, race, and place. In chapter 16, M. Gloria de Sá brings us back to the direct confrontation of Donald Taft's depictions of the Portuguese in New England, challenging his assumptions and providing a sound comparative analysis of women's occupational structure all through the twentieth century. Moving through the different waves of migration, and using a comparative framework, De Sá shows how factories were a gateway to economic success among Portuguese migrant women with low levels of education but were also a trap in that there was no incentive to enhance their education. Yet while Portuguese immigrant women continued to be predominantly factory workers toward the end of the twentieth century, American-born women of Portuguese descent had moved away from the century-old tradition of industrial production work and become virtually indistinguishable from their European-American counterparts in terms of occupational structure. Finally, in chapter 17, Feldman-Bianco brings us a fresh view on the late twentieth-century New Bedford Portuguese by analyzing the aftermath of the 1983 infamous case known as the "Big Dan gang rape"—with which the media reinforced negative stereotypes of the Portuguese that almost echoed the older, racialist notions of degeneration and lowliness. Feldman-Bianco places the event and its aftermath into the social history of New Bedford, contextualizing its occurrence in a period marked by Portuguese immigration renewal and a new downscaling of this city at a time when class-based politics were being replaced by identity politics.

Visualizations of mill work and the afterlives of the mills as buildings and as spaces of labor appear throughout the volume and complete our approach to the imbricate relation of migrants and mill work. Lewis Hine's photographs provide views of the cotton mill interiors and machinery and the children and youth who worked there in the early twentieth century. Filipe Leal de

Faria's watercolors capture the materiality of mill-centered landscapes while evoking some aspects of their ruination. Andrea Klimt's Fall River Portraits Project reveals the continuities and reutilizations of mill spaces in the forms of production and labor in our days. In those reinventions and emergences of life and work among what might have been regarded as ruins and rubble, we can foresee the promise of an unpredictably creative continuation for the closure of the mill economy historic cycle, the one addressed in this book through the lens of the Portuguese migrants. As always, learning about the past may empower us a little bit more to act upon the future, and thus we invite you the readers to cruise the sections and chapters, learn from them, challenge them, and continue to ask questions and search for clues, interpretations, narratives, and testimonies that help us know who we are.

Works Cited

Bastos, Cristiana. "Portuguese in the Cane: The Racialization of Labour in Hawaiian Plantations." In *Changing Societies: Legacies and Challenges,* edited by Sofia Aboim, Paulo Granjo, and Alice Ramos, 1:65–96. Lisboa: Imprensa de Ciências Sociais, 2018.

Beechert, Edward D. *Working in Hawaii: A Labor History.* Honolulu: University of Hawaii Press, 1985.

Burkholder, Zoë. "From 'Wops and Dagoes and Hunkies' to 'Caucasian': Changing Racial Discourse in American Classrooms During World War II." *History of Education Quarterly* 50 (2010): 324–58.

Dillingham, William Paul. *Dictionary of Races of Peoples—Volume 5 of Reports of the Immigration Commission.* U.S. Government Printing Office, 1911.

Eno Jr, Arthur L. *Cotton Was King: A History of Lowell, Massachusetts.* Lowell, MA: Lowell Historical Society and New Hampshire Publishing Company, 1976.

Feldman-Bianco, Bela. *Saudade* 59'. Watertown, MA: Documentary Educational Resources, 1991.

Felix, John Henry, and Peter Senecal, eds. *The Portuguese in Hawaii.* Honolulu: Centennial Edition, 1978.

Holton, Kimberly DaCosta, and Andrea Klimt, eds. *Community, Culture and the Makings of Identity. Portuguese-Americans along the Eastern Seaboard.* Dartmouth, MA: Tagus Press, 2009.

Ignatiev, Noel. *How the Irish Became White.* New York: Routledge, 1995.

Jacobson, Mathew Frye. *Whiteness of a Different Color: European Immigrants and the Alchemy of Race.* Cambridge, MA: Harvard University Press, 1998.

Jung, Moon-Kie. *Reworking Race: The Making of Hawaii's Interracial Labor Movement.* New York: Columbia University Press, 2006.

Lai, Walton Look. *Indentured Labor, Caribbean Sugar: Chinese and Indian Migrants to the British West Indies, 1838–1918.* Baltimore: Johns Hopkins University Press, 1993.

Newitt, Malyn. *Emigration and the Sea: An Alternative History of Portugal and the Portuguese.* Oxford: Oxford University Press, 2015.

Nóvoa, André, ed. "Ocean Crossings." Special issue, *Portuguese Literary and Cultural Studies* 33 (2020).

Ripley, William Z. *The Races of Europe: A Sociological Study.* London: Kegan Paul, Trench, Trübner, 1913. First published in 1899 by D. Appleton and Company (New York).

Stoddar, Lothrop. *The Rising Tide of Color: The Threat against White World-Supremacy.* New York: Charles Scribner and Sons, 1920.

Takaki, Ronald. *Pau Hana: Plantation Life and Labor in Hawaii 1835–1920.* Honolulu: University of Hawai'i Press, 1983.

Thompson, Edgar T. *The Plantation.* Columbia: University of South Carolina Press, 2010.

Taft, Donald R. *Two Portuguese Communities in New England.* New York: Longman, Green and Company, 1923; republished by Arno Press and the *New York Times,* 1967, 1969.

Teelock, Vijaya. *Bitter Sugar: Sugar and Slavery in 19th Century Mauritius.* Moka, Mauritius: Mahatma Gandhi Institute, 1998.

Vermette, David. *A Distinct Alien Race: The Untold Story of Franco-Americans.* Montréal: Baraka Books, 2018.

Warrin, Donald. *So Ends This Day: The Portuguese in American Whaling 1765–1927.* Dartmouth, MA: Center for Portuguese Studies and Culture, 2010.

Williams, Jerry. *In Pursuit of Their Dreams: A History of Azorean Immigration to the United States.* Dartmouth, MA: Tagus Press, 2007.

Notes

1. The *Colour of Labour—The Racialized Lives of Migrants* is a large-scale, multisite, multi-period, interdisciplinary project that addresses the nexuses of plantation-racialization and plantation-factory and that is funded by the European Research Council with Advanced Grant no. 695573, hosted at ICS-ULisboa. http://colour.ics.ulisboa.pt/.

2. Among an extensive literature, see Donald Warrin, *So Ends This Day: The Portuguese in American Whaling 1765–1927* (Dartmouth, MA: Center for Portuguese Studies and Culture, 2010); Jerry Williams, *In Pursuit of Their Dreams: A History of Azorean Immigration to the United States* (Dartmouth, MA: Tagus Press, 2007); Malyn Newitt, *Emigration and the Sea: An Alternative History of Portugal and the Portuguese* (Oxford: Oxford University Press, 2015); André Nóvoa, "Ocean Crossings," special issue, *Portuguese Literary and Cultural Studies,* 33 (2020). For a full immersion in the history of whaling and New Bedford's

centrality in the whale oil global economy, the New Bedford Whaling Museum provides a wealth of learning resources. For a contemporary comprehensive analytical collection on Portuguese American matters, see Kimberly DaCosta Holton and Andrea Klimt, *Community, Culture and the Makings of Identity. Portuguese-Americans along the Eastern Seaboard* (Dartmouth, MA: Tagus Press, 2009).

3. Among others, John Henry Felix and Peter Senecal, *The Portuguese in Hawaii* (Honolulu: Centennial Edition, 1978); Cristiana Bastos, "Portuguese in the Cane: The Racialization of Labour in Hawaiian Plantations," in *Changing Societies: Legacies and Challenges*, edited by Sofia Aboim, Paulo Granjo, and Alice Ramos, 1:65–96 (Lisboa: Imprensa de Ciências Sociais, 2018).

4. See Arthur L. Eno Jr, *Cotton Was King: A History of Lowell, Massachusetts* (Lowell, MA: Lowell Historical Society and New Hampshire Publishing Company, 1976). The contemporary city of Lowell offers a variety of learning resources—from the very musealization of the Boott-Mills complex, managed as a state park, to the research and community actions promoted to highlight the city's social history of work and migration.

5. For the plantation as a race-making device, see Edgar T. Thompson, *The Plantation* (Columbia: University of South Carolina Press, 2010).

6. E.g., Zoë Burkholder, "From 'Wops and Dagoes and Hunkies' to 'Caucasian': Changing Racial Discourse in American Classrooms during World War II." *History of Education Quarterly* 50 (2010): 324–58; Mathew Frye Jacobson, *Whiteness of a Different Color: European Immigrants and the Alchemy of Race* (Cambridge, MA: Harvard University Press, 1998); David Vermette, *A Distinct Alien Race: The Untold Story of Franco-Americans.* (Montréal: Baraka Books, 2018).

7. E.g., Edward D. Beechert, *Working in Hawaii: A Labor History* (Honolulu: University of Hawaii Press, 1985); Moon-Kie Jung, *Reworking Race: The Making of Hawai'i's Interracial Labor Movement* (New York: Columbia University Press, 2006); Walton Look Lai, *Indentured Labor, Caribbean Sugar: Chinese and Indian Migrants to the British West Indies, 1838–1918* (Baltimore: Johns Hopkins University Press, 1993); Ronald Takaki, *Pau Hana* (Honolulu: University of Hawaii Press, 1983); Vijaya Teelock, *Bitter Sugar: Sugar and Slavery in 19th Century Mauritius* (Moka, Mauritius: Mahatma Gandhi Institute, 1998).

8. The fact that a number of the Portuguese whalers and sailors who settled in New England were originally from Cape Verde further complicates the classificatory ambiguities for the local Portuguese: Portuguese mainlanders identify themselves as white; the Azores and Madeira were settled mostly by Portuguese mainlanders, and their descendants also see themselves as white; Cape Verde was settled by both Europeans and Africans, and the population tends to be depicted and self-depicted as "mixed," or "creole," sometimes emphasizing the distinctiveness between themselves and mainland Africans. Cape Verde would in 1975 become independent from Portugal in a temporary partnership with Guiné Bissau, which brought the islands closer to an African sphere of influence. The Azores and Madeira remained regions of Portugal. The degree to which the Cape Verdean demographics in New England influenced the perception of the Portuguese as nonwhite

is a matter of debate. The perception of the Portuguese as nonwhite is recurrent throughout the English literature, and the slurs "Portuguee," "Potagee," "Potygee," etc. are widely spread throughout the diaspora in English-speaking places—regardless of the existence of a part-African contingent among those Portuguese.

Fall River Mills

Filipe Leal de Faria

Figure 1. Fall River Mill, May 2013.

Figure 2. Fall River Mill, May 2013.

Figure 3. Fall River Mill, May 2013.

Figure 4. Fall River Mill, May 2013.

Figure 5. Fall River Mill, May 2013.

SECTION 1

Deconstructing Racialist Paradigms

CHAPTER 1

Migrants, Inequalities, and Social Research in the 1920s

The Story of *Two Portuguese Communities in New England*

......

CRISTIANA BASTOS

A Science of Society in Times of Racialism and Racism

In this chapter I address the production and the mixed reception of Donald Taft's *Two Portuguese Communities in New England,* a doctoral dissertation submitted at Columbia University in 1923 and published that same year by Longman, Green and Company in New York. The book got positive reviews in academic journals, one of them signed by no less than Robert E. Park, the central reference of the Chicago school of sociology.[1] But elsewhere the book was loathed. The Portuguese community leaders throughout southern New England responded to it with anger, claiming that the book was offensive to their nationality. They encouraged meetings to protest against the book and called for the drafting of an official note of disapproval about the way in which the Portuguese were depicted. When community associations, consuls, and other representatives scheduled a meeting to make a formal protest in March 1924, the extraordinary number of six thousand people allegedly turned up for the demonstration, forcing it to be held outside.

To understand the scale and intensity of that protest, we need to discuss the core tensions of the book, of the communities it depicted, and of the society that produced it. In this, the concept of coproduction of science and society, borrowed from science and technology studies, is useful.[2] "Science" corresponds here to the early social sciences, particularly as practiced at Columbia University at the time, in the wider context of the institutionalization of sociology and anthropology. It also stands for the racialist knowledge that hierarchized human types into complex taxonomies of color, nationality, belonging, customs, intelligence, aptitude, and other features under the category of "race."[3] "Society" stands for a tense, unequal socioeconomic system that relied on an industrial development that was mostly supported by immigrant labor. Immigrant groups entered the mills of New England in the lower positions and eventually moved into better jobs; historically, they also moved from racialized positions as nonwhite to ethnic white and, eventually, mainstream white.[4] Yet, at the very moment Taft was exploring and writing about the Portuguese communities in New England, the United States was about to regulate its borders and distinguish those groups who were allowed to move freely into the country from those who would be subject to severe restrictions through the Immigration Act of 1924. This fact provides a key to explaining the passion and number of demonstrators in New Bedford: they were highly anxious about the position allocated to them in the racial hierarchies, which provided a measure of their distance from full citizenship. And while they regarded themselves as white, Taft had candidly said that they were not.

To analyze that tension, we ought to revisit the sort of racialism—and racism—that pervaded in society and academia in the 1920s. We tend to think of those times as the coming of age of social sciences. It is a time often associated with the narratives of founders who promoted epistemological and methodological shifts: Franz Boas and students guiding anthropology through the shift from race to culture at Columbia;[5] Robert Park and fellows guiding sociology into community studies in Chicago;[6] Malinowski defining ethnographic fieldwork at the London School of Economics;[7] Marcel Mauss establishing a new paradigm for social relations with his essay on the gift.[8] But the history of anthropology and sociology is far more complex. And, at that time, even the scholars most committed to explaining the social with social and cultural variables were not immune to the racialist ideas that prevailed.

At the turn of the century, a repertoire of racial categories had been added to the old established black/white racialism. While that had gone hand-in-hand with plantation economies supported by the traffic of enslaved Africans into the Americas and had lingered afterward in inhuman actions, beliefs, and laws, the new racialism was adjusted to the demands of an industrial economy based on immigrant labor recruited from the poorer fringes of

Europe.[9] Elaborate taxonomies about European races became "science" through works like Ripley's *Races of Europe* (originally published 1899), the Dillingham Commission's *Dictionary on the Races and People of Europe* (1911), and Lorthrop Stoddar's *The Rising Tide of Color* (1920), a radical manifesto for white supremacy.[10] Although dynamic—for the groups moved along the color line when moving up in the labor hierarchies—these racialized taxonomies and hierarchies were naturalized and internalized via somatic, anthropometric, psychological, and cultural criteria affecting different groups.

In this chapter I argue that the new racialism was omnipresent and easily enmeshed in the early works of social scientists. Donald Taft's *Two Portuguese Communities in New England,* meant to be a study of the determinants of differential health patterns in migrant communities, is a good example of the contamination of social knowledge by racialism. The author explicitly aimed to address the social structures of inequality. He defined infant mortality rates as his central research problem, outlined the social variables that could account for the variation in infant mortality, and studied extensively those indexes and variables in two actual communities of Portuguese background in southern New England. Most of the time, he kept the analysis at a sociological level. But he also used Ripley's racialist literature and ended up assigning to race the same heuristic powers he ascribed to the carefully researched social variables, implying that migrants themselves—with their constitutions and their ways—were at least as responsible for their fate and their poor health as were the dreadful conditions in which they lived and worked.

Columbia's Quantitative Sociology

At the time Donald Taft was working on his dissertation at Columbia University, sociology had already gone a long way to affirm its importance as a discipline within the Faculty of Political Science. History, economics, law, and political theory had been established as independent departments in the 1890s.[11] Social science had gained independence from economics in 1904.[12] Sociology at Columbia was slow to take off, particularly when one considers that the University of Chicago had been founded in 1890 with an independent department of that discipline. At Columbia, both its president, Seth Low, and the economics professor and statistics pundit, Richmond Mayo-Smith, agreed on the importance of the discipline, which they saw as a subject "that dealt with questions of public concern," albeit with a somewhat fuzzy description of what it entailed.[13] Dean Burgess was more explicit about its contents, suggesting that sociology covered issues like ethnology, penology, charity, and poor relief, and he began requesting a chair in the discipline from 1891.[14] That same year Franklin Giddings came from Bryn Mawr, Philadelphia, where he had started his academic career in 1888 by taking Woodrow Wilson's position when he moved on to Wesleyan. Giddings temporarily replaced Mayo-Smith at Columbia during the latter's leave of absence. Giddings's position was renewed on a temporary basis until, finally, in 1894 he received the newly founded chair of sociology, thanks to negotiations conducted by Low.[15] Giddings was a charismatic, argumentative character who supervised dozens of students and explored his own original views on society in his courses and seminars—some would say in a more experimental than scholastic mode.[16] Like Durkheim across the Atlantic, Giddings was interested in what held society together and also developed his own conceptual tools.[17] His student Taft, when addressing labor organizations in his MA thesis, chose the concept of "sympathy" rather than Durkheim's "solidarity."[18]

Columbia contributed significantly to the development of sociology in the United States. Its trademark was a quantitative and statistical orientation,[19] while the Chicago school was famous for its ethnography-inspired, and inspiring, community studies,[20] and Harvard became known for the all-encompassing theories of social action and social structure produced by its sociologists.[21] Aldon Morris's recent account of the history of American sociology has highlighted the role of yet another school, mentored by W. E. B. Du Bois in Atlanta. Morris argues that academic racism was responsible for the erasure of Du Bois from the history of the discipline and that, more than being simply credited as the first black sociologist in the country, Du Bois—who had studied in Germany and developed his own original thinking—should be acknowledged as the inspiration for the Chicago school and the true ancestor of the discipline in America.[22]

Donald Taft was a long way from the influence of Du Bois and, for that matter, from the Chicago school. He adopted the positivist type of sociology practiced at the time in New York. We can speculate whether Taft had some exposure to the race/culture epistemological tensions that were at the core of the neighboring discipline of cultural anthropology and that evolved exactly at that time in Columbia around the influential Franz Boas. However, we do not know if the influence of Boas reached further than his chair at the American Museum of Natural History to inspire, formally or informally, the students of Franklin Giddings and other sociologists.[23] *Two Portuguese Communities* does not reveal the influence of the embryonic cultural anthropology growing across campus: the book is filled with references to "nation," "people," and "race" rather than "culture." It should be noted that Boas and his students pursued the potential of the concept of culture mostly among exotic indigenous societies,[24] while sociologists addressed migrants and urban communities, whether ghettoes or middletowns, in the United States.[25]

A Scientist in the Making

Although Donald Taft used the sort of proximity fieldwork that characterized ethnography and anthropological research, *Two Portuguese Communities* is a work of sociology—a discipline that was still struggling to establish itself as a science. In his 1924 article about the emergence of sociology in the United States, Albion Small referred to the discipline as "in the process of becoming."[26] Like other social disciplines, sociology demanded legitimacy, institutional space, and acknowledgment as a specific branch of knowledge that could qualify as science and have its own academic space. During that process of becoming, the social sciences "lacked stable corporate identities."[27] In the absence of a stable identification with a disciplinary status, it is understandable that Taft referred to himself somewhat nonspecifically as of "the author" or "the writer" in his dissertation.

Regardless of whether he qualified himself as a sociologist or simply as an author, Taft was an experienced scholar when he conducted the New England research. He was in his mid-thirties and had already seen some of the world. He had worked in the economy of his native Massachusetts; attended college in Massachusetts and graduate school in New York City; taught in the states of Pennsylvania, Ohio, Massachusetts, and New York; and spent years reading theory, compiling data, and formulating problems. He had been born in Worcester, Massachusetts, in 1886. Between the time he finished high school and entered college, he worked for eight years in the paper business and for the Whitney Manufacturing Company. He graduated from Clark University in 1914 and moved on to Columbia on a Bancroft scholarship. In 1915, he was granted a master's degree for his thesis, "Sympathy in Labor Organizations." The following year he remained at Columbia on another fellowship and worked toward his doctorate. He attended the sociology seminars of Frank Giddings and Alan Tenney, plus their lectures and those of Robert Chaddock,

Henry Seager, John B. Clark, James Robinson, and James Stowell.[28] Taft promoted the social sciences in other settings as well: at the Carnegie Institute of Technology in Pittsburgh, Pennsylvania (1916–17), at Ohio State University in Columbus (1917–19), at Wellesley College in Massachusetts (1919–20), and at Wells College in Aurora, New York (1920–28). He moved to the University of Illinois at Urbana-Champaign in 1928 and remained there for good, retiring in 1955.[29]

Tools for Social Analysis and Intervention

For many of the aspiring social scientists at that time, interest in a science of society coincided with an interest in intervening in its problems—be that via social reform or via social eugenics. The laboring classes lived in extreme conditions, as documented in Jacob Riis's photojournalist account of New York tenements at the turn of the century, *How the Other Half Lives*.[30] And, while there is no American equivalent to the depictions of the English working classes during their industrial revolution presented by authors like Friedrich Engels and Charles Dickens, some poignant novels like Upton Sinclair's *The Jungle*, about Lithuanians in Chicago's slaughterhouses, and Thomas Bell's *Out of This Furnace*, on Slovaks in the steel industries of Pennsylvania, provide a close approach to the harsh conditions endured by U.S. laboring immigrants at that time.[31]

Many of the sociology students worked toward the mitigation of such suffering by engaging with progressive churches and other social-oriented organizations; they aspired for reform, not necessarily for a revolution of the kind that was happening in Soviet Russia at the time. But not all of those who worked toward the scientific understanding of social inequalities dreamed of an equalitarian society. Nor were all of them ready to engage with the philosophical, sociological, and political consequences of the assumption that inequalities between humans were an effect of social constraints. Some actually endorsed the principles of white supremacy and other variations of racialist and racist worldviews. In sum, motivation for social intervention could be backed by progressive humanism or by its very opposite, as epitomized by eugenics.

It is not entirely clear which one of the tendencies appealed the most to the author of *Two Portuguese Communities*. In part he emphasized the devastating impact of harsh labor and living conditions on the health of the members of the communities, allowing for sympathy toward progressive policies that could improve their lives. But he also accepted that their lower destiny was conditioned by their own racial constitution, even while allowing the possibility that it worked as a social stigma rather than a fatality of biology. It should be noted that Taft's supervisor, Giddings, held a Spencerian attitude regarding the limitations for the improvement of the disenfranchised.[32] In fact, Eduardo Bonilla-Silva and Gianpaolo Baiocchi depict Giddings as nothing less than a racist sociologist.[33] We can speculate whether Giddings's influence pushed Taft toward racialist options, neutralizing other possible analytic choices the doctoral student might have had. With no access to Taft's field notes, diaries, chapter drafts, preliminary analyses, revisions, advisor's criticisms, or other materials that might help us go further in the analysis of his choices and constraints, we can only speculate on the matters behind and beyond the published book.

The Structure, Contents, and Social Life of the Book

Taft designed his research project around the problem of health inequalities, as represented by infant mortality rates. Statistics showed that some migrant communities had higher infant mortality rates than others. Such was the case for the Portuguese, which was why Taft chose to study two New England communities with significant populations of Portuguese migrants: Fall River, Massachusetts, and Portsmouth, Rhode Island, situated next to each other along the state line. Both sites were marked by the presence of recently arrived Portuguese islanders from the Azores. The social, cultural, and material circumstances in the two sites were, however, very different. In rural Portsmouth, the Portuguese had mostly old-stock white American families as neighbors.[34] In industrial Fall River, they coexisted with other groups of migrants who had arrived earlier to supply the labor-intensive cotton industry: French Canadians, Irish, Italians, Russians, Syrians, Poles, and so on. At the time of the research, the Azorean Portuguese were at the lower strata of the textile mill hierarchies, had low-paying jobs, and lived in the least attractive parts of town. "In Fall River they can expect but low real wages, albeit higher than those they have been accustomed," notes Taft, adding that "if they marry they must live on a very low plane and expect their wives and children to continue to work outside the home"—with little chance of advancement in the mills.[35] He also mentions that "the Portuguese are the lowest paid nationality in Fall River with the exception of the Poles."[36] As for their housing, Taft notes that "the sections of the city where most of the Portuguese live are unattractive" and that, in general, "housing conditions of mill workers in Fall River are not ideal," being unattractive, without a bath, sometimes with a toilet in the corner of the pantry separated only by a curtain, and owned by landlords who hardly ever undertook much-needed repairs. In that aspect, life in rural Portsmouth seemed easier than that of the city dwellers.[37]

Taft used the appropriate research tools to approach the subject. He talked to people, combed the historical and economic sources, used all the statistical data he could find, crunched numbers, and tested hypotheses to explain the high rates of infant mortality in those communities. He observed and evaluated their living headquarters, labor conditions, surrounding environment, nutrition patterns, and education levels. In other words, he measured, counted, mapped, and described with fair accuracy the lives in those communities. He sorted out indicators of social, economic, and environmental constraints associated with ill health, such as poor housing, low wages, extensive working schedules, illiteracy, toxic atmospheres, and the pervasiveness of tuberculosis. His research was sound: he consulted multiple sources, compiled statistics, explored possible answers, and depicted the harsh work conditions that people endured in the cotton mills of Fall River and the farms of Portsmouth. All in all, Taft performed a proficient social analysis, combining qualitative observations with the heavy statistical work that was the trademark of sociology at Columbia.[38] The resulting monograph, *Two Portuguese Communities*, was a typical academic work of the time, filled with references, sources, numeric tables, graphs, and maps.

The book was organized into seven chapters: (1) a short introduction (pp. 17–20); (2) "The Racial Composition of the Portuguese Nationality" (pp. 21–50); (3) "The Continental and Island Background" (pp. 51–87); (4) "Immigration and Distribution in the United States" (pp. 88–136); (5) "Infant Mortality of the Portuguese" (pp. 137–93); (6) "The Portuguese of Portsmouth, R.I., and Fall River, Mass." (pp. 194–342); and a final chapter (7) "Limitations and Conclusions" (pp. 343–50). The bulk of the empirical research was concentrated in chapters 5 and 6, much lengthier than the others. Chapter 5 addressed and analyzed the data on infant mortality among the Portuguese, and chapter 6 presented the detailed results of the empirical research conducted in the field and among archival resources. In these two chapters, the author emerges as a sociologist, as someone with a predominantly quantitative orientation but who does not shy away from dense and accurate descriptions and comments based on the field research he had conducted through visiting Portuguese homes and interviewing the residents with the assistance of a nurse who could speak their language.

The other chapters are thinner in size and lighter in data. In them, Taft mostly discusses the literature that provides the background to the problem and to the subject of study and presents a brief introduction to the problem, the specificities of the Portuguese nationality, and the differences between mainlanders and islanders, plus an overview of immigration to America. However, after presenting his research, Taft's final remarks are frustrating and do not explore the findings. Instead, he returns to the racialized themes of the introduction and ends with a short and deceptive set of inconclusive conclusions. Overall, there is a tension between two different analytic and interpretive directions—each of them with different political implications—in the book. In chapters 5 and 6, the author identifies social variables related to infant mortality that were along the lines of those followed by pioneers of public health and that are still valid in contemporary studies of the social determinants of health and illness today: housing and working conditions, environment, hygiene, economic status, parental education levels, and so on. But throughout the book, particularly in chapters 1, 2, and 7, Taft interweaves his analysis with fixed racial categories. In spite of his sound empirical and analytical work, he starts and ends with racialist comments, suggesting that if the Portuguese in New England exhibited health patterns that were closer to those seen in black communities than to those seen in white communities, then this was perhaps not unrelated to the fact that the Portuguese were not really white to begin with, that they were—as one of Taft's (non-Portuguese) informants claimed—"half negroes anyhow."[39] For Taft and his white interlocutors from the mill-owning classes of Fall River and from the academic world, the Portuguese were another dark migrant group who came from a dark corner of the world, just like the Irish and Italians who came before them.[40] He used the racialist authors of the moment as sources and depicted the Portuguese as nonwhite: "Not only are they Southern Europeans but, as we shall show, some of them seem to be of a semi-negroid type."[41] He made clear that this was not just the case for the "Bravas" (from Cape Verde), who had Portuguese nationality and were classified as colored in the U.S. census, but also for the "so-called white Portuguese."[42]

Taft eventually confronted the possibility of framing race as a social operator of inequalities when he questioned what the consequences of "this infusion of negro blood" would be for the Portuguese immigrants' social welfare and admitted that being perceived as "negro" could lead to being "relegated to ostracism."[43] Nonetheless, he still used race as a biological entity in spite of the evidence on social disadvantages that he collected and addressed in the analytic chapters of the book. He went to the most exquisite lengths—supported by existing bibliography and a mix of prevailing perceptions regarding the Portuguese in general and the islanders in particular—to argue that the Portuguese had a racial type with African blood. He made an exception for those from the island of Fayal in the central cluster of the Azores, who were supposedly "whiter" than the other islanders due to "special infusions of Northern European blood" via a reputedly Flemish influence.

The Fayal/São Miguel rivalry was an Azorean motif that Taft took at face value.[44] Had he been a contemporary anthropologist he might have elaborated on island rivalries and seen the people of Fayal as claiming a Flemish ticket to whiteness vis-à-vis their Mediterranean counterparts from the main island of São Miguel. But although he paid attention to this particular ideological trait among the communities, he did not explore further the contrasts between the health patterns of the São Miguel–descent Portuguese of Fall River and the Fayal-descent Portuguese of Portsmouth, as the data were hardly comparable.[45] Instead, Taft indicated an occasional appreciation of the more suitable living conditions offered in rural Portsmouth, where the Portuguese could excel in farming and interacted only with native-born Americans, as opposed to the harsh urban dwellings of Fall River, where they had to compete with many other migrants. He also referred to a microracial differentiation between islanders, as suggested by Frederic Hoffman, and indulged ambiguously with what the implications of a contrast between Micaelenses and Western islanders might be.[46] But in the end that was not the point, and it did not affect the general racialization of the Portuguese.

The ease with which Taft racialized the "so-called white Portuguese" also evokes a tradition in English literature—epitomized by Lord Byron's poetry and Richard Burton's colonial adventure narratives—that represented the Portuguese as some sort of mixed, mongrelized people. It was a perception perhaps shared by Taft and other New England white Protestants, including the Fall River millowners with whom he interacted during fieldwork. Portuguese leaders who later contested Taft's findings blamed his distorted views on the fact that he had interacted with the wrong people: local authorities and millowners who were highly prejudiced about the Portuguese.

Those racialist assumptions about the Portuguese were shared throughout the English-speaking world. Writing on the former British Caribbean, Robert Harney noted that there was an ingrained Anglophone tradition of regarding the Portuguese as nonwhite and it is likely that a sense of this was also shared by the predominantly white academics that were Taft's main audience.[47] Outside the walls of academia, however, the racial categories used in the book were challenged, precisely by those who were its subjects.

In the decades that followed the publication of *Two Portuguese Communities*, Taft shifted his interests toward other subfields of social science, such as criminology and the broad patterns of international migration.[48] We do not know if he ever returned to Fall River and Portsmouth or if he considered revisiting his data, but there was no major publication as a result if he did. The original book, however, was republished almost fifty years later, in a double reprint (1967 and 1969) within the American Immigrant Collection series.[49] This was an epic collection promoted by the *New York Times* showcasing the contributions of Afro-descendants and different European nations to the making of contemporary America. It is an ultimate irony that *Two Portuguese Communities* was chosen to stand for a community that, as we shall see, disliked it so much.

We do not have data on the impact of the 1960s editions, other than the fact that they made the book more easily accessible in the secondhand market supplied by libraries discarding dormant volumes. But we do have elements on the reception of the original 1923 edition. *Two Portuguese Communities* had positive reviews in academic journals.[50] Clifford Kirkpatrick from Brown University recommended the book enthusiastically "to social workers in contact with the Portuguese" and to all students of social science not only for its valuable material but also for its exemplary application of the scientific method.[51] He also observed that "a dominant note in the book is the unanswered question as to whether the social inadequacy is due to lack of native intelligence or to environmental causes," as converging data on the Californian Portuguese inclined him to believe in the inferior intelligence of the Portuguese.[52] Robert Park accepted easily that the Portuguese were racially admixed and that they were "a low-grade people, and one that responds very slowly to supposedly better economic and living conditions of the American environment." Yet he acknowledged that the inferiority could not be explained in racial terms: "Inferiority in physical stamina, in culture, and in living conditions seems to be less due to fundamental racial than to local and historical factors."[53] In other words, Park could detect an argument for social determinants of health and illness beneath Taft's racialist paragraphs. In summary, for the academics who read *Two Portuguese Communities,* Taft had done a great job in the scientific study of a group that was clearly seen as remote from mainstream America. The Portuguese in New England, however, had other ideas on the matter.

The Portuguese Response

Who were the Portuguese depicted by Taft, and who were the Portuguese in New England that ultimately contested his findings? For centuries, Portuguese migrants came to the shores of New England to engage in a number of activities, from whaling and fishing to cranberry picking and other farming chores, and to work in a range of environments, from the cotton mills to construction work and from smaller and larger businesses to education, music, recreation, and food industries. The Portuguese became an important component of southern New England's population, particularly in the New Bedford area.[54] They came from different regions of mainland Portugal and from the Atlantic islands of Azores, Madeira, and Cape Verde. Place of origin, time of arrival, community of residence, all contributed to distinctions, differences, and potential antagonisms among the Portuguese. Some of those rivalries continue to be played out today. Oppositions are relational, playing islands against mainland, one archipelago against another, western islands against eastern islands, and a number of other possibilities that are about the present yet use the language of an imagined place of origin.

The complex history of the islanders in particular would contribute to confusion within the United States, as officials tried to classify Portuguese migrants according to racial categories. Before the arrival of Portuguese sailors (starting in the fifteenth century) to the Azores, Madeira, and Cape Verde, none of the three archipelagoes had indigenous populations. The Azores and Madeira were settled predominantly by mainland Portuguese peoples and occasionally by Northern Europeans (reputedly Flemish and French). Some of the islands had highly stratified plantation systems, such as the main island of Madeira and São Miguel in the Azores. Throughout the nineteenth century, rampant poverty pushed large numbers of Madeirans onto Caribbean and Guianese plantations; later, both Madeirans and Azoreans were contract laborers on Hawaiian sugar plantations.[55] Toward the end of the century, many Azoreans joined the labor force in New England's mills and other places in North America.[56] The islands of Cape Verde, off the coast of Guinea, had served as a platform in the Atlantic slave trade, and its population had both European and continental African ancestry. Cape Verdeans had been crossing the Atlantic into New England as whalers and sailors since the eighteenth century. Known as Bravas after the name of one of the western Cape Verde islands, they challenged the racial and social classifications in the United States by being free African migrants and also black Portuguese. For census purposes, they counted as "colored."[57] Anthropologist Miguel Moniz suggests that such plural identifications definitely distinguished the Portuguese migrants from other southern Europeans.[58] So complex and unsettling was the matter that there is even evidence of ambiguities in census data collection at that time. The Portuguese qualified as white for official purposes, but some data collectors for the 1920 U.S. household surveys thought otherwise. Many filled the box for "race" for Portuguese households with a handwritten *O* (for "other"). This was later overwritten, presumably by a supervisor, with a *W* (for "white"; see fig. 1).

New Bedford was the one place where Portuguese from all backgrounds—mainlanders, Azoreans, Madeirans, Cape Verdeans—had settled. It was home to Portuguese whalers, sailors, tailors, mill laborers, shopkeepers, health professionals, musicians, and others. And it was there that the anti-Taft voices were most strident. Fall River was different, and Taft had chosen it as the center for his study because of the homogeneous character of the Portuguese community there: it was predominantly Azorean and composed of recently arrived laborers. The industrial development of Fall River started later than its northern counterparts of Lowell and Manchester. At the time of Taft's research, Fall River was an industrial hub with a large number of cotton mills and a wealthy class of Yankee families who owned them.[59] The cotton industry devoured human labor, and by that time it had already depleted local generations around the main industrial poles of Lowell, Massachusetts, and Manchester, New Hampshire. It had attracted English and Scottish men and women whose lives had already been affected by the rise and fall of the cotton industry of northern England.[60] These were followed by Irish workers making their way across the Atlantic and impoverished French Canadians coming down from Quebec. The vibrant economy of New England had also

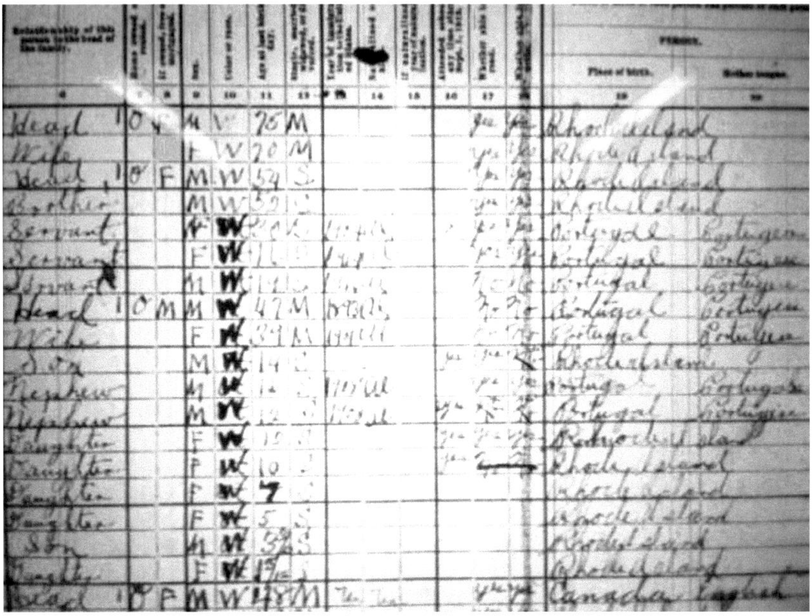

Figure 1. U.S. census. Portuguese immigrant families. Note the "race" column, with O for "other" replaced by W for 'white." Photograph of microfilm, New Bedford Public Library.

made room for Poles, Russian Jews, Syrians, Italians, and, ultimately, the Portuguese. The migrants were employed in a range of unskilled and skilled tasks as weavers, doffers, spinners, spoolers, scrubbers, sweepers, and card strippers; speeders, slubbers, warpers, beamers, and slasher tenders; and loom fixers, trimmers, and dyers, among others.[61] Mill owners and managers were not shy of employing underage children, both in some of the above positions and as table boys, bobbin boys, braiders, winder tenders, fillers, harness makers, cloth handlers, and sometimes office boys.[62] In the 1910s Lewis Hine photographed child laborers from several sectors of the economy, including from the cotton mills of Fall River. His photographs from Fall River reveal no shortage of Portuguese names among the children depicted (see fig. 2).

The waves of European migrants that fed the cotton industry in New England moved through categories of color as they moved up the ladder of the mill economy and of the social hierarchies outside the mills. Jews, Italians, Irish, and others faced a long path to whiteness, itself a dynamic entity.[63] Groups could rise in the hierarchies only when others came in to fill the lower positions. In Fall River's industrial economy in the 1920s, the Azorean

Figure 2. Working boys, some of them Portuguese, at a Fall River mill, photographed by Lewis Hine in January 1912, with the legend "Young doffer and spinner boys in Seaconnet Mill. The youngest are Manuel Perry, 111 Pitman St. John E. Mello, 229 Alden St. Manuel Louis. None of these could write their own names. The last couldn't spell the street he lives on. They spoke almost no English. Location: Fall River, MA." Collection of Lewis Wickes Hine (1874–1940), photographer, Library of Congress.

Portuguese were the late arrivals. When Taft conducted his research, they were stuck in the lower strata and appeared as a homogeneous group. The Portuguese of New Bedford would have been far more challenging to depict, to measure, and to assess due to the wide variety in their provenance, time of arrival, identifications, professions, socioeconomic class, and education.

Contested Knowledge: The Book, Its Author, and the Subjects

While applauded by academics as exemplary research and as a potential resource for social workers, *Two Portuguese Communities* was utterly disliked by the Portuguese communities in New England. The book became the target of public disputes and was loathed on the streets and in the newspapers of southern New England. Community leaders declared war on its author out of indignation at the way in which he represented the Portuguese. In New Bedford alone, on March 23, 1924, allegedly six thousand people gathered in the streets with the sole purpose of demonstrating against a book that they might not even have read but that they still found offensive to their own sense of self.

The meeting was originally supposed to be held indoors on the assumption that it would attract a restricted number of participants. However, so many people sent letters and telegrams of support for the cause, and so many people expressed their desire to participate, that the meeting was relocated to successively larger venues, until it was finally scheduled for the large headquarters of the Club Recreativo Portuguez.[64] On the day of the meeting, however, more and more people flocked into the place, forming a crowd so big that it had to move outdoors. It was most likely a typically cold March Sunday as the crowd gathered in Grove Park, by the waterfront of the city's south end. The following day's papers reported on the event. The page-wide front headline of the *A Alvorada* newspaper referred to the "big protest demonstration of the New Bedford Portuguese colony," while its subhead reported that six thousand Portuguese people came to state their protest against the insulting book by Dr. Taft: "Cerca de 6.000 Portuguezes acorrem a lavrar o seu protesto contra o livro insultuoso do Dr. Taft." Later that day, the English-language *New Bedford Evening Standard* also reported on the demonstration, albeit on the last page: "Portuguese Government asked by 6000 to answer to Dr. Taft."

Support for the demonstration came in all forms. Mrs. Simão, resident and owner of 402 Front Street, for example, offered her porch as a podium for the speakers. The prestigious philharmonic City Band began the day with the national anthems of the United States and Portugal. The crowd cheered and applauded. The consul of New Bedford, Madureira e Castro, made an inspired speech, claiming that the book had wounded and offended the Portuguese but that no insult or offense should follow in return. He declared that, as the committee in Fall River had suggested, the book should be sent to the Portuguese universities so that Portuguese academics—whom he praised very much—could respond to it word for word. Before an enthusiastic crowd, the consul read aloud the motion:

> The Portuguese of New Bedford, with no distinction of class, political affiliation or religious beliefs, gathered in Grove Park, made the deliberation of protesting against some of the statements of Professor Donald Taft in his recently published book "Two Portuguese Communities in New England," in which the Portuguese race is considered inferior and ignorant—something that not only hurts an entire race that proved itself along the

> centuries as a race of brave conquerors, explorers, navigators, colonizers, as is proved by the great republic of Brazil, by the vast colonies that make for the third empire in the world, a race to whom the civilization owes so much, which has an epopee that is pair to Eneida and Ramayana, translated in 23 languages, now creates dissent among the races that constitute the great nation of the United States of America; [and also of] sending to the Portuguese government via its representative in Washington the will of New Bedford that our government takes the task of responding to the book in question, either as suggested by the colony of Fall River or other, to raise up the morals amongst the Portuguese and give moral support to the targeted communities of Fall River and Portsmouth.[65]

The next speaker, Dr. Pitta, was met with cheers as he took issue with the book's approach to fertility, mortality, the care of the mothers and, of course, the racialist criteria. After a digression on the shades of the Latin (Mediterranean) peoples, their exposure to the sun, and their sailing habits, he questioned Taft's generalizations as being the private opinions of a restricted number of Fall Riverites who were prejudiced against the Portuguese. He added that a memo of protest should also be addressed to Columbia University because of this shameful work written by one of its associates.

Many other speakers followed, praising the Portuguese community and invoking the most valued aspects of Portuguese identity—literary epics, pioneering sea discoveries, and the glorious distant past. Last to speak was the teacher of Portuguese in Fall River, Mr. Sá Couto, who had been actively involved in writing newspaper articles against Taft. He called for a scientific reply from Portuguese academics that could unequivocally dismiss Taft's statements. The crowd cheered the speakers, using the opportunity to boost their national pride. Yet throughout most of the speeches and actions there was a racialist credo that they all shared with the very book they loathed. The speakers did not reject racism and racial thinking; they just demanded a better place in the hierarchy it implied.

That this usually low-profile community gathered to rally against one academic dissertation is remarkable. Understanding the reasons why they did so leads us to the complexities they lived in southeastern New England at the time: the class structure they were part of, their inner divisions, the prejudice they were subject to, the harsh labor and living conditions endured by many of them, the high infant mortality rates that captured the sociological interest of Donald Taft in the first place, and their struggles over color, race, class, and access to citizenship. While the protests reveal disputes over representation and authorship—in some ways anticipating debates that would flourish in academia in the late twentieth century—the passion that carried them suggests that Taft's use of racial categories triggered social anxieties that were particularly intense at that political moment. Indeed, the United States was about to produce the Immigration Act, which established quotas according to a hierarchy of nations—one in which the Portuguese had a fragile position.

Disputes over Representation

Two Portuguese Communities stirred the ground and angered the communities, who demanded to know who was that sociologist who spoke of them and got it all wrong. More than half a century later, anthropologists engaged in a wave of self-criticism regarding the limitations and authoritarian character of ethnographic (or sociological) writing; the very notion of representing other peoples via ethnography had been anchored on the social and geographical distance between the author and the subject, itself an echo of a past world of empires that created "natives," "races," and "cultures."[66] But the 1924 New Bedford demonstration against Taft was not just an outburst about who is entitled to speak for whom, who can represent and be represented in narratives and in sciences. It was above all about clashing understandings regarding the place of the Portuguese in the racial hierarchies of that place and time, a problem of no little importance at that troubled moment in border governance and immigration law. They wanted to make sure they were not left out.

In other words, New Bedford's anti-Taft demonstration was not solely the dismissal of a product of knowledge by subjects of that knowledge who happened to know otherwise. The passionate response of the communities revealed the intensity of New England's social fractures at that moment and the enmeshment of the pseudoscience of race in the political debates regarding immigration. As one analyst pointed out years later, Taft's book "reflects the pseudo-scientific racism of the times to a point that verges on the pornographic."[67] The book turned out to be the ultimate catalyst for the public expression of the feelings of a community on edge.

To summarize, race was a very sensitive issue for the Portuguese in New England. It was not simply that their classification in an unwanted position in the racial hierarchies of the day was like adding insult to the injuries endured in the past and present.[68] It also threatened their future as migrant communities. What followed, thus, was not an antiracist demonstration, but a racialized display of the Portuguese as a worthy "race" that deserved a better place in the symbolic hierarchies that permeated their lives and shaped their collective predicament. The speakers at the demonstration referred to the Portuguese in New England collectively, but they were far from being a homogeneous community. Some of them had settled in the circles of mainstream whiteness, or so they thought, and some hadn't, or so claimed Taft. Had the book been titled "Two Azorean Communities," perhaps the demonstration would not have taken place.[69] It was not the Azorean mill workers from Fall River or the farmhands from Portsmouth who spoke out at the demonstration, but the most literate of their representatives—consuls, teachers, journalists—most of whom came from mainland Portugal. It was not just the people from Fall River and Portsmouth, not just the recently arrived Azoreans who worked in the worst paid jobs who were affected by Taft's depiction of them; all Portuguese were, including the white-collar leaders who took up the microphone and spoke out. And while they rejected Taft's comments, they did not reject his hierarchized understanding of a society that cultivated white supremacy; they just disagreed with the place assigned to the Portuguese nationality.

At the time, there was no incipient articulation of what became later the lusotropicalist claims regarding the color blindness of the Portuguese and their multiracial, pluricontinental nation, which euphemized a late empire.[70] The offended Portuguese spoke of their nationality using raw imperial signs and evoked a mythical epic past. Nor was there any antiracist, pancontinental drive for solidarity; the repertory of the disenfranchised was meagre, and the bonds between the different groups in the community were volatile.

The community's demand for an official response from Portuguese scientists would never be met. Perhaps the impressionistic and laudatory monograph about the Portuguese of New England written a few years later by Boston's Portuguese consul Eduardo Carvalho was thought of as a reply to Taft, but it in no way matched Taft's solid empirical research.[71] In years to come, the identity struggles of the Portuguese in New England persisted and took many forms.[72]

Final Remarks

Two Portuguese Communities did not make it into the canon of early works of American sociology, nor did its author enter the pantheon of pioneering social scientists, in spite of the laudatory comments on his work by sociology's tsar Robert Ezra Park. We can speculate whether the crude and racialist passages that marked the beginning and end of the book condemned it to obsolescence in the very academic settings of which it was a product, as times changed, and the social sciences moved away from racialism. Interestingly, however, it was precisely its crude and racist component that gave the book a parallel life—albeit an infamous one. Even today, the book figures in scholarship on the Portuguese in America more for its offensive elements than for its knowledge about past communities.[73]

We could also speculate on what other life the book might have had if it had been solely composed of the analytic chapters 5 and 6, with a minimalist introduction on the capacities and limitations of quantitative sociological analysis. It might have turned into a reference for the history of those communities, or it might have led to further sociological studies on a fairly invisible migrant group. Either way, *Two Portuguese Communities* had a complex life, achieved a second edition, and every now and then gets renewed attention. From today's perspective, it is worth revisiting the book for the tension it leaves open. On the one hand, there is an accomplished effort to identify social variables, sound statistical work around them, and a sophisticated formulation of social hypotheses that could account for the problem of high infant mortality. On the other hand, there is an upfront adoption of race as biology, as fate, and as explanation for ill health.

That tension opens two meaningful avenues for analysis. By reading Taft's description of the working and housing conditions of the migrants and adding to them other sources of local history, we can enumerate a variety of hazardous factors that influenced their ill health: toxic work environments (e.g., in the production of the cotton print calicoes that Fall River was so famous for), toxic living quarters with still waters and other vehicles for infection, mothers' inability to maintain regular breastfeeding due to long working hours, difficulties in communication in a new social and cultural setting, the breaking of community structures and support, and so on. In spite of the racialist introduction and conclusion, the descriptive chapters provide enough good material for us to get to know the materiality of life and health problems in the communities in the 1920s.

The other reason to revisit this obscure book is the one used in the present article: *Two Portuguese Communities* offers a magnified historical parallel to contemporary trends of reinscription of race in the health sciences.[74] *Two Portuguese Communities* is particularly revealing of how society and knowledge coproduce each other in given circumstances. At that time and place, racialism and immigration control were coproduced in ways that become more distinctively clear when we look back at them from today. Even Taft—a well-equipped social scientist who pointed out all the reasons for ill health among migrant communities—did not prevent his book from letting racialism in, bringing to his own book the widespread hostility of the communities.

Acknowledgments

A version of this chapter was originally published as an article in the journal *History and Anthropology*, which kindly consented to its reproduction with minimal changes. Preliminary research was conducted during the author's appointment as the Hélio and Amélia Pedroso Endowed Chair of Portuguese Studies at the University of Massachusetts Dartmouth, Massachusetts, in spring 2013. I thank Frank Sousa for the invitation, and challenge, to explore, as an anthropologist, Taft's accounts of the early twentieth-century Portuguese communities in Fall River and Portsmouth. I thank my colleagues at the Center for Portuguese Studies and Culture at UMass Dartmouth for their warm support and for the chance to present a preliminary analysis of the data. Familiarity with New England communities was built over the years with a series of appointments as FLAD Visiting Professor at the Portuguese and Brazilian Studies Department at Brown University in Providence, Rhode Island. I thank Onésimo Almeida and colleagues for many rich discussions and the ongoing learning experience, recently revived in discussions with Miguel Moniz. The Workshop on Global Health and Science and Technology Studies jointly organized by Maastricht University and the University of Oxford in November 2013 allowed me to go further in the analysis. I very much thank Nora Engel, Salla Sariolla, and Patricia Kingori for their invitation, support, and excellent comments, and I also extend thanks to the workshop participants for the rich debates. A visiting position and fellowship at the Research Group Twentieth Century Histories of Knowledge about Human Variation at the Max Planck Institute for the History of Science in Berlin, October 2015, helped consolidate the research and expand the reference literature. I thank Veronika Lipphardt and Samüel Coghe for the invitation and the wonderful researchers who discussed my paper and provided feedback. Further discussions on the data—particularly with Virginia Dominguez—at the Society for the Anthropology of North America meetings in New York City, April 2015, expanded the scope of analysis. I also presented advanced versions of the current chapter at Brown University (with cosponsorship of the Departments of Anthropology and Portuguese and Brazilian Studies) and at the Saab-Pedroso Center for Portuguese Studies at the University of Massachusetts at Lowell, both in November 2015. I thank the organizers and the audience for the wonderful questions and debates. In April 2016, I had the privilege of being part of the workshop Racial Conceptions in the Twentieth Century: Comparisons, Connections and Circulations in the Portuguese-Speaking Global South, organized by Warwick Anderson, Ricardo Roque, and Ricardo Ventura Santos in Rio de Janeiro. I thank the organizers and the participants, particularly Pamila Gupta, Peter Wade, and Sarah Walsh, for their great comments. All through the process I had the privilege of being helped by excellent librarians in superb collections: the Ferreira-Mendes Portuguese Archives at UMass Dartmouth, New Bedford Public Library, Fall River Historical Society, New Bedford Whaling Museum, Rockefeller Library at Brown, the Rare Books and Manuscripts Library at Columbia, the Silva and Baiocchi Max Planck Institute for the History of Science Library and its famous interlibrary loan system, and my own Institute of Social Sciences at the University of Lisbon, whose library, inspiration, and support over the years have been invaluable. The research involved in the making of this article influenced the final format of the proposal "The Colour of Labour—the Racialized Lives of Migrants," which was awarded a European Research Council Advanced Grant (ERC-2015-AdG 695573) in 2016. The analysis was finalized in the context of that project. A word of thanks for the comments to the prefinal version by the careful reader Kay Celtel plus the members of the project "The Colour of Labour" Rita Kantu, Colette Le Petitcorps, Marta Macedo, Nicholas Miller, André Nóvoa, and Irene Peano.

Funding

This work was supported by the Hélio and Amélia Pedroso Endowed Chair of Portuguese Studies (University of Massachusetts Dartmouth, 2013) and by the European Research Council Advanced Grant "The Colour of Labour—the Racialized Lives of Migrants" (grant number ERC-2015-AdG-695573, 2016–21).

Works Cited

Almeida, Onésimo T. *O Peso do Hífen. Ensaios sobre a experiência luso-americana.* Lisboa: Imprensa das Ciências Sociais, 2010.

Almeida, Onésimo T. *Tales from the Tenth Island.* Seagull: Faoileán, 2006.

Bastos, Cristiana. "Intersections of Empire, Post-Empire, and Diaspora: De-Imperializing Lusophone Studies." *Journal of Lusophone Studies* 5 (2020): 27–54.

Bastos, Cristiana. "Portuguese in the Cane: The Racialization of Labour in Hawaiian Plantations. In *Changing Societies: Legacies and Challenges,* edited by Sofia Aboim, Paolo Granjo, and Alice Ramos, 1:65–96. Lisboa: Imprensa de Ciências Sociais, 2018.

Bell, Thomas. *Out of This Furnace.* Boston: Little, Brown and Company, 1941.

Benedict, Ruth. *Patterns of Culture.* New York: Houghton Mifflin, 1934.

Boas, Franz. *Race, Language, and Culture.* New York: Macmillan, 1940.

Bonilla-Silva, Eduardo, and Gianpaolo Baiocchi. "Anything but Racism: How Sociologists Limit the Signification of Racism." In *Handbook of Sociology of Racial and Ethnic Relations,* edited by Hernan Vera and Joe R. Feagin, 79–100. New York: Springer, 2007.

Burkholder, Zoë. "From 'Wops and Dagoes and Hunkies' to 'Caucasian': Changing Racial Discourse in American Classrooms during World War II." *History of Education Quarterly* 50 (2010): 324–58.

Camic, Charles. "Three Departments in Search of a Discipline: Localism and Interdisciplinary Interaction in American Sociology, 1890–1940." *Social Research* 62 (1995): 1003–33.

Camic, Charles, and Yu Xie. "The Statistical Turn in American Social Science: Columbia University, 1890 to 1915." *American Sociological Review* 59 (1994): 773–805.

Carvalho, Eduardo. *Os Portugueses na Nova Inglaterra.* Rio de Janeiro: A Leitura Colonial, 1931.

Conforti, Joseph A. *Another City upon a Hill: A New England Memoir.* Dartmouth, MA: Tagus Press, 2013.

Cordeiro, Graça I., and Frederic Vidal. "Entre o gueto e a cidade: perspectivas cruzadas da 'colónia' portuguesa na região de Boston no início do século XX." *Actas do Congresso Português de Sociologia* 2012. http://historico.aps.pt/vii_congresso/papers/finais/PAP1534_ed.pdf

De Sá, M. Gloria, and David Borges. "Context or Culture: Portuguese-Americans and Social Mobility." In *Community, Culture and the Makings of Identity: Portuguese-Americans along the Eastern Seaboard,* edited by Kimberly DaCosta Holton and Andrea Klimt, 265–90. Dartmouth, MA: Tagus Press, 2009.

Dickens, Charles. *Hard Times.* Serialized in *Household Worlds,* 1854.

Dillingham, William Paul. *Dictionary of Races of Peoples—Volume 5 of Reports of the Immigration Commission.* U.S. Government Printing Office, 1911.

Du Bois, W. E. B. *The Souls of Black Folk.* Chicago: A. M. McClurg, 1903.

Dunwell, Steve. *The Run of the Mill.* Boston: D. Godine, 1978.

Durkheim, Emile. *De la Division du Travail Social.* Paris: Presses Universitaires de France, 1968.

Duster, Troy. "A Post-Genomic Surprise. The Molecular Reinscription of Race in Science, Law and Medicine." *British Journal of Sociology* 66 (2015): 1–27

El-Haj, Nadia Abu. "The Genetic Reinscription of Race." *Annual Review of Anthropology* 36 (2007): 283–300

Engels, Friedrich. *The Condition of the Working Class in England.* London: Allen & Unwin, 1845.

Eno Jr, Arthur L. *Cotton Was King: A History of Lowell, Massachusetts.* Lowell, MA: Lowell Historical Society and New Hampshire Publishing Company, 1976.

Feldman-Bianco, Bela. "Multiple Layers of Time and Space: The Construction of Class, Ethnicity and Nationalism among Portuguese Immigrants." In *Community, Culture and the Makings of Identity: Portuguese-Americans along the Eastern Seaboard,* edited by Kimberly DaCosta Holton and Andrea Klimt, 51–94. Dartmouth, MA: Tagus Press, 2009.

Felix, Charles Reis. *Through a Portagee Gate.* North Dartmouth, MA: Tagus Press, 2004.

Frazier, E. Franklin. *The Negro Family in Chicago.* Chicago: University of Chicago Press, 1932.

Freyre, Gilberto. *Aventura e Rotina.* Rio de Janeiro: Jose Olympio, 1953.

Fullwiley, Duana. "Race, Genes, Power." *British Journal of Sociology* 66 (2015): 36–45.

Giddings, Franklin H. *The Elements of Sociology.* New York: Macmillan, 1901.

Giddings, Franklin H. *The Principles of Sociology.* New York: Macmillan, 1896.

Giddings, Franklin H. *The Theory of Socialization.* New York: Macmillan, 1897.

Gillin, John Lewis. "Masters of Social Science: Franklin Henry Giddings." *Social Forces* 5 (1926): 197–214.

Grant, Madison. *The Passing of a Great Race: The Racial Basis of European History.* New ed. New York: Charles Scribner's Sons, 1916.

Hagendijk, Rob. "Sense and Sensibility: Science, Society, and Politics as Co-production." In *Science and Democracy: Making Knowledge and Making Power in the Biosciences and Beyond,* edited by Stephen Hilgartner, Clark Miller, and Rob Hagendijk, 220–38. New York: Routledge, 2015.

Halter, Marilyn. *Between Race and Ethnicity: Cape Verdean American Immigrants, 1860–1965.* Urbana: University of Illinois Press, 1993.

Harney, Robert F. "'Portygees and Other Caucasians': Portuguese Migrants and the Racialism of the English Speaking World." In *Portuguese Migration in Global Perspective,* edited by David Higg, 113–35. Toronto: Multicultural Society of Ontario, 1990.

Hoffman, Frederic. "The Portuguese Population in the United States." *Publications of the American Statistical Association* 6 (1899): 327–36.

Holton, Kimberly DaCosta, and Andrea Klimt, eds. *Community, Culture and the Makings of Identity: Portuguese-Americans along the Eastern Seaboard.* Dartmouth, MA: Tagus Press, 2009.

Hullet Jr, Edward J. "Donald Reed Taft, 1866–1970." *American Sociologist* 6 (1971): 185–86.

Ignatiev, Noel. *How the Irish Became White.* New York: Routledge, 1995.

Jacobson, Mathew Frye. *Whiteness of a Different Color: European Immigrants and the Alchemy of Race.* Cambridge, MA: Harvard University Press, 1998.

Jasanoff, Sheila, ed. *States of Knowledge: The Co-production of Science and the Social Order.* New York: Routledge, 2004.

Kirkpatrick, Clifford. "Review: *Two Portuguese Communities in New England* by Donald R. Taft." *Journal of Social Forces* 2 (1924): 450–51.

Kuper, Adam. *Anthropology and Anthropologists.* 2nd ed. London: Routledge, 1983.

Leal, João. *Azorean Identity in Brazil and the United States: Arguments about History, Culture, and Transnational Connections.* Dartmouth, MA: Tagus Press, 2011.

Leal, João. "Travelling Rituals. Azorean Holy Ghost Festivals in Southeastern New England." In *Community, Culture and the Makings of Identity: Portuguese-Americans along the Eastern Seaboard*, edited by Kimberly DaCosta Holton and Andrea Klimt, 127–44. Dartmouth, MA: Tagus Press, 2009.

Lynd, Robert S., and Helen M. Lynd. *Middletown: A Study in Contemporary American Culture.* New York: Harcourt, Brace, and Company, 1929.

Marcus, George, and Michael Fischer. *Anthropology as Cultural Critique.* Chicago: University of Chicago Press, 1986.

Mauss, Marcel. "Essai sur le don: Forme et raison de l'échange dans les sociétés archaïques (1902–1903)" *Année Sociologique* (1923–24), republished in *Sociologie et Anthropologie.* Paris: Les Presses Universitaires de France, 1968.

McCabe, Marsha, and Joseph D. Thomas, eds. *Portuguese Spinner: An American Story.* New Bedford: Spinner Publications, 1998.

Mead, Margaret. *Coming of Age in Samoa.* New York: Morrow, 1928

Merton, Robert K. "Social Structure and Anomie." *American Sociological Review* 3 (1938): 672–82.

Merton, Robert K. *Social Theory and Social Structure.* New York: Simon and Schuster, 1968.

Moniz, Miguel. "The Shadow Minority: An Ethnohistory of Portuguese and Lusophone Racial and Ethnic Identity in New England." In *Community, Culture and the Makings of Identity: Portuguese-Americans along the Eastern Seaboard*, edited by Kimberly DaCosta Holton and Andrea Klimt, 409–30. Dartmouth, MA: Tagus Press, 2009.

Morris, Aldon. *The Scholar Denied: W.E.B. Du Bois and the Birth of Modern Sociology.* Berkeley: University of California Press, 2015.

Northcott, Clarence H. "The Sociological Theories of Franklin H. Giddings." *American Journal of Sociology* 24 (1918): 1–23.

Painter, Nell Irvin. *The History of White People.* New York: Norton, 2010.

Pap, Leo. *The Portuguese-Americans.* Boston: Twayne Publishers, 1981.

Park, Robert E. "Review: *Two Portuguese Communities in New England,* by Donald R. Taft." *American Journal of Sociology* 31 (1925): 272.

Park, Robert E., Ernest Burgess, and Roderick McKenzie. *The City.* Chicago: University of Chicago Press, 1925.

Parsons, Talcott. *The Structure of Social Action.* New York: McGraw-Hill, 1937.

Riis, Jacob. *How the Other Half Lives: Studies among the Tenements of New York.* New York: Scribner's, 1890.

Ripley, William Z. *The Races of Europe: A Sociological Study.* London: Kegan Paul, Trench, Trübner, 1913.

Roediger, David R. *The Wages of Whiteness: Race and the Making of the American Working Class.* London: Verso, 1991.

Rogers, Francis. *Americans of Portuguese Descent: A Lesson of Differentiation.* Beverly Hills: Sage Publications, 1974.

Shenton, Herbert N. "The Giddings Sociology." *Social Forces* 11 (1932): 137–39.

Sinclair, Upton. *The Jungle.* New York: Doubleday, 1906.

Small, Albion W. "Some Contributions to the History of Sociology: The Emergence of Sociology in the United States." *American Journal of Sociology* 30 (1924): 310–36.

Stocking Jr., George W. *Race, Culture, and Evolution: Essays in the History of Anthropology.* New York: Free Press, 1968.

Stoddar, Lothrop. *The Rising Tide of Color: The Threat against White World-Supremacy.* New York: Charles Scribner and Sons, 1920.

Taft, Donald R. *Criminology.* New York: Macmillan, 1942.

Taft, Donald R. *Human Migration: A Study of International Movements.* New York: Ronald Press, 1936.

Taft, Donald R. "Sympathy in Labor Organizations." MA thesis, Columbia University, 1915. Rare Books and Manuscripts Collection.

Taft, Donald R. *Two Portuguese Communities in New England.* New York: Longman, Green and Company, 1923; republished by Arno Press and the *New York Times,* 1967, 1969.

Taft, Donald R., and Richard Robbins. *International Migrations: The Immigrant in the Modern World.* New York: Ronald Press, 1955.

Thomas, William Isaac, and Florian Znaniecki. *The Polish Peasant in Europe and America: Monograph of an Immigrant Group.* Boston: Gorham Press, 1918.

Wallace, Robert W. "Starting a Department and Getting It under Way: Sociology at Columbia University, 1891–1914." *Minerva* 30 (1992): 497–512.

Wätjen, Hermann. "Review: *Two Portuguese Communities in New England* by Donald R. Taft." *Journal of Institutional and Theoretical Economics* 80 (1925): 380–81.

Williams, Jerry. *In Pursuit of Their Dreams: A History of Azorean Immigration to the United States.* Dartmouth, MA: Tagus Press, 2007.

Wirth, Louis. *The Ghetto.* Chicago: University of Chicago Press, 1928.

Notes

1. Robert Park, "Review: Two Portuguese Communities in New England, by Donald R. Taft." *American Journal of Sociology* 31 (1925): 272.

2. Sheila Jasanoff, ed., *States of Knowledge* (New York: Routledge, 2004); Rob Hagendijk, "Sense and Sensibility: Science, Society, and Politics as Co-production," in *Science and Democracy*, ed. Stephen Hilgartner, Clark Miller, and Rob Hagendijk, 220–38 (New York: Routledge, 2005).

3. William Ripley, *The Races of Europe: A Sociological Study* (London: Kegan Paul, Trench, Trübner, 1913); William Dillingham, *Dictionary of Races of Peoples—Volume 5 of Reports of the Immigration Commission* (U.S. Government Printing Office, 1911); Madison Grant, *The Passing of a Great Race: The Racial Basis of European History* (New York: Scribner, 1916); Lothrop Stoddar, *The Rising Tide of Color: The Threat against White World-Supremacy* (New York: Charles Scribner and Sons, 1920).

4. David Roediger, *The Wages of Whiteness: Race and the Making of the American Working Class* (London: Verso, 1991); Noel Ignatiev, *How the Irish Became White* (New York: Routledge, 1995); Zoë Burkholder, "From 'Wops and Dagoes and Hunkies' to 'Caucasian': Changing Racial Discourse in American Classrooms during World War II," *History of Education Quarterly* 50 (2010): 324–58; Mathew Frye Jacobson, *Whiteness of a Different Color: European Immigrants and the Alchemy of Race* (Cambridge, MA: Harvard University Press, 1998); David Vermette, *A Distinct Alien Race: The Untold Story of Franco-Americans* (Montréal: Baraka Books, 2018).

5. The departure from racial or other biological and psychological explanations for social facts was a goal shared by the different social disciplines seeking epistemological autonomy and academic maturity in the early twentieth century; and the prospect of using "culture" instead of "race" to account for differences between human groups was the keystone of cultural anthropology since its early days in North America, having its most visible expressions in the nurture versus nature debates. Among the cultural anthropologists of Columbia, see, e.g., Ruth Benedict, *Patterns of Culture* (New York: Houghton Mifflin, 1934); Franz Boas, *Race, Language, and Culture* (New York: Macmillan, 1940); George Stocking Jr., *Race, Culture, and Evolution* (New York: Free Press, 1968).

6. Robert Park, Ernest Burgess, and Roderick McKenzie, *The City* (Chicago: University of Chicago Press, 1925); Louis Wirth, *The Ghetto* (Chicago: University of Chicago Press, 1928).

7. Adam Kuper, *Anthropology and Anthropologists,* 2nd ed (London: Routledge, 1983).

8. Marcel Mauss, "Essai sur le don: Forme et raison de l'échange dans les sociétés archaïques (1902–1903)," *Année Sociologique* (1923–24).

9. Jacobson, *Whiteness of a Different Color.*

10. See note 3.

11. Robert Wallace, "Starting a Department and Getting It Under Way: Sociology at Columbia University, 1891–1914," *Minerva* 30 (1992): 497.

12. Wallace, "Starting a Department," 506.

13. Wallace, "Starting a Department," 500.

14. Wallace, "Starting a Department," 498.

15. John Gillin, "Masters of Social Science,": Franklin Henry Giddings," *Social Forces* 5 (1926): 201; Wallace, "Starting a Department," 502.

16. Giddings's correspondence and personal papers, kept at Columbia Rare Books and Manuscripts Library, reveal an active, engaged, and hard-working professor and researcher who supervised dozens of students at the same time as he taught his courses and led his seminars, while also promoting empirical research and publishing. Some of the papers suggest that his classes were exciting and passionate but occasionally lost structure and focus as the speaker elaborated freely on new ideas rather than reciting established knowledge. See Clarence Northcott, "The Sociological Theories of Franklin H. Giddings," *American Journal of Sociology* 24 (1918): 1–23, and Herbert Shenton, "The Giddings Sociology," *Social Forces* 11 (1932): 137–39. Scholars who later analyzed the development of sociology in the United States suggested that Giddings was known for anti-Semitic remarks, which could have been behind his uneasy relationship with Seligman at Columbia (Wallace, "Starting a Department"); others describe him as the epitome of racist sociology (Eduard Bonilla-Silva and Gianpaolo Baiocchi, "Anything but Racism: How Sociologists Limit the Signification of Racism,") in *Handbook of Sociology of Racial and Ethnic Relations*, ed. Hernan Vera and Joe R. Feagin (New York: Springer, 2007), 82.

17. Franklin Giddings, *The Principles of Sociology* (New York: Macmillan, 1896); *The Theory of Socialization* (New York: Macmillan, 1897); *The Elements of Sociology* (New York: Macmillan, 1901).

18. Émile Durkheim, *De la Division du Travail Social* (Paris: Les Presses Universitaires de France, 1968). Donald Taft, "Sympathy in Labor Organizations," MA thesis, Columbia University, 1915.

19. Charles Camic, "Three Departments in Search of a Discipline: Localism and Interdisciplinary Interaction in American Sociology, 1890–1940," *Social Research* 62 (1995): 1003–33; Charles Camic and Yu Xie, "The Statistical Turn in American Social Science: Columbia University, 1890 to 1915," *American Sociological Review* 59 (1994): 773–805.

20. Park et al., *The City*; Wirth, *The Ghetto*; Franklin Frazier, *The Negro Family in Chicago* (Chicago: University of Chicago Press, 1932).

21. Talcott Parsons, *The Structure of Social Action* (New York: McGraw-Hill, 1937); Robert Merton, "Social Structure and Anomie," *American Sociological Review* 3 (1938): 672–82; *Social Theory and Social Structure* (New York: Simon and Schuster, 1968).

22. W. E. B. Du Bois, *The Souls of Black Folk* (Chicago: A. M. McClurg, 1903); Aldon Morris, *The Scholar Denied: W.E.B. Du Bois and the Birth of Modern Sociology* (Berkeley: University of California Press, 2015).

23. Brazilian scholar Gilberto Freyre, who was at the time an MA student at Columbia, claimed that Boas's classes were hard to follow but that the master interacted profusely with students and informal audiences in coffee shops and bars around campus. Interview given by Freyre to Elide Rugai Bastos in the 1980s. I am thankful to Elide Rugai Bastos for sharing with me this information and insight in August 2015.

24. E.g., Margaret Mead, *Coming of Age in Samoa* (New York: Morrow, 1928).

25. Wirth, *The Ghetto*; Frazier, *The Negro Family in Chicago*; William Thomas and Florian Znaniecki, *The Polish Peasant in Europe and America* (Boston: Gorham Press, 1918); Robert Lynd and Helen Lynd, *Middletown: A Study in Contemporary American Culture* (New York: Harcourt, Brace, and Company, 1929).

26. Albion Small, "Some Contributions to the History of Sociology. Section XIX. The Emergence of Sociology in the United States," *American Journal of Sociology* 30 (1924): 323.

27. Camic, *Three Departments*, 1010

28. Taft, *Two Portuguese Communities*, 359.

29. After retiring he would take visiting professor positions in different places, maintaining a base in Illinois until his death in 1970. He had become a specialist on criminology and international migrations. He also worked at length on a book on the sociology of international conflict that aimed to be a major theoretical contribution, but the outcome was never satisfactory enough to be sent out for publication. See Edward Jullet Jr., "Donald Reed Taft, 1866–1970," *American Sociologist* 6 (1971): 186.

30. Jacob Riis, *How the Other Half Lives: Studies among the Tenements of New York* (New York: Scribner's, 1890).

31. Friedrich Engels, *The Condition of the Working Class in England* (London: Allen & Unwin, 1845); Charles Dickens, *Hard Times*, serialized in *Household Worlds* (1854); Upton Sinclair, *The Jungle* (New York: Doubleday, 1906); Thomas Bell, *Out of This Furnace* (Boston: Little, Brown and Company, 1941).

32. Gillin, Masters of Social Science, 204.

33. Bonilla-Silva and Baiocchi, "Anything but Racism," 82.

34. Taft, *Two Portuguese Communities*, 207

35. Taft, *Two Portuguese Communities*, 247

36. Taft, *Two Portuguese Communities*, 254; see also Marsha McCabe and Joseph Thomas, *Portuguese Spinner: An American Story* (New Bedford: Spinner Publications, 1998); Jerry Williams, *In Pursuit of Their Dreams: A History of Azorean Immigration to the United States* (Dartmouth, MA: Tagus Press, 2007); Gloria De Sá and David Borges, "Context or Culture: Portuguese-Americans and Social Mobility," in *Community, Culture and the Makings*

of Identity: Portuguese-Americans along the Eastern Seaboard, ed. Kimberly DaCosta Holton and Andrea Klimt, 265–90 (Dartmouth, MA: Tagus Press, 2009).

37. Taft, *Two Portuguese Communities,* 225, 227.

38. Camic and Xie, "The Statistical Turn."

39. Taft, *Two Portuguese Communities,* 139.

40. Sicilians and other southern Europeans were classified at the bottom of the hierarchy. Jacobson narrates a telling episode from the same period: a black man who was accused of the crime of interracial sex ended up being acquitted as it was proved that the women in question was Sicilian; thus they were not from different "races." Jacobson, *Whiteness of a Different Color,* 4.

41. Taft, *Two Portuguese Communities,* 18.

42. Taft, *Two Portuguese Communities,* 18.

43. Taft, *Two Portuguese Communities,* 18.

44. A few short periods of residence in southern New England made me aware of this tension. When in 2013 I engaged in the project of revisiting Taft's monograph, I had two different invitations for local TV programs and both interviewers raised the (unsupported) issue that Taft would have favored the residents of Portsmouth over those of Fall River on a racialist basis.

45. Taft, *Two Portuguese Communities,* 287.

46. Frederic Hoffman, "The Portuguese Population in the United States," *Publications of the American Statistical Association* 6 (1899): 327–36; Taft, *Two Portuguese Communities,* 303.

47. Robert Harney, "'Portygees and Other Caucasians': Portuguese Migrants and the Racialism of the English Speaking World," in *Portuguese Migration in Global Perspective,* ed. David Higg, 113–35 (Toronto: Multicultural Society of Ontario, 1990). At the time Taft graduated from Columbia, comments and jokes with explicit racist contents were a common presence in the literature that circulated on campus. Alumni reunions at commencement ceremonies featured costume parties and parades, which might include anything from orientalist phantasies to uniformed prisoners to the Ku-Klux-Klan burning a straw dummy. Reported as enjoyable, funny moments of recreation and celebration in terms that are shocking to contemporary readers, those parades reveal much of where the students and alumni of those years stood. I am thankful to the Rare Books and Manuscripts collection of Columbia University for giving me access to the university's yearbooks and other relevant documents.

48. Donald Taft, *Human Migration: A Study of International Movements* (New York: Ronald Press, 1936); *Criminology* (New York: Macmillan, 1942); Donald Taft and Richard Robbins. *International Migrations: The Immigrant in the Modern World* (New York: Ronald Press, 1955).

49. Donald Taft, *Two Portuguese Communities in New England* (New York: Arno Press and the *New York Times,* 1967, 1969).

50. Clifford Kirkpatrick, "Review: Two Portuguese Communities in New England by Donald R. Taft," *Journal of Social Forces* 2 (1924): 450–51; Herman Wätjen, "Review: Two

Portuguese Communities in New England by Donald R. Taft," *Journal of Institutional and Theoretical Economics* 80 (1925): 380–81; Park, "Review."

51. Kirkpatrick, "Review," 451.

52. Kirkpatrick, "Review," 450

53. Park, "Review," 272.

54. Eduardo Carvalho, *Os Portugueses na Nova Inglaterra* (Rio de Janeiro: A Leitura Colonial, 1931); Francis Rogers, *Americans of Portuguese Descent: A Lesson of Differentiation* (Beverly Hills: Sage Publications, 1974); Leo Pap, *The Portuguese-Americans* (Boston: Twayne Publishers, 1981); Onésimo Almeida, *Tales from the Tenth Island* (Seagull: Faoileán, 2006); João Leal, "Travelling Rituals. Azorean Holy Ghost Festivals in Southeastern New England," in *Community, Culture and the Makings of Identity*, 127–44; *Azorean Identity in Brazil and the United States* (Dartmouth, MA: Tagus Press, 2011); De Sá and Borges, "Context or Culture"; Bela Feldman-Bianco, "Multiple Layers of Time and Space: The Construction of Class, Ethnicity and Nationalism among Portuguese Immigrants," in *Community, Culture and the Makings of Identity*, 51–94.

55. Harney, "Portygees"; Williams, *In Pursuit of Their Dreams*; Cristiana Bastos, "Portuguese in the Cane: The Racialization of Labour in Hawaiian Plantations," in *Changing Societies: Legacies and Challenges*, ed. Sofia Aboim, Paulo Granjo, and Alice Ramos, 65–96 (Lisboa, Imprensa de Ciências Sociais, 2018); "Intersections of Empire, Post-Empire, and Diaspora: De-Imperializing Lusophone Studies," *Journal of Lusophone Studies* 5 (2020): 27–54.

56. Holton and Klimt, *Community, Culture and the Makings of Identity*.

57. Marilyn Halter, *Between Race and Ethnicity: Cape Verdean American Immigrants, 1860–1965* (Urbana: University of Illinois Press, 1993).

58. Miguel Moniz, "The Shadow Minority: An Ethnohistory of Portuguese and Lusophone Racial and Ethnic Identity in New England," in *Community, Culture and the Makings of Identity*, 415.

59. Joseph Conforti, *Another City upon a Hill* (Dartmouth, MA: Tagus Press, 2013).

60. Steve Dunwell, *The Run of the Mill* (Boston: D. Godine, 1978); Arthur Eno Jr, *Cotton Was King: A History of Lowell, Massachusetts* (Lowell, MA: Lowell Historical Society and New Hampshire Publishing Company, 1976).

61. Taft, *Two Portuguese Communities*, 212, 214, 253.

62. Taft, *Two Portuguese Communities*, 232.

63. Roediger, *The Wages of Whiteness*; Ignatiev, *How the Irish Became White*; Jacobson, *Whiteness of a Different Color*; Burkholder, "From 'Wops and Dagoes and Hunkies' to 'Caucasian'"; Nell Painter, *The History of White People* (New York: Norton, 2010).

64. Data gathered from the collections of the Ferreira-Mendes Portuguese Archives at the University of Massachusetts Dartmouth, the New Bedford Public Library, and the New Bedford Whaling Museum Library.

65. *A Alvorada*, March 24, 1924.

66. George Marcus and Michael Fischer, eds., *Anthropology as Cultural Critique* (Chicago: University of Chicago Press, 1986).

67. Harney, "Portygees," 123.

68. Charles Felix, *Through a Portagee Gate* (Dartmouth, MA: Tagus Press, 2004); Conforti, *Another City*.

69. For this point I am thankful to the discussion on a talk at Casa dos Açores da Nova Inglaterra (New England House of Azores) in 2013, hosted by its president Nélia Alves.

70. That ideology would be developed by Freyre after touring the Portuguese colonies in Africa and was later adopted by the Portuguese government as a way to embellish the colonial governance; the core idea was that the Portuguese were more prone to inhabit the tropics, less racist than other Europeans, and more suited to having friendly and amenable relationships with peoples around the world. The mantra of the inexistence of racism among the Portuguese was so thoroughly diffused that many Portuguese people continue to swear by it. Gilberto Freyre, *Aventura e Rotina* (Rio de Janeiro: Jose Olympio, 1953).

71. Carvalho, *Os Portugueses na Nova Inglaterra;* Graça Cordeiro and Frédéric Vidal, "Entre o gueto e a cidade: perspectivas cruzadas da 'colónia' portuguesa na região de Boston no início do século XX," *Actas do Congresso Português de Sociologia*, 2012

72. Onésimo Almeida, *O Peso do Hífen. Ensaios sobre a experiência luso-americana* (Lisboa: Imprensa das Ciências Sociais, 2010); De Sá and Borges, "Context or Culture"; Feldman-Bianco, "Multiple Layers of Time and Space"; Moniz, "The Shadow Minority."

73. Harney, "Portygees"; Moniz, "The Shadow Minority"; Almeida, *O Peso do Hífen.*

74. Nadia Abu El-Haj, "The Genetic Reinscription of Race," *Annual Review of Anthropology* 36 (2007): 283–300; Troy Duster, "A Post-Genomic Surprise. The Molecular Reinscription of Race in Science, Law and Medicine," *British Journal of Sociology* 66 (2015): 1–27; Duana Fullwiley, "Race, Genes, Power," *British Journal of Sociology* 66 (2015): 36–45.

CHAPTER 2

Place Matters

The Portuguese Community in 1900 New Bedford, Massachusetts

••••••

ROSE P. RODRIGUES

The narrative of Portuguese immigration to the United States is not one story.[1] It is made up of many stories, which are part of historical time. A multilayered narrative comes engraved with each place of settlement. It is possible to discuss the "Portuguese experience" in very broad terms; however, the richness of migrants' journeys is far more distinct. For the people who have left their homeland, the search for a place to build a life, even temporarily, is unquestionably shaped by multiple factors. Douglas S. Massey argues for the need to "build a comprehensive model of international migration."[2] The conditions that migrants walk away from, or walk into, individual and familial motivations for moving, labor demands in destination places, human capital of migrants, and government policies are interconnected in complex ways.[3] These migration features have shaped and continue to shape Portuguese communities, with differing outcomes, including the Portuguese who made their way to New Bedford, Massachusetts, in the latter part of the nineteenth century. They initially arrived aboard whaling vessels as largely illiterate "ordinary seamen." With the decline of the whaling industry, the Portuguese moved into the manufacturing sector of the economy, predominantly within the textile mills, where they were clustered in the lowest-paying jobs along with many of their children. Occupational mobility of the Portuguese (group, career and intergenerational) was minimal between 1870 and 1900, but property mobility (homeownership) was made possible largely through "family income"[4] and was very significant when compared to previous migrant groups who settled in New Bedford.

The degree to which any migrant group is perceived as "having made it" (or not) in a specific place during a specific historical period is subject to quite different measurements and interpretations. For example, social scientists have a long tradition of relying on multiple measures to assess achievement (i.e., success) including labor force participation, income, wealth, occupational prestige, educational attainment, and political participation. Homeownership patterns as a measure of "buying into the American Dream" have received less attention. Government documents and reports often compare economic mobility rates within the migrant population and between migrant groups and the native-born population. In addition, historical documents, biographies, and news accounts often lead to valuable paths for exploring how migrants are perceived and treated in multiple settings. The discussions brought about from the sources referred to above, on migration as a group, have derived clashing narratives on the constructs of accomplishment and identity.

Similar to the experiences of many people who leave their place of origin, nineteenth- century Portuguese immigrants in New Bedford, Massachusetts, were economically, politically, and socially shaped by place—birthplace, place of destination, workplace, and residential place. Whaling vessels, textile mills, and three-decker houses are each physical/geographical spaces and places embedded with multiple levels of meaning. In addition, it is important to note that the Portuguese were not merely victims within the social arrangements constructed by the holders of economic, cultural, and social capital. A description of their journey requires explanations that combine structural forces as well as agency, context as well as culture, socially constructed identities as well as self-identities.

Following a brief discussion of New Bedford's transition from whaling to textile manufacturing in the latter part of the nineteenth century, this chapter provides a descriptive analysis focusing on the following three narratives: (1) Portuguese migration to the city, (2) Portuguese occupational status from 1870 to 1900 combined with property acquisition, and (3) Portuguese mill workers in 1900. These narratives are related in several aspects. Migration theory and occupational mobility theory help explain these relationships. In addition, some of the social patterns highlighted in this discussion are supported by digital maps. It can be argued that mapping "space" does not fully explain the meaning and value of "place."[5] However, some scholars view spatial analysis via maps and an understanding of "place" as not mutually exclusive.[6] The maps created for this research project bridge both of these perspectives by not only delineating the specific location but also by rendering a base for exploring and elucidating the Portuguese experience in late nineteenth-century New Bedford, Massachusetts.

Methodology

The following discussion on the New Bedford Portuguese relies extensively, albeit not exclusively, on data compiled by the author from the Population Schedules of the Ninth (1870), the Tenth (1880), and the Twelfth (1900) Census of the United States.[7] Undercounting and statistical errors need to be recognized in these primary sources, although a page-by-page examination of the manuscripts yielded 1,528 individual Portuguese households (i.e., 1528 household heads) in 1900.[8] A separate file was created for each boarder (n = 344 cases) and each nonfamily employee from the household head (n = 64 cases). It can be reasonably argued that almost two thousand cases are sufficient for constructing a profile of the Portuguese at the turn of the twentieth century. In addition, when spouses, children, and extended family members living in the household are added to the count, this study captured a total of 4,586 individuals out of the 4,802 aggregate figure.

Upon discussing the constraints of relying on aggregate statistical data to analyze historical social phenomena, Kurt Schlichting, Peter Tuckel, and Richard Maisel argue that Geographical Information System technology in combination with manuscript census data allows research to be conducted at a significantly smaller geographical level (e.g., neighborhood or street) and "information can include large numbers of individual-level, historic census data."[9] Following Schlichting et al.'s method, mapping the data discussed in this chapter first required building an historical Geographical Information System map of New Bedford by creating a 1900 digitized street map.[10] This process involved comparing a 2010 digital street map of New Bedford with paper maps of the city included in the *Atlas of the City of New Bedford, Massachusetts 1911*,[11] deleting streets that did not exist in 1900 and adding streets that existed in 1900 but were eventually eliminated. The next step involved attaching address ranges to every street segment in the city. Each street address of New Bedford Portuguese residents listed in the U.S. Bureau of the Census Population Schedules of 1900 was then matched against the street segment file—the process of geocoding. The address records show up as points on digital maps. In addition to plotting the residential location of the Portuguese, individual-level data attached to each record were mapped by Jonathan Delgado and the author.[12]

From Whaling to Weaving in Late Nineteenth-Century New Bedford

New Bedford faced dramatic social and economic changes during the last three decades of the nineteenth century as the whaling industry declined, and textile mills and other manufacturing enterprises proliferated, causing a large number of immigrants to move in and out of the city. Daniel Ricketson, Zepheniah W. Pease, and Joseph R. Anthony tell the story of whaling owners who were predominantly native born of English ancestry and who for many generations inhabited the city, acquiring the top social, political, and economic positions.[13] Samuel Eliot Morison describes the enthusiasm of these early capitalists: they "went out after oil with a spirit and perseverance that made their town within six years the first whaling port of North America."[14] With reference to their character, he states that "they were as tight-fisted, cruel, and ruthless a set of exploiters as you can find in American history, these oil kings of New Bedford."[15]

Surnames such as Russell, Rotch, Howland, Tabor, Wing, Bourne, Knowles, Swift, Morgan, and Grinnell were synonymous with the industry. All were sole owners of whaleships and owned stock in other whaling vessels. Whaling reached its peak in capital, vessels, and tonnage in 1857. During that year New Bedford's fleet of 329 ships and whaling outfits was worth more than $12 million and required ten thousand seamen.[16] Morison describes this period as a "golden age for owners" and that "the whaling vessel *Lagoda,* belonging to Jonathan Bourne and others, netted them an average of ninety-eight per cent for each of the six voyages she made between 1841 and 1860."[17] During the Civil War years, "the Lagoda netted her owners 219 and 363 percent profit."[18]

Much has been written about the decline of the whaling industry. The works of Reginald B. Hegarty and Everett Allen highlight the following contributing factors:[19] (1) the discovery of petroleum in 1859; (2) the capture and destruction of whaling vessels during the Civil War; and (3) the loss of twenty-plus New Bedford vessels during the 1871 Arctic Disaster. But the decline of whaling did not drive these prominent men out of the city, although they were reluctant at first to invest in mills. Henry Beetle Hough argues that the wealthy whaling merchants at first "clung to the oily tradition of the city, and scorned factories."[20] Hough notes that Joseph Grinnell, who established New Bedford's original mill in 1847, was the first of these merchants in what eventually would be a long line of investors who would transfer their capital to manufacturing, most heavily to the production of textiles, causing New Bedford to grow to be the third largest textile city in the country by 1900.[21] Those who had become wealthy from whale oil were now sitting on the boards of directors of countless mills. Seymour L. Wolfbein meticulously describes the intertwined relationships between the executive committee of the cotton mills and the banks.[22]

By 1892, thirteen mills had been established.[23] Compared to 11 percent in 1870, almost a third (i.e., 32%) of the city's male labor force toiled as mill operatives in 1900.[24] At the turn of the century, the Yankee presence could clearly still be felt in New Bedford, but an abundance of migrants had made their way to the city. The foreign-born population swelled to 41 percent by 1900.[25] Following the English, the next wave of immigration brought the Irish and French Canadians. Along with the growth in textile manufacturing, the Portuguese population also increased to almost one-fifth of the foreign-born population by 1900 (i.e., 19%).

Portuguese Immigration

The first wave of Portuguese immigrants in New Bedford claimed the Azores, Cape Verde, and Madeira Island as their homelands. Massey argues in his comprehensive framework that "structural forces in sending societies" and "structural forces in receiving nations" are two features of international migration.[26] Theories built on the first feature highlight populations fleeing from their living conditions and seeking a better life. Theories emphasizing the second feature focus on the demand for migrant workers, including active recruitment.[27] The evidence on Portuguese migration to New Bedford strongly supports both of these theoretical perspectives. Francis M. Rogers points out that Cape Verdean droughts and the scarcity of Madeiran plowable land explain Portuguese migration.[28] Jerry Williams reports that the 1850s were the beginning of extensive migration from the Azores due to crop failure—potato rot struck first, and then a deadly fungus to the grape vines.[29] These disasters were followed by a decline in the citrus crop in the 1880s. Williams also highlights universal conscription as a factor contributing to migration. The islanders migrated as a survival strategy, but the argument that migrants leave their place of origin because of active recruitment by host countries, which are frequently in demand for cheap labor, needs to be accounted for in this case. The Portuguese were actively recruited by Yankee captains to fill out a skeletal crew aboard a whaler that would leave New Bedford for what would be frequently a two-year journey. Supplies, including fresh fruits and vegetables, would also be picked up from the Atlantic islands. The Portuguese islanders' fishing background was considered an advantage along with other personal characteristics. An 1870 labor bulletin stresses their boat management skills from early childhood and elaborates on the frugality of Portuguese seamen and their proclivity for saving money:

> *It must not be supposed that these Western Island Portuguese who so largely aid to man the most of our whale ships, are as seamen mere makeshifts, for want of better material. On the contrary, they constitute, in the main, the best part of the crews trained to the management of the boats from early childhood, they need to serve no apprenticeship as to that material part of the business, while the fact that their pay is dependent on their success, appealing to their shrewd, acquisitive habits of mind, induces them to be wide awake and keen-sighted when on the lookout for whales and eager and persevering in the pursuit of them.*
>
> *But it is far different with the Portuguese. Brought up, through dire necessity, in habits of severe economy; early taught the value of money, and how to keep it when acquired, these men, as a class, are as provident as they are shrewd. They are not imposed on by "outfitters," to any great extent, and they desire little or no "liberty money," in the ports they may visit; and of the money deposited in the savings banks by the seamen from our whaling ships, nine-tenths is the savings of the Portuguese.*[30]

These stereotyped views about the Portuguese seamen are mirrored in the words of George Brown Goode,[31] assistant secretary of the Smithsonian, who describes the Azorean fishermen in New England as "industrious and daring," adding that they made good cooks and stewards.[32] Nevertheless, he notes that they were "looked down upon and avoided by the native population, but this is apparently the result of race prejudice, for they are honest and unobtrusive."[33]

A discussion on the lay system appears frequently in the expansive body of whaling literature. According to Elmo Paul Hohman,[34] earnings consisted of a fractional share, known as a lay, of the total net profits of a voyage. Captains typically came away with 1/8th to 1/16th of the profits; mates, boat steerers and coopers received lays ranging from 1/20th to 1/100th.[35] These lays are in marked contrast to what a seaman earned—1/160th of the proceeds, with stewards and cooks garnering even less, 1/100th and 1/140th, respectively.[36] In *So Ends This Day: The Portuguese in American Whaling 1765–1927,* Donald Warrin writes at length about the Portuguese who actually held the position of captain and he lists invaluable detailed information about American whaling regions, Portuguese masters, and the voyages they commanded.[37] Performing some rather simple calculations of the data on these lists leads to several striking findings. First, approximately one-third of all whaling voyages between 1754 and 1927 (i.e., 5,146 out of a grand total of 15,795 voyages) departed from New Bedford. Second, out of all the captains of these voyages, only 85 were Portuguese/Portuguese American masters, 57 of which were captains of vessels that departed from New Bedford over the course of 103 years (between 1824 and 1927). Third, of these New Bedford masters, 31 percent began their voyages after 1880—long after the peak of the whaling industry. Despite their long history with the sea, the overwhelming majority of Portuguese whalemen were "ordinary seamen" who at best could only hope to become boat steerers and possibly a third mate. Of course, the occupation of seaman was not exclusively a Portuguese domain, but data compiled from the 1870, 1880, and 1900 population schedules strongly indicate that the Portuguese were overrepresented in this low-paying position. In 1870, 56 percent of the employed Portuguese residing in the city worked as seamen, compared to only 10 percent of the total labor force.[38] In the following decade, the Portuguese were overrepresented as seamen by seven times.[39] The figures for 1900 indicate an overall rapid decline of New Bedford males in whaling, but the Portuguese still remained in this occupation for longer than the general population.[40]

The overrepresentation of Portuguese on whaling crews had a striking impact on their future lives with regard to occupational mobility. Being an "ordinary seaman" on a New Bedford whaling vessel proved to be a "trap" job for most of the Portuguese. Warrin states that "the poverty of the Portuguese islanders [crewmen], their lack of education, and even their religion added to their being discriminated against."[41] He attributes their low level of education and high rates of illiteracy to the negligence of the islanders by Lisbon and the Catholic Church's emphasis on educating the elite and priests. The lack of education of the nineteenth-century Portuguese became to a large degree a barrier for high-paying positions on the whaling vessels. However, placing irons on crewmen for speaking Portuguese during voyages and physically isolating Cape Verdeans on vessels echo ethnic/racial animosity.[42] The Portuguese seamen were lauded for their industriousness but faced sanctions for their perceived cultural and racial inferiority.

As whaling was replaced by textile manufacturing, the Portuguese found their way into the mills, again finding themselves predominantly in the lowest-paying positions. The industries had changed, but the captains of these industries did not. There was also little movement for the Portuguese immigrants. For them, this economic transition resulted from a horizontal shift in the lowest-paying whaling positions to the unskilled positions within the textile mills; the unskilled nonmill workers became for the most part "common laborers."

Portuguese males between 1870 and 1900 were mainly located in unskilled occupational positions (see fig. 1). As a group, they experienced some degree of upward mobility, usually into semiskilled occupations, with a small percentage into higher-paying skilled manual jobs; but any movement toward nonmanual labor classifications was negligible. The lowest-status occupations (e.g., common laborers) in New Bedford during these years were disproportionately Portuguese.[43] Generally speaking, foreigners were not as occupationally successful as the native born, although the Portuguese were even underrepresented in skilled manual occupations to a greater extent, even compared to other immigrant groups residing in the city.[44] Tracing patterns of career and intergenerational occupational mobility during this thirty-year period clearly paints the same picture.[45] Gains were modest from one generation to the next, downward mobility existed for some during their own lifetime, and most strikingly, occupational hierarchical arrangements remained intact.

A Portrait of the New Bedford Portuguese in 1900[46]

New Bedford was spatially segregated in 1900—90 percent of foreigners lived in Wards 1 and 6; the Portuguese resided predominantly in Wards 5 and 6 in the South End of the city. Much can be learned about Portuguese everyday life

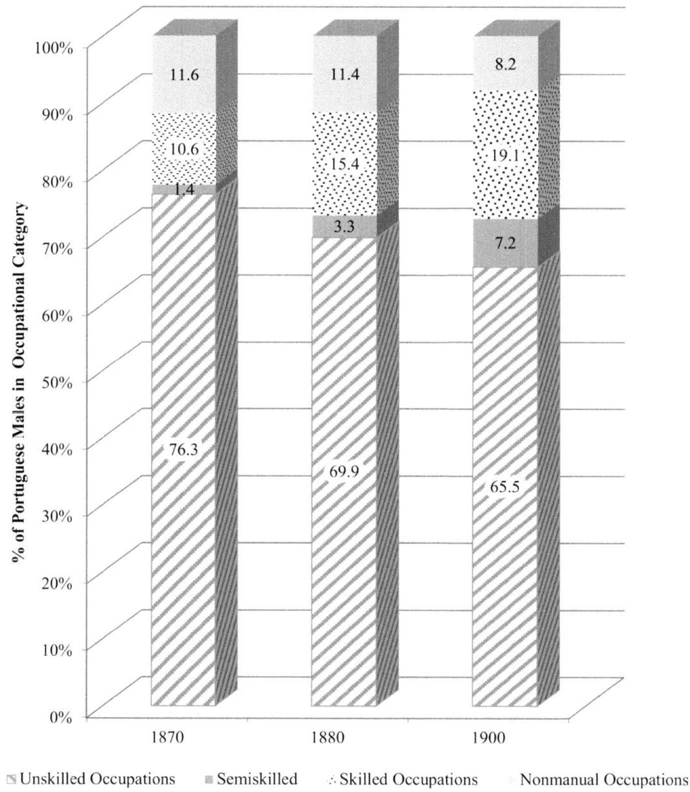

Figure 1. Occupational group mobility of New Bedford Portuguese: 1870–1900.

at the turn of the century by looking at the geographic location of the Portuguese in 1900 New Bedford (see fig. 2). The clustering of Portuguese in the South End made it relatively easy to walk to work at one of the many factories that dotted the area. Residential proximity to one another reinforced the connections within biological extended families and helped to create new relationships with those perceived as having a similar background. The Portuguese neighborhoods were close enough to the Acushnet River so that one would pass small family-owned grocery stores on the way. Portuguese Catholics could walk to the first St. John the Baptist Catholic Church located at the intersection of Wing and Fifth Streets—not only a place that provided pastoral services and religious instruction to children but a place through which a sense of community was built by fostering bonds between individuals who saw themselves as Portuguese (in all its complexity) and by creating social networks.[47]

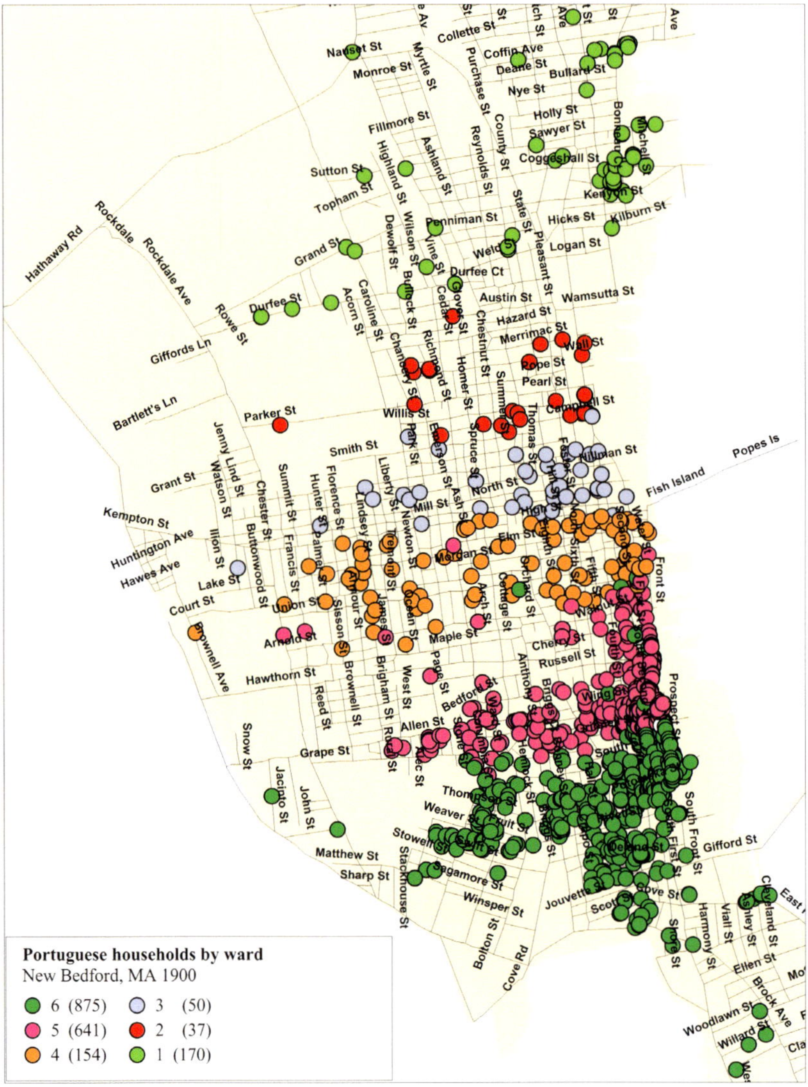

Figure 2. Residence of Portuguese households in 1900 New Bedford, Massachusetts.

Slightly over 50 percent of the Portuguese living in New Bedford in 1900 had arrived during the previous decade, an additional one-third migrated during the 1880s, and a low percentage arrived prior to 1870 (death and outmigration account for this figure). By 1900, not quite 10 percent of Portuguese household heads were native-born, yet it is important to keep in mind that when children are taken into account, this figure significantly increases. The data on citizenship in the population schedules are somewhat spotty. The best estimate that can be selected from the 1900 census information is that 16.5 percent of the cases in this study were listed as having citizenship (i.e., were naturalized).

With regard to race, 93 percent of the Portuguese population in New Bedford were enumerated in the 1900 census as white and the remainder as black. It was common practice for census takers to fill in the race section on the sheet based on the enumerator's own perceptions of household members. The Azoreans, Madeirans, and continental Portuguese were marked with a *W* in the population schedules; the residents who cited Cape Verde as their birthplace were identified as *B*. It is critical to note that the names of racial categories in census enumeration and what groups fit into each category vary historically and geographically. In other words, census categorizations of race are not static. The Portuguese in the United States have been identified as "white," "nonwhite," "black," and "other," and even their placement within any census category in a given year varied by region of the country. Relying on the perspective that race is a social construct, Michael Omi and Howard Winant argue that the U.S. census "variation both reflects and in turn shapes racial understanding and dynamics."[48] According to Omi and Winant, defining racial categories is "an intensely political process"[49] and "the census's racial classification reflects prevailing conceptions of race."[50] Although census enumerators in 1900 New Bedford wrote *W* on the census sheets next to the surnames of Azoreans, Madeirans, and continentals, was "whiteness" officially granted to these specific groups of Portuguese migrants because there were darker-skinned Portuguese, the Cape Verdeans, residing in the city during the same historical era who could be placed by the enumerators in the black category? A comprehensive analysis of the complex dynamics in the emergence of racial and ethnic identities of migrants in general and the Portuguese specifically are beyond the scope of this chapter; nevertheless it is crucial to highlight an important point. According to Miguel Moniz, "articulations of social identity among Lusophone migrants emerged through a relational and co-dependent social process that made the existence of a 'white' Portuguese category dependent upon the existence of a 'black' Portuguese category and vice-versa."[51]

The compiled 1900 New Bedford census data also offer an essential glimpse of family structure. Out of all the case files in this study, 73 percent were married, 8 percent were widowed, and the remaining 19 percent were single. Not surprisingly, the majority of the boarders were in this last category. Almost one-third of households had no living children; this figure is correlated with the relatively young age of the more recent immigrants. Out of the households with children, 16 percent had one child, 14 percent had two, 12 percent had three, 15 percent had families of four or five children, and an additional 8 percent fell within the category of six to eight children.

The census population schedules make it possible to analyze the occupational hierarchy of a place and the specific status of segments of the population within that arrangement. At the turn of the twentieth century, two-thirds of the Portuguese earned wages that were among the lowest in the city. They toiled as mill workers (42%), common laborers (27%), and seamen (8%). One-fifth occupied skilled manual positions, mainly as artisans (63% of the skilled) and as higher wage earners in the textile industry (30% of the skilled). Manual skilled labor positions in the mills accounted for 6 percent of all Portuguese labor.

Where one ended up in this hierarchy appears to be, at least in part, a function of time residing in the United States and age. The Portuguese who managed to enter nonmanual occupations (i.e., professions, proprietors, clerk/sales) had migrated prior to 1880. By contrast, over half of the unskilled manual workers arrived between 1890 and 1900.

Where did the Portuguese of these varying occupational statuses live? It appears next door to one another (see fig. 3). Although there is a robust body of literature devoted to the discussion of residential segregation by race, ethnicity, and social class in the United States, much territory has yet to be explored. If one were Portuguese, you resided in the South End, but there are multiple stories and questions embedded in this map. For example, occupation status is only one measure of social class, although ownership of property also needs to be considered. William Clark highlights this point in his extensive analysis of upward mobility trends among recent immigrants to the United States.[52] As opposed to their slight occupational mobility during the last three decades of the 1900s, the city's Portuguese made notable advances in the acquisition of property. It can reasonably be argued that purchasing a house was proof to oneself, to one's neighbors in the South End of New Bedford and to one's relatives back home, that indeed success had been achieved.[53] In 1900, 31 percent of all Portuguese families were homeowners. In contrast, only 27 percent of all household heads in Bristol County, Massachusetts, were owners.[54]

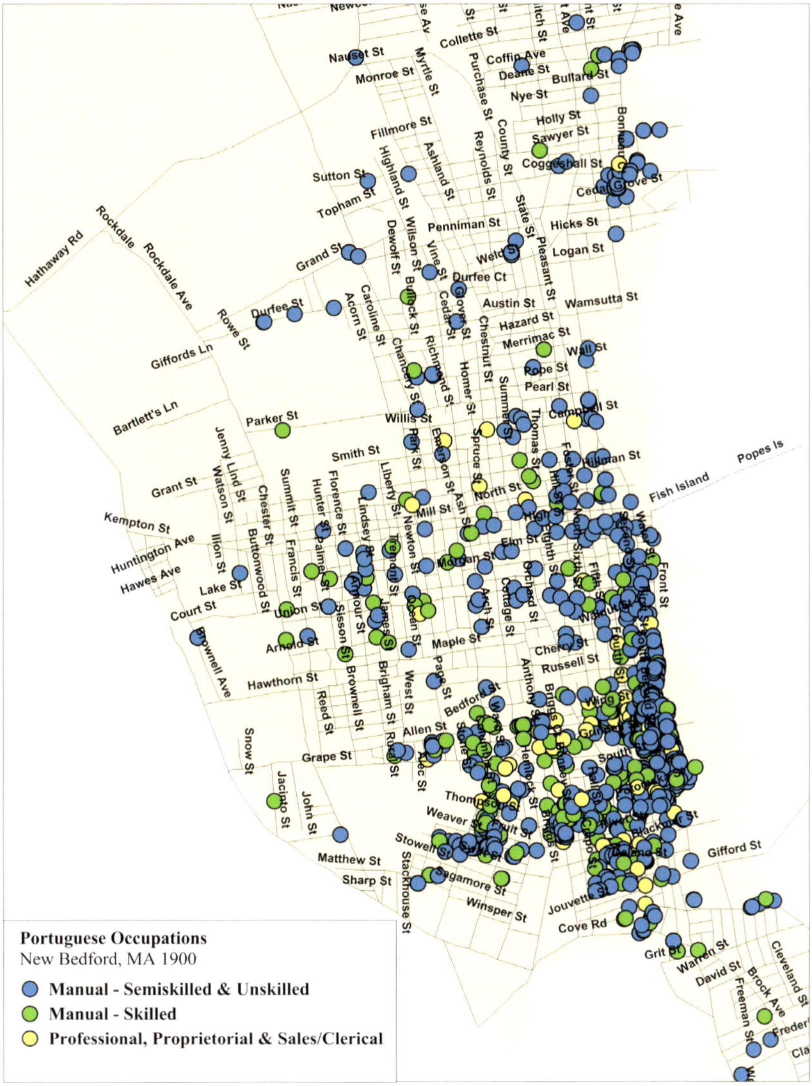

Figure 3. Residence of Portuguese by occupational status in 1900 New Bedford, Massachusetts.

With the exception of the native born, the Portuguese were more likely than the English (26%) and French Canadians (15%) to purchase a home and as likely as the Irish (30%), even though the Portuguese settled in New Bedford after these other groups.[55] Not surprisingly, the largest percentage of Portuguese homeowners (49%) came to the United States prior to 1880.

An additional one-quarter arrived between 1881 and 1890, and 8 percent migrated during the last decade of the nineteenth century. Mapping ownership and rental data for the Portuguese residents provides a clear picture of their desire to acquire property (see fig. 4). What is striking about the Portuguese homeownership pattern is that over half of these owners had semi-skilled and unskilled jobs. For example, Manuel Francis,[56] an immigrant from the Azores and father of nine children, was listed in the 1900 Federal Census Schedules as a "laborer" and most likely earning a daily wage of $1.80.[57] This was less than half the wages paid to skilled machinists, bricklayers, and toolmakers,[58] yet Francis managed to purchase a home. By 1900, he had lived in New Bedford for forty years, but time spent saving does not alone explain the high rate of homeownership. Overall, 73 percent of the Portuguese families in 1900 who were owners had at least one working child over the age of twelve living in the household; those parents who migrated prior to 1880 were most likely to have working children (see fig. 5).

Family income surely made paying for necessities less burdensome, but it also facilitated the purchase of a home. Joseph Santos,[59] a city laborer, was listed in the census as owning a home—mortgage free; his sixteen-year-old son and fourteen-year-old daughter were not in school but found employment in a cotton textile mill and a shirt factory, respectively. The young teenage children of Paul Enos,[60] a day laborer, were mill hands. Five sons of John Jason,[61] another day laborer, lived with their parents while working in the mills. Ranging in age from sixteen to twenty-one, four were spoolers and the oldest a machinist. Jason, like Enos, was a mortgage-free homeowner. How was this possible? It was a common practice for children in Portuguese families to leave school in order to enter the workforce. The Portuguese came to the United States with lower literacy rates compared to the total foreign-born population in Massachusetts. In 1900, 23 percent of foreign-born males twenty years old and over in Massachusetts were illiterate compared to 51 percent of the foreign-born Portuguese in New Bedford.[62] The native-born Portuguese children were more adept at reading and writing compared to their parents but not as proficient as their peers from other ethnic backgrounds.

There is not enough evidence to suggest that the Portuguese had low regard for education, or disdain for those in the community in higher status occupations than themselves. Is this practice of school-age children entering the workforce rooted in culture, or is it a response to real and perceived

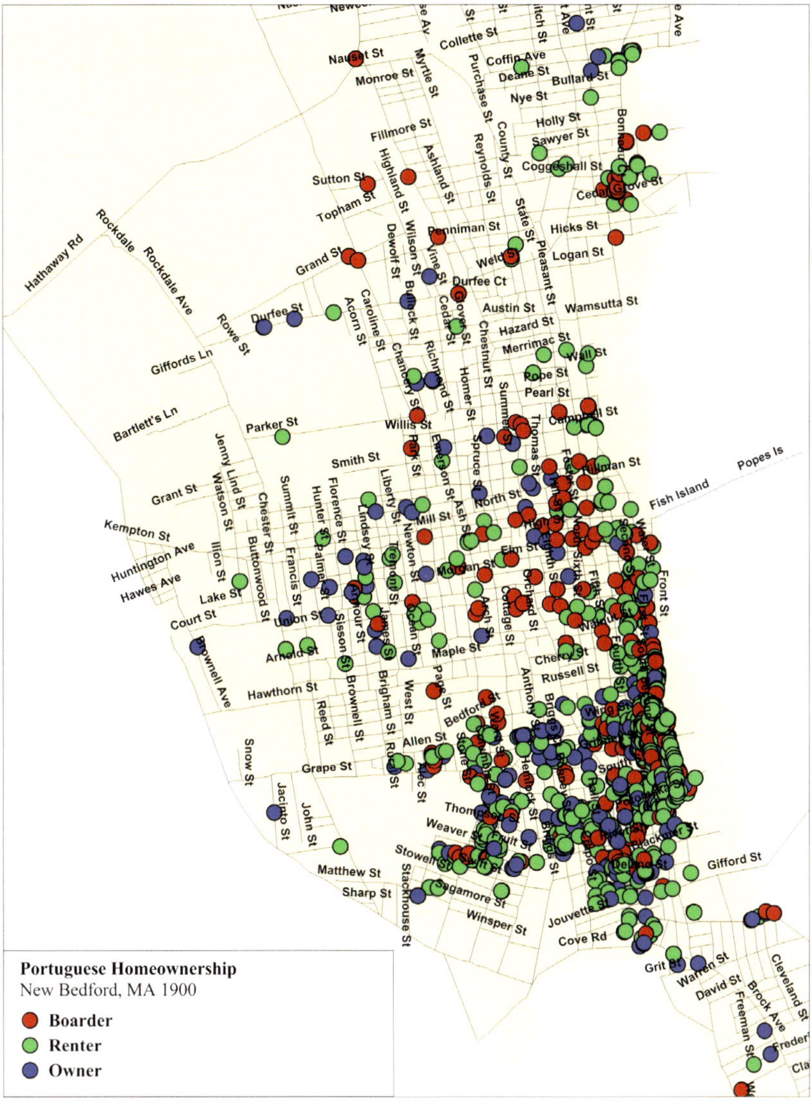

Figure 4. Portuguese homeownership in 1900 New Bedford, Massachusetts.

occupational barriers existing within the city? Initially, Portuguese migrants got stuck in the whaling industry and then again when they entered textile manufacturing. They mainly occupied the lowest-paying positions on vessels and in mills, largely explained by the complex interplay of migration factors, structural barriers, and prevailing negative racial/ethnic stereotypes.

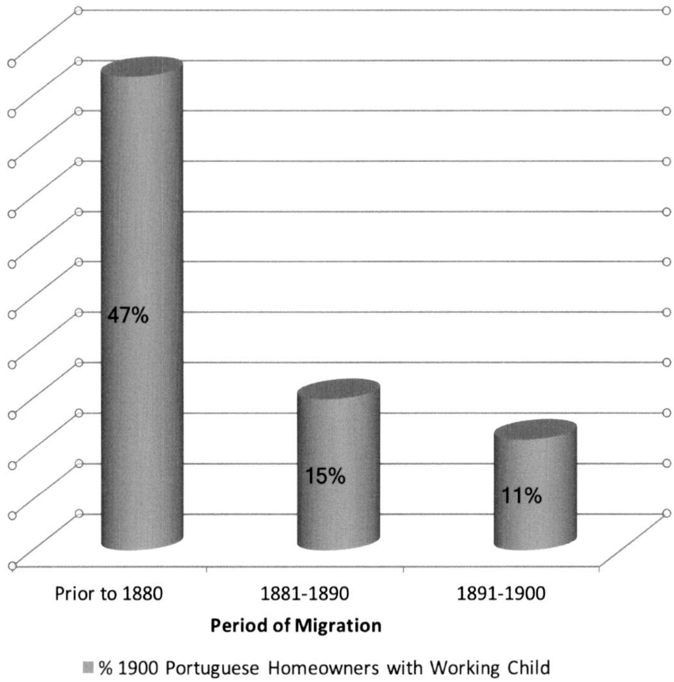

Figure 5. Portuguese homeowners with working children in 1900 New Bedford, Massachusetts.

Occupational mobility during the last three decades of the nineteenth century was minimal for the New Bedford Portuguese, but aiming for homeownership was clearly not viewed as an impossible goal to attain. Clark states that "homeownership has always been a part of the American Dream of upward mobility and financial security."[63] Clark found that purchasing a home increases with occupational mobility among immigrants—that is, attaining high levels of education leads first to entry into high-status occupations and then to homeownership. Contrary to Clark's finding that education is an effective strategy for eventually buying a home, many Portuguese, in the face of limited occupational opportunities in New Bedford, relied on family income as the vehicle for investing in residential "place." Pooling the earnings of parents, children, and other relatives in the household contributed to property mobility, but the forfeiture of education had long-term consequences in terms of occupational mobility. Portuguese fathers rarely saw their sons do substantially better than themselves.[64] The sons of seamen in the whaling industry became fishermen or back boys and doffers in the mills. For a small percentage of sons, a vertical move meant one or two steps within the manual occupational categories but seldom a leap into nonmanual positions.[65] Thus, an analysis of the relatively high rates of homeownership among the New Bedford Portuguese clearly requires a contextual framework, but the possibility of a cultural emphasis on purchasing property ought not be discounted as a contributing factor in this discussion. Data compiled from the city's federal population schedules indicate that the Portuguese owned homes at an overall rate equal to that of Irish immigrants,[66] but when controlling for years spent in the United States, Portuguese ownership exceeded that of property acquisition by the Irish.[67] In addition, a striking difference between these two groups is that one-third of Irish unskilled and semiskilled workers in 1900 became homeowners but over half of the Portuguese in these lowest paid jobs managed to acquire property.[68] Working children enabled ownership for both the Portuguese and the Irish, but the percentage of Portuguese homeowners with working children was significantly higher (75%) compared to Irish owners with employed children (45%).[69]

A Portrait of the Portuguese Mill Workers in 1900[70]

For the most part, the Portuguese mill workers in 1900 both lived and worked in the South End of New Bedford, where they resided mainly in the blocks closest to the Potomska and Acushnet mills and City Manufacturing Corporation (see fig. 6). In the early era of textile manufacturing, the industry relied on male skilled workers from England and other New England villages, but with a shift to more efficient looms caused by technological advancements and, thus, increased profits, another boom in mill construction and heavy recruitment of unskilled workers occurred, cutting across ethnicity, sex, and age.

The Portuguese presence in this industry included men, women, and children. Data compiled from the 1900 U.S. Census Population Schedules indicate the following: 20 percent of all household heads, 56 percent of boarders (more males than females), 70 percent of working wives, and 58 percent of all working male and female children living with parents were employed by the mills. Almost three-fourths (73.9%) of children 15 years of age or less who worked were employed in the mills.

By far, the largest percentage of Portuguese in the mills was composed of recent immigrants; 58 percent migrated to the United States during the last decade of the nineteenth century compared to the 27 percent who migrated

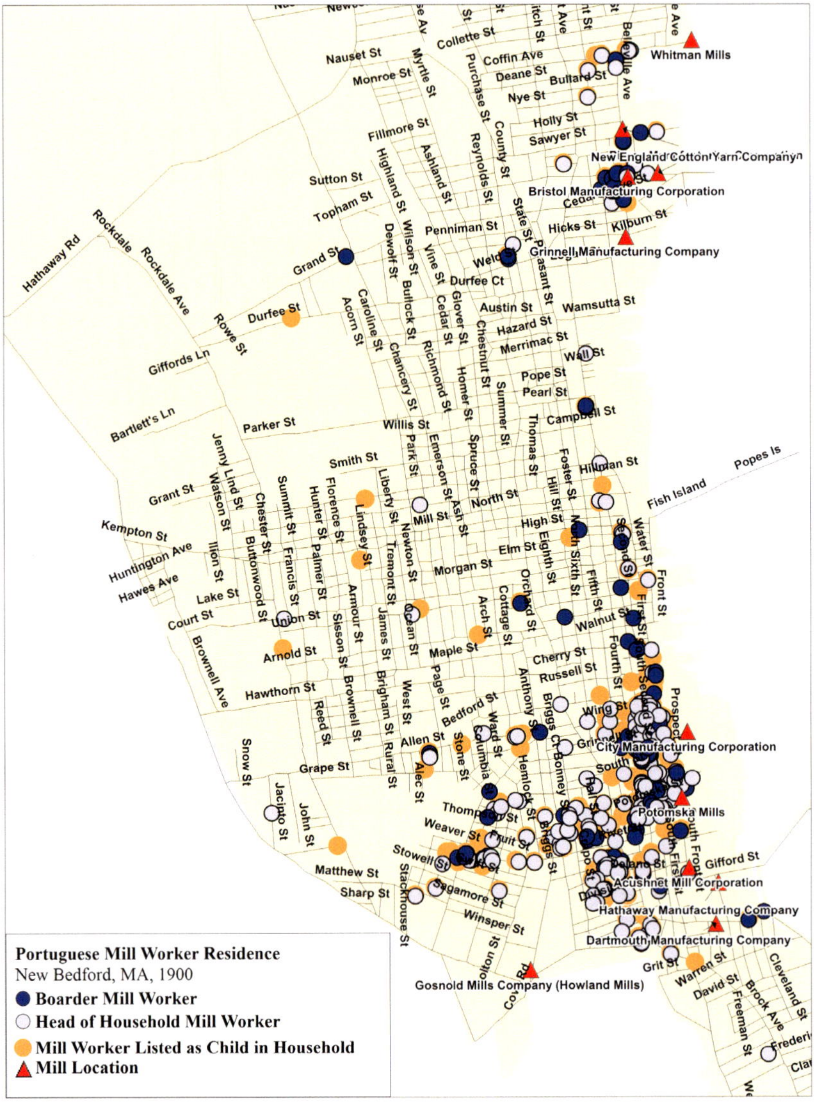

Figure 6. Residence of Portuguese mill workers in 1900 New Bedford, Massachusetts.

between 1881 and 1890; slightly less than 7 percent were native-born Portuguese. Period of immigration also impacted occupational status in the mills. Migrating in the 1890s significantly increased the likelihood of earning the lowest wages; 90 percent of these most recent immigrants occupied the bottom rungs of the mill wage ladder.

The Portuguese were mainly hired to fill the lowest-paying jobs in the mills—operative, carder, doffer, twister, back boy, picker, oiler, comber, and sweeper. The skilled mill workers were mainly weavers and spinners, and a handful became foremen, machinists, loom fixers, or slasher tenders, the highest paid mill employees. Overall, less than 3 percent of all the Portuguese mill workers earned the highest wages in 1900. This pattern of underrepresentation can be explained, at least in part, by occupational gatekeeping.

The Portuguese followed one another into the cotton textile industry as they had into the whaling industry. Relying on coethnics was paramount for newcomers seeking employment.[71] Someone already settled into mill work could speak to the foreman about filling an opening with a relative who had recently arrived in the city. Thirty-four percent of the total Portuguese labor force in 1900 were in textile manufacturing and lived in close proximity to one another. This is compelling evidence for arguing that Portuguese kin, friends, and neighbors were a widely used channel for obtaining employment in the mills.

Equally outstanding is the finding that the Portuguese who first entered this industry did so at the bottom and few among them managed to become higher status gatekeepers—thus, further limiting the opportunities of their children and other relatives to acquire the higher-paying jobs. Thomas Dublin points out that over 70 percent of women with Yankee relatives already employed in the Lowell mills were initially hired to work in the high-paying weaving rooms.[72] Having kin in the higher-paying mill jobs positively impacted job placement for the continued flow of Yankee newcomers. It can plausibly be argued that the Portuguese did not have the connections to power brokers in the mills and therefore found themselves again trapped at the bottom of the major industry controlling New Bedford's economy.

A lack of connections to skilled occupational gatekeepers, however, does not fully explain their exclusion from these positions. The Report of the Immigration Commission to the U.S. Congress, *Immigrants in Industries*,[73] is telling. In comparing the American, English, Irish, French Canadian, North Italian, Polish, South Italian, and Syrian "racial groups," the mill superintendents ranked the Portuguese as first for "industriousness" and "tractability" but as fifth in "general efficiency" and "progress."[74] In addition, the superintendents did not perceive the Portuguese mill workers as particularly "adaptable," having ranked them below all the other groups with the exception of the Syrians and the Polish.[75] The report also notes that the "low ranking of

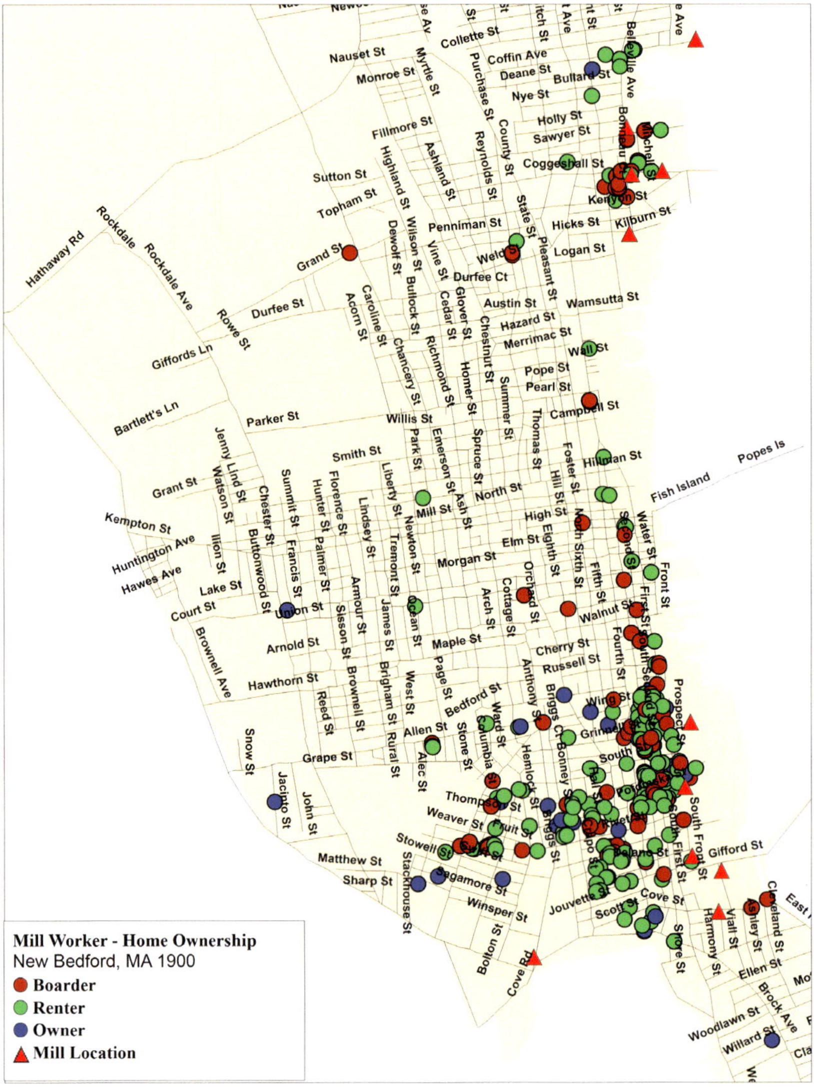

Figure 7. Residence of Portuguese mill workers in 1900 New Bedford, Massachusetts: homeowners, renters and boarders.

American, English, and Irish racial groups as to tractability in the above summary is due to the employers' objection to these races on the ground that they organize and take an active interest in labor unions."[76]

In sum, according to this congressional report, superintendents rated the Portuguese mill workers as moderately efficient and not very adaptable but highly industrious and controllable (i.e., "they don't join unions"). It is difficult to deconstruct these rankings with absolute certainty, but they appear to contradict one another. For example, why would a group of workers who are rated as very hardworking and not prone to making demands on their employers not be viewed in more overall favorable terms? Perhaps allocating low scores in efficiency, progress, and adaptability became a justification and strategy by the superintendents for not moving the Portuguese into higher-paying jobs in the mills.

The growing number of New Bedford mills in the late nineteenth century necessitated more living quarters for workers. Kingston Wm. Heath meticulously documents the shift from earlier brick four tenements to wooden two- and three-story tenements and single-family cottages, from company-owned housing to privately built and owned residences.[77] Although Portuguese mill workers in 1900 predominantly occupied the lowest-paid positions and were not owners, some did manage to purchase a house (see fig. 7); a two-story three tenement with "Portuguese dormers" grew in popularity during the late 1890s.[78] The 1900 Census Population Schedules tell a story of Portuguese owners living in one flat (often with boarders) and renting the remaining flats to other Portuguese families.

Places of residence, whether owned or rented, are built by a raft of decision makers—architects, engineers, politicians, power brokers—and "rebuilt" by users to fit their daily needs and reflect their cultural values. As New Bedford entered the twentieth century, the predominantly South End working-class Portuguese neighborhoods heavily occupied by mill workers had become communities built on similar job experiences as well as cultural, social, and religious bonds.

Conclusions

An understanding of Portuguese migration to New Bedford, Massachusetts, during the latter part of the nineteenth century rests upon a discussion of challenging economic conditions in their homelands as well as the active recruitment into the lowest rungs of the whaling industry, which offered little opportunity for Portuguese seamen to move up. High illiteracy rates do not fully account for their low rates of mobility—prevailing ethnic and racial stereotyping must also be taken into account. With the decline of whaling and the rise of textile manufacturing, the Portuguese again found themselves heavily clustered in the lowest-paying positions within the mills and as common laborers in the city. A contextual framework is helpful in order to explain and understand this pattern. The high demand for technological changes in the textile industry became a structural impediment for accomplishing performance in the workplace; in addition, negative perceptions by the mill supervisors (e.g., Portuguese are inefficient and nonadaptable albeit industrious) often ruled out the Portuguese from being moved to or promoted into higher-paying positions. Although context is essential for understanding their occupational immobility during this time period in New Bedford, it is not sufficient for adequately explaining Portuguese success at homeownership. Not unlike other migrant groups residing in the city, Portuguese children often left school to work and contribute to family income, but they did so in greater numbers. For example, the New Bedford Irish arrived prior to the Portuguese, and thus, by 1900 they would have had more time to save for a home, but the Portuguese outpaced them in this regard. In other words, a cultural emphasis on homeownership as "success" is not an improbable component of the narrative laid out here. Was the Portuguese emphasis on owning property a cultural value that compromised the path for occupational mobility by forfeiture of education? Was the high rate of homeownership within the Portuguese population in New Bedford a direct reaction to real and perceived barriers to achieving higher occupational status? An unequivocal response of "yes" to either of these queries can lead to oversimplified cause/effect conclusions. The compiled data instead support a more multifaceted portrayal of the Portuguese experience in late nineteenth-century New Bedford. This depiction requires an amalgam of contextual and cultural factors and an understanding of structural forces and agency within a framework that represents them as not mutually exclusive.

The evidence presented in this chapter supports the notion that place matters in peoples' everyday lives. When, how, and why individuals leave their place of origin deeply affects their future. The extent to which a place of destination offers historically specific economic opportunities to newcomers, makes use of their human capital, or constructs impediments based on prevailing racial/ethnic attitudes not only impacts achievement rates of migrants but also shapes the meaning of "success" itself. In addition, the significance of place can be highlighted by mapping social patterns. These digital maps enable one to visualize place not as a static point but as an ongoing process of constructing life in the arenas of work, neighborhood, and home.

Works Cited

Allen, Everett S. *Children of the Light: The Rise and Fall of New Bedford and the Death of the Arctic Fleet.* Boston: Little Brown, 1973.

Anthony, Joseph R. *Life in New Bedford a Hundred Years Ago: A Chronicle of the Social, Religious and Commercial History of the Period.* New Bedford, MA: Reynolds Printing, 1922.

Atlas of the City of New Bedford, Massachusetts. Boston: Walker Lithograph & Publishing, 1911.

Burgy, Herbert, J. *The New England Textile Industry: A Study in Industrial Geography.* Baltimore: Waverly, 1932.

Clark, William. *Immigrants and the America Dream: Remaking the Middle Class.* New York, Guilford Press, 2003.

Dublin, Thomas. *Women at Work: The Transformation of Work and Community in Lowell, Massachusetts, 1826–1860.* New York: Columbia University Press, 1979.

Enos, Paul. Sheet 18 (handwritten), line 72, Enumeration District 204, New Bedford, Bristol County, Massachusetts Census of the Population. In *Twelfth Census of the United States, 1900.* National Archives Microfilm Publication T623, roll 637, Records of the Bureau of the Census, record group 29.

Gieryn, Thomas, F. "A Space for Place in Sociology." *Annual Review of Sociology* 26 (2000): 463–66.

Goode, George Brown. *The Fisheries and Fishery Industries of the United States.* Washington, DC: Government Printing Office, 1887.

Heath, Kingston Wm. *Patina of Place: The Cultural Weathering of a New England Industrial Landscape.* Knoxville: University of Tennessee Press, 2001.

Hegarty, Reginald B. *New Bedford and American Whaling.* New Bedford, MA: Reynolds Printing, 1960.

Hohman, Paul E. *The American Whaleman.* New York: Longmans, Green and Company, 1929.

Hough, Henry B. *Wamsutta of New Bedford, 1846–1946.* New Bedford: Wamsutta Mills, 1946.

Jason, John. Sheet 4 (handwritten), line 81, Enumeration District 199, New Bedford, Bristol County, Massachusetts Census of Population. In *Twelfth Census of the United States, 1900,* National Archives Microfilm Publication T623, roll 637, Records of the Bureau of the Census, record group 29.

Logan, John R. "Making a Place for Spaces: Spatial Thinking in Social Science." *Annual Review of Sociology* 38 (August 2012): 507–24.

Manual, Francis. Sheet 12 (handwritten), line 14, Enumeration District 194, New Bedford, Bristol County, Massachusetts Census of the Population. In *Twelfth Census of the*

United States, 1900. National Archives Microfilm Publication T623, roll 637, Records of the Bureau of the Census, record group 29.

Massey, Douglas, S. "Building a Comprehensive Model of International Migration." *Eastern Journal of European Studies* 3, no. 2 (2013): 9–35.

Massey, Douglas S. "A Missing Element in Migration Theory." *Migration Letters* 12, no. 3 (September 2015). www.tplondon.com/journal//index.php/ml/article/view/568.

Massachusetts Bureau of Statistics of Labor. *1895 Census of Massachusetts, Manufacturing,* vol. 5. Boston: Wright and Potter Printing Company, 1898.

Massachusetts Bureau of Statistics of Labor. *Labor Bulletin of Commonwealth of Massachusetts,* no. 22. Boston: Wright and Potter Printing Company, 1902.

Moniz, Miguel. "The Shadow Minority: An Ethnohistory of Portuguese and Lusophone Racial and Ethnic Identity in New England." In *Community Culture and the Makings of Identity: Portuguese Americans along the Eastern Seaboard,* edited by Kimberley DaCosta Holton and Andrea Klimt, 409–28. Dartmouth, MA: Tagus Press, 2009.

Morison, Samuel E. *The Maritime History of Massachusetts, 1738–1860.* Boston: Houghton Mifflin, 1921.

Omi, Michael, and Winant Howard. *Racial Formation in the United States.* New York and London: Routledge, 1994.

Pap, Leo. *Portuguese American Speech: An Outline of Speech Conditions among Portuguese Immigrants in New England and Elsewhere in the United States.* New York: Kings Crown Press, 1949.

Pease, Zepheniah W., and George Hough A. *New Bedford Illustrated: Its History, Industries, Institutions and Attractions.* New Bedford, MA: Mercury, 1889.

Piore, Michael J. *Birds of Passage: Migrant Labor and Industrialized Societies.* Cambridge and New York: Cambridge University Press, 1979.

Ricketson, Daniel. *The History of New Bedford.* New Bedford, MA: Daniel Ricketson, 1858.

Rodrigues, Rose. "Occupational Mobility of Portuguese Males in New Bedford Massachusetts 1870–1900." PhD diss., New School for Social Research, 1990.

Rogers, Francis M. "Americans of Portuguese Descent: A Lesson in Differentiation." *Sage Research Papers in Social Sciences* 2, no. 90-013 (1974): 17–68.

Santos, Joseph. Sheet 6 (handwritten), line 89, Enumeration District 191, New Bedford, Bristol County, Massachusetts Census of Population. In *Twelfth Census of the United States, 1900.* National Archives Microfilm Publication T623, roll 637, Records of the Bureau of the Census, record group 29.

Schlichting, Kurt, Peter Tuckel, Richard Maisel. "Residential Segregation and the Beginning of the Great Migration of African Americans to Hartford, Connecticut. A GIS-Based Analysis." *Historical Methods* 39 no. 3 (2006): 132–43.

Thernstrom, Stephan. *Poverty and Progress.* New York: Atheneum, 1971.

United States Bureau of the Census. *Twelfth Census of the United States, 1900.* National Archives Microfilm Publication T623, rolls 637, 638, record group 29.

United States Bureau of the Census. *Population,* vol. 1, pt. 1. Washington DC: Government Printing Office, 1901, 931.

United States Census Bureau. *Ninth Census of the United States, 1870.* National Archives Microfilm Publication M593, roll 605, record group 29.

United States Census Bureau. *Occupations of the Twelfth Census.* Washington, DC: Government Printing Office, 1904.

United States Census Bureau. *Population,* vol. 2, pt. 2. Washington, DC: Government Printing Office, 1902.

United States Census Bureau. *Population Schedules of New Bedford 1870, 1880, and 1900.* Washington DC: National Archive Microfilm Publication, n.d.

United States Census Bureau. *Social Statistics of Cities,* vol. 2, pt. 1. Washington DC: Government Printing Office, 1886, 356.

United States Census Bureau. *Tenth Census of the United States, 1880.* National Archives Microfilm Publication MT9, roll 525, record group 29.

Warrin, Donald. *So Ends This Day: The Portuguese in American Whaling, 1765–1927.* Dartmouth, MA: Tagus Press, 2010.

Williams, Jerry. *And Yet They Come: Portuguese Immigration from the Azores to the United States.* New York: Center for Migration Studies, 1982.

Wolfbein, L. Seymour. *The Decline of the Cotton Textile City.* New York: Columbia University Press, 1944.

Notes

1. Portuguese ethnicity in this study was determined by one or more of the following ways using U.S. census manuscripts: (1) surname, (2) place of birth for each listed name, or (3) place of father's and/or mother's birthplace for each listed name. Leo Pap, *Portuguese American Speech: An Outline of Speech Conditions Among Portuguese Immigrants in New England and Elsewhere in the United* States (New York: Kings Crown Press, 1949), discusses Portuguese surnames being anglicized and Americanized; census manuscript surnames that illustrated these two practices were also included in this study. The description of the New Bedford Portuguese mobility patterns in the transition from the whaling industry to the textile manufacturing industry is explored in detail in Rose P. Rodrigues, "Occupational Mobility of Portuguese Males in New Bedford, Massachusetts: 1870–1900" (PhD diss., New School for Social Research, 1990), 126–226. The original data collected from the *Twelfth Census of the United States, 1900* (Population Schedules) were more recently utilized for the construction of digital maps included in this paper.

2. Douglas S. Massey, "Building a Comprehensive Model of International Migration," *Eastern Journal of European Studies* 3, no. 2 (2013): 9–35.

3. Douglas S. Massey, "A Missing Element in Migration Theory," *Migration Letters* 12, no. 3 (September 2015): 281–82, http://www.tplondon.com/journal//index.php/ml/article/view/568.

4. Family income consisted of earnings from employment of heads of households, spouses, children, and other relatives living within the household. These earnings were supplemented by taking in boarders.

5. Thomas F. Gieryn, "A Space for Place in Sociology," *Annual Review of Sociology* 26 (2000): 463–66.

6. John R. Logan, "Making a Place for Space: Spatial Thinking in Social Science," *Annual Review of Sociology* 38 (August 2012): 507–24.

7. United States Bureau of the Census, *Ninth Census of the United States, 1870,* National Archives Microfilm Publication M593, roll 605; *Tenth Census of the United States, 1880,* National Archives Microfilm Publication MT9, roll 525; *Twelfth Census of the United States, 1900,* National Archives Microfilm Publication T623, rolls 637, 638, Records of the Bureau of the Census, record group 29.

8. The original compiled household data from the 1900 U.S. census manuscripts were more recently entered into a computer data program and analyzed using the Statistical Package for the Social Sciences.

9. Kurt Schlichting, Peter Tuckel, and Richard Maisel, "Residential Segregation and the Beginning of the Great Migration of African Americans to Hartford, Connecticut: A GIS-Based Analysis," *Historical Methods* 39, no. 3 (Summer 2006): 132.

10. Building a digital map of 1900 New Bedford was made possible through the instruction of Kurt Schlichting, Department of Sociology and Anthropology, Fairfield University, and the assistance of undergraduate students with the following tasks: (1) data entry, (2) historical paper maps and contemporary maps comparisons, (3) geocoding, and (4) frequency/cross-tabulation calculations.

11. Tiger, U.S. Census Bureau Tiger/Line Geodatabase. *Atlas of the City of New Bedford, Massachusetts* (Boston: Walker Lithograph and Publishing Company, 1911). The atlas contains forty-seven plates and was purchased by Fairfield University from Historic Map Works, Portland, Maine, in support of this research project.

12. Jonathan Delgado, a Fairfield University MPA graduate student, plotted the compiled individual-level census data and translated the ideas of the author into digital maps. MapInfo (a geographical information system company in Troy, New York).

13. Daniel Ricketson, *The History of New Bedford* (New Bedford: Daniel Ricketson, 1858); Zepheniah W. Pease and George A. Hough, *New Bedford Illustrated, 1889: Its History, Industries, Institutions and Attractions* (New Bedford: Mercury, 1889); Joseph R. Anthony, *Life in New Bedford a Hundred Years Ago: A Chronicle of the Social, Religious and Commercial History of the Period,* ed. Zephaniah W. Pease (New Bedford: Reynolds Printing Company, 1922).

14. Samuel Eliot Morison, *The Maritime History of Massachusetts, 1738–1860* (Boston: Houghton Mifflin, 1921), 315.

15. Morison, *Maritime History*, 315.

16. United States Census Bureau, *Social Statistics of Cities*, vol. 2, pt. 1 (Washington, DC: Government Printing Office, 1886), 356.

17. Morison, *Maritime History*, 319.

18. Morison, *Maritime History*, 319, footnote.

19. Reginald B. Hegarty, *New Bedford and American Whaling* (New Bedford: Reynolds Printing Company, 1960); Everett S. Allen, *Children of the Light: The Rise and Fall of New Bedford and the Death of the Arctic Fleet* (Boston: Little, Brown, 1973).

20. Henry Beetle Hough, *Wamsutta of New Bedford, 1846–1946* (New Bedford: Wamsutta Mills, 1946), 19.

21. There is a robust body of literature that focuses on the desirability of New England for establishing cotton mills. For example, Herbert J. Burgy, *The New England Textile Industry: A Study in Industrial Geography* (Baltimore: Waverly, 1932), 4–5. Burgy cites a number of factors, including the high demand for cotton textiles, abundance of small power sites, easy transportation provided by eastern ports, dwindling farming opportunities, and New Bedford's ideal moist atmosphere for spinning finer yarns and fabrics.

22. Seymour L. Wolfbein, *The Decline of the Cotton Textile City* (New York: Columbia University Press, 1944), 93.

23. Massachusetts Bureau of Statistics of Labor, *1895 Census of Massachusetts, Manufacturing*, vol. 5 (Boston: Wright and Potter Printing Company, 1898), 63.

24. United States Census Bureau, *Ninth Census of the United States, 1870* (n7); United States Census Bureau, *Occupations of the Twelfth Census* (Washington, DC: Government Printing Office, 1904), 626.

25. United States Census Bureau, *Population*, vol. 2, pt. 2 (Washington, DC: Government Printing Office, 1902).

26. Massey, "A Missing Element in Migration Theory," 281.

27. Also see Michael J. Piore, *Birds of Passage: Migrant Labor and Industrialized Societies* (Cambridge: Cambridge University Press, 1979).

28. Francis M. Rogers, "Americans of Portuguese Descent: A Lesson in Differentiation," *Sage Research Papers in the Social Sciences* 2, no. 90–013 (1974): 19.

29. Jerry Williams, *And Yet They Come: Portuguese Immigration from the Azores to the United States* (New York: Center for Migration Studies, 1982), 67–69.

30. Massachusetts Bureau of Statistics of Labor, *Labor Bulletin of Commonwealth of Massachusetts*, no. 22 (Boston: Wright and Potter Printing Company, 1902).

31. George Brown Goode, *The Fisheries and Fishery Industries of the United States* (Washington, DC: Government Printing Office, 1887), 21.

32. Goode, *The Fisheries,* 21.

33. Goode, *The Fisheries,* 22.

34. Elmo Paul Hohman, *The American Whaleman* (New York: Longmans, Green and Company, 1929).

35. Hohman, *The American Whaleman,* 231.

36. Hohman, *The American Whaleman,* 231.

37. Donald Warrin, *So Ends This Day: The Portuguese in American Whaling, 1765–1927* (Dartmouth, MA: Tagus Press, 2010), 317–50.

38. Calculated by author using the *Ninth Census of the United States, 1870* (Population Schedules) of New Bedford, Massachusetts (n8).

39. Calculated by author using the *Tenth Census of the United States, 1880* (Population Schedules) of New Bedford, Massachusetts (n8).

40. Calculated by author using the *Twelfth Census of the United States, 1900* (Population Schedules) of New Bedford, Massachusetts (n8).

41. Warrin, *So Ends This Day,* 60.

42. Warrin, *So Ends This Day,* 59–62.

43. United States Census Bureau, *Occupations at the Twelfth Census* (Washington, DC: Government Printing Office, 1904), 624–66. Underrepresentation was calculated by the author.

44. United States Census Bureau, *Occupations,* 624–26. The following frequencies were calculated by the author: (1) the Irish by parentage (12 percent of 1900 New Bedford population) had equal representation as machinists, painters, and shoemakers; (2) the French Canadians by parentage (22 percent of population) were overrepresented as carpenters; and (3) the Portuguese by parentage (11 percent of population) were underrepresented in the skilled occupations of machinists, painters, shoemakers, and carpenters.

45. Rodrigues, "Occupational Mobility of Portuguese," 126–226. The dissertation lays out a much fuller discussion of group, intergenerational and career mobility trends among the New Bedford Portuguese between 1870 and 1900.

46. Unless otherwise noted, the statistical data in this section of the paper were calculated by the author using the *Twelfth Census of the United States, 1900* (Population Schedules) of New Bedford, Massachusetts (n8).

47. A robust body of sociological literature focuses on the social functions of ethnic churches in the United States, including assisting new immigrants in their search for employment and housing.

48. Michael Omi and Howard Winant, *Racial Formation in the United* States (London: Routledge, 1994), 3.

49. Omi and Winant, *Racial Formation,* 3.

50. Omi and Winant, *Racial Formation,* 3.

51. Miguel Moniz, "The Shadow Minority: An Ethnohistory of Portuguese and Lusophone Racial and Ethnic Identity in New England," in *Community, Culture and the Makings of Identity: Portuguese-Americans Along the Eastern Seaboard*, ed. Kimberly DaCosta Holton and Andrea Klimt (Dartmouth, MA: Tagus Press, 2009), 427.

52. William Clark, *Immigrants and the American Dream: Remaking the Middle Class* (New York: Guilford Press, 2003).

53. Clark, *Immigrants and the American Dream*, chap. 5.

54. United States Bureau of the Census, *Population*, vol. 2, pt. 2 (Washington DC: Government Printing Office, 1902), 678.

55. United States Bureau of the Census, *Population*, 746. The figures of homeownership for the English, French Canadians, and Irish are state figures.

56. Manual Francis, sheet 12 (handwritten), line 14, Enumeration District 194, New Bedford, Bristol County, Massachusetts Census of Population, *Twelfth Census of the United States, 1900*, National Archives Microfilm Publication T623; Records of the Bureau of the Census, record group 29.

57. Massachusetts Bureau of Statistics of Labor, *Labor Bulletin of Commonwealth of Massachusetts*, 41.

58. Rodrigues, "Occupational Mobility of Portuguese," 63.

59. Joseph Santos, sheet 6 (handwritten), line 89, Enumeration District 191, New Bedford, Bristol County, Massachusetts Census of Population, *Twelfth Census of the United States, 1900*.

60. Paul Enos, sheet 18 (handwritten), line 72, Enumeration District 204, New Bedford, Bristol County, Massachusetts Census of Population, *Twelfth Census of the United States, 1900*.

61. John Jason, sheet 4 (handwritten), line 81, Enumeration District 199, New Bedford, Bristol County, Massachusetts Census of Population, *Twelfth Census of the United States, 1900*.

62. United States Bureau of the Census, *Population*, vol. 1, pt. 1 (Washington, DC: Government Printing Office, 1901), 931; the illiteracy rates of the foreign-born Portuguese in New Bedford were calculated from the United States Bureau of the Census, *Twelfth Census of the United States* (Population Schedules).

63. Clark, *Immigrants and the American Dream*, 128.

64. Rodrigues, "Occupational Mobility of Portuguese," 239–40.

65. Higher rates of property mobility compared to occupational mobility were also found by Stephan Thernstrom, *Poverty and Progress* (New York: Atheneum, 1971).

66. Calculated by author using *Twelfth Census of the United States, 1900* (Population Schedules) of New Bedford, Massachusetts (n8).

67. Rose P. Rodrigues, "Homeownership Patterns among Irish Immigrants in 1900 New Bedford, Massachusetts," presented at Eastern Sociological Association Annual Meeting, March 3, 2001, Philadelphia, Pennsylvania.

68. Calculated by author using the *Twelfth Census of the United States, 1900* (Population Schedules) of New Bedford, Massachusetts (n8).

69. Calculated by author using the *Twelfth Census of the United States, 1900* (Population Schedules) of New Bedford, Massachusetts (n8).

70. Unless otherwise noted, the statistical data in this section of the paper were calculated by the author using the *Twelfth Census of the United States, 1900* (Population Schedules) of New Bedford, Massachusetts (n8).

71. Coethnics in this study include all those groups in late nineteenth-century New Bedford who identified themselves as Portuguese—Azoreans, Madeirans, continental Portuguese, and Cape Verdeans. Analyzing coethnic contacts as a strategy for finding employment is not intended to underestimate the complexity of Portuguese identity including the divergences between self-identities and identities constructed by "outsiders."

72. Thomas Dublin, *Women at Work: The Transformation of Work and Community in Lowell, Massachusetts, 1826–1860* (New York: Columbia University Press, 1979), 48.

73. United States Immigration Commission, *Immigrants in Industries,* "Cotton Goods Manufacturing in the North Atlantic States," This S. Doc. 61-633, at 178–79 (1911).

74. S. Doc. 61-633, at 179 (1911).

75. S. Doc. 61-633, at 179 (1911).

76. S. Doc. 61-633, at 179 (1911).

77. Kingston Wm. Heath, *Patina of Place: The Cultural Weathering of a New England Industrial Landscape* (Knoxville: University of Tennessee Press, 2001), 119–61.

78. Heath, *Patina of Place,* 138.

CHAPTER 3

Neither Slum nor "Elite" Suburb

The Emergence of a Portuguese Colony in Cambridge, Massachusetts, in the Early Twentieth Century

• • • • • •

GRAÇA ÍNDIAS CORDEIRO

Introduction

The eastern part of the city of Cambridge, in Massachusetts, is an almost unremarkable area that is densely populated by Portuguese signs, sounds, smells, and tastes through a myriad of discreet places such as stores, coffee shops, restaurants, bakeries, the Manuel Rogers funeral home, the MAPS (Massachusetts Alliance of Portuguese Speakers), the social clubs Faialense and Filarmónica de Santo António, and Saint Anthony's church. Between Inman Square and Lechmere, Cambridge Street is the backbone of a broader network of relationships and interactions that draws together the routines of daily life, as well as celebrations and all sorts of rituals. The "Portuguese Boulevard," as the *Boston Globe*'s journalist Lynda Morgenroth named the east side of this street in her gastronomic guide through the "ethnic enclaves in and around Boston,"[1] seems to be the Portuguese hub of Boston, drawing individuals, families, associations, musical bands, and schools from communities settled by Portuguese immigrants scattered throughout Massachusetts and Rhode Island to gather in periodic festivities.

This "Portuguese-flavored enclave," consisting of the unique, highly central, global, cosmopolitan, and tolerant city of Cambridge, has triggered my interest since 2009.[2] Furthermore, there are not enough studies about this particular place, which remains on the periphery of the literature about the Portuguese in New England. As a matter of fact, unlike other ethnic minorities in Boston, such as the Italian minority,[3] the Portuguese in Boston have never been considered for major sociological or anthropological studies.[4] Yet the relationship between the less-studied urban Portuguese communities and the well-known urban Italian communities in the greater Boston is particularly interesting, given the proximity between the two communities in a number of matters, including residential settlement patterns (first in the North End,[5] later in East Cambridge), religious affinities, and other similarities. Still, despite the erasure of the Portuguese ethnicity resulting from the impact of gentrification, many traits of Portuguese heritage remain visible in the area.

Upon inquiring about the history of the city of Cambridge, I became acquainted with the recent memories of Portuguese immigration during the 1960s and '70s. Furthermore, the research took me to the earlier wave of Portuguese immigration at the turn of the twentieth century. The Portuguese parish of Saint Anthony's was founded in Cambridge in 1902 with the building of a church on Portland Street, one of the first Catholic churches in this city, a significant landmark signaling the arrival of many Portuguese in that period—just a step away from the current church inaugurated eighty years later, resting on an everlasting historical landmark.

The Zone of Emergence: One Book, Two Moments, and Many Voices

I came across the book that inspired this chapter while exploring local archives at the Cambridge Public Library during a short stay in 2013.[6] *The Zone of Emergence: Observations of the Lower Middle and Upper Working-Class Communities in Boston* was written before World War I by a group of social workers and urban reformers under the coordination of Robert A. Woods and Albert J. Kennedy, and it was concerned with the life of working-class and "emergent" lower-middle-class districts in the Boston area. It would be a lost manuscript if it had not been discovered fifty years after it was undertaken and fortunately published for the first time in 1962 by the urban historian Sam Bass Warner Jr., under the auspices of the new Joint Center of Urban Studies MIT/Harvard. As he wrote in the foreword to the second edition (1969), this study provides a "systematic coverage of (such) quarters which are neither slum nor elite suburb."[7]

East Cambridge is one of those quarters, among the six relatively more prosperous neighborhoods analyzed in this study, representing the so-called zone of emergence. In the beginning of the twentieth century, Portuguese, Irish, Polish, and Armenians were the most prominent immigrant groups living in this area, attracted by an industrial and residential district, and they came either from other parts of the metropole or directly from their homelands. The prevailing idea that "new Portuguese immigrant enclaves in Cambridge" began in the 1960s and 1970s[8] is not supported by this and other studies,which point out that by 1912, the Portuguese "had risen to 25 percent of the population of East Cambridge . . . and by 1920, they were the majority of the foreign-born residents living there.[9] In fact, a 1970s City of Cambridge report said "that Portugal has contributed to Cambridge the second-largest foreign-born group . . . concentrated in Census Tracts along Cambridge Street between Inman and Lechmere Squares."[10] This indicates a dense preexisting network of relatives, friends, and countrymen who were able to welcome more recent immigrants into what are today the broader contours of this Portuguese neighborhood in the Boston area.

The fundamental method of reading and analyzing this chapter in *The Zone of Emergence* is to verify how the Portuguese were represented, which led to the more intensive focus on the chapter dedicated to East Cambridge as a zone of emergence. Besides the voice coming from the beginning of the twentieth century, the editor's voice, that of Sam Bass Warner Jr., fifty years later provides another vision of the Boston old inner suburbs, shaping the representation of the European immigrants including those "emergent assimilated Portuguese." For this reason, the book encompasses multiple narratives among two different periods: one from an insider's point of view, a voice coming from the 1905–14 report about a zone of emergence of a lower middle class in the old inner suburbs of Boston, and another from the editor, almost fifty years later. The first one is an original voice, the only one of its kind registered in this period; it is the product of the interactions of the authors experimenting in the field with a guided questionnaire in order to situate the writing, showing the eminently microlocal character of the knowledge produced. The other voice comes from the 1962 preface written by a renowned urban historian specializing in the history of the American city; it is an analysis supported on a larger urban scale as the main guiding tool for this reading across the city of Boston and its emerging suburbs.

Boston Old Inner Suburbs: "This is about the recently assimilated, not the newly arrived . . ."

Robert A. Woods and Albert J. Kennedy, who between 1905 and 1914 coordinated the study that resulted in *The Zone of Emergence*, were two urban reformers, and the most prominent men in the South End House, the first settlement house created in Boston; it was founded in 1891 under the name of Andover House. They were both graduates of theological schools, were imbued with the Social Gospel, and led research activities at Andover House.[11]

Inspired by the English settlement house experience, the American settlement movement started in the Lower East Side of Manhattan, with the creation of a settlement house in 1886, followed by Hull House in Chicago, the best-known case, which was initiated by Jane Addams.[12] In 1897 there were already seventy-four American settlements, and in 1910, "there were 413 U.S. settlement houses in 33 states and Hawaii, with particularly dense concentrations in the major cities—NY, Chicago, Boston, Philadelphia, Los Angeles and San Francisco."[13] This information is based on the compilation made by Robert Woods and Albert Kennedy in their *Handbook of Settlements* (1911), one of a series of texts published between 1898 and 1922 and dedicated to slum life and settlement house movement. However, different from these other books, *The Zone of Emergence* is an odd text among those written by these groups of researchers and activists among South End House in Boston.

The typewritten manuscript of 335 double-spaced pages, on which the most recent penciled editorial marks bear the date 1920, was discovered in 1958 in a coal bin of the South End House after being in dead storage since 1929, when Albert Kennedy, one of the authors, "left Boston to become headworker at the University Settlement in New York City."[14] It includes Kennedy's handwritten table of contents, identifying the authors of the introduction, and six chapters on specific localities in the *Zone of Emergence*—Charlestown, Cambridge Port, East Cambridge, Roxbury and Dorchester, South Boston, East Boston—plus three chapters on Swedes, Canadians, and "Negros,"[15] which were never written,[16] and a map (fig. 1).

The beginning of World War I in 1914 interrupted the work of publishing the book, and after the war, Robert Woods and Albert Kennedy shifted their priority from this study to the publication of one of the great works on the settlement house movement—*The Settlement Horizon* (1922). *The Zone of Emergence* was about to be lost permanently, but, fortunately, it was saved fifty years later.

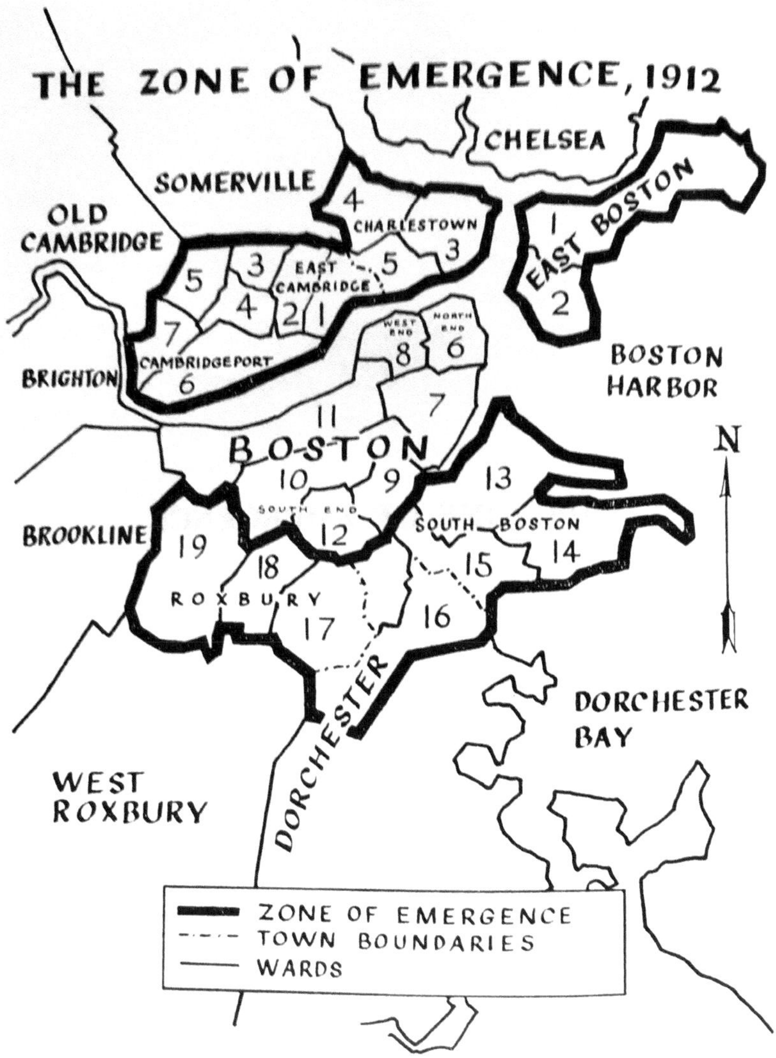

Figure 1. Map of The Zone of Emergence (Woods and Kennedy, *The Zone of Emergence*, page 30). Reprinted from The Zone of Emergence: Observations of the Lower Middle and Upper Working Class Communities of Boston, 1905-1914 by Robert A. Woods and Albert J. Kennedy, courtesy of The MIT Press.

Thus, *The Zone of Emergence* was published for the first time in 1962, with a grant from the Joint Center of Urban Studies MIT/Harvard, created in 1959, which merged the urban studies centers of both universities.[17] The small, 219-page book is abridged and edited by Sam Bass Warner Jr., who was working on this recently created center and who wrote a remarkable preface. As an expert in the history of the American city, author of *The Urban Wilderness: A History of the American City* (1972) and of *American Urban Form,* (2012), and as "an old plain citizen of Cambridge,"[18] Sam Bass Warner Jr. had studied the patterns of suburban growth in Boston, focusing on Dorchester and Roxbury, in the scope of what later became a classic of urban studies, first published in the same year as *The Zone of Emergence, Streetcar Suburbs* (1962).

Indeed, *The Zone of Emergence,* written almost fifty years before today's classic *Streetcar Suburbs,* seems to anticipate the concerns with the suburban development of this city, but with different purposes. It is part of the series of studies, in the setting of South End House, on the real life of growing neighborhoods in an industrial town undergoing a transformation at the turn of the nineteenth and twentieth centuries. Warner pointed to it as the groundbreaking moment in urban research set in South End House in the opening of the preface to the first edition of this book:

> Boston's first settlement house, the South End House, established a national reputation in the opening decades of this century with a series of studies of urban life. . . . The series began in 1898 with an examination of the slum, *The City Wilderness,* and closed in 1922 with a summary of the settlement house movement and its techniques, *The Settlement Horizon.* Taken as a whole the series constitutes an impressive body of pioneer studies of urban poverty.[19]

However, this book brings us not the world of the slum but that of the more prosperous residential and industrial neighborhoods, located in the first ring of suburban growth, the old inner suburbs, where the authors analyze a lower middle class emerging among an upper working class in the process of social mobility: "What the authors meant by 'emergence' was emergence from the slum to the mainstream of American life."[20] Actually, *The Zone of Emergence* is concerned with the life of the "working class and lower-middle-class districts in Boston area, beyond the core city of Boston."[21]

For Warner, the true originality of *The Zone of Emergence,* in relation to the rest of the series of studies on slums, is the focus on the "recently assimilated, not the newly-arrived, as being the city's major problem."[22] The relationship between newcomers and old inhabitants was mediated by the settlement workers, heirs of New England's democratic spirit. This was the turning point in a relationship of conflict and transformed the "village churches and the village government, formerly the symbols of a united community, in bastions of minority interest." The role of the "politicians, representatives of ethnic minorities . . . was to put together coalitions of the minority clusters of their districts."[23]

The description of community life in *The Zone of Emergence,* in "which traditional ways were twisted or destroyed,"[24] challenged previous books. The hot topic is the Americanization of these immigrants in a process of rapid assimilation, the "recognition of the cultural weakness of a native American life,"[25] and, above all, "an interrogation of common life."[26] In a particularly perceptive way, Warner sees a multiculturalist, *avant la lettre* position in this book, which he calls "cultural pluralism." He remarked that Kennedy himself defended a policy of encouragement of "hyphenated American groups," promoting self-education and citizenship to make the most of the cultural qualities of each group.[27]

In this sense, the study is seen by Sam Bass Warner as confused and contradictory, standing apart from other books on slums. In this zone of emergence, (some of) the dormitories were characterized not by their economic problems but by the fact that they were not structured into "integrated communities, but fast-changing clusters of people in one income group or another."[28] The belief in the "revival of America's traditional small-scale institutions (voluntary associations of church and club),"[29] which covers the whole ring of small towns around Boston, seems to clash with the authors' neighborhood orientation, focused on the description and careful analysis of social life in the streets, clubs, and churches and in small social and political groups. In a fuller version of the quotation cited above, "As such this is the only book, I've ever seen which gives anything like a systematic coverage of these vast stretches of the American metropolis, quarters which are neither slum nor elite suburb."[30]

Moreover, the findings of this study may be among the reasons why it was not published earlier. This view of the more prosperous working-class and lower-middle-class suburbs shows how "the escape from the slum led to a place of unsatisfactory religious, educational, work and community relations." Consequently, "the logical conclusion of *The Zone of Emergence* could only have been a general call for the reform of American life. The South End authors were not prepared to take this final step."[31]

The Emergent Portuguese Colony in East Cambridge: "a distinct feature of the social structure"

The chapter on East Cambridge,[32] one of six in the book, was written by Eugene L. Sheldon (born in 1885 in Springfield, MA; graduated from Harvard in 1906; died in 1957) between 1906 and 1908, during his time doing graduate work at Harvard and also while he was working for the *Boston Globe*.[33] Later, this text was reviewed and rewritten by Ordway Tead (born in 1891, son of a Somerville, MA, Congregational minister) when he was at the South End House from 1912 to 1914 as an Amherst College Fellow.

The brief profile of this area, which would become one of the most important industrial poles in the Boston area, tells us that until the beginning of the nineteenth century, East Cambridge was almost an island, a wide zone of cattle pasture. After 1807 it drastically changed, thanks to the fact that this land was bought first by Andrew Craigie to build the Boston Porcelain and Glass Company (1814) and later by other manufacturers, as well as due to the influence of construction of transport access to Boston (bridges and viaducts). In just a few years, East Cambridge, one of the most peripheral parts of the city of Cambridge, became simultaneously a strategic, central, and suburban space that, beginning after the Civil War, dramatically expanded.[34]

According to the authors of this chapter, the industrial expansion promoted the arrival of the first two colonies of European immigrants to East Cambridge: the Irish and the Portuguese. The differences between the two communities, however, are stressed, as the "character of the people in these years became more uniformly working-class and more uniformly Irish," while the Portuguese colony "forms a distinct feature of the social structure," different from the dominant Irish character.[35] Moreover, "it still remains true that the qualities and traits of the Portuguese are not such that their advance or achievement is at all spectacular, brilliant, or in any way exceptional."[36]

In fact, other historical sources refer to the arrival of the Portuguese in East Cambridge from the nineteenth century. Boston, including Cambridge, is the third "Portuguese colony" of seven listed by Henry Lang in the article "The Portuguese Element in New England" (1892).[37] Leo Pap, in *The Portuguese-Americans* (1981), included several references to Cambridge,[38] as well as to the Portuguese leaving the North End for Cambridge and Somerville, fleeing ethnic conflicts between Italians and Irish inhabitants.[39]

George Hanford also traced a brief history of all the populations that immigrated to Cambridge from 1639. However, the Cantabrigian ethnic landscape would change in the twentieth century: during the nineteenth and early twentieth centuries, the major immigrant groups were the Irish, the Italians, the French Canadians, and the Portuguese, who settled in "discrete neighborhoods" around their own parishes and churches and maintained their native languages.[40]

The Ethnic Landscape: Irish, Poles, Portuguese, and Armenians

Irish, Poles, Portuguese, and Armenians made up the prevailing migrant groups in East Cambridge in the early years of the twentieth century: "The sons of Ireland have become the aristocracy, and practically all the substantial homes are in their hands . . . this is the hard but royal road that has been traveled by the Irish and that must be traveled by every other race that would become a component of the nation."[41]

This characterization led to the identification of the notorious visibility and rooting of the first comers, which, in this case, was seen as an ethnic rooting model to be copied by the communities that followed, in this case, the Portuguese.

Directly from the "Azores and from the St. Michael's Islands" as well as from New Bedford, "which harbors the largest and most prosperous colony in the state," the Portuguese are following this path, although "as a group they have not yet established themselves as firmly or as powerfully as have the Irish."[42] One of the reasons was their lack of knowledge of English; the other reason was related to what was characterized as their temperament, particularly against the "political game," which made them incapable of leading politically:

> They are handicapped, of course, by an ignorance of our language which often seems to denote a degree of diffidence and unaggressiveness that is easily mistaken for lack of energy, acuteness, and ambition. For this reason, also their life has remained slightly distinct and colonized. They entered East Cambridge soon after the Civil War, but whether the first comer was a barber, or a cabinetmaker is not clear. However, we do know that the first dozen families came from Boston—a beginning of the dispersion that has now emptied the North End of this nationality. A furniture factory that was the means of support for an increasing number of Portuguese.[43]

The prevailing idea that the Italians preceded or accompanied the arrival of the Portuguese in East Cambridge, as stated in some of the more recent works on local history,[44] deserves some comment. In those early years of the twentieth century, the intensity and volume of arrival of new immigrants to these urban territories was such that sometimes the population changed very fast, causing rapid transformation to a populace in a certain place. Sam Bass Warner himself states in his preface: "Since the nineteenth century was the century not only of industrial change but also of European immigration, the shift from one income to the next lower one was often associated with a radical change in ethnic composition."[45]

Knowing that both the Portuguese and the Italians who occupied East Cambridge in these early times were fleeing poor living conditions in the North End (one of the "three Boston Ends"—North End, West End, South End, i.e., the slums), it is natural that there might have been some confusion between the two populations. If, on the one hand, a number of years separated the time of these groups' migration (the mass arrival of the Italians could have come after the two-year period in which the author did his fieldwork, 1906–8), on the other hand, we know, also from this source, that there were several different types of mobility, including commuting, which already was a common practice. This type of detailed and thorough analysis reports these nuances in the different ways of occupying the social space.

The Community: "life here is a real step forward"

One of the most valued aspects stressed in the chapter of *The Zone of Emergence* on East Cambridge is the direct relationship between work and workers. Through the "waves and the nature of the population we should understand the contemporary industrial conditions, for life here has always depended intimately upon the economic forces at work." In these years operations either were begun or became firmly established in the woodworking concerns, pump and bridge manufactories, rubber work, sugar refinery, publishing house, and gasworks. Those firms that deal in the bulky commodities received by water—coal, lumber, and stone—were also started in this period or even earlier. Structurally, therefore, until very recently, the district has undergone little change, except in the deterioration of property.[46]

The urban centrality of East Cambridge is stressed: a mile from the state house, the tunnel to Park Street, the viaduct to North Station, and the subway from Cambridge Street—these connections "make the business sections of Boston only five minutes away" and "communication with the suburbs on the other side of the city is easy." The close to 30 corporations counted here during this period (1906–8, maybe updated in 1914) each employed more than 25 people: four factories employed more than 800 men, nine factories employed 100–400 men, and 2,900 men and 700 women were doing unskilled machine work.[47] A wide range of commodities were distributed, from six woodworking establishments, four metalworking, and two printing; there were three factories of pork products, sugar, and syrups; eight coal or lumber dealers, as well as marble, granite, and stone dealers.

Social mobility is a distinctive feature between the several types and classes of workers, with a specification for the female gender. The majority of Portuguese, men and women, are unskilled workers, like the Irish and Polish, "of the first or second generation." But there are also a few Portuguese who are "skilled men—the machinists, woodcarvers, upholsterers, typesetters, etc."—along with Americans, older Irish, Swedes, and Germans.[48]

The least qualified lived mostly in East Cambridge, and the most qualified usually lived outside the neighborhood, commuting there daily. There was, however, a special relationship with Cambridgeport in the daily journey to work as "about 75 percent of the unskilled men and 85 percent of all women make their homes either in the district or nearby. But, the artisans, the clerks, and those who do the light, clean work come almost without exception from out of the town."[49]

Even though the physical conditions of living are better than in the congested parts of Boston, "It is hard to say whether these unskilled Portuguese, Poles, and Armenians are more victims of unduly low wages or of their own ignorance of better standards."[50] It would be unjust to the better families to generalize about home life in Cambridge: "For the Portuguese colony it can be safely affirmed that life here is a real step forward. For those from Boston there is more room and air, and as houses are smaller and cheaper, the thrifty ones become property owners in a short time. For those from abroad there is offered a wider horizon and a broader field of endeavor, if not for the adults at least for their children."[51]

Public Sociability: Streets, Clubs, Churches, Small Social and Political Groups

The Zone of Emergence shows clearly how churches are the backbone of migrating communities—and in Cambridge even more so, in comparison with other districts in this study. Indeed, Saint Anthony Church was founded on Portland Street in 1902, and the Portuguese had abandoned the prior Portuguese church located in the North End, while the first Italian church only appeared in East Cambridge in 1917. Until then the reference for the Italian community, with its origins in the south of Italy, was still Saint Leonard's Church in the North End where, in fact, the celebration of Santo António de Pádua started a few years later, nowadays considered one of the most important Catholic celebrations in the United States.

> Until 1902 many of the faithful were communicants of the Portuguese church in the North End. In that year, a parish was organized in Cambridge, and the building on Portland Street just over the line into the Port, that had been built by the Portuguese Fraternity in 1897, was purchased for a church. . . . At present with its rebuilt front and new parish house, the church gives a fairly accurate indication of the prosperity of its members. The Portuguese are now scattering from East Cambridge to the extent that a considerable number of the older church people come from the upper parts of Cambridge and from all over Somerville.[52]

But other churches like the "small Portuguese mission in the Methodist Church [call] attention to the fact that as a people they are by no means the devoted churchmen that the Irish are."[53]

Other spots of daily urban interaction, in the public and semipublic domain, deserve our attention. If we look at the factory, street, and night school, we can "get a clue about the assimilative influences that are in operation" in the frame of social and industrial forces.[54] In these places, "the workers are thrown into contact with other nationalities." In the Portuguese civic center and in the Armenian boarding house there is educational work: "The older Polish residents—and this is true of Portuguese and Armenians as well—make a very gracious and fraternal effort toward adjusting matters of all sorts for the immigrants."[55]

Among the Portuguese, the Luso-American Club is the distinctive organization. This is a men's club with rooms, called a "civic center," which are used for a general gathering place.[56] But there are others. As "the Portuguese Fraternity, a benefit society to which some six hundred men belong, holds its meetings here, and the club aims in every way to preserve the interest of the Portuguese people," and the "immigrants from St. Michael's Island . . . have their own fraternal organization numbering about two hundred, and there are two similar societies among the women."[57]

The more evident social life of East Cambridge is that of the young people. "There are nearly twenty young men's clubs, many of which hire a room that they fit up with card tables, chairs and a few posters. These rooms serve as hangouts where the fellows come in the evenings to smoke and amuse themselves."[58]

There are also references to "an annual dance and political contests, poolrooms and bowling alleys, a *moving-picture theater*, gambling between boys 17 to 21 years old, some signals of delinquency. . . . Cambridge Street seems to be the hot spot at night, comparable to the "Fifth Avenue and Rialto of this section."[59]

The small scale of city life was, in fact, the predominant point of view of this study, and it allowed certain details of daily life to be understood with great accuracy, as well as their impacts on the forms of urban social organization on another scale.

According to the future editor of the book, Sam Bass Warner, these perceptions, among others, on the smallest scale of city life allowed for an understanding of how the "industrial pattern determined the class of people who came to live in a district."[60] Also, the phenomenon of commuting ("many of the residents of *The Zone of Emergence* worked outside their town boundaries") contributed to a more general understanding of how the "interaction of the industrial and traffic patterns of Greater Boston caused . . . radical change in ethnic composition."[61]

Portuguese in Cambridge: A Shadow of the City?

Sam Bass Warner writes in the foreword to the second edition that "this is the best social science survey I've found to accompany the early twentieth-century naturalistic novel."[62] The local descriptions of the inner residential quarters and towns that surround Boston and the analysis of the "lower middle class and working class life are rare for any city in any period," along with the fact that the authors "valued accuracy enough to seek empirical data, to walk the streets, to count the churches, schools, and clubs, to talk to neighbors, to go to local politicians"[63] all make this book a precious source.

First and foremost, the value of the book lies in its insider point of view. Most authors of *The Zone of Emergence* were, or had been, residents of South End House and, in certain cases, brought experience in journalism or religious activities. In general, the settlement residents were mostly young middle-class students or professors who were imbued with the spirit of social reform and tried to help poorer European immigrants living in miserable conditions to be fully integrated into American society and, at the same time, to better know the "foreign lands of the slums of great cities."[64] Their practices combined what we would now classify as "social work" and "research in social sciences" with a hands-on involvement in urban poverty and unknown living spaces. Even though this book is not about slum areas, the authors' descriptions, through scientifically framed analysis, were based on an empathetic interaction with a world of "otherness" that they wished to know from the inside, from its daily routines. We can consider *The Zone of Emergence* a study comparable to the urban monographs later undertaken by the University of Chicago, which were inspired by notions such as "natural area," the process of assimilation, supervised by Robert Park, who is considered today as a pioneer in the history of urban ethnography.[65]

Next, related to this insider point of view, *The Zone of Emergence* is worthy for its microlocal analysis, defining each neighborhood as a unit of analysis. The empirical observational subject is territorial not ethnic or national, which is related to the interest in studying the "small scale of the city." This is indubitably one of the most interesting examples of this approach. It is an accurate firsthand description based on meticulous observations making this information livelier and more colorful than many other theoretically oriented academic studies. Yet this centennial report, including the two Cambridge neighborhoods (Cambridgeport and East Cambridge) populated by Portuguese immigrants and their descendants, has traditionally been framed as "small local history." *The Zone of Emergence* was lost in the so-called "cumulative history" of science, particularly regarding the studies on Portuguese immigration to the United States. The representations of the Portuguese "colony" presented in *The Zone of Emergence* contrast strikingly with later works such as Donald Taft's *Two Portuguese Communities in New England* (1969; written in 1923).[66]

Finally, the study and its subsequent publications provide an indispensable source of the knowledge of local and social history as well as of the cognitive contexts, which mold the advances and setbacks of knowledge. This report emerged from local—microlocal, I should say—observations of an area that is still, to paraphrase Topalov, "unknown territory"[67]—that of studies about Portuguese immigration to the most central and urban area of Boston, especially Cambridge. In the words of the authors themselves, East Cambridge emerges as something that "embodies in miniature all the aspects of the larger industrial world; it is a complete microcosm that because of its comparative unity can be studied more readily and more accurately than would otherwise be possible"; they conclude, "In East Cambridge the hopes and fears of our American progress are met."[68] This continues to surprise, as it is an area of intersection between the history of one of the most famous American cities and one of the least known or studied ethnic groups in the United States. This may help us gain a more accurate perspective of the still-hidden role played by Portuguese immigrants in the rise of the "American middle class urban culture," as Sam Bass Warner pointed out, through the twentieth century in New England—and find out why the Portuguese are almost eradicated from cutting-edge discussions on urban life and ethnicity processes carried out in mainstream American social sciences.

Thus, the city could be the privileged field site, simultaneously the "object and the venue of study . . . the empirical referent of analysis and the physical site where investigation takes place . . . in short: a scientific truth-spot," according to Thomas Gieryn in his explanation of the *paradox of place and truth:*

> All scientific knowledge-claims have a provenance: they originate at some place and come from there. However, as they become truth, these claims shed the contingent circumstances of their making, and so become transcendent (presumably true everywhere, supposedly from nowhere in particular). Turning the argument around: scientific claims are diminished in their credibility as they are situated somewhere, as if their truthfulness depended upon conditions located only there.[69]

This relatively unknown description of the East Cambridge neighborhood exemplifies the diversity of the roles played by Portuguese migrants to New England. The case of the Portuguese in Cambridge provides a privileged example to discuss the relationship between residence and ethnicity. The inclusion of the Portuguese label in the "cumulative texture" of this part of the city, expressed in "images, typifications and collective representations"[70] for such a long time, deserves more attention.

Works Cited

Adams, Jane. *Twenty Years at Hull-House.* New York: Macmillan, 1910.

Bastos, Cristiana. "Migrants, Inequalities and Social Research in the 1920s: The Story of Two Portuguese Communities in New England." *History and Anthropology* 29, no. 2 (2018): 163–83.

Birch, Eugénie L. "Making Urban Research Intellectually Respectable: Martin Meyerson and the Joint Center for Urban Studies of Massachusetts Institute of Technology and Harvard University 1959–1964." *Journal of Planning History* 10, no. 3 (2011): 219–38.

Boyer, Sarah. *All in the Same Boat: Twentieth-Century Stories of East Cambridge.* Cambridge, MA: Cambridge Historical Commission, 2005.

Carvalho, Eduardo. *Os Portugueses da Nova Inglaterra.* Rio de Janeiro: A Leitura Colonial, 1931.

Conzen, Kathleen Neils. "Immigrants, Immigrant Neighborhoods, an Ethnic Identity: Historical Issues." *Journal of American History* 66, no. 3 (December 1979): 603–15.

Cordeiro, Graça I. "Belongings and Interactions: Negotiating Portuguese-Speaking Identities in Boston." *Portuguese Literary and Cultural Studies* 26 (2012): 111–26.

Cordeiro, Graça I. "A cidade à escala da rua. Usos e significados do passado na afirmação de 'tradições' locais urbanas." In *Patrimônio cultural: memória e intervenções urbanas,* edited by Renato Cymbalista, Sarah Feldman, and Beatriz M. Kuhl, 71–86. São Paulo: Anna Blume, 2017.

Cordeiro, Graça I., and Frédéric Vidal. "Entre o gueto e a cidade: perspetivas cruzadas sobre a 'colónia' portuguesa na região de Boston no início do século XX." *VII Congresso Português de Sociologia,* Universidade do Porto, 19–22 Junho (2012). http://historico.aps.pt/vii_congresso/papers/finais/PAP1534_ed.pdf.

Cornell, Stephen, and Douglas Hartmann. *Ethnicity and Race: Making Identities in a Changing World.* Thousand Oaks, CA: Pine Forge Press, 1988.

Gans, Herbert. *The Urban Villagers.* New York: Free Press, 1962.

Gieryn, Thomas F. "City as Truth-Spot: Laboratories and Field-Sites in Urban Studies." *Social Studies of Science* 36, no. 1 (2006): 5–38.

Gieryn, Thomas F. "Three Truth Spots." *Journal of History of the Behavioral Sciences* 38, no. 2 (2002): 113–32.

Hanford, George H. "The Immigrants of Cambridge Massachusetts." In *A City's Life and Times. Cambridge in the Twentieth Century,* edited by Daphne Abeel, 13–25. Cambridge, MA: Cambridge Historical Society, 2007.

Hannerz, Ulf. *Exploring the City: Inquiries to an Urban Anthropology.* New York: Columbia University Press, 1980.

Harney, Robert F. "'Portygees and other Caucasians': Portuguese Migrants and the Racialism of the English-Speaking World." In *Portuguese Migration in Global Perspective,* edited by David Higgs, 113–35. Toronto: MHSO, 1990.

Lang, Henry R. "The Portuguese Element in New England." *Journal of American Folklore* 5 (1892): 9–18.

Lengermann, Patricia, and Gillian Niebrugge. "Thrice Told: Narratives of Sociology's Relation to Social Work." In *Sociology in America: A History,* edited by Craig Calhoun, 63–114. Chicago: University of Chicago Press, 2007.

Lindner, Rolf. "The Imaginary of the City." In *Sensing the City: A Companion to Urban Anthropology,* edited by Anja Schwanhausser, 114–19. Basel: Birkhauser Verlag, 2016.

Maycock, Susan E. *East Cambridge. Survey of Architectural History in Cambridge.* Rev. ed. Cambridge, MA: MIT Press, Cambridge Historical Commission, 1988.

Morgenroth, Lynda. *Boston Neighborhoods. A Food Lovers Walking, Eating and Shopping Guide to Ethnic Enclaves in and around Boston.* Guilford, CT: Globe Pequot Press, 2001.

Pap, Leo. *The Portuguese-Americans.* Boston: Twayne Publishers, 1981.

Rogers, Francis M. *American of Portuguese Descent: A Lesson in Differentiation.* Sage Research Papers in the Social Sciences. Beverly Hills and London: Sage Publications, 1974.

Stave, Bruce M. "A Conversation with Sam Bass Warner, Jr." *Journal of Urban History* 1, no. 1 (1974): 85–110.

Suttles, Gerald D. "The Cumulative Texture of Local Urban Culture." *American Journal of Sociology* 90 (1984): 283–304

Taft, Donald Reed. *Two Portuguese Communities in New England.* New York: Arno Press and *New York Times,* 1969.

Topalov, Christian. "La ville, «terre inconnue». L'enquête de Charles Booth et le peuple de Londres, 1886–1891." *Genèse* 5 (1991): 4–34.

Warner Jr., Sam Bass. "Foreword." In *The Zone of Emergence,* edited by Robert A. Woods and Albert J. Kennedy, v–vi. 2d ed. Cambridge, MA: MIT Press, 1969.

Warner Jr., Sam Bass. "Preface to the First Edition." In *The Zone of Emergence,* edited by Robert A. Woods and Albert J. Kennedy, 1–27. 2d ed. Cambridge, MA: MIT Press, 1969.

Whyte, William Foote. *Street Corner Society, The Social Structure of an Italian Slum.* Chicago: University of Chicago Press, 1943.

Woods, Robert A. *The City Wilderness. A Settlement Study by Residents and Associates of the South End House.* Boston: Houghton, Mifflin & Company, 1898.

Woods, Robert A., and Albert J. Kennedy. *The Zone of Emergence: Observations of the Lower Middle and Upper Working Class Communities of Boston, 1905–1914.* 2d ed. Cambridge, MA: MIT Press, 1969.

Notes

1. Lynda Morgenroth, *Boston Neighborhoods. A Food Lovers Walking, Eating and Shopping Guide to Ethnic Enclaves in and around Boston* (Guilford, CT: Globe Pequot Press, 2001), 169–93.

2. This chapter is part of an ethnographic research project on the uses and representations of the Portuguese-speaking category in Greater Boston. See Graça Índias Cordeiro, "Belongings and Interactions: Negotiating Portuguese-Speaking Identities in Boston," *Portuguese Literary and Cultural Studies* 26:111–26; and "A cidade à escala da rua. Usos e significados do passado na afirmação de 'tradições' locais urbanas," in *Patrimônio cultural:*

memória e intervenções urbanas, ed. Renato Cymbalista, Sarah Feldman, and Beatriz M. Kuhl (São Paulo: Anna Blume, 2017), 71–86.

3. Such as the well-known urban ethnographies *Street Corner Society* (North End, by William Foote Whyte, 1943) or *The Urban Villagers* (West End, by Herbert J. Gans, 1962).

4. Although the small towns of Cambridge and Somerville do not belong to Boston administratively, they are usually included in the same urban universe as the mother city.

5. Leo Pap, *The Portuguese-Americans* (Boston: Twayne Publishers, 1981), 61; Robert A. Woods and Albert J. Kennedy, *The Zone of Emergence: Observations of the Lower Middle and Upper Working Class Communities of Boston, 1905–1914* (Cambridge, MA: MIT Press, 1969), 101–2

6. With Frédéric Vidal, historian, who did a first overview and analysis of the most relevant historical sources, supported by a FLAD grant.

7. Sam Bass Warner Jr., "Foreword," in *The Zone of Emergence: Observations of the Lower Middle and Upper Working Class Communities of Boston, 1905–1914,* ed. Robert A, Woods and Albert J. Kennedy (Cambridge, MA: MIT Press, 1969a), v.

8. Robert F. Harney, "Portygees and Other Caucasians: Portuguese Migrants and the Racialism of the English-Speaking World," in *Portuguese Migration in Global Perspective,* ed. David Higgs (Toronto: MHSO), 113–35.

9. Sarah Boyer, *All in the Same Boat: Twentieth-Century Stories of East Cambridge* (Cambridge, MA: Cambridge Historical Commission, 2005), 12.

10. Francis M. Rogers, *American of Portuguese Descent: A Lesson in Differentiation* (Beverly Hills and London: Sage Publications, 1974), 42.

11. Sam Bass Warner Jr, "Preface to the First Edition," in *The Zone of Emergence,* ed. Robert A. Woods and Albert J. Kennedy (Cambridge, MA: MIT Press, 1969), 4.

12. Jane Adams, *Twenty Years at Hull-House* (New York: Macmillan, 1910).

13. Patricia Lengermann and Gillian Niebrugge, "Thrice Told: Narratives of Sociology's Relation to Social Work," in *Sociology in America: A History,* ed. Craig Calhoun, 63–114 (Chicago: University of Chicago Press, 2007).

14. Warner, "Preface," 3.

15. Sam Bass Warner contextualizes the uses of stereotypes: "Because of the antique tone of this book some mention should be made of this modern reader's reaction to the racial stereotyping found in the text (which) were commonplace for the day. They were neither kinder nor more unjust than normal prewar collegiate discourse. When this text was read to Mr. Kennedy in 1962, some forty years after he had last seen it, he too was shocked by some of the statements made about immigrants and Negroes." Warner, "Foreword," vi.

16. Warner, "Preface," 3.

17. Eugénie L. Birch, "Making Urban Research Intellectually Respectable: Martin Meyerson and the Joint Center for Urban Studies of Massachusetts Institute of Technology and Harvard University 1959–1964," *Journal of Planning History* 10, no. 3 (2011): 219–38.

18. Bruce M. Stave, "A Conversation with Sam Bass Warner, Jr.," *Journal of Urban History* 1, no. 1 (1974): 87.

19. Warner, "Preface," 1.

20. Warner, "Preface," 1.

21. Warner, "Foreword," v.

22. Warner, "Preface," 4. Actually, the relationship between the concentration of immigrants in slums and ghettos and ethnic identity, related to their process of assimilation, or Americanization, has been discussed for decades, even before the famous race relations cycle developed by Robert E. Park at the University of Chicago (called the "Chicago school of sociology") in the1920s, explaining that immigrant groups went through a series of phases as they gradually melt into the larger society. Stephen Cornell and Douglas Hartmann, *Ethnicity and Race: Making Identities in a Changing World* (Thousand Oaks, CA: Pine Forge Press, 1988). In 1898, Robert Woods characterized Boston's North End as a place where immigrants were not assimilated since they had remained foreign and isolated from other immigrants from other countries. In this slum the immigrant "does not become American for the simple reason that the North End is not American. It is Italian, Jewish, Irish, or Portuguese; and naturally the mere contiguity of these several elements, with the least possible association among them, has not produced an American type." Robert A. Woods, *The City Wilderness. A Settlement Study by Residents and Associates of the South End House* (Boston: Houghton, Mifflin & Company, 1898). But in *The Zone of Emergence*'s neighborhoods, the process of assimilation of the same national immigrants, as the Portuguese, has advanced a step. The slum appears here "as a temporary way-station on the path toward assimilation." Kathleen Neils Conzen, "Immigrants, Immigrant Neighborhoods, an Ethnic Identity: Historical Issues," *Journal of American History* 66, no. 3 (December 1979): 603–15.

23. Warner, "Preface," 21.

24. Warner, "Preface," 22.

25. Warner, "Preface," 15.

26. Warner, "Preface," 27.

27. Warner, Preface, 14. This point reminds Eduardo Carvalho's 'distressed' reflections on the rapidity of the Americanization of the Portuguese—those who gave up their nationality. Eduardo Carvalho, *Os portugueses da Nova Inglaterra* (Rio de Janeiro: A Leitura Colonial, 1931).

28. Warner, "Preface," 2.

29. Warner, "Preface," 18.

30. Warner, "Foreword," v

31. Warner, "Preface," 7.

32. Woods and Kennedy, *The Zone of Emergence*, 95–115.

33. Warner, "Preface," 5.

34. Woods and Kennedy, *The Zone of Emergence*, 97–98.

35. Woods and Kennedy, *The Zone of Emergence*, 98.

36. Woods and Kennedy, *The Zone of Emergence*, 102.

37. Henry R. Lang, "The Portuguese Element in New England," *Journal of American Folklore* 5 (1892): 9.

38. Pap, *The Portuguese-Americans*, 22, 55–57, 60, 85, 100.

39. Pap, *The Portuguese-Americans*, 61.

40. George H. Hanford, "The Immigrants of Cambridge Massachusetts." In *A City's Life and Times. Cambridge in the Twentieth Century*, ed. Daphne Abeel (Cambridge: Cambridge Historical Society, 2007), 18.

41. Woods and Kennedy, *The Zone of Emergence*, 100–101.

42. Woods and Kennedy, *The Zone of Emergence*, 102.

43. Woods and Kennedy, *The Zone of Emergence*, 101.

44. Susan E. Maycock, *East Cambridge. Survey of Architectural History in Cambridge* (Cambridge, MA: MIT Press, Cambridge Historical Commission (revised edition), 1988); Sarah Boyer, *All in the Same Boat: Twentieth-Century Stories of East Cambridge* (Cambridge, MA: Cambridge Historical Commission, 2005); Hanford, George H., "The Immigrants of Cambridge Massachusetts," in *A City's Life and Times. Cambridge in the Twentieth Century*, ed. Daphne Abeel (Cambridge: Cambridge Historical Society, 2007), 13–25; among others.

45. Warner, "Preface," 20.

46. Woods and Kennedy, *The Zone of Emergence*, 98.

47. Woods and Kennedy, *The Zone of Emergence*, 98–99.

48. Woods and Kennedy, *The Zone of Emergence*, 99.

49. Woods and Kennedy, *The Zone of Emergence*, 99.

50. Woods and Kennedy, *The Zone of Emergence*, 103–4.

51. Woods and Kennedy, *The Zone of Emergence*, 102.

52. Woods and Kennedy, *The Zone of Emergence*, 102.

53. Woods and Kennedy, *The Zone of Emergence*, 108.

54. Woods and Kennedy, *The Zone of Emergence*, 111.

55. Woods and Kennedy, *The Zone of Emergence*, 109.

56. Woods and Kennedy, *The Zone of Emergence*, 108.

57. Woods and Kennedy, *The Zone of Emergence*, 108.

58. Woods and Kennedy, *The Zone of Emergence*, 110.

59. Woods and Kennedy, *The Zone of Emergence*, 112.

60. Warner, "Preface," 20.

61. Warner, "Preface," 20.

62. Warner, "Foreword," v.

63. Warner, "Preface," 27.

64. Warner, "Preface," 8.

65. Ulf Hannerz, *Exploring the City: Inquiries to an Urban Anthropology* (New York: Columbia University Press, 1980), chap. 2.

66. See Cristiana Bastos, "Migrants, Inequalities and Social Research in the 1920s: The Story of Two Portuguese Communities in New England," *History and Anthropology* 29, no. 2 (2018): 163–83; and Graça I. Cordeiro and Frédéric Vidal, "Entre o gueto e a cidade: perspetivas cruzadas sobre a 'colónia' portuguesa na região de Boston no início do século XX," *VII Congresso Português de Sociologia,* Universidade do Porto, 19–22 Junho (2012).

67. Christian Topalov, "La ville, «terre inconnue». L'enquête de Charles Booth et le peuple de Londres, 1886–1891," *Genèse* 5 (1991): 4–34.

68. Woods and Kennedy, *The Zone of Emergence,* 114.

69. Thomas F. Gieryn, "Three Truth Spots," *Journal of History of the Behavioral Sciences,* 38, no. 2 (2002): 113; see also "City as Truth-Spot: Laboratories and Field-Sites in Urban Studies," *Social Studies of Science* 36, no. 1 (2006): 5–38.

70. Rolf Lindner, "The Imaginary of the City," in *Sensing the City. A Companion to Urban Anthropology,* ed. Anja Schwanhausser (Basel: Birkhauser Verlag, 2016): 116; see also Gerald D. Suttles, "The Cumulative Texture of Local Urban Culture," *American Journal of Sociology* 90 (1984): 283–304.

CHAPTER 4

The Portuguese of Fall River and the Fight for White Working-Class Status

PAULA CELESTE GOMES NOVERSA

This chapter examines the Portuguese community of Fall River, Massachusetts, in the 1920s. In contrast to Donald Taft's *Two Portuguese Communities* (1923), which focused on a single neighborhood of Fall River and a specific health issue affecting the Portuguese, it will use a broader approach to the Portuguese community as a whole, seeking to understand what factors shaped and gave support to the development of this community. This study will show that the Portuguese, like other immigrants of the time, were confronted with the difficult task of proving themselves deserving of the benefits of whiteness in a racially hierarchically structured society. It will accomplish this by (1) studying the history of the first Portuguese mass migration to the United States between 1870 and 1921, (2) focusing on the settlement patterns and community dynamics that shaped the 1920 Portuguese community in Fall River, and (3) examining the1920 doffers strike as evidence of the Portuguese community's emergence into ranks of the white American working class.

This chapter also argues that the Portuguese immigrants of this study hardly fit in the now classic history *The Uprooted* by Oscar Handlin.[1] The series of psychological shocks followed by the loneliness and despair that Handlin attributes to the immigrant experience does not reflect the experiences of the Portuguese arriving in Fall River at the turn of the twentieth century. In large measure, the expected "cultural trauma" was curbed by the existence of the ethnic neighborhoods that Fall River's Portuguese immigrants created for themselves.[2] Their experience of both change and continuity is closer to that depicted by historian John Bodnar's *The Transplanted*.[3] Bodnar grants the immigrant an agency both within the home and the neighborhood that escapes Handlin's interpretation. The Portuguese immigrant in this study experienced that same agency, as revealed in their settlement patterns, the founding of their churches, and the creation of their social clubs as well as their marriage patterns,

This study also examines the 1920 Fall River Portuguese immigrant in the workplace, namely the cotton textile mills of Fall River. Traditionally, historians of migration have led the discussion regarding the role that the workplace played in the lives of immigrants often identifying work and the workplace as a vehicle through which immigrants become "Americanized." Susan Glenn's *Daughters of the Shtetl* and James Barrett's *Americanization from the Bottom Up* both reflect this model of interpretation.[4]

Most recently, immigrant workplace mobility and trade unionism have received attention from labor historians, who are offering a new interpretation of these phenomena.[5] The dean of this new interpretation is David R. Roediger. In his seminal work, *The Wages of Whiteness*, Roediger argues that it is because the American industrial working class took shape in a slave-holding republic that "whiteness" conditions class consciousness in America.[6] Roediger's study focuses on the first sixty-five years of the nineteenth century. Through cultural analysis, he shows how the "wage slave" was transformed into the "free laborer." By the end of the Civil War and with the passage of the Thirteenth Amendment and the consequential end to institutional slavery in America, Irish Americans who earlier on had been categorized as nonwhite eagerly embraced the distinction of "whiteness" and all of the privileges that came with it. In some ways, Roediger is building on W. E. B. Du Bois's argument that white laborers are compensated for low wages by a "public and psychological wage" that grants them "public deference and titles of courtesy . . . [admittance to] public functions, public parks, and the best schools."[7]

In *Working towards Whiteness*—the follow-up to *Wages of Whiteness*—Roediger focuses on Jewish, Italian, and Polish immigrants and their efforts to be seen as white by turn of the twentieth-century American society. He points out that in some Southern educational districts Italian immigrants were assigned to black schools. In 1902 Minneapolis, the Washington League of Knights and Ladies excluded both "Negroes and Italians." After the Lawrence textile strike of 1912, Boston newspapers reported the news of the arrest of Italian American labor leaders as the renewed "ascendancy of the white-skinned races."[8] The first great wave of American immigrants (1870–1924) was confronted by this racialization of the American working class, and the Portuguese of Fall River were no exception.

Portuguese Immigration, 1870–1921

There are sparse predecessors to Portuguese mass migration to North America. The earliest known Portuguese settler was Mathias de Sousa, a resident of Maryland in 1634.[9] Although Britain's oldest ally, Portugal wasted no time after the American Revolution in reestablishing strong economic ties with the new republic.[10]

It was not until the whaling industry took root in nineteenth-century New England that a steady stream of Portuguese began to arrive on U.S. shores. Conditions on whaling vessels were harsh—long voyages, mean rations, and low wages. It became difficult for American captains to fit out their ships. Instead, they would set out with only a minimal crew of about twelve. Once they reached a way station in the Atlantic, they would take on supplies and sailors. The two most frequent stops were on the islands of Fayal (Azores) and Brava (Cape Verde). After the voyage, many of the Cape Verdean Bravas remained as seamen, but most of the Azorean Fayalense turned to other means of employment in New England.[11]

The California gold rush of 1849 also drew the Portuguese to the United States. This time they came from both the continent and the Atlantic islands. Regardless of whether they found their fortune in gold, many of these adventurers stayed on in California as farmers.[12] It was not until the post–Civil War period, however, that the Portuguese began to migrate to the United States in what can be called a mass migration. This first mass migration began circa 1870 and continued until 1921 when quota restrictions reduced migration to a minimum. The following graph (fig. 1) breaks down the number of documented immigrants for this time period by decade.[13]

Nearly three-quarters of Portuguese immigration occurred between 1901 and 1921. The majority of these immigrants were from the Azores (63%), with a smaller number coming from continental Portugal (26%) and the island of Madeira (11%).[14]

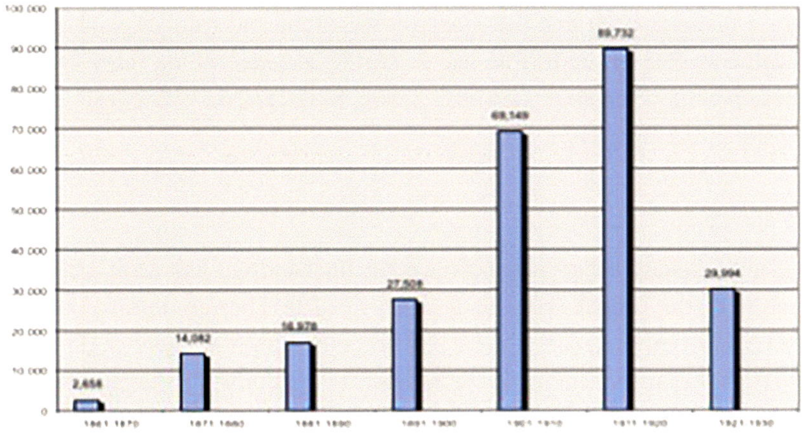

Figure 1. First Wave of Portuguese Immigration.

Borrowing from the perspective of migratory "pull factors," there are three main reasons for Portuguese emigration: (1) to escape economic stagnation in the homeland, (2) to avoid a peacetime draft, and (3) to reunite families separated by earlier migration. Many Portuguese saw no opportunity for economic growth at home. This was principally caused by the land tenure system in Portugal. In some regions, farmworkers could not own the land outright; they were either dispossessed or inherited the possibility of working on those lands, owned by a very small number of landlords. This situation coupled with high taxes and poor crop yields left many farmers desperate for a way out. Emigration offered a viable outlet for these laborers.[15]

The peacetime draft of able-bodied young men was a sore point with many Portuguese. The term of enlistment was three years at eight cents a day minus the cost of a uniform. Although a substitute could be hired, this was not an option available to the poor. For the Azoreans this was especially disturbing since they had often felt neglected by the mainland government. Emigration was seen as an opportunity to circumvent this unpopular law.[16]

Finally, there was a migration stream created by the early Azorean seamen on the whaling vessels. What began as intermittent recruitment became a regular point of direct labor recruitment for these ships. As noted earlier, once on land the Fayalense soon turned to other economic pursuits. After establishing themselves in a community, they would then send for other family members.[17] At first these voyages were long and arduous, with immigrants traveling for up to a month on small passenger sailing ships, but the development of the steamship lines greatly facilitated travel between Portugal and the United States.

The Era of the Steamship

It is no coincidence that the era of the ocean liner and the "first wave" of immigration to the United States both began in 1870. They are interconnected. By 1870, inventions such as the screw propeller, the compound engine, and the triple-expansion engine made transoceanic shipping on a large scale possible. The demand for these large-scale ocean liners increased to meet the needs of immigrants crossing the Atlantic. Over the decades that make up the "first wave," millions of men and women crossed the Atlantic Ocean on the newly established steamship lines. This demand resulted in many steamship lines. Naturally, the development of the steamship lines also facilitated travel between Portugal and the United States. Two outstanding trans-Atlantic ocean liner fleets of the day were the White Star Line and the Fabre Line.

By 1917 both the Fabre Line and the White Star Line were making regular trips to mainland Portugal, the Azores, and Madeira. The White Star Line offered round-trip first-class and second-class passage from Boston to Egypt along their Mediterranean cruise voyage. On the return voyage, the same ship served as an immigrant transit ship for third-class (or steerage) passengers. One of these was the steamship RMS *Cretic* pictured below (fig. 2).[18]

Figure 2. R.M.S. Cretic, 1905.

Figure 3. 1917 White Star Line Advertisement.

The White Star Line regularly ran advertisements in the Portuguese-language paper of Fall River. It boasted superior accommodations and an average passage of only six days. The White Star Line advertisement, pictured above (fig. 3), encouraged recent immigrants to "Bring your friends from the Islands" and guaranteed all third-class passengers inclusive train tickets to "Fall River, New Bedford, Taunton, Providence, Newport, etc, etc."[19]

Inducements like this both facilitated immigration and helped to increase the pace of immigration to the United States at the turn of the twentieth century. Rapid industrial expansion in the United States created a need for inexpensive labor, which could be filled more easily by immigrants traveling via steamship.

Settlement: Home, Church, and Neighborhood

The 1920 Census of the United States revealed that in Fall River there were 42,421 foreign-born out of a total population of 120,458, roughly one-third.[20] While just about half of the population of Fall River were between the ages of 15 and 44 (prime working age), nearly 80 percent of the population of Fall River was under the age of 45.[21] Of the age group over fifteen, the census also revealed that Fall River had nearly the same number of males as females, a third of whom were single.[22]

Based on this census data, it is clear that Fall River was a draw to immigrants seeking a new life in the United States. The Fall River of 1920 was a large urban center, with a youthful and ethnically diverse population. Of the 42,421 foreign-born residents of Fall River in 1920, 12,103 were of Portuguese descent.[23] In the case of Fall River, direct recruitment of mill hands from the island of São Miguel in the Azores explains the unusually high concentration of Micaelenses in the Fall River textile industry.[24] The typical Portuguese immigrant was between the ages of 14 and 44 years old, unskilled, and illiterate.[25]

Upon arriving in Fall River, the average Portuguese immigrant immediately set about finding employment, usually as a textile mill hand, and a place to live, usually in a nearby apartment—more commonly first as a boarder and then as a renter. The process of leaving the islands would quickly transform the immigrant from someone living in a distinctly rural community to someone living in an urban space, from working in farm labor to industrial labor, from a Portuguese-speaking to an English-dominated society, and from the comfort of familial surroundings to that of a relatively unknown world. All this after a short six-day steamship voyage.

How well these individuals adjusted to life and work in Fall River was directly related to the ethnic community that awaited them. The foundation of this community was the large extended patriarchal family. As Agnes Conforti, the daughter of a Portuguese immigrant noted, "Everything was home. Home was the most important center of the family."[26] Children lived with their parents until they were married and were essential contributors to the family's economy.

A child of fourteen could expect to work in the mills for eight to twelve hours a day at an average pay of seven to eight dollars per week. Gertrude Rogers, a weaver in the Fall River textile mills in 1922, recalls, "The pay I was getting at fourteen [was] eight dollars a week. I used to get fifty cents a week spending money and I thought that was wonderful! I was always waiting for payday to get that fifty cents a week."[27] The eight dollars a week would have been an economic imperative for the family because parents did not earn much more than their children. In order for the family to survive—to pay rent, to buy coal, food, and clothing—everyone in the family had to work.

Beyond the family unit, there were the ethnic neighborhoods. Each neighborhood was typically organized by ethnic group. In Fall River these ethnic divisions were many: English, Irish, Polish, Italian, French (who were actually Quebecois), and Portuguese, to name but a few. The most densely populated and longest established Portuguese neighborhood in Fall River was the Columbia Street area. It spanned over fifteen city blocks and was home to Santo Christo Church. The second largest Portuguese neighborhood was in the city's "North End" and was home to St. Michael's Church. Finally, there was the Flint neighborhood for which Espirito Santo Church was built.

The following three maps are of Fall River in 1923, and they illustrate the contemporary settlement patterns of the Portuguese (figs. 4–6). These settlement maps were created by the author with the use of the 1925 City Directory. By studying the family names of the city residents, going street by street, it was possible to create a map that reflected these Portuguese enclaves. The streets in pink represent streets in which the overwhelming number of residents were Portuguese. The areas in green represent the streets in which there was a fifty-fifty ratio of Portuguese and other (predominantly French Canadian) ethnicities—most of which eventually became pink.[28]

These neighborhoods included local grocers, confectioners, barbers, bars and social clubs, and, as mentioned above, churches. The proprietors of these establishments were former Portuguese immigrants themselves who could speak to their clients in their own native tongue. Take, for example, the Columbia Street neighborhood. At the center of this neighborhood was, of course, Santo Christo Church located on the corner of Canal and Columbia Streets, but there were numerous Portuguese-owned businesses on Columbia Street alone. A Portuguese immigrant could get their groceries from the Portuguez [sic] Wholesale Grocery on 77 Columbia Street. At 249 Columbia Street, home of the local Portuguese-language newspaper, *As Novidades,* they could not only buy a copy of the paper but also talk to the editor. If they needed new furnishings, they could stop in at Cavaco Furniture Company at 295 Columbia Street. They had the services of a trained dentist, Dr. Joseph C. Carvalho, at 422 Columbia Street. They could obtain the assistance of a barber, William F. Almeida, at 444 Columbia Street. If, sadly, they needed the services of an undertaker, they need go no further than Rogers & Oliveira (undertakers) on 299 Columbia Street. In effect, a broad range of the immigrant's practical necessities could be met within the confines of the neighborhood.[29]

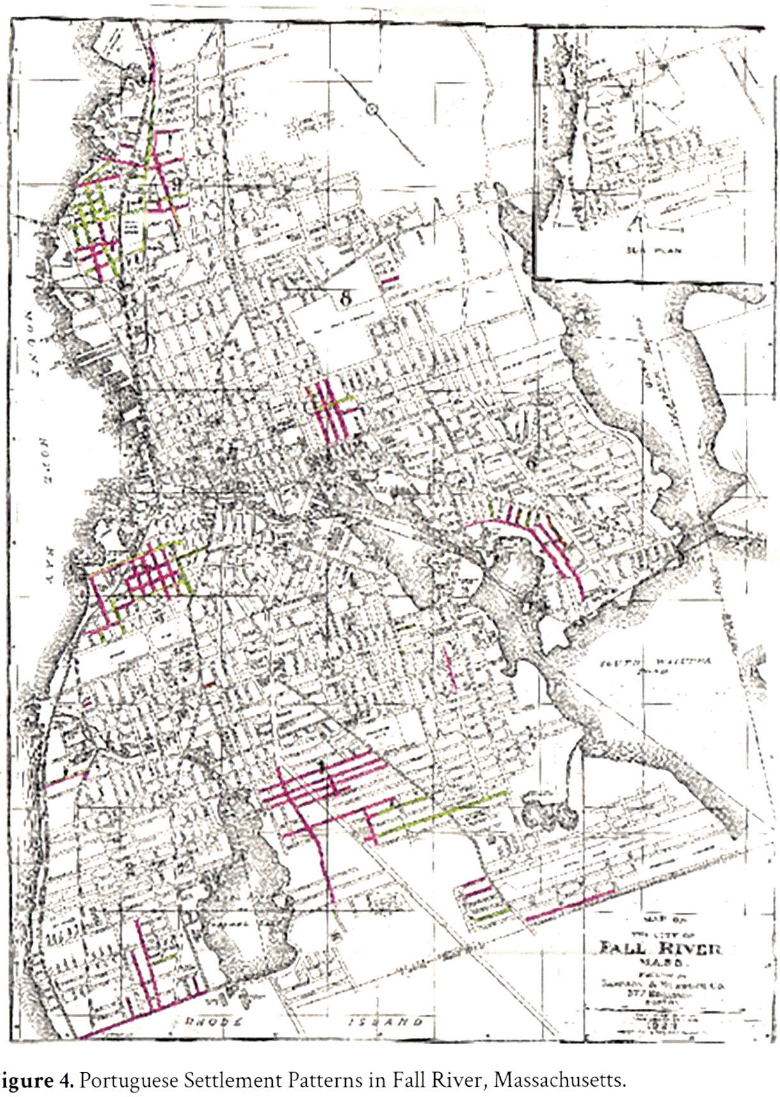

Figure 4. Portuguese Settlement Patterns in Fall River, Massachusetts.

Each neighborhood in Fall River was, to a certain extent, marked by its ethnic makeup. A stranger walking down the street would hear the native language of its occupants, smell the scents of ethnic cooking, and even witness children playing games particular to their native lands. John Camara, a Portuguese immigrant to Fall River, recalled that in his youth, "If a neighbor was sick, everybody took turns going over to see how they were doing and

Figure 5. North End Neighborhood (Ward 9) and the Columbia Street Neighborhood (Ward 3).

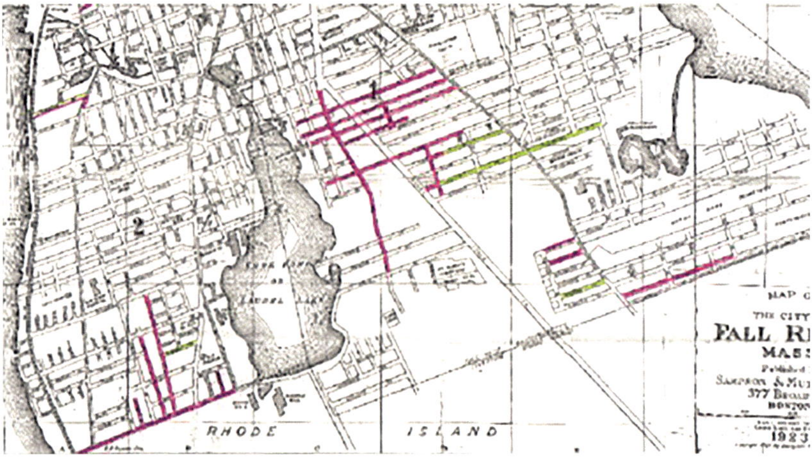

Figure 6. Flint Neighborhood (Ward 6).

would help them with the housework or cooking."[30] All of this made for a very tight-knit community.

This is not to say that other ethnic groups did not socialize at all within these neighborhoods. To an extent, they had to because even in the three neighborhoods mentioned above there were some streets that were not ethnically exclusive. In other words, some streets had exclusively Portuguese residents, while others had a mix of Portuguese and some other ethnicity. When asked how well different ethnic groups associated with each other, John Camara—whose mother had lived on Flint Street, a predominantly French-speaking street in the Flint—remarked, "Not too close . . . there was always friction between the French and the Portuguese but eventually they became the closest of all the nationalities."[31]

The limits of this interethnic association can be measured by studying the rate of out-marriages within the Portuguese community in Fall River at the turn of the century. The table below clearly shows that, even after the wave of Portuguese immigration began to diminish in the mid-1920s, only a small number of Portuguese married outside of their ethnic group (table 1). In 1916, when the largest number of marriages took place, only eight involved marriages of mixed ethnic background. Thus, although they lived in proximity to one another, there were no clear social ties binding one ethnic group to another.[32]

Of course, although most of the immigrants in Fall River were Roman Catholic and thereby shared the same religious beliefs, they did not pray in the same churches. Each group had their own national churches. These churches were an integral part of the neighborhood. By 1925 Fall River had

Table 1. Marriage Patterns

	1888	1902	1909	1916	1923	1930
No. of Port. immigrants who were married	21	233	404	712	618	208
No. of marriages involving at least one Port. immigrant	11	132	206	360	330	110
No. of marriages involving a Port. immigrant and a non-Port.	1	11	16	8	42	12
No. of marriages in which both parents of one spouse were Port. and neither parent of the other spouse were Port.	1	13	12	12	70	46

no fewer than seven of these Portuguese national churches. The following is a list of those parishes including their year of founding (table 2).

These churches provided the setting for some of the highpoints in an immigrant's life. This is where the immigrants would marry, have their children baptized and confirmed, give their daughters away in marriage, and say goodbye to their deceased loved ones. It was here that they joined with their neighbors in faith and bore witness to each other's joys and sorrows.

The masses were celebrated in Latin, but the homily was always in Portuguese and delivered by well-educated Portuguese priests. These priests often acted as a liaison between the parishioners and the outside, that is, English-speaking community. Indeed, after 1911, among the first contacts a passenger on the Fabre Line steamships would meet upon disembarking in Providence would be a representative of the Roman Catholic Church. These Church agents offered the passengers translating/interpreting services and assistance with exchanging currency, as well as ensuring they found correct train lines

Table 2. Portuguese National Churches

1876	Santo Christo
1902	St. Michael
1904	Espirito Santo
1911	St. Anthony of Padua
1915	St. Elizabeth
1915	Our Lady of the Angels
1924	Our Lady of Health

Note. Data taken from Francis M. Rogers, *Americans of Portuguese Descent: A Lesson in Differentiation* (London: Sage Publications, 1974), 27.

to reach their destination. They also paid particular attention to caring for young single ladies who they thought were the Fabre Line's most vulnerable passengers.[33]

National churches were able to organize church feasts according to the customs practiced in their parishioners' homeland. These would involve solemn processions, festive costumes, music, and dance. It was a great opportunity for the entire parish to socialize as well as a reaffirmation of ethnic identity. The Portuguese had such close ties with their churches that some practiced a costly tradition. John Camara described it thus: "When we worked, the first pay we got we used to have to send it to the old country, to the church. I remember my grandmother was living in the old country then, in the Azores, and my first pay was at the mill. I was getting seven dollars and my mother sent that to her mother to give to the church out there. It was a tradition. Our first pay, so God would give us luck."[34]

There were also many social clubs and associations which were formed by the Portuguese community. Some of these were strictly recreational, for example, the Moonshiner's Club.[35] Others were fraternal benevolent societies, such as the Associação Portuguesa Beneficente de São Miguel Arcanjo, Inc., and the St Joseph's Portuguese Protective and Benevolent Society. These fraternal societies served an important networking service within the Portuguese community that helped strengthen the bonds of community. They were also founded as a means to aid fellow Portuguese in times of family sickness or death and, thereby, could help keep families financially stable during periods of economic loss.[36]

Thus, within their homes, their neighborhoods, their churches, and their social clubs, Portuguese immigrants found a refuge from American society, places where Old World traditions of kinship and faith were maintained. They provided places where Portuguese was spoken, and homemade wine was shared with neighbors over a friendly game of cards or dominos.

Work and Union Participation

Immigrants were drawn out of their enclave by their employment. Nowhere else was this more true than in the textile mills in Fall River. Many of the immigrant groups in the city were well represented in these factories because the textile mills were the leading employers. Although it is true that the different departments in the mills were often divided along ethnic lines, these were not strict divisions. Any given department would have a majority of one or two ethnic groups as workers. Arthur G. Wilson, a retired cotton mill supervisor, explained it this way:

> There was a lot of what you call Syrians and Lebanese. They used to be in the weave room a lot. The Poles and the Portuguese people used to be in the carder [carding department]. In the spinning room, it was dominated by mostly French people. They hung in clans. The reason was, like, say you worked on the spinning frame. So you would say I got a son or a daughter and you would bring him into the mill. The boss would accept him on account of you. You would teach him for nothing and when he got to know the job then the overseer would give him a job. It was a family.[37]

The extent of the textile mill operation in Fall River was described by local historian Philip T. Silvia:

> By the turn of the century, forty-two cotton textile corporations were valued at more than $45 million, while three other corporations, capitalized at nearly $7 million, were engaged in the closely associated processes of textile dyeing and finishing. Furthermore there were 26,371 textile workers in 1900. And despite intermittent periods of depression, the number of spindles in place rose from 2,164,664 in 1890 to 3,246,468 in 1904. Its residents understandably boasted in 1901 that the Spindle City [nickname for Fall River] mills were weaving slightly more than 843 million yards of cloth per year. On a typical work day its total output was an extraordinary 1,571 miles of cloth.[38]

By 1920 those numbers had grown. Fall River was now home to fifty cotton manufacturing corporations operating 111 mills. Fall River's textile industry employed nearly 35,000 operatives and distributed over $400,000 weekly in wages.[39]

Textile unions in Fall River were associated with the United Textile Workers of America (UTW). The UTW was predominantly a union of native-born male workers of English, Scottish, and Irish descent.[40] In Fall River, only 16–19 percent of textile workers were unionized.[41] This number may seem low, but the reality was that while the bulk of the textile workers were not skilled craftsmen, these were craft unions—that is, skilled worker unions.[42]

Union membership rolls in Fall River reflected the national trend at the time. English and Irish workers dominated union membership in Fall River. Early on, Portuguese laborers proved to be willing to make personal sacrifices for the greater workers' good. An example of this was their willingness to support the Fall River textile mill strike of 1904. John Golden, president of the UTW, was quoted in a July 25, 1904, *Fall River Daily Globe* article: "I cannot help but compliment the French, Portuguese, Italian and Polish people for the splendid way in which they stood by their English-speaking brothers and sisters."[43]

Despite their relatively recent arrival in Fall River and their small numbers as skilled craftsmen, by 1925 the Portuguese participated in these craft unions to a surprising degree. Of the six unions associated with the UTW, the Portuguese held executive offices in three—the Bleachers' Union, the Weavers' Union, and the Doffers' Union. In the latter, the Portuguese were the majority and held all three offices—president, secretary, and treasurer. They also held offices in the Print Workers' Union and the Central Labor Union.[44] Their willingness not only to join labor unions but also to take leadership roles within those unions reflects an understanding of what union membership meant. This was not simply job security. It meant social mobility and respect as well.

In 1920 it was the Portuguese themselves who led a strike. As stated earlier, many Portuguese were doffers. It was the task of the doffer to doff, or remove, the filled bobbins from the spinning frames and replace them with empty ones. On March 13, 1920, the Cotton Manufacturers' Association (CMA) rejected a 17.5 percent increase in wages as requested by the Doffers' Union. This increase reflected the UTW's goal of standardized wages within the textile mill payroll. The Doffers' Union was affiliated with the UTW and worked closely with it over the next three months. The Doffers' Union thought this increase a reasonable request as mill profits had been strong in the first quarter of that year, and nine other mills in Fall River were already paying their doffers at this increased rate. When the CMA rejected the offer and countered with a much lower rate of increase, the Doffers' Union voted to strike.[45]

The first day of the strike, Monday, March 15, 1920, saw the closing of two mills, the Merchants and the American Linen Mills. It is no coincidence that these mills are both within walking distance of a Portuguese neighborhood.[46] The Merchants Mill is in the North End neighborhood, and the American

Linen Mills is in the Columbia Street neighborhood. That same day, the *Fall River Daily Globe* reported that the northern section of the city was the hardest hit by the strike. The Doffers' Union reported that thirteen other mills were without any doffers, while the Border City Mills only had 50 percent of its doffers reporting for work.[47]

The next day saw two more mills close. John L. Campos, secretary of the Doffers' Union, was quite confident when he reported, "It is true that many of the mills are operating but it is only on yarns they have stored up before the strike began. When these yarns are used up the whole plant will have to close down."[48] Since it was the job of the doffer to remove the filled bobbins of yarn from the spinning machines, these mills could only weave cloth from yarns on bobbins that had been filled prior to the strike.

On Wednesday the Emergency Board of the UTW met in New York City to endorse the Doffers' Union strike in Fall River, known to them as Local 1057. They also recommended that the Central Labor Union of Fall River endorse the strike as well.[49] Meanwhile, in Fall River, it was alleged that some mill superintendents were using "unfair methods" to break the strike. The union claimed that superintendents were not only threatening strikers with permanent loss of their jobs but were also insisting that husbands "compel their wives and daughters to become strikebreakers."[50] Concurrently, the CMA released a statement saying they would "fight [the] strike to a finish." The millowners were confident because stocks in their companies were maintaining a steady price on the market regardless of the strike. Indeed, the first two mills to close—American Linen and the Merchants mills—were not financially threatened. American Linen showed an increase to $160 per share, while Merchants was holding at $260 per share.[51]

Tempers flared when four picketing strikers were arrested outside of the Flint Mills. The president of the Doffers' Union, James Foley, along with three other union members—Manuel R. Costa, Antone F. Oliveira, and Manuel E. Mello—were arrested by Captain Patrick Connors and two assisting officers on March 25, 1920, and charged with obstructing the sidewalk. Secretary Campos witnessed the arrest, "We were walking quietly along two by two when Capt. Connors and his men came up to us and told us to keep moving. We had just started to cross over the street, when four of our men were put under arrest." Campos was beside himself. He went on to say, "If all the policemen of the city acted the same way as Capt. Connors did this noon there would be a revolution in the city very soon."[52]

When the four arrived in Second District Court the following Tuesday, the courtroom was packed to capacity, and the crowd of spectators, strikers all, spilled out into the hallways of the courthouse. Many of these spectators had come as witnesses for the defense. They were not needed, as Deputy Chief Barker immediately asked that the complaint be dismissed. Judge Hanify complied, and the men were released forthwith.[53]

As the months passed, tensions were mounting throughout the city without either side showing signs of capitulation. The CMA and the Doffers' Union officials continued to issue conflicting reports as to the effects of the drawn-out strike. The union continued to have regular meetings with its membership to keep them appraised and to issue strike benefits. Naturally the hardest hit were the laborers' families.

Father Manuel A. Silva, third pastor of the Santo Christo Church, was well aware of the hardship this strike wrought on his parishioners. On Saturday, May 29, 1920, Father Silva met with representatives of the CMA in an effort to reach a compromise. The following day a meeting was held of the Doffers' Union. Officers were told that the CMA had agreed to a 15 percent increase for doffers "and improvements of conditions for third hands and other operatives in the spinning rooms." A general meeting of the Doffers' Union was held on the following Tuesday in which Father Silva himself presented the CMA's offer. A vote was taken, and the offer was accepted.[54] It would, however, take nearly six more weeks before all of the strikers were off of the strike list and back to their original positions.

Portuguese-Language Newspapers: Strike Coverage and Reaction

The Portuguese weekly *As Novidades* had remained fairly silent during the entire length of the protracted strike. When in mid-July the last of the doffers finally went back to work, the editor had only this to say: "The Iron Works Factory suffered the greatest absence of personnel because the Spinners of this factory are almost exclusively Portuguese and this strike, it can well be said, was inaugurated and carried by the Portuguese element."[55] As noted above, the factories that were most affected by the strike were those in Portuguese neighborhoods. Excluding President Foley, the union men who were arrested as picketing strikers were Portuguese. The secretary and most vocal officer of the Doffers' Union, John L. Campos, was also Portuguese.

A critical part of the union leadership, and active on the picket lines, the Portuguese were at the forefront of the strike. These laborers had previously been landless peasants, and now they were affiliated with a national American union (UTW) that represented scores of workers from different backgrounds. The strike did not weaken their commitment to being a part of the labor movement in the United States; on the contrary, applications for union membership in Fall River increased during the strike.[56] The 1920 Doffers' Union strike affirmed the Portuguese laborer's ability to conduct himself within the standards and expectations of the American labor movement.

It is interesting to underline how the Portuguese workers resisted the objections of their own community as expressed in local media. Evidence of this can be found in the tenacity of the doffers when faced with disapproval from their own ethnic newspapers. Ethnic newspapers tend to reflect the values of the ethnic community from which they spring. They give voice to the group. They help interpret news and events both within and outside of the community.[57]

The two Portuguese-language newspapers of the day in this region were *As Novidades* and *A Alvorada.* Neither paper supported the strike. The relative silence of *As Novidades* spoke volumes. Fundamentally, it reported only the beginning of the strike and its end. As noted earlier, the *As Novidades* publishing house was located on Columbia Street. That placed it just up the street from the American Linen Mills and on the same street as Santo Christo Church. Yet it did not once report on the impact of the strike on the workers or its impact on the Columbia Street neighborhood merchants. It never published an interview with the millowners, the striking doffers, or Father Silva. It chose not to report on an event that for months adversely impacted both its readership and its neighbors.

On the other hand, from the beginning, *A Alvorada* was openly critical of the doffers' decision to strike. It continued its criticism throughout the duration of the strike. On March 18, 1920, it reported the start of the strike with the following comment: "We do not agree with this idea [of striking] as a result of the high cost of living."[58] As the strike continued so did the reports, "The strike continues . . . the result being thousands of workers are without employment."[59] One week later the paper increased its critique of the strike stating, "What is certain is that the situation is terrible and that the times are not opportune for strikes."[60] When the strike was finalized, *A*

Alvorada reported on the union vote and ended the brief article by pointing out to its readership that "since the year 1916, the factories of Fall River have raised their workers' salaries by 169 per cent."[61] Clearly, the editorial staff of both papers did not approve of the decision by these Portuguese laborers to strike. Nevertheless, in the face of disapproval and even open criticism from members of their own ethnic community, the Portuguese doffers were loyal members of their union.

Conclusion

In their homes and in their neighborhoods, the Portuguese reinforced their culture at every turn. They spoke Portuguese. They ate Portuguese food. They participated in Portuguese choral and folkloric groups. They prayed in Roman Catholic Churches in Latin and Portuguese.

Nonetheless, in the textile mills the Portuguese worked side by side with other ethnic groups. If they were to succeed economically, they had to learn to speak English so that they could train for better positions within the mills. In the labor unions they not only worked with other European ethnic groups but also, and more importantly, with white Anglo-Saxon, Protestant, English-speaking individuals.

More than anywhere else, it was in the workplace and in the skilled labor unions such as the UTW that the Portuguese were drawn out of their immigrant community and into white American society. It was in their union participation that they reached beyond ethnic ties to a new working-class identity. This union working-class identity was distinctly white.

At the very time when the Portuguese were joining the unions and leading a strike, national labor unions such as the American Federation of Labor and its affiliate the UTW were at the forefront of the nativist movement. They were demanding new immigration legislation that would require literacy tests (1917) of new arrivals and, later, immigration quotas (1921 and 1924) meant to put an end to the immigration of southern and eastern European immigrants, including the Portuguese. By 1924, this legislation had succeeded in putting an end to the historic first great wave of American immigration.

That same year, publication of Taft's study *Two Portuguese Communities in New England* was met with outrage from the Portuguese community. Donald R. Taft earned his PhD at Columbia University in 1923. As such, his academic training as a sociologist and his research were influenced by the now infamous eugenics movement. His study of the Portuguese in Fall River, *Two Portuguese Communities in New England,* is a reflection of the best and worst aspects of this movement.[62] His methodology was solid—extensive use of primary sources, including vast data collection through the use of interviews. His theory was flawed because it was racially biased. In the very first paragraph of his introduction, Taft states that the high infant mortality rates of the Portuguese in New England first drew his attention to this community. For Taft, this then begged the question, Did the infants die "because of racial and nationalistic traits, or because the Portuguese chanced to be exposed to peculiarly adverse surroundings?"[63] His pursuit of the answer to this question led him to study two Portuguese communities, one in Portsmouth, Rhode Island (as a rural case study), and one in Fall River, Massachusetts (as an urban case study).

On March 23, 1924, an estimated six thousand members of the surrounding Portuguese communities gathered in New Bedford's Grove Park. Organized by the Club Portuguez Recreativo, this was meant to be a meeting held within the clubhouse. The turnout was so large that, at the last minute, organizers had to get city permission to take the meeting outdoors. There were a multitude of prominent speakers present including consular representatives from the Portuguese Consulates of New Bedford and New Haven, Connecticut.[64]

The next day the protest meeting made front-page news in the newspaper *A Alvorada.* The paper reported that the protest was due to certain affirmations made by Taft in his book "in which the Portuguese race is considered inferior and ignorant."[65] Taft did conclude that the Portuguese were ignorant, in that the majority of them were illiterate and did not keep their children in school after that period required by law.[66] He did not state outright that they were inferior. He did, however, dedicate the entirety of his second chapter to the composition of the Portuguese race, which he argued had had no less than four "infusion[s] of negro or negroid blood," especially those of the "Island Portuguese."[67] The inference being made was that the Portuguese were inferior because of these four "infusions." That was not lost on the Portuguese who gathered in protest at Grove Park.

With a stroke of a pen, Taft undermined decades of Portuguese immigrant effort within the workplace to earn that coveted place among the white working class by identifying them or linking them by blood to the "Negro" race.[68] The six thousand Portuguese that gathered that Sunday afternoon in New

Bedford's Grove Park wanted vindication. The lengthy protest statement that was addressed to Taft and read aloud to the public began by stating that the Portuguese were "a race of intrepid conquerors, [and] navigators . . . [with] vast colonies that even today constitute the third largest colonial empire in the world."[69] Clearly, the distinction being made was that the Portuguese were the conquerors—like the British and the Dutch, white Europeans—not the conquered, that is, black Africans.

The term "inferior race" that had earlier been associated with and used to justify the enslavement of blacks within the United States was, at the turn of the twentieth century, often used to describe immigrants from southern and eastern Europe. The eugenics movement emboldened racist thought in the United States by offering a "scientific" basis to racial classification. The Portuguese of Fall River experienced this firsthand with the publication of *Two Portuguese Communities in New England.* Their reaction was an acknowledgement of what was at stake for them as a community in the racially charged United States.

Works Cited

Primary Sources

Archives

Ferreira-Mendes Portuguese-American Archives, University of Massachusetts Dartmouth, Portuguese Alliance Benevolent Association (Associação Beneficiente Aliança Portuguesa) Records, 1924–2004, MC50/PAA, Dartmouth, MA.

Documents

Fall River Directory Massachusetts, 1915–1925.

U. S. Department of Commerce, Bureau of the Census. *The Fourteenth Census of the United States: 1920.* Vols. 1–3.

Newspapers

As Novidades. 1917–25.
Fall River Evening Herald. 1915–25.
Fall River Daily Globe. 1915–25.
A Alvorada, 1920, 1924.

Interviews

Ana Camara, Rose Sousa, Olive Farias, John Camara. Interview by John Conforti, Lisa Boyle, Carol Picard, and Lisa St. Pierre. August 16, 1979. Tape recording. B. M. C. Durfee High School of Fall River Library.

Agnes Conforti. Interview by Lori Miozza and David Polseli August 10, 1981. Tape recording. B. M. C. Durfee High School of Fall River Library.

Gertrude Rogers. Interview by Nanette Durette, Nancy Tones, and Sandra Silva. July 21, 1980. Tape recording. B. M. C. Durfee High School of Fall River Library.

Arthur G. Wilson and Ray Gaskell. Interview by Paula Noversa and Randy Chabot. July 27, 1981. Tape recording. B. M. C. Durfee High School of Fall River Library.

Secondary Sources

Dissertations

Baganha, Maria loannis Benis. "International Labor Movements: Portuguese Emigration to the United States, 1820–1930." PhD diss., University of Pennsylvania, 1988.

Leite, Joaquim da Costa. "Portugal and Emigration, 1855–1914." PhD diss., Columbia University, 1994.

Rosa Borges, Aluisio Medeiros de. "The Portuguese Working Class in the Durfee Mills of Fall River, Massachusetts: A Study of the Division of Labor, Ethnicity, and Labor Union Participation, 1895–1925." PhD diss., State University of New York, Binghamton, 1990.

Whitehead, Paul Charles. "The Assimilation of the Portuguese in Fall River, Massachusetts." PhD diss., University of Massachusetts, Amherst, 1966.

Books

Bernard, William S. "A History of the U. S. Immigration Policy." In *Immigration*, edited by Richard A. Easterlin et al. Cambridge, MA: Belknap Press of Harvard University, 1982.

Bettencourt, José de Sousa. *O Fenómeno da Emigração Portuguesa.* Luanda: Instituto de Investigação Científica de Angola, 1961.

Bodnar, John. *The Transplanted: A History of Immigrants in Urban America.* Bloomington: Indiana University Press, 1985.

Cameron, Ardis. *Radicals of the Worst Sort: Laboring Women in Lawrence, Massachusetts, 1860–1912.* Chicago: University of Illinois Press, 1993.

Carpenter, Niles. *Immigrants and Their Children.* The American Immigration Collection. New York: Arno Press and the *New York Times*, 1969.

Chapin, Francis W. *Tides of Migration: A Study of Migration, Decision-Making and Social Progress in São Miguel, Azores.* New York: AMS Press, 1989.

Cumbler, John T. *Working-Class Community in Industrial America—Work, Leisure and Struggle in Two Industrial Cities, 1880–1930.* Westport, CT: Greenwood Press, 1979.

Daniel, Clete. *Culture of Misfortune: An Interpretive History of Textile Unionism in the United States.* Ithaca, NY: Cornell University Press, 2001.

Du Bois, W. E. B. *Black Reconstruction in the United States: An Essay toward a History of the Part Which Black Folk Played in the Attempt to Reconstruct Democracy in America, 1860–1880.* Edited by Henry Louis Gates, Jr. New York: Oxford University Press, 2007. First published 1935

Evangelista, João. *Um Século de População Portuguesa (1864–1960).* Lisbon: Publicações do Centro de Estudos Demográficos, I.N.E., 1971.

Glenn, Susan A. *Daughters of the Shtetl: Life and Labor in the Immigrant Generation.* Ithaca, NY: Cornell University Press, 1990.

Goulart, Tony, Coordinator. *Capelinhos, A Volcano of Synergies: Azorean Immigration to America.* San Jose: Portuguese Heritage Publications of California, 2008.

Handlin, Oscar. *The Uprooted: The Epic Story of the Great Migrations That Made the American People.* Boston: Little, Brown and Company, 1951.

Hareven, Tamara K. and Randolph Langenbach. *Amoskeag: Life and Work in an American Factory City.* New York: Pantheon Books, 1978.

Hayman, Robert W. *Catholicism in Rhode Island and the Diocese of Providence.* Vol. 2. Providence, RI: Diocese of Providence, 1995.

Lane, A. T. *Solidarity or Survival? American Labor and European Immigrants, 1830–1924.* Contributions in Labor Studies 21. New York: Greenwood Press, 1987.

Morison, Samuel Eliot. *The Maritime History of Massachusetts 1783–1860.* Northeastern Classics Edition. Boston: Northeastern University Press, 1979.

Pap, Leo. *The Portuguese-Americans.* Boston: Twayne Publishers, 1981.

Pereira, M. Halpern. *Política e Economia (Portugal nos Séculos XIX e XX).* Lisbon: Livros Horizonte, 1979.

Roediger, David R. *Wages of Whiteness: Race and the Making of the American Working Class.* New York: Verso, 1991. Reprinted, 1993.

———. *Working towards Whiteness: How America's Immigrants Became White, The Strange Journey from Ellis Island to the Suburbs.* New York: Basic Books, 2005.

Roediger, David R., and Philip S. Foner. *Our Own Time: A History of American Labor and the Working Day.* Contributions in Labor Studies 23. New York: Greenwood Press, 1989.

Rogers, Francis. *Americans of Portuguese Descent: A Lesson in Differentiation.* London: Sage Publications, 1974.

Sowell, Thomas. *Ethnic America: A History.* New York: Basic Books, 1981.

Taft, Donald R. *Two Portuguese Communities in New England.* New York: Columbia University Press, 1967.

Tavares, Belmira E. *Portuguese Pioneers in the United States.* Fall River, MA: R. E. Smith Printing, 1973.

Warrin, Donald, and Geoffry L. Gomes, *Land as Far as the Eye Can See: The Portuguese in the Old West.* Spokane, WA: A. H. Clark Co., 2001.

Webster's New Collegiate Dictionary. Springfield, MA: G & C Merriam Company, 1977.

Williams, Jerry. *And Yet They Come: Portuguese Immigration from the Azores to the United States.* North Dartmouth, MA: University of Massachusetts, 2005.

Articles and Chapters

Barrett, James R. "Americanization from the Bottom Up: Immigration and the Remaking of the Working Class in the United States, 1880–1930." *Journal of American History* 79, no. 3 (December 1992): 996–1020.

Bastos, Cristiana. "Migrants, Inequalities and Social Research in the 1920s: The Story of *Two Portuguese Communities in New England.*" *History and Anthropology* 29, no. 2 (2018).

Brody David. "Reconciling the Old Labor History and the New." *Pacific Historical Review* 62, no. 1 (February 1993): 1–18.

Godinho, Vitorino Magalhães. "L'Émigration Portugaise (XVe—XXe Siècles) une constante structurale et les réponses aux changement du monde." *Revista de História Económica e Social* 1 (1978): 5–32.

Hill, Herbert. "The Problem of Race in American Labor History." *Reviews in American History* 24, no. 2 (June 1996): 189–208.

Justino, David. "A evolução do produto nacional bruto em Portugal, 1850–1910—algumas estimativas provisórias." *Análise SociaL* 22, no. 97 (1987): 451–61.

Lang, H. P. "The Portuguese Element in New England." *Journal of American Folklore* 5 (1892): 9–17.

Lauck, W. Jett. "Cotton Mill Operatives in New England." *Atlantic Monthly* 109 (1912): 706–13.

Moniz, Miguel. "The Shadow Minority: An Ethnohistory of Portuguese and Lusophone Racial and Ethnic Identity in New England." In *Community, Culture, and the Making of Identity: Portuguese-Americans along the Eastern Seaboard,* edited by Kimberly DaCosta Holton and Andrea Klimt. Portuguese in America Series 2. North Dartmouth, MA: University of Massachusetts Dartmouth, 2009.

Olzak, Susan, and Elizabeth West, "Ethnic Conflict and the Rise and Fall of Ethnic Newspapers." *American Sociological Review* 56, no. 4 (August 1991): 458–74.

Pereira, M. Halpern. "Niveaux de Consommation, Niveau de Vie au Portugal (1874–1922). *Annales E. S. C.* (March 1975), 610–31.

Segal, Martin. "Interrelationship of Wages under Joint Demand: The Case of the Fall River Textile Workers." *Quarterly Journal of Economics* 70 (August 1956): 464–77.

Silvia, Philip T. "The Position of the 'New' Immigrant in the Fall River Textile Industry." *International Migration Review* 13, no. 1 (1976): 221–32.

Suárez-Orozco, Marcelo M. "Everything You Ever Wanted to Know about Assimilation but Were Afraid to Ask." *Daedalus* 129, no. 4 (Fall 2000): 1–30.

Walker, Timothy. "Atlantic Dimensions of the American Revolution: Imperial Priorities and the Portuguese Reaction to the North American Bid for Independence (1775–83)." *Journal of Early American History* 2 (2012): 247–85.

Waters, Mary C., and Tomás R. Jimérez, "Assessing Immigrant Assimilation: New Empirical and Theoretical Challenges." *Annual Review of Sociology* 31 (2005): 105–25.

Notes

1. Oscar Handlin, *The Uprooted: The Epic Story of the Great Migrations That Made the American People* (Boston: Little, Brown and Company, 1951).

2. Throughout this paper the term "ethnic" is defined as of or relating to a minority group or a member of a minority group who retain the customs, language, or social views of their group. See *Webster's New Collegiate Dictionary* (Springfield, MA: G & C Merriam Company, 1977), 393.

3. John Bodnar, *The Transplanted: A History of Immigrants in Urban America* (Bloomington: Indiana University Press, 1985).

4. In their studies, workplace and union participation facilitate assimilation by offering the immigrant an alternative identity separate from their ethnic identity. Susan A. Glenn, *Daughters of the Shtetl: Life and Labor in the Immigrant Generation* (Ithaca, NY: Cornell University Press, 1990); James R. Barrett, "Americanization from the Bottom Up: Immigration and the Remaking of the Working Class in the United States, 1880–1930," *Journal of American History.* 79, no. 3 (December 1992): 996–1020.

5. There is a definitive shift away from the Commons school (also known as the Wisconsin school) of labor history beginning in the 1960s. For a discussion of the changing discourse in labor history see the following historiographical essays: David Brody, "Reconciling the Old Labor History and the New," *Pacific Historical Review* 62, no. 1 (February 1993): 1–18; and Herbert Hill, "The Problem of Race in American Labor History," *Reviews in American History* 24, no. 2 (June 1996): 189–208.

6. David R. Roediger, *Wages of Whiteness: Race and the Making of the American Working Class* (New York: Verso, 1991).

7. W. E. B. Du Bois, *Black Reconstruction in the United States: An Essay Toward a History of the Part which Black Folk Played in the Attempt to Reconstruct Democracy in America, 1860–1880,* ed. Henry Louis Gates, Jr. (New York: Oxford University Press, 2007), 573; originally published in 1935.

8. David R. Roediger, *Working towards Whiteness: How America's Immigrants Became White, The Strange Journey from Ellis Island to the Suburbs* (New York: Basic Books, 2005): 47–49.

9. Leo Pap, *The Portuguese-Americans* (Boston: Twayne Publishers, 1981), 9. This work, as well as other studies, has argued that the Portuguese explored the eastern American coastline as early as 1502 with the voyage of Miguel Corte-Real. The controversy arises from the fact that D. Miguel never returned from his voyage. In 1928, Edmund B. Delabarre published a work, *Dighton Rock* (New York: Walter Neale), in which he claimed to have discovered evidence of D. Miguel's travels in the form of stone markings left on a rock in the Taunton River in Massachusetts in 1511.

10. To study the extent of commercial exchange between these two countries, see Thomas Jefferson's "Report on Commerce." All three reports—released in 1792 and 1793—discuss the commercial exchange of goods in both dollars and tonnage. For a thoughtful analysis of Portuguese-American trade relations during the Revolutionary War, see Timothy Walker, "Atlantic Dimensions of the American Revolution: Imperial Priorities and the Portuguese Reaction to the North American Bid for Independence (1775–83)," *Journal of Early American History* 2 (2012): 247–85.

11. Samuel Eliot Morison, *The Maritime History of Massachusetts 1783–1860,* Northeastern Classics Edition (Boston: Northeastern University Press, 1979), 322–23. For a brief but comprehensive view of the patterns of Azorean emigration as a whole see José Isaac Ávila and Luís Mendonça, "Azorean Emigration: Causes, Waves and Destinations, a Brief Historical Summary," in *Capelinhos, A Volcano of Synergies: Azorean Immigration to America,* coordinated by Tony Goulart (San Jose, CA: Portuguese Heritage Publications of California, 2008). For a thorough discussion of Azorean immigration to the United States see Jerry R. Williams, *In Pursuit of their Dreams: A History of Azorean Immigration to the United States* (Dartmouth, MA: University of Massachusetts Dartmouth, 2005).

12. An interesting overview of Portuguese immigration to the Old West can be found in Donald Warrin and Geoffry L. Gomes, *Land as Far as the Eye Can See: The Portuguese in the Old West* (Spokane, WA: A. H. Clark Co., 2001).

13. *Immigration and Naturalization Service, 1976 Annual Report* (Washington, D.C., 1977), 86–88. The figures for 1921–30 include 19,195 for the year 1921.

14. Pap, *The Portuguese-Americans,* 36.

15. Aluisio Medeiros da Rosa Borges, "The Portuguese Working Class in the Durfee Mills of Fall River, Massachusetts: A Study of the Division of Labor, Ethnicity, and Labor Union Participation, 1895–1925" (PhD diss., University of New York at Binghamton, 1990), 43.

16. Donald R. Taft, *Two Portuguese Communities in New England* (New York: Columbia University Press, 1967), 94.

17. Maria Ioannis Benis Baganha, "International Labor Movements: Portuguese Emigration to the United States 1820–1930" (PhD diss., University of Pennsylvania, 1988), 23.

18. Wikimedia Commons, "Cretic.jpg", accessed February 18, 2015, https://upload.wikimedia.org/wikipedia/commons/0/0b/Cretic.jpg.

19. *As Novidades,* December 6, 1917, 4.

20. Department of Commerce, Bureau of the Census, *Abstract of the Fourteenth Census of the United States, 1920* (Washington, DC: Government Printing Office, 1923), 324.

21. Department of Commerce, Bureau of the Census, *Abstract of the Fourteenth Census of the United States, 1920,* 170.

22. Department of Commerce, Bureau of the Census, *Abstract of the Fourteenth Census of the United States, 1920,* 244–45.

23. This number is derived by adding the "country of birth: Portugal" figure and the "country of birth: Atlantic Islands" figure. Department of Commerce, Bureau of the Census, *Abstract of the Fourteenth Census of the United States, 1920,* 314–15.

24. Pap, *The Portuguese-Americans,* 62.

25. Rosa Borges, "The Portuguese Working Class," 67.

26. Agnes Conforti, interview by Lori Miozza and David Polseli, August 10, 1981, tape recording, B. M. C. Durfee High School of Fall River Library.

27. Gertrude Rogers, interview by Nanette Durette, Nancy Tones, and Sandra Silva, July 21, 1980, tape recording, B. M. C. Durfee High School of Fall River Library.

28. *The Fall River Directory Massachusetts, 1925 Containing a General Directory of the Citizens, House Directory, Business Directory, Street Directory and Record of the City Government, Institutions, etc. with New Map.* No. 51 (Boston, MA: Sampson & Murdock Company, 1925).

29. *The Fall River Directory Massachusetts, 1921 Containing a General Directory of the Citizens, House Directory, Business Directory, Street Directory and Record of the City Government, Institutions, etc. with New Map.* No. LI (Boston, MA: Sampson & Murdock Company, 1921), 699–700.

30. John Camara, interview by John Conforti, Lisa Boyle, Carol Picard, and Lisa St. Pierre, August 16, 1979, tape recording, B. M. C. Durfee High School of Fall River Library.

31. John Camara, interview by John Conforti et al.

32. Paul Charles Whitehead, "The Assimilation of the Portuguese in Fall River, Massachusetts" (PhD diss., University of Massachusetts, Amherst, 1966), 153. These figures were originally abstracted from the Marriage Registers of Fall River.

33. Robert W. Hayman, O.P. *Catholicism in Rhode Island and the Diocese of Providence, 1886–1921,* vol. 2 (Providence, RI: Diocese of Providence, 1995), 547. These tasks were first performed by members of the St. Vincent de Paul Society, then by members of the St. Raphael Society, and finally by two parishioners of Holy Rosary Church in Providence.

34. John Camara, interview by John Conforti et al.

35. *The Fall River Directory Massachusetts, 1921,* 52.

36. Whitehead, "The Assimilation of the Portuguese in Fall River, Massachusetts," 115. A later, but no less significant, organization was the Associação Beneficente e Aliança Portuguesa (PAA). It offered mortuary and disability benefits to those of Portuguese descent who were its members. Founded in 1924, the PAA was not dissolved until 2004. The

records of this important organization can be located at the Ferreira-Mendes Portuguese-American Archives at the University of Massachusetts Dartmouth, MC50/PAA.

37. Arthur G. Wilson and Ray Gaskeil, interview by Paula Noversa and Randy Chabot, July 27, 1981, tape recording, B. M. C. Durfee High School of Fall River Library.

38. Philip T. Silvia, Jr., "The Position of 'New' Immigrants in the Fall River Textile Industry," *International Migration Review* 13, no. 1 (1976): 221–32.

39. *The Fall River Directory Massachusetts, 1921,* 31.

40. Clete Daniel, *Culture of Misfortune: An Interpretive History of Textile Unionism in the United States* (Ithaca, NY: Cornell University Press, 2001): 19.

41. Martin Segal, "Interrelationship of Wages under Joint Demand: The Case of the Fall River Textile Workers," *Quarterly Journal of Economics* 70 (August 1956): 467.

42. It should be noted that after the strike of 1904 a sliding scale was established so that if the craft unions negotiated an increase in wages, nonunion members would also receive an increase. This increase would be scaled according to the degree of their skills. Segal, "Interrelationship of Wages under Joint Demand," 469.

43. Silvia, "The Position," 229.

44. *The Fall River Directory of 1925,* 69–70.

45. "Doffers' Strike closes the Merchants and Linen Mills," *Fall River Daily Globe,* March 15, 1920, 1.

46. See the settlement maps, appendix A and B, which show the locations of each of the Fall River textile mills.

47. "Doffers' Strike closes the Merchants and Linen Mills."

48. "Two More Mills Forced to Close," *Fall River Daily Globe,* March 16, 1920, 1.

49. "MIII Men Claim More Help Back," *Fail River Evening Herald,* March 18, 1920, 1.

50. "Police To Make Arrest in Strike," *Fall River Daily Globe,* March 19, 1920, 1.

51. "Say They Will Fight Strike to a Finish," *Fail River Daily Globe,* March 20, 1920, 1.

52. "Four Members of Doffers Arrested," *Fall River Evening Herald,* March 25, 1920, 1.

53. "Complaints against Doffers Dismissed," *Fall River Daily Globe,* March 30, 1920, 1.

54. "Fr. Silva Trying to Settle Strike of Union Doffers," *Fall River Daily Globe,* June 1, 1920, 9.

55. "Greve dos Doffers," *As Novidades,* July 15, 1920, 1.

56. "Two More Mills Forced to Close."

57. Susan Olzak and Elizabeth West, "Ethnic Conflict and the Rise and Fall of Ethnic Newspapers," *American Sociological Review* 56: 4 (August 1991), 460.

58. "—Segundo nos consta . . ." *A Alvorada,* March 18, 1920, 2.

59. "—Ainda continua . . ." *A Alvorada,* April 1, 1920, 3.

60. "—Continua em grande progresso . . ." *A Alvorada,* April 8, 1920, 6.

61. "A Gréve em Fall River," *A Alvorada*, May 20, 1920, 3.

62. Taft, *Two Portuguese Communities in New England.*

63. Taft, *Two Portuguese Communities in New England*, 17.

64. For a thoughtful and detailed study on the reaction to the publication of Taft's book by the Portuguese community see Cristiana Bastos, "Migrants, Inequalities and Social Research in the 1920s: The Story of *Two Portuguese Communities in New England*," *History and Anthropology* 29, no. 2 (2018), accessed October 11, 2018, doi.org/10.1080/02757206.2017.1359586.

65. Originally, "no qual a raça portugueza é considerada inferior e ignorante." Translation mine. "A Manifestação de Protesto da Colonia Portugueza de New Bedford," *A Alvorada*, March 24, 1924, 1.

66. Taft, *Two Portuguese Communities in New England*, 346–47.

67. Taft, *Two Portuguese Communities in New England*, 26–33 et passim.

68. For a nuanced anthropological study of the efforts of the Portuguese to be recognized as white in America see Miguel Moniz, "The Shadow Minority: An Ethnohistory of Portuguese and Lusophone Racial and Ethnic Identity in New England," in *Community, Culture, and the Making of Identity: Portuguese-Americans along the Eastern Seaboard*, ed. Kimberly DaCosta Holton and Andrea Klimt (North Dartmouth, MA: University of Massachusetts Dartmouth, 2009), 409–30.

69. Originally, "uma raça de intrepidos conquistadores, navegadores . . . vastas colonias que ainda hoje constituem o terceiro imperio colonial do Mundo." Translation mine. "A Manifestaçâo de Protesto da Colonia Portugueza de New Bedford," *A Alvorada*, March 24, 1924, 1.

Mill Workers of New England
Lewis Wickes Hine

Lewis Wickes Hine (1874 –1940) was an American sociologist and photographer whose combined skills helped promote awareness of social issues; since 1908, he joined the National Child Labor Committee and photographed boys and girls working in mills, factories and fields all over the United States, including southern New England. Some of his photographs picture Portuguese children and youth working in the mills.

Figure 1. Hine, Lewis Wickes, photographer. *Manuel Miranda, 229 Alden St. Very young boy, has been doffer in card room of Cornell Mill for 6 months. Said, "I'm goin' on 16" but didn't say when he would reach it. Cornell Mill. Location: Fall River, Massachusetts.* United States Fall River. Massachusetts Fall River, 1912. January. https://www.loc.gov/item/2018676972/.

Figure 2. Hine, Lewis Wickes, photographer. *Cornell Mill. Smallest girl in group is Jennie Sylvia, 522 Alden St., a doffer in card room of Cornell Mill. I saw a girl, apparently as young, running a loom in weave room there. Location: Fall River, Massachusetts.* United States Fall River. Massachusetts Fall River, 1912. January. https://www.loc.gov/item/2018676974/.

Figure 3. Hine, Lewis Wickes, photographer. *General view of the spinning room, Cornell Mill, showing some of the young boys and girls employed there. See names on other photo. Cornell Mill. Location: Fall River, Massachusetts.* United States Fall River. Massachusetts Fall River, 1912. January. https://www.loc.gov/item/2018676970/.

Figure 4. Hine, Lewis Wickes, photographer. *Portuguese Spinner. Location: Fall River, Massachusetts / Lewis W. Hine*. United States Fall River. Massachusetts Fall River, 1916. https://www.loc.gov/item/2018675608/.

Figure 5. Hine, Lewis Wickes, photographer. *Cleaner and Sweeper—Spinning Department of American Linen Co. Location: Fall River, Massachusetts / Lewis W. Hine*. United States Fall River. Massachusetts Fall River, 1916. https://www.loc.gov/item/2018678099/.

Figure 6. Hine, Lewis Wickes, photographer. *Jose de Sousa Magano. Refused certificate at Certificate Office. Location: Fall River, Massachusetts /Lewis W. Hine*. United States Fall River. Massachusetts Fall River, 1916. https://www.loc.gov/item/2018678124/.

Figure 7. Hine, Lewis Wickes, photographer. *Evening recreation of the "Young Holy Ghosters"—Ages 15–25, average is 18—all mill workers—all Portuguese. Whole House on George Street. Great need of leadership. Location: Fall River, Massachusetts /Lewis W. Hine*. United States Fall River. Massachusetts Fall River, 1916. https://www.loc.gov/item /2018675596/.

Figure 8. Hine, Lewis Wickes, photographer. *Applying for certificate—Menuel Cabral—Portuguese. 15 years old Oct. 9, 67 Aetna St. Been spinning 1 month Laurel Lake and sweeper 1 month American Linen. Now to be a braider at Estes Mill. Location: Fall River, Massachusetts / Lewis W. Hine.* United States Fall River. Massachusetts Fall River, 1916. https://www.loc.gov/item/2018678243/.

Figure 9. Hine, Lewis Wickes, photographer. *Marian Viera – 101 Columbia St., Doffer - Says he gets $7.74 a week. Location: Fall River, Massachusetts / Lewis W. Hine.* United States Fall River. Massachusetts Fall River, 1916. https://www.loc.gov/item/2018676903/.

SECTION 2

Participation In Labor Movements

CHAPTER 5

The Position of "New" Immigrants in the Fall River Textile Industry

PHILIP T. SILVIA JR.

Fall River, Massachusetts, made a heroic contribution to American manufacturing supremacy. During the course of the nineteenth century, Yankee efficiency, ingenuity, technical ability, self-confidence, and energy, assisted by favorable environmental and market conditions, nurtured an infant mill industry and shaped the Spindle City, as Fall River came to be called, into the country's largest cotton textile center. Its prominence could also be credited to the thousands of factory operatives, whose efforts turned a raw cotton staple into millions of yards of finished cloth. Their coordinated effort had brought about undreamed-of growth.

Fall River's dominance of the textile industry showed few signs of decay before 1905. Capital continued to be drawn by its cotton mill investment opportunities. Operatives were attracted to the Spindle City, and the population swelled from 74,398 in 1890 to 89,203 in 1895, and passed the 100,000 mark two years later.[1] By the turn of the century, forty-two cotton textile corporations were valued at more than $45 million, while three other corporations, capitalized at nearly $7 million, were engaged in the closely associated processes of textile dyeing and finishing.[2] Furthermore, there were 26,371 textile workers in 1900.[3] And, despite intermittent periods of economic depression, the number of spindles in place rose from 2,164,664 in 1890 to 3,246,468 in 1904.[4] Fall River, consequently, was outstripping all competitors in the value of its finished cotton goods.[5] Its residents understandably boasted in 1901 that the Spindle City mills were weaving slightly more than 843 million yards of cloth per year.[6] On a typical workday its total output was an extraordinary 1,571 miles of cloth.[7]

Despite these satisfying statistics, Fall River citizens had not always been able to depend upon a typical workday. Manufacturing growth had been paralleled by a burgeoning trade unionism sustained by immigrant employees from the British Isles. Their aggressive dedication to the protection of labor rights had led to six major conflicts with capital in the last three decades of the nineteenth century. Strike-marred industrial relations reached an ugly climax in July 1904, when more than five thousand members of local trade unions, bound together by a common affiliation with the United Textile Workers of America (UTWA), staged a protest walkout against an announced wage reduction. They were immediately joined by three times their number of unorganized mill hands.[8] The strikers endured twenty-six poverty-stricken and harrowing weeks. Industrial peace was finally restored by an agreement that Governor William Douglas negotiated. Prior to this dramatic clash of 1904, Fall River had achieved distinction as a major center of immigration in the United States.[9] No municipality of comparable size held such an array of emigrants who came from eighteen different nations.[10] Among its 12,762 male textile operatives, only 3.6 percent had native-born parents, while native parentage among female employees was even smaller.[11]

The French Canadian influx most fully explains the displacement of natives and "old" European immigrants in Fall River's textile industry.[12] Despite their slow start, French Canadian males joined their womenfolk in mill work at such an accelerated pace that, after 1885, this nationality dominated the city's textile labor force just as it did elsewhere in New England. By 1895, when approximately 30 percent of the total number of employees in Massachusetts cotton textiles were of French Canadian origin, 69 percent of Fall River's gainfully employed French Canadians were in manufacturing,[13] and they comprised 45.5 percent of the state's cotton mill operatives five years later.[14] Statistics compiled by two separate investigatory bodies revealed the French Canadians far surpassed all other ethnic groups in percentage and numbers engaged in New England mill work toward the end of the first decade of the twentieth century. Contained within the 1911 immigration report, the Dillingham Commission study, was information about 12,654 Fall River operatives, 3,553 of whom were foreign-born French Canadians or native-born of

Canadian fathers.[15] The English had slipped to second place, while the Irish had dropped into fourth.[16] Spindle City mills were filling vacancies created by Irish and English departures with "new" immigrants from southern and eastern Europe. In this category there were 596 Polish workers and 2,401 Portuguese foreign-born, which included emigrants from the Azores.[17] The Portuguese had the largest percentage of males in this sampling of factory operatives. Statistics, then, confirmed that a significant shift in the source of immigrant labor was well underway.

The Portuguese who trickled into Fall River during the 1870s for the most part had drifted over from New Bedford where they had initially settled after being recruited for jobs on American whaling vessels.[18] Most of them attended St. Joseph's Catholic Church during that decade, and a few immediately gained employment in the mills.[19] As late as 1880, however, all but forty textile employees—who were lumped together as being from "other countries"—were either native-born or from northern and western Europe; and only 132 immigrants from southern and eastern Europe, including 104 Portuguese, settled in the Spindle City.[20] Although the new immigrant total jumped to 1,017 in 1890, this number was still barely perceptible in an urban population of 74,398. This figure was made up almost exclusively of Portuguese and Russians,[21] whose influx became more noticeable in 1891, when as many as twenty began arriving at one time.[22] The *Fall River Daily Herald* worried over the prospect of Russian Jews infiltrating mill work, although the newspaper acknowledged that they displayed little interest in textile employment and were demonstrating that "the tendency of the race is towards trade."[23]

During this decade of the 1890s, the new immigration assumed substantial proportions for the first time. Creating the greatest splash, and dramatizing this trend, the Portuguese steamship *Olinda* arrived at Fall River in 1895. It carried 150 emigrants, eighty of whom had booked passage for Fall River, and was the first European vessel to travel directly to the Spindle City in years.[24] By 1900 there were nearly five thousand immigrants from southern and eastern Europe living in Fall River,[25] and five years later this number had surpassed ten thousand, a rise that was primarily due to arrivals from the Azores, who comprised one-half of this total.[26] In 1910, one-fifth of urban residents were either Portuguese, Hebrew, Polish, or Italian.[27]

Millowners welcomed this influx, especially the Portuguese and Polish, among the immigrants. They had good reason. Thousands of operatives and their families had left for other localities during the strike of 1904–5. Nor could employers continue to depend on the earlier sources of English, Irish, and French Canadian immigrations. Finally, the Italians rivaled Jewish newcomers in shunning textile employment,[28] hence the turn to the Portuguese and Polish as replacements.[29] Further data collected by the Immigration Commission about 8,024 Fall River operatives verified such occupational mobility. While French Canadian mill workers were still numerically dominant, 44.3 percent of 2,403 residents sampled resided in the United States before 1891. Only 16.6 percent had emigrated from Canada in the decade preceding this Immigration Commission study, and only 6 percent within the most recent five-year period.[30] More than half of the English-born total of 1,531 had arrived before the 1890s, with only 9.3 percent emigrating to Fall River in the last five years.[31] The Irish exodus from the mills was most pronounced, as only 673 textile workers were listed, and of this small number, three-quarters had been in the United States by 1890, long enough to presume that they had secured upper-echelon mill positions. Only 2.2 percent reported an arrival during the most recent five years.[32]

In 1895, in a paper delivered before an audience of Southern cotton manufacturers in Atlanta, Edward Atkinson declared that New England was not going to concede its cotton textile supremacy. Obviously disturbed by the slowdown in French Canadian immigration from Quebec, northern manufacturers would soon begin recruiting "Georgia crackers" and North Carolina mountaineers.[33] Atkinson's prediction was never acted upon by Fall River management because the Portuguese, and to a lesser extent the Poles, became the major source of unskilled operatives after 1900—as the French Canadians had been in the 1870s. About half of Fall River's entire Portuguese and Polish population was working in the mills by 1910.[34] Nearly four-fifths of the 2,343 Portuguese and 580 Polish mill operatives studied by the Immigration Commission had emigrated after 1901, while fewer than 3 percent had lived in the United States before 1891.[35]

Now that trade unions had won greater approval and become an acceptable part of the American scene, the Dillingham Commission feared that the new immigrants would retard organized labor's quest for higher wages and improved working conditions. More than a decade earlier, Fall River trade union officials had expressed a similar concern. How could the labor force be united when manufacturers employed an ethnic conglomeration that was separated by language and cultural variations?[36] Many of the female and adolescent operatives were unable to speak English. These new immigrants could not even protect themselves. Secretary James Whitehead of the Fall River Weavers' Progressive Association swore that the mills shortchanged hundreds of defenseless weavers of part of their earnings.[37] In 1898, James Tansey, leader of the organized carding room employees, declared that the Portuguese were a menace to the labor movement because they accepted substandard wages.[38] The Irish, having escaped from the mills after more than a half century of effort and having achieved community acceptance, lent their voices to the chorus of criticism. At an Irish Catholic interparish debate of 1901, the winning debaters argued that the new immigrants were vastly inferior to those who had come to Fall River prior to 1875.[39]

W. Jett Lauck, an ardent immigration restrictionist, summed up nativistic criticism of the new cotton textile operatives in a 1912 *Atlantic Monthly* article that read much like an anti–French Canadian diatribe printed by the Massachusetts Bureau of Statistics of Labor in its 1881 annual report. Gone were the days of the "attractive, well-educated" native New England working women and their "sober, intelligent, and reliable" male counterparts.[40] Times had changed, Lauck insisted, and now, with the installation of automatic machinery, even the "ignorant" newcomers could be trained to operate it.[41] These southern and eastern European immigrants were driving the better class of English, Irish, and French Canadians out of the mills, the natives having already departed.[42] They worked for lower wages and sought immediate economic gains. Because their purpose was to save money and to return to the motherland in a few years, they refused to participate in strikes that interfered with their opportunity to save.[43] They lived on a miserably low scale, Lauck claimed. "A normal family life—wife and children dependent entirely upon the husband for support—is unusual."[44]

But "a normal family life" had always been the exception for all nationalities. Nor do Lauck's other assertions withstand close scrutiny. Because of their earlier arrival, for example, the French Canadians were classified with the "superior" element by neatly piecing them into that ethnic mix comprising the "old" nationalities. Unlike the southern and eastern Europeans, then, the French Canadians were "Americans" even before entering the United States.[45] Their ancestors were from Normandy, so ran the argument, making them of Nordic stock, and therefore among the elite.[46] But the claims are forced and inaccurate. Except for a longer period of assimilation, the Canadians were the counterparts of the Portuguese and Polish peoples coming into the mills in the twentieth century. They had the same religion, their culture was distinct from the "native" standard, and they held tenaciously to their French language.[47] The Immigration Commission was uneasily aware of these differences. It bestowed equal but separate status upon this ethnic group by stating that recent immigrants "do not yet constitute a steady and reliable trade-union class as do the English, Irish, and Americans. This does not apply to the French Canadians who have become well Americanized and are strong trade unionists."[48] Not strong enough perhaps! For according to an accompanying sampling of 1,693 male New England operatives, English-born labor markedly led in trade union membership, but only 10 percent of the French Canadians were affiliated with textile craft unions.[49]

Although the new immigrants lacked awareness of trade union principles, their interest was being awakened at least as rapidly as it was among the French Canadians. The latter, according to several Spindle City residents, were just beginning to join the textile trade unions.[50] Until the turn of the century it had been virtually impossible to organize them.[51] Indeed, the new immigrants had a relatively higher enrollment at this early date, and once in the unions the Portuguese, for one, were less likely to drop out.[52] French Canadian names did not appear in a 1902 listing of twenty-nine Fall River trade union executives.[53] Among delegates at conventions of the UTWA between 1901 and 1922, only ninety-two had French names, sixty-one of them appearing in the years from 1917 to 1922.[54] Cotton textile sentiment, then, rested where it always had: 2,069 convention delegates were English, Irish, and Scottish.[55]

Trade unions were not particularly eager to add the Portuguese and Polish operatives to their rolls because these immigrants usually worked in low-paying occupational categories that had never been organized.[56] Not competing for the same skilled jobs, they did not undercut wages paid in those industrial departments where workers were generally unionized. When newcomers did advance to better positions, efforts were made to break down the language barrier and to organize them.[57] But their reluctance to join, as President John Golden of the UTWA understood, was matched by the refusal of great numbers of English-speaking operatives, who thereby set a poor example.[58]

Rather than displaying hostility or indifference, these new immigrants, when first tested, supported trade union efforts (in Fall River and other localities) to preserve the wage standard.[59] Lauck's assumption that all new immigrants drove wages downward, much like the Dillingham Commission claim that the Portuguese harbored "socialistic ideas," was simply erroneous.[60] When the mass of Spindle City operatives walked out together with the majority of trade unionists in July 1904, John Golden, who did not find it easy to divorce the Canadians from the new immigrants, said, "I cannot help but compliment the French, Portuguese, Italian, and Polish people for the splendid way in which they stood by their English-speaking brothers and sisters."[61] A sliding scale that was adopted shortly after the termination of this strike guaranteed all operatives a minimum wage base, and in effect was a pledge by management that cheap new immigrant labor would not undercut the earning potential of trade unionists.[62]

When none of the new immigrants made the rapid vocational advance to department overseer, the Immigration Commission suggested why this was so without invoking the usual argument of innate inferiority. The newcomers had not had sufficient time to acquire experience at the most skilled jobs, and even if the time factor had not been a consideration, management preferred appointing old immigrants to overseer positions because they would in turn recruit experienced operatives from the ranks of their own nationality to work under them. Consequently, new immigrants were discriminated against by this ethnic selectiveness, much as the French Canadians had been in the 1870s and 1880s.[63] Furthermore, employers were aware that racial and cultural animosity would lead English and Irish, as well as many French Canadian, operatives to quit the mills rather than work under Portuguese or Polish supervision. Mill superintendents nevertheless had a fairly high regard for the new immigrants, especially the Portuguese, and predicted they would work themselves into top positions. When asked to evaluate employees according to nationality, the New Bedford and Fall River treasurers' score sheet tallied as follows: "General efficiency and progress—American, English and Irish, French Canadian, North Italian, Portuguese, Polish, South Italian, Syrian. Industriousness—Portuguese, French Canadian, North Italian, American, English, Irish, Polish, South Italian, Syrian."[64]

It was difficult to distinguish French Canadians from the "inferior" immigrants in many aspects of work and social behavior. While living down their "Annual Canadian" image, by 1900 they had a greater percentage of returnees to the homeland than any of the new ethnic groups.[65] Despite the Immigration Commission's contention that French Canadian women were becoming discontented by work in the low-paying cotton industry, which was attracting southern and eastern Europeans, their number far exceeded those of any other nationality employed in New England cotton mills. Figures compiled about textile operatives in four New England states reveal that Portuguese males and females over sixteen years of age were competitive in proficiency and wages with French Canadian and even American-born doffers, ring spinners, speeder tenders, and spoolers.[66] Regarding child labor, a large sampling—over twenty-one thousand New England textile workers—indicates that more than one-half of all operatives under sixteen were French Canadians, while the Portuguese and Polish had the fewest minors among nationalities with substantial numbers.[67] Because of absolute numbers, this figure is deceiving. Nevertheless, in proportion to the total number of child workers in each ethnic group, the Polish and Portuguese percentage of minors was almost identical with that of the English and French Canadians.[68] Critics, then, could not single out new immigrant parents for blame in sending offspring into the mills.

In sum, while the impact of the new immigrants was pronounced by 1910, the cotton textile industry had not been taken over by them. Although native-born labor, as well as workers of Irish and to a lesser extent of English descent, had left the mills in large numbers by 1910, they had not been forced out by economic competition.[69] The new immigrants were not imported as strikebreakers, they did not compete for the higher-paying jobs, and, if anything, they were pushing other groups to better positions within the mills.[70] The chronological line between old and new immigration could more properly have been drawn in the 1870s, when Canadians speaking the French language had descended on New England by the trainload. The later Portuguese, Polish, and other southern and eastern European arrivals essentially represented more of the same.

Fall River's Irish- and English-dominated trade unions should be credited with maintaining the New England wage scale, which might have been reduced to the Southern level if mills had been able to operate solely with foreign-language operatives.[71] However, the latter reciprocated with the 1904 walkout when they joined the organized minority.

These newest arrivals, especially attracted by mill desertions following this strike, gained the security of sure employment, despite their initial lack of skill. They did not hurt other workers but were themselves injured by the low wages paid in the unskilled cotton textile mill occupations.[72] Their very status as recent immigrants also worked against them. Substantial numbers of other ethnic groups, including French Canadians, had resided in Fall River long enough to advance up and out of the mills, but the new immigrants were almost universally stationed at the bottom occupational rung of the mills' ladders. When Southern competition overwhelmed these textile mills, beginning in the 1920s, Fall River lost its industrial base, and the occupational progress of its newest immigrant groups, especially the Portuguese, was impeded. To a great extent, it still is.

Works Cited

Abrams, Richard M. *Conservatism in a Progressive Era. Massachusetts Politics, 1900–1912.* Cambridge, MA: Harvard University Press, 1964.

Brewer, Daniel C. *The Conquest of New England by the Immigrant.* New York: G Putnam and Sons, 1926.

Brooks, Roberts R. "The United Textile Workers of America." PhD diss., Yale University, 1935.

Dublin, Louis I. "Infant Mortality in Fall River, Massachusetts." *American Statistical Association Journal* 14 (June 1915): 516–17.

Earl, Henry H. *Fall River and Its Manufactories, 1803–1904.* Fall River, MA: G. E. Bamford, 1904.

Keith, E. Gordon, "The Financial History of Two Textile Cities: A Study of the Effects of Industrial Growth and Decline upon the Financial Policies and Practices of Lowell and Fall River, Massachusetts." PhD diss., Harvard University, 1936.

Fall River Daily Globe, January 13, 1898.

Fall River Daily Globe, September 1, 1891.

Fall River Daily Herald, September 2, 1891.

Fall River Daily Herald, February 12, 1895.

Fall River Daily Herald, March 20, 1901.

Fall River Daily Herald, May 25, July 6, July 12, July 19, 1902.

Fall River Daily Globe, July 25, 1904

Fall River Daily Globe, October 17, 1905.

Hard, William, and Theta Childe Dorr. "The Woman's Invasion: Fall River and Outpost On the Edge of the Future." *Everybody's Magazine,* November 1908, 579–91.

Lahne, Herbert. T*he Cotton Mill Worker.* New York: Farrar & Rinehart, 1944.

Lauck, W. Jett, "The Cotton Mill Operatives of New England." *Atlantic Monthly,* May 1912, 706–12.

Lower, A. R. M. "New France in New England." *New England Quarterly* 2 (April 1929): 294.

Massachusetts Bureau of Statistics. *Forty-Third Annual Report* (1912): 39.

Massachusetts Bureau of Statistics of Labor. *Massachusetts Labor Bulletin*, 39 (January 1906): 39.

Massachusetts Bureau of Statistics of Labor. *Massachusetts Bureau of Statistics of Labor Bulletin* 37 (September 1905): 328–30.

New England Cotton Manufacturers' Association. *Transactions* 49 (1896): 119–12.

New York Times. "Textile Workers to Strike. 30,000 Employees of Fall River Cotton Mills to Walk Out." New York Times, July 21, 1904, 5.

Segal, Martin. "Interrelationship of Wages under Joint Demand: The Case of the Fall River Textile Workers (1873–1955)." *Quarterly Journal of Economics* 70 (August 1956): 464–67.

United Textile Workers of America. *Convention Proceedings* (1903): 11.

———. *Convention Proceedings* (1904): 30.

———. *Convention Proceedings* (1905): 9.

U.S. Bureau of the Census. *Twelfth Census of the United States: 1900.* Vol. 1, *Population.* Washington, DC: U.S. Bureau of the Census, 1901.

U.S. Bureau of the Census. *Twelfth Census of the United States: 1900.* Vol. 8, *Manufactures.* Washington, DC: U.S. Bureau of the Census, 1901.

Notes

1. Henry H. Earl, *Fall River and Its Manufactories, 1803–1904* (Fall River, MA: G. E. Bamford, 1904), 23.

2. U.S. Bureau of the Census, *Twelfth Census of the United States: 1900*, vol. 8, *Manufactures* (Washington, DC: U.S. Bureau of the Census, 1901), 2:382–83. Fall River's entire industrial valuation rested at $58.5 million. U.S. Bureau of the Census, *Manufactures,* 2:382–83. In 1904, listed forty-one textile corporations with a capitalization of $25,565, 000. Earl, *Fall River*, 35

3. U.S. Bureau of the Census, *Manufactures,* 2:382–83.

4. A convenient reproduction of this growth, as listed by E. Gordon Keith, reads as follows:

E. Gordon Keith, "The Financial History of Two Textile Cities: A Study of the Effects of Industrial Growth and Decline upon the Financial Policies and Practices of Lowell and Fall River, Massachusetts" (unpublished PhD diss., Harvard University, 1936), 310.

Year	Population	Value of Cotton Manufactures	Capital in Cotton Manufactures	Spindles
		unit: 1,000	unit: 1,000	
1890	74,398	24,926	32,104	2,165
1895	89,203	26,403	38,743	
1900	104,863	29,080	45,641	3,042
1905	105,762	32,308	51,170	

5. In 1905, all but 1.8 million of 21.4 million spindles in operation in the United States were located in New England and the South. Of the 13.9 million in New England, Massachusetts contained 8.4 million. U.S. Senate, Report on Conditions of *Woman and Child Wage Earners in the United States,* S. Doc. 61-645, at 20 (1910). Hereinafter referred to as U.S. Senate, *Woman and Child Wage Earners.*

6. *Fall River Daily Herald,* March 20, 1901.

7. *Fall River Daily Herald,* March 20, 1901.

8. Robert R. Brooks, "The United Textile Workers of America" (unpublished PhD diss., Yale University, 1935), 54; United Textile Workers of America, *Convention Proceedings,* 1903, 11; 1904, 30; *"Textile Workers to Strike. 30,000 Employes of Fall River Cotton Mills to Walk Out," New York Times,* July 21, 1904, 5.

9. It contained the highest percentage of immigrants for cities with populations exceeding one hundred thousand. U.S. Bureau of the Census, *Twelfth Census of the United States: 1900, vol. 1, Population* (Washington, DC: U.S. Bureau of the Census, 1900), 1:609–46.

10. U.S. Senate, *Woman and Child Wage-Earners,* 1:216–17.

11. U.S. Senate, *Woman and Child Wage-Earners,* 10:175; William Hard and Theta Childe Dorr, "The Woman's Invasion: Fall River and Outpost on the Edge of the Future," *Everybody's Magazine* 19 (November 1908): 579–91.

12. In round numbers, the first- and-second generation French populace rose from 8,200 in 1885 to 17,000 in 1895 and would reach 36,000 by 1910. Massachusetts Bureau of Statistics, *Forty-Third Annual Report* (1912), 39. Herbert J. Lahne, *The Cotton Mill Worker* (New York: Farrar & Rinehart 1944), 179.

13. U.S. Senate, *Woman and Child Wage-Earners,* 1:107; Massachusetts Bureau of Statistics of Labor, *Massachusetts Labor Bulletin* 39 (January 1906), 39.

14. Lahne, *The Cotton Mill Worker,* 179.

15. S. Doc 61-633 (1911), hereinafter referred to as U.S. Senate, Immigration Commission, *Reports,* 10:18.

16. U.S. Senate, Immigration Commission, *Reports,* 10:18.

17. U.S. Senate, Immigration Commission, *Reports,* 10:19.

18. Massachusetts Bureau of Statistics, *Forty-Third Annual Report,* 39.

19. St. Joseph's Church (Fall River), Baptismal and Marriage Registers. One John Mello, a mill operative for twenty-five years who became chief engineer at the Shove mill no. 1, passed away in 1898. *Fall River Daily Globe,* January 13, 1898.

20. U.S. Senate, Immigration Commission, *Reports,* 10:32.

21. The only exceptions were forty-eight immigrants from Italy and thirty-nine from Poland. U.S. Senate, Immigration Commission, *Reports,* 10:34.

22. *Fall River Daily Globe,* September 1, 1891.

23. *Fall River Daily Herald,* September 2, 1891.

24. *Fall River Daily Herald,* June 10, 1895. This proved unfortunate, for soon after disembarking from Fall River for New York, the *Olinda* crashed against offshore rocks. *Fall River Daily Herald,* June 12, 1895, 17.

25. Of 5,974 immigrants, 805 came from Portugal, 1,095 from the Azores, and 1,095 from Russia. U.S. Senate, Immigration Commission, *Reports,* 10:37.

26. There were 10,000 Portuguese, 6,500 Jews, 4,000 Poles, and 500 Italians. U.S. Senate, Immigration Commission, *Reports,* 10:37.

27. U.S. Senate, Immigration Commission, *Reports,* 10:37.

28. U.S. Senate, Immigration Commission, *Reports,* 10:40.

29. Massachusetts Bureau of Statistics of Labor, *Massachusetts Labor Bulletin* 37 (September 1905), 328, 330; *Fall River Daily Herald,* May 25, July 6, 1901, July 12, 19, 1902; *Fall River Daily Globe,* October 17, 1905.

30. U.S. Senate, Immigration Commission, *Reports,* 10:40.

31. U.S. Senate, Immigration Commission, *Reports,* 10:55.

32. U.S. Senate, Immigration Commission, *Reports,* 10:55.

33. New England Cotton Manufacturers' Association, *Transactions* 59 (1896): 119–12.

34. U.S. Senate, Immigration Commission, *Reports,* 10:40.

35. U.S. Senate, Immigration Commission, *Reports,* 10:55.

36. *Fall River Daily Herald,* February 12, 1895.

37. *Fall River Daily Herald,* May 9, 1900.

38. *Fall River Daily Herald,* February 17,1898.

39. *Fall River Daily Herald,* December 3, 1901.

40. W. Jett Lauck, "The Cotton Mill Operatives of New England," *Atlantic Monthly* 109, May 1912), 706.

41. Lauck, "The Cotton Mill Operatives," 711.

42. Lauck, "The Cotton Mill Operatives," 709, 711.

43. Lauck, "The Cotton Mill Operatives," 709–10.

44. Lauck, "The Cotton Mill Operatives," 712.

45. Daniel Chauncey Brewer, *The Conquest of New England by the Immigrant* (New York: G. Putnam and Sons, 1926), 163, 165.

46. A. R. M. Lower, "New France in New England," *New England Quarterly* 2 (April 1929): 294.

47. Leon E. Truesdell, *The Canadian Born in the United States: An Analysis of the Canadian Element in the Population of the United States, 1850 to 1930* (New Haven, CT: Yale University Press; Toronto: Ryerson Press, 1943).

48. U.S. Senate, Immigration Commission, *Reports,* 10:125.

49. U.S. Senate, Immigration Commission, *Reports,* 10:122–23.

50. H. Doc 57-184 (1901). Hereinafter referred to as U.S. Congress, House, *Report of the Industrial Commission,* 15:421.

51. U.S. Congress, House, *Report of the Industrial Commission,* 15:421.

52. U.S. Congress, House, *Report of the Industrial Commission,* 15:421.

53. Massachusetts Bureau of Statistics of Labor, *Massachusetts Labor Bulletin* 33 (August 1902): 118.

54. Brooks, "The United Textile Workers of America," 76.

55. Brooks, "The United Textile Workers of America," 76. The total number of delegates was 2,296.

56. U.S. Senate, Immigration Commission, *Reports,* 10:124.

57. U.S. Senate, Immigration Commission, *Reports,* 10:124. United Textile Workers of America, *Convention Proceedings* (1904), 3–4. There were at least some "new" immigrants in each of the Fall River textile unions by 1910. U.S. Senate, Immigration Commission, *Reports,* 10:125.

58. United Textile Workers of America, *Convention Proceedings,* 9.

59. U.S. Senate, Immigration Commission, *Reports,* 10:1.

60. U.S. Senate, Immigration Commission, *Reports,* 10:1.; see Thomas O'Donnell's testimony in U.S. Congress, House, *Report of the Industrial Commission,* 14:569.

61. *Fall River Daily Globe,* July 25, 1904

62. U.S. Senate, Immigration Commission, *Reports,* 10:125. As Martin Segal has noted, if the organized minority won the support of nonunion help, the latter were at the same time beholden to the trade unionists. This was because the organized operatives occupied the more skilled or "key jobs" within each section of textile mill production. Whenever the mule spinners, as the "key" craft unionists and "reference group" won a concession, the other unionists, because of social and occupational proximity, were aware of this and sought similar concessions. Although Segal had no way of knowing that the mule spinners had received special, unique favoritism on five different occasions previous to 1897, his relationship concept is valid beginning with that year. By uniting as a textile council and gaining manufacturer recognition, the organized craft workers created a type of industrial unionism and could expect similar wage scale adjustments. The unskilled nonunionist jobs were totally integrated with those of the skilled key job workers in completing the production process in all but the cloth room department—i.e., in carding, spinning, weaving, and warp and filling preparation. The technology of the cotton textile process meant that their functions were essential and directly related to the work of the unionists. Even though the unorganized were excluded from the bargaining table, the working relationship between skilled and unskilled led to a parallel wage structure for all operatives, which was formalized in the sliding scale agreement of 1905. Martin Segal, "Interrelationship of Wages under Joint Demand: The Case of the Fall River Textile Workers (1873–1955)," *Quarterly Journal of Economics* 70 (August 1956): 464–67.

63. U.S. Senate Immigration Commission, *Reports,* 10:178.

64. U.S. Senate Immigration Commission, *Reports,* 10:179.

65. U.S. Senate Immigration Commission, *Reports,* 10:168; U.S. Senate, *Woman and Child Wage-Earners,* 1:114; U.S. Congress, House, *Report of the Industrial Commission,* 14:544.

66. U.S. Senate, *Woman and Child Wage-Earners,* 1:726–27.

67. U.S. Senate, *Woman and Child Wage-Earners,* 1:100.

68. U.S. Senate, *Woman and Child Wage-Earners,* 1:100.

69. The Massachusetts Bureau of Statistics' summary of volume 10 of the Industrial Commission report focused on the reasons for this egress: low pay; education, which fostered a desire to find less noisy, monotonous, confining mechanical work; and status, which had eroded because the influx of new immigrants made life as a mill operative "less worthy and respectable." Massachusetts Bureau of Statistics, *Forty-Third Annual Report* (1912), 46.

70. U.S. Senate, Immigration Commission, *Reports,* 10:39, 124, 177.

71. In a letter addressed to a member of President William H. Taft's cabinet, one Massachusetts employer presumed that "of course, you understand, we cannot run the mills of New England without immigrants." Richard M. Abrams, *Conservatism in a Progressive Era: Massachusetts Politics, 1900–1912* (Cambridge, MA: Harvard University Press, 1964), 226.

72. The rate of mortality for infants of mothers from Portugal and the Azores was a frightening 299 per thousand, as compared with 172 and 153 per thousand for infants of French Canadian and native-born American mothers, respectively. More than twice as many of these Portuguese women worked in the mills during pregnancy than expectant mothers of any other ethnicity. Louis I. Dublin, "Infant Mortality in Fall River, Massachusetts," *American Statistical Association Journal* 14 (June 1915), 14:516–17.

CHAPTER 6

The Strike of '28

......

DANIEL GEORGIANNA AND ROBERTA HAZEN AARONSON

Whaling to Textiles

On Monday, April 9, 1928, the day after Easter, the New Bedford Cotton Manufacturers' Association announced a 10 percent wage cut to take effect the following Monday. The city's thirty thousand textile workers, angry from years of low wages and speedups, decided to strike rather than accept another wage cut. Shutting down the mills was the easy part; keeping the mill workers on strike would prove more difficult.

The outlook was not very promising for the city's mill workers and their unions. Few unions existed elsewhere in the United States. By the mid-1920s the striking mill workers stood alone. When they worked, New Bedford's mill workers were paid about one-half of subsistence wages, and they were divided on the job and in the union halls by nationality, religion, and gender.

But through resourceful leadership and their own courage, the city's mill workers kept the mills closed for six months and forced the millowners to negotiate with them until starvation and the approach of winter drove them to accept a compromise of a smaller pay cut. The story begins with the wealth accumulated when New Bedford was the whaling capital of the world. After the discovery of petroleum, whaling became riskier and less profitable. New Bedford's whaling merchants shifted their money from whaling ships to cotton mills, but they continued to tightly control economic and political power in the city. They procured labor from the immigrants flooding into America in the late 1800s, and by the turn of the twentieth century, New Bedford had become the largest producer of fine cloth in the United States, transforming the town from a small port village to a bustling manufacturing city with large mill complexes and vibrant working-class neighborhoods. In the decades after the Civil War, the New Bedford whaling merchants, weary of the risk and low profits from whaling, followed the siren song to textiles. In order to avoid competition with the rest of New England and the South, they decided to specialize in fine cotton cloth.[1]

Most of the newcomers were immigrants. In 1865, only 14 percent of the city's population was foreign-born, but by 1900, the percentage had grown to over 40 percent.[2] Three-quarters of New Bedford's mill workers were immigrants.[3] Although they carried with them a complex array of cultures and religions, immigrant groups in the mills usually were classified into simple nationalities: English, Irish, and German, who arrived first, followed by French Canadian, Polish, Syrian, and Portuguese.[4] Typically, Polish meant any European from east of Germany, and Syrian meant someone from the Middle East. However, by the end of the century most of the immigrants coming to New Bedford were from Portugal or its islands—Madeira, the Azores, and Cape Verde—and almost always went directly into the mills.

Very few African Americans worked in the early cotton mills. In 1900, only twenty-five of the city's 11,006 mill workers were African Americans, although this probably didn't include Cape Verdeans.[5] Earlier, in 1860, New Bedford had a larger percentage of African Americans than any other New England city. New Bedford, because of its port and its Quaker heritage, was a station on the underground railroad leading slaves to freedom, and African Americans were a common sight on city streets and in city schools.[6] In 1837 Frederick Douglass escaped from Maryland to New Bedford, found friends there, and began his career as an abolitionist, women's rights supporter, and labor advocate. But Douglass faced discrimination on the docks, his skin color often costing him employment, and he left the city in 1841. The discrimination he left behind continued in the cotton mills, where African Americans could find employment only if no European could be found for the job.

Although mills generally occupied the centers of early industrial cities, most of New Bedford's mills were built in the north and south sections of the city along the river and the railroad lines. Finance and commerce left over from whaling continued to dominate the center, and most of the city's elite continued living in spacious neighborhoods near the financial district, free from the noise, grime, and congestion of industrial life.[7] Densely populated working-class neighborhoods grew around the mills in the city's north and south ends. In order to attract the skilled workers needed to manufacture fine cloth, owners of the early mills built nearby housing.[8]

During the period of New Bedford's largest growth, almost all new housing was supplied by small-scale landlords, often mill workers themselves, who built two- and three-decker tenements. Most apartments were crowded, and many people took in boarders.[9] Cots in the kitchen were a common sight. The increase in housing drove down rents and reduced the profits to landlords. The quality of mill-owned housing deteriorated along with the decline in profits, and by the end of World War I the millowners had sold their few remaining tenements.[10]

New Bedford's mill workers usually preferred but sometimes were forced to live among their own kind, and they settled into a mosaic of ethnic neighborhoods centered around the mills.

> *We had ghettos. The South End of the city was where most of the English workers lived. The Portuguese also lived in the South End, but also in the North End. The Cape Verdeans were mostly in the South End; there was a ghetto of Cape Verdeans within that ghetto. Then you had the Poles. Most of the Poles were spread out, but the biggest Polish group was in the North End of the city.*[11]
>
> —*Joe Figueiredo*

To afford the barest necessities, both parents and their children had to work in the mills. Men held the better jobs at higher pay, but neither men nor women could support a family on a single wage.[12] Children, sometimes as young as ten years old, doffed the full bobbins off the spinning frames, cleaned around the machinery, and did other repetitive, simple tasks. Children learning a skill such as weaving were taught by their parents or other relatives on the job without pay.[13]

Many children, especially those of Portuguese, Polish, and French Canadian descent, didn't survive to work in the mills. Infant mortality rates were very high in mill cities, and New Bedford had one of the highest rates of infant deaths. One out of every five children born into low-wage mill families in New Bedford died before their first birthday, whereas in the highest income bracket only one out of seventeen died in infancy.[14] Children's deaths from gastric, respiratory, and intestinal diseases, usually associated with poverty and preventable through better nutrition, were among the highest in the country.[15] Pay was low, hours were long, and work was hard.

Textile Mill Workers and Their Unions

The number of mill workers in New Bedford doubled in the period after 1898, mostly from Portuguese immigration, but the English mill workers maintained their tight hold on union leadership and skilled jobs. French Canadians held most of the remaining skilled jobs. Although one-half of the mill workers were Portuguese or Cape Verdean, in 1926 they held less than 10 percent of the skilled jobs.[16]

> *As a matter of fact, [tradesmen were] made up primarily of Anglo-Saxons. They had the better jobs and the whole relationship in the plant was that you got a job through the foreman, and the foreman kept the better jobs for the elite, which were the Anglo-Saxons. And that's the way it worked.*[17]
>
> —*Jack Rubenstein*

> *The slavery department of a cotton mill was the card room. You never sat down. You always had plenty of work to do and were never paid much money. Mostly Portuguese and Cape Verdean people worked there. They would never hire a colored guy and put him in the spinning room. They would never make a weaver out of him. The management kept the colored people in the card room. You saw very few white people in there, except for the boss.*[18]
>
> —*Pete Fauteux*

Following their success in gaining skilled jobs, French Canadians also did well in city politics. Between 1912 and 1930, about 20 percent of city aldermen and 10 percent of Common Council members were French Canadian.[19] The Portuguese did not share in these political successes, however. During the same period, no Portuguese aldermen were elected, and only 6 percent of the Common Council members were Portuguese.[20] French Canadian and British voters probably supported each other in elections, keeping out the Portuguese candidates. The Portuguese, alienated in the mills, in unions, and in political life, also were less likely to become citizens.

Conservative leadership in the Textile Council firmly held power by 1901, when New Bedford's textile unions joined with those in Fall River and elsewhere to form the United Textile Workers (UTW), an affiliate of the AFL under the leadership of John Golden of Fall River. But the city's craft unions resisted the national association, opposing Golden's use of their dues to build a stronger national union.[21] With a solid English mistrust of anything foreign, the New Bedford and Fall River craft unions were reluctant to tax themselves to support textile workers elsewhere. By 1916, all local craft unions in Fall River and New Bedford had left the UTW to form the National Amalgamation of Textile Operators. Eventually the group became the American Federation of Textile Operatives, a weak national organization with low per capita dues.[22] More militant unions like the Industrial Workers of the World (IWW) failed to make any headway in the city. In 1912, fresh from its victory in the bitter "Bread and Roses" strike in Lawrence, the IWW tried to interest New Bedford's mill workers in a strike over working conditions. The organization attracted a few hundred members and was isolated by the established union leaders, who actively opposed the IWW's goals and tactics.[23]

The textile industry boomed during World War I as it had in previous wars, calling for ever-increasing amounts of textiles for bandages, uniforms, blankets, airplane covering, and cotton tire cord. Production and profits in textile manufacture rose sharply. During the war years, sales more than quadrupled, and profits increased sixfold.[24] Labor shared in the wartime boom. Five thousand more people were employed in the mills, where the average wage more than doubled.[25] New Bedford's population had tripled in three decades to one hundred thousand, and the city's commerce flourished on a diet of full employment and higher wages. Wartime prosperity wasn't based on a permanent foundation, however. When the war ended, demand for military products dropped, and the mills began accumulating unsold cloth rather than profits.

The Textile Council didn't give in easily. During the spring of 1920, eleven of the thirteen unions in New Bedford voted to join the loom fixers in a strike calling for a wage increase. The unions claimed to represent over half of New Bedford's textile workers and, encouraged by the pattern set during the war, expected a quickly negotiated settlement. The millowners, tired of wartime concessions, proved the unions wrong. They refused to negotiate, claiming that the unions were influenced by radical elements and were trying to establish a "soviet system." The unions quickly learned that the days of easy victories and rising wages were over. After Mayor Ashley failed to bring the owners to the bargaining table, a short, weakly supported strike forced union leaders to cave in. The few mill workers who remained on strike straggled back to work.

In the fall of 1920, the cloth market collapsed, and the mill workers' situation deteriorated further. The owners laid off thousands of mill workers, and production trickled to a stop. The Cotton Manufacturers' Association, representing New Bedford's cotton millowners, asked for a 30 percent wage cut to take effect in December, when they planned to reopen the mills. The Textile Council objected but was powerless because almost all the city's textile workers were out of work. Abraham Binns, the council's president and head of the weavers' union, called unsuccessfully for a congressional inquiry into the wage reduction. Binns, as a member of the Overseers of the Poor, also begged for more relief funds. When the mills reopened in February 1921, mill workers were forced to accept a 20 percent wage cut.

The Strike Begins

> *The mill owners were making a lot of money, but they were obviously never satisfied, no matter how much they made. They always wanted to make more, and the way they did it was by taking it off the hides of the workers by increasing their production with less workers. This was called speedup in which they would speed the operation of the various machines and increase their workload. The workers used to resist it.*
>
> *The ten-cent wage cut imposed by the mill owners broke the camel's back—workers were real angry, and even though most of the workers were unorganized they poured out of the mills fighting mad. They were fed up with the wage cuts and the speedups, and it was almost as if everything was organized beforehand, but it wasn't. When the Textile Council rejected the ten percent cut and announced that they were gonna strike, all the unskilled people that they paid no attention to go out there. And they became the main force of the strike.*[26]
>
> —*Joe Figueiredo*

The city's merchants realized that lower wages would depress the local economy. Over 80 percent of the city's working population was employed in the manufacture of cotton textiles. Mill workers filled the city's churches and spent their wages in local stores. Nor could the millowners count on the media for support. A typical editorial at the beginning of the strike said of the millowners, "Among the newspapers of their own city, they could not find a single editorial comment in their favor."[27] Most local advertising came from the city's merchants, whereas almost none came from the mills because cloth produced in New Bedford was sold not locally but in New York and other commercial centers.

The millowners countered that competition had forced their hand.[28] They pointed to the general 10 percent wage cut that began in Lawrence late in 1927 and quickly spread through Maine and New Hampshire.[29]

Between Monday's announcement of the pay cut and the following Monday when it was to take effect, William E. G. Batty, leader of the Textile Council, pressed for a strike vote. Batty was the youngest of New Bedford's labor leaders. Born in England and educated as a young man for missionary work, he became an officer in the Salvation Army. When this didn't suit him, he went into the textile mills, working as a weaver and loom fixer. In 1920, at the age of thirty, he became secretary of the loom fixers union and two years later was elected secretary of the Textile Council. Batty was an energetic organizer and a forceful speaker. Although his union wasn't in the major national union, Batty was becoming a force in national textile organization. He traveled throughout the Northeast, offering New Bedford's help to striking textile workers.

Another, deeper split was developing within the mill workers' ranks. Fred Beal from Lawrence and William Murdoch from Providence, militant labor organizers with a vision of an industrial union that would unite all textile workers, arrived in New Bedford a few days before the strike vote armed with ten thousand leaflets urging the textile workers to strike. Veterans of other New England strikes, they were trying to build the Textile Mill Committees (TMC), an organization that had originated in a Passaic, New Jersey, strike two years earlier. Beal and Murdoch warned the mill workers that delaying the count would allow the Textile Council leaders to count the ballots in secret and then announce that the vote had been against a strike. Many at the meeting supported the TMC's vision of one union in the industry, and most of the audience wanted the votes counted publicly.

With the audience shouting, "Count the ballots," the Textile Council's leaders agreed to open the sealed ballots and tabulate the votes from each of the unions. The result was 2,571 to 188 in favor of a strike on the following Monday, the day of the wage cut. Every union had voted overwhelmingly to strike. No one doubted for a minute that the 2,571 union members who voted to strike were speaking for the 27,000 workers employed in the mills at the time, and the greatest strike in the history of the city and perhaps the textile industry was imminent. [30]

—John McKenna

The Textile Council had done little to put its plan for a strike into action, and no one knew how effective the strike would be. Batty and Binns drove together from mill to mill to assess the situation. Delighted and somewhat surprised, they found crowds of mill workers at every gate, with hardly anyone going into work. Workers had set up informal pickets at many of the mill gates, but the general scene resembled a celebration more than a tense confrontation. Some brought late breakfasts to the mills, and many wore their best clothes. At a time when they usually hurried into work, the mill workers chatted, laughed, and sang songs.

There was some uncertainty about whether or not to go work. Some hoped they might find a sign, "No Cut," posted to cancel the strike. A few workers entered the mill to get personal belongings. Others were overheard to say, "If you'll go in, I'll go in too," but no one started in. Machines could be heard running near the doors where the crowd gathered. The noise gave the impression that some workers were in the mills, but with four or five cars in the parking lot, it was obvious the bosses were running the machines [31]

— *Evening Standard*

A New Bedford Kind of Strike

After the millowners closed their gates on the second day of the strike, the Textile Council paid little attention to picketing. William Batty and Abraham Binns, as secretary and treasurer of strike relief funds for the council, were content to make the rounds of the mills every day to make sure that the gates were closed. The Textile Council held rallies for all textile workers once a week, where union leaders encouraged the thousands in attendance to keep up the fight. Notices were printed on the front pages of the city's newspapers, and the press carefully reported on discussions at the meetings. Batty was especially eloquent, contrasting the millowners' tyranny with the democratic political system. He entertained the crowd by playing his cornet and led the singing of strike songs that he composed himself.[32]

The craft unions distributed strike funds directly to their members and organized a Citizens Strike Relief Committee to distribute relief to mill workers who were not members. The committee was composed of clergy, owners of small businesses, and local professional people interested in "the cause of humanity and the desire to do civic duty as good citizens."[33] The committee looked to the middle classes for funds, promising independence from the Textile Council and impartiality in the battle between millowners and workers, but it received most of its funds from the council's collections. The committee gave out the money as vouchers for groceries from local storekeepers. Most relief for nonunion strikers came from the city's public and private agencies, however. During the strike's second week, Batty, Binns, and Textile Council president Joseph Harrison met with the city's Board of Public Welfare. They convinced the board that because the millowners had closed the mill gates, nonunion workers couldn't work and therefore were eligible for public relief.[34] In order to focus city welfare payments on the nonunion strikers, the Textile Council leaders gave the board a list of union members so they could be excluded from receiving welfare.

Applicants had to demonstrate they were destitute, without property, cars, or money. This was true for most strikers, and thousands flooded the office. The Welfare Board gave out about $10,000 per week to the strikers, several times as much as the Citizens Relief Committee did.[35] Private organizations, such as New Bedford Family Welfare, the Catholic Welfare Bureau, and the Soldiers and Sailors Relief, also gave small amounts of aid to striking workers not receiving strike pay from the craft unions.[36]

The strikers received help from the property owners and merchants in their neighborhoods. Sam Collins, the local boxing promoter who owned the Bristol Arena, refused to charge the Textile Council rent for its meetings.[37] "It was for a good cause and I could not see myself taking the money which could be used to better advantage by the textile operatives."[38] Collins later donated a railroad carload of potatoes to the council.[39] Grocery stores extended credit to strikers, pharmacies and other small shops cut prices, barbers offered free haircuts, and landlords reduced rents, in some cases cutting them in half.[40] But most mill workers stopped paying rent and many moved during the strike to avoid rent collection, some moving in with relatives and other families.[41] Landlords, many of whom were mill workers themselves, felt the pinch especially toward the end of the strike in the fall, when city tax payments came due. Landlords tried to reduce rents further in hope of collecting something, but most collected little or nothing during the strike.[42]

Support for the strikers came also from their own organizations. The Washington Club, a workingmen's club founded by the English textile workers in 1892, quickly opened a soup kitchen where children received soup, bread, and lollipops. The club operated daily when the crowd of children grew from eight hundred to fifteen hundred. In the South End near both the English and Portuguese neighborhoods, the mostly English club members took pride that they didn't discriminate against Portuguese children. Because almost all members of the club were striking textile workers, the treasury soon ran out, but the soup kitchen continued on with donations from city grocers and merchants.[43] By the end of the strike the club was feeding two thousand to three thousand children per day, and Fred Duckett, the club's president, estimated that it had given out 250,000 loaves of bread during the strike.[44] Smaller soup kitchens operated in the North End at the Workingmen's Club and at the Canadian Club.

> *Everybody had a sense of commitment. Store owners let people run up tremendous bills. Landlords cut rents until they barely met their tax and water bills. There was support for the worker because the worker was just about getting along, treading water, and no one could see how he could make ends meet with a 10 percent cut. People felt that the strikers were justified in what they were doing.*[45]
>
> — *Beatrice Pacheco*

The council needed allies to pressure the millowners to withdraw the pay cut. The democratic ideals of fairness and justice still existed in the city's small-town atmosphere, and the millowners were susceptible to moral as well as economic arguments.[46] The council also called on the political support it had built over the years.

At the start of the strike, public officials, including Mayor Ashley, trod lightly in the conflict, trying to walk a fine line between the millowners and the Textile Council. Over the previous thirty years, the Textile Council had won its place in New Bedford political life. Samuel Ross had served in the state legislature for twenty years and at the time of the strike was a member of the State Board of Arbitration and Conciliation, which either party in a labor dispute could call in to mediate conflict.

Each of the city's three newspapers, the *Evening Standard*, the *Morning Mercury*, and the *Times*, opposed the wage cut, objecting to the workers' low wages and the detrimental effect the wage cut would have on local business. The press aided relief efforts by praising contributors to the Citizens Relief Committee, usually on the front page. The newspapers also questioned the mills' finances and criticized the millowners' greed and their outdated methods of management, advertising, and sales. Editorials called for state intervention, asked why mill managers' salaries were not included in the cut, and called on the millowners to justify the wage cut.

Unlike the millowners, who never were available to the media at the start of the strike, Batty and the other Textile Council leaders gave daily interviews and had exceptionally good relations with the press.

The Textile Council also published a twelve-part series by nationally renowned labor economist Dr. Norman Ware in the newspapers, showing that the wage cut was both unnecessary and unfair. Dr. Ware argued that the wage cut was unnecessary because New Bedford's major product, finely woven cloth, was not in competition with low-wage mills in the South and other areas that produced coarse cloth. He stated that wage cuts were unfair because profits were rising, not falling.

Newspaper articles by Frank Manning and Donald Thompson, who came from the Boston branch of the Young People's Socialist League to work for the Textile Council, spurred stockholders to enter the struggle. Newspapers and magazines outside New Bedford covered the strike. The *New Republic* and the *Nation* charged that the New Bedford millowners were using the wage cuts in coarse cloth to line their pockets. The *New Republic* also reported that the low wages in New Bedford contrasted with the high cost of living. The magazine quoted a 1923 study of living conditions in New Bedford: "In few cities of the United States do the necessaries of life cost so much as in New Bedford."[47]

Although national coverage never approached the yellow journalism of the 1898 strike, occasional articles tried to characterize the strike as a violent confrontation between destitute workers and greedy owners. The local newspapers perceived these reports as attacks on their city and took pride in the businesslike behavior of the Textile Council. The editor of the *Evening Standard* poked gentle fun at attempts to sensationalize the strike: "The writers who are satisfied with nothing short of clubs and bullets and bloodshed must have found New Bedford distinctly disappointing."[48]

The strike was 100 percent effective in closing the mills. Industry analysts concluded that the strike had saved the owners from having to close the mills for the summer. Two days after the strike's start, the Cotton Manufacturers' Association bought a full-page advertisement in each of the city's newspapers, arguing that other textile centers had cut wages and that it would be ruinous for them to pay more than a competitive wage. Nevertheless, if Textile Council leaders maintained discipline within their ranks they could look forward to more favorable conditions for negotiations when market conditions changed. This strategy required that the unorganized workers, who formed a majority in the mills, follow the council's leadership. But the lower-paid, mostly Portuguese, Cape Verdean, and Polish workers had suffered long enough from their second-class status in the mills. This time they weren't willing to quietly follow the lead of the craft unions that long had excluded them: the TMC came to New Bedford to challenge the Textile Council.

The Textile Mill Committees

The roots of the TMC reached back to the founding of the Communist Party in the United States. In 1919, encouraged by the success of the Bolsheviks in Russia, a group split from the Socialist Party to form the Communist Party. The new organization joined the Communist International, a worldwide organization formed to unite the various national communist parties.

A struggle quickly developed within the International between two labor strategies: forming militant labor unions in opposition to the existing unions or working from within the established unions to shift them toward more militant tactics and more revolutionary goals. V. I. Lenin, the leader of the Bolsheviks and the founder of the International, decided in favor of working from within the established unions.

For the U.S. Communist labor leaders, this meant joining with the conservative AFL. Less than ten years earlier, in 1912, the UTW had fought the IWW in the Lawrence Bread and Roses strike. John Golden, president of the UTW, denounced the strike as a revolution. At a U.S. congressional hearing, Golden defended the clubbing and bayoneting of women and children by the police during the strike. During the following years, the UTW vigorously fought the various spinoffs from the IWW and other left-wing unions.

In 1926, Albert Weisbord, a young Harvard Law School graduate and Communist labor leader, welded together an impressive organization of women and men from several different mills spread throughout the Passaic region. Sixteen thousand strikers of many different nationalities closed the mills through mass picketing.[49] Weisbord tried to bring the UTW into the strike several times, but the union refused to work with the Communists. As the Communist leaders watched the UTW abandon the strike, spending most of its efforts to discredit Weisbord and the party, they realized that their strategy of working within the UTW couldn't succeed. In February 1928, the International reversed its earlier decision and directed its members to form unions to rival the AFL, focusing on the lower-paid, mostly immigrant workers that the AFL long had ignored.[50]

Selected by the Communist Party to organize textile workers in New England, Fred Beal and William Murdoch went to New Bedford to organize a strike.[51] After printing leaflets urging workers to strike, they left for New Bedford and began passing them out at mill gates the next morning.[52] Beal and Murdoch had traveled similar roads in different countries to become labor organizers for the Communist Party. Beal had worked in the woolen mills of Lawrence, a down-on-his-luck Yankee amidst the sea of recent immigrants, and joined those immigrants in the Bread and Roses strike in 1912. After the war, he returned to the mills and the militant labor movement. Murdoch, born the tenth of eleven children in Inverness, Scotland, was apprenticed to a machinist before he enlisted in the military to fight in World War I. After the war he emigrated to Providence, where he worked in several mills and became increasingly involved in labor organizing.[53]

Their paths crossed in Boston in 1927 when both joined the international movement to stop the execution of Nicola Sacco and Bartolomeo Vanzetti, labor organizers accused of armed robbery and murder in Braintree. Beal and Murdoch were attracted by the Communist Party's worldwide connections and its ability to organize large groups of workers. For their part, party leaders wanted Beal and Murdoch to implement their new strategy of forming militant textile unions in opposition to the AFL unions.

Beal and Murdoch found a welcome reception in New Bedford from the twenty thousand Portuguese, Polish, and other immigrant mill workers who had long been excluded from the craft unions. A few Portuguese workers, some of whom had been union organizers in Portugal and others who had been members of the IWW, helped Beal and Murdoch distribute leaflets.[54]

On Monday, April 16, the first day of the strike, Murdoch and Beal were joined by several veterans of the Passaic strike. They set up headquarters in the South End and announced a mass meeting for that Wednesday. Although Batty and Binns bitterly denounced the group and warned workers to stay away from the meeting, over five hundred mill workers attended. The TMC quickly took the alienation and frustration of the unskilled, lower-paid workers, who had been excluded from the craft unions, and turned it into an enthusiasm unrivaled in previous New Bedford textile strikes. Daily picketing, meetings, rallies, and soup kitchens created excitement, purpose, and unity behind the strike in the Portuguese and Polish communities. Thousands walked the picket lines and attended rallies organized to educate and entertain. The TMC concentrated its efforts in the immigrant neighborhoods located around the mills in the north and south ends of the city and left the center of town, where the millowners lived and commerce reigned, to the Textile Council. Organizers went to people's homes to encourage participation. Families picketed as groups—women with babies in their arms, young children walking alongside.

The TMC's message did not end with opposing the 10 percent wage cut. The group demanded a 20 percent wage increase, a forty-hour work week, equal pay for equal work, an end to the speedup, no discrimination against union members, and an end to child labor.[55] Their plans called for a single union covering all textile workers in the city and a democratically elected executive committee.

> *We wanted a union that would take in all of the textile workers. We called for an industrial type of union instead of a craft union, and that was quite progressive at that time because most of the unions in the United States at that time were craft unions. The whole idea was to get all of the textile workers to belong to a single textile union.*[56]
>
> —*Eula Mendes*

> *There is no question in my mind that we put the backbone into the strike. . . . The people were very much incensed. They were living very close to the marginal line. We told the people that they were going to win or lose the strike because of what they done and not because of what we as leaders told them. We told them the strike would be won on the picket line, as a result we were able to build a great feeling and desire and need for attending the picket lines.*[57]
>
> —*Jack Rubenstein*

The frantic pace of the strike didn't allow time for a complicated internal structure. Beal and Murdoch directed activities, while labor organizers from Passaic teamed with local grassroots leaders to direct strike activities. The

TMC's goal was to unite workers from all mills into a single union; workers were told to picket the mills closest to their homes, whether they worked there or not.

Picket lines often would march from mill to mill before gathering for a mass meeting at TMC headquarters. After hearing local and sometimes national leaders, everyone would march to one of the mills and continue picketing. Hundreds and often thousands of mill workers and their families would spend the day on the picket lines and at TMC rallies. Many more people would troop to the mills to watch and shout encouragement.

TMC leaders included women and children in the strike activities. Ann Washington Craton, a New York labor organizer and writer, told TMC members, "Make the strike a family affair. Women are better at this sort of thing than the men. They are more courageous than men. They will do more and suffer more. . . . You women who cannot leave your children at home, bring them with you. Let them understand what the strike means, so that when they have to go hungry, and when they have to go to school in ragged shoes, they will know why. Educate them to be good union men and women for they are the workers of the future."[58] Children were led on the picket lines, and at TMC headquarters taught the meaning of the strike. When the number of children increased and more space became necessary Mayor Ashley refused, saying, "No, you cannot have any playground or anything else that I have any control over for your damnable work with children, as long as I am in the mayor's chair."

The newspapers sided with Ashley against the TMC. They contrasted the children being fed by the Textile Council members at the Washington Club with the children marching in the TMC picket lines. An *Evening Standard* editorial titled "Children First" went further: "We recall nothing more shameful unless it is the tactics of an invading army which forces the children of the defenders to march ahead of it."[59]

Stung by the newspapers' rhetoric, the TMC changed tactics. Children no longer marched alone but joined their parents on picket lines for the remainder of the strike. Young women in their teens especially were drawn to the TMC. Before the strike, their lives were spent at work or at home. But during the strike, for the first time in their lives, they were allowed out on their own.

Because the TMC had no treasury and most members couldn't collect from the Textile Council or its relief organizations, strike relief became a major activity for the new union. When Police Chief William Cole would not allow the TMC to collect money in the city, Murdoch replied that he expected harassment from local police. "The opposition to us here is very strong. Permits might be issued and then revoked; so, we shall not try it. We will obtain our funds from other cities."[60]

Chief Cole also notified police chiefs in other cities that the Textile Council collectors were the official representatives of New Bedford strikers, and he asked them to stop the TMC representatives from collecting for strike relief in their cities. The communist relief organization, the Workers' International Relief (WIR), promised large donations. However, like the UTW and the other AFL unions that promised much, it didn't deliver. Little money from the WIR actually reached the city.

> *The TMC established committees on picketing with picket captains. They also established a relief committee which tried to get food and financial support. Carloads of us would go to Fall River to working-class neighborhoods. We knew the majority of the people living in these areas were textile workers. We would go to their homes. They had a little sticker on them which said, "Support and relief for the New Bedford strikers." We would also go to places like Brockton, Lawrence, Malden, Pawtucket and Providence.*[61]
>
> —*Joe Figueiredo*

The city's relief agencies and private charities also chose the Textile Council over the TMC. Batty and Binns maintained close contact with city welfare officials, and strikers needed cards signed by the Textile Council to apply to the Citizens Relief Committee.[62] The police took photographs of people on the TMC picket lines and distributed them to the city agencies and the Citizens Relief Committee so they could stop TMC members from getting strike relief.[63] Later in the strike, when property and bank books were used to bail out arrested TMC picketers, the court gave city agencies the names of people supplying bail to show that they owned property and shouldn't collect strike relief.[64]

The TMC relied mainly on the tightly knit Portuguese and Polish communities that always had provided for their own in need. Most families were used to poverty because they earned subsistence wages and had learned to do without. Although rent and other payments could be stopped with little effect, people still had to eat. Family gardens helped, and Portuguese dairy farmers, bakers, and fishermen donated milk, bread, and fish, which were distributed from TMC headquarters on Scott Street.

> *We had a few trucks, and they'd go to Rhode Island to the little grocery stores and get the bones that they would throw out to make soup with. It was all filled with maggots . . . but they would come back and put that in the great big vats that they got. They would boil that and the scum would come on top. They would skim that. The rest of it was the broth that they used to make soup. Then they'd go out and pick up whatever they could get to make it, give it a body. And that's what you had to eat. You'd have to bring your own dish, and you could get one cup of soup, including the kids.*[65]
>
> —*Al Saulnier*

The Textile Council Responds to the TMC and the Millowners Strike Back

The council leaders vigorously opposed the new union. The TMC's attraction for unorganized workers and even for some Textile Council members weakened the council's control over the strike. Over the past thirty years, Batty, Binns, Ross, and the other leaders successfully had used the unity of the skilled workers to confront millowners when they could, and to accommodate them when they couldn't. They would not give up these gains easily to accept the TMC leaders and their mostly Portuguese and Polish followers, who threatened the council's social, political, and economic status as labor leaders in New Bedford.

At first the Textile Council leaders publicly ridiculed the TMC effort. Binns, expecting a small turnout for the TMC's first mass meeting, said, "We'll let the Textile Mill Committees conduct their own funeral."[66] At the same time, Council leaders joined the growing chorus in the city's newspapers in calling Beal, Murdoch, and the other TMC leaders communist invaders and outside troublemakers leading a revolution in New Bedford.[67]

> *The word "reds" was used a lot in the commercial press. They tried to take the focus away from the strike and what it was all about. They tried to portray it that we had an enemy here when the real enemy was the mill owners. They fabricated and exaggerated and invented. What happened, however, was it boomeranged as far as the mass of the textile workers were concerned. They were involved in the strike, and it didn't happen the way these newspapers presented it.*[68]
>
> —*Joe Figueiredo*

Although these strategies may have influenced the council's members, they had little effect on Portuguese and Polish mill workers. Many didn't speak English, and those who did interpreted these attacks as evidence that the Textile Council and the city's elites were united against them. Also, some Portuguese workers, especially those from the Continent, knew the difference between a labor strike for higher wages and a political revolution to overthrow the government. Shrill denunciations of communism and emotional appeals to American values didn't convince the Portuguese mill workers to leave the TMC. For them, the TMC was fighting for higher wages and equality with other workers, principles easily identified with American democracy.

> *And people were not concerned because the way we approached them was, "They call us communist because we fight for you."*[69]
>
> —*Jack Rubenstein*

When the TMC's picket lines began to build, the council's leaders had to win back the leadership of the strike. The council had stopped picketing after the millowners closed their gates on the first day of the strike, but the TMC used mass picketing and daily rallies to build up its membership. While making his daily rounds of the mill gates, Batty came upon a large TMC picket line at the Wamsutta Mills and spotted Beal. He walked up to Beal and punched him in the face. A wild melee followed. TMC supporters attacked Batty, and, according to Beal's statement in the newspapers, Beal and Murdoch tried to defend him. Batty told the newspapers, "I would have done the same to him if I had found Beal in New York, Boston, or anywhere else. In a story, he called me a traitor to the cause of labor. . . . I warned Murdoch to tell Beal to keep out of my way or I'd punch his nose."[70]

In response to the TMC's daily actions, the Textile Council broadened its vision of strike activities. The council held weekly open meetings in the Bristol Arena and rallies at Buttonwood Park in the city's center that thousands of mill workers and their families attended. National union leaders and well-known politicians addressed huge crowds, who quietly listened to long speeches. In contrast to the council's practice, many of the speakers spoke openly in favor of socialism and the unity of all workers.

Women, who numbered about half of New Bedford's mill workers, long had been ignored by the Textile Council. Although about one-third of the council members were women, all of the council leaders were men.[71] The council tried to counter the TMC's focus on women by bringing in women speakers, encouraging women to come to membership meetings, and holding special events for them. Rose Schneiderman, president of the Women's Trade Union League, told her audience, "In the old days, women always would work more cheaply than men. And as long as they held themselves cheap, they were cheap. You women who do men's work have got to remember that and organize along with your husbands. . . . Don't let them divide you. One big union in the textile industry is its only salvation."[72]

Occasional assemblies and picnics also were held on other afternoons and evenings. At festivals, several thousand mill workers listened to the speakers and the music, ate, chatted, and sang, while children played, and young people courted.

The soup kitchens for children, operated by Textile Council members, fed council and TMC families alike. The Textile Council leaders also tried to attract the Portuguese, Cape Verdean, Polish, and French Canadian men and women, whom they long had excluded. Manuel Silva, secretary-treasurer of the Ring Twisters' Union, which represented the lowest-paid craft union workers, was given more prominence within the leadership of the council. He spoke in Portuguese at mass meetings and asked Portuguese workers, whatever their jobs in the mills, to join his group or at least attend its meetings. But Silva never was successful in attracting Portuguese workers to the council. At the special council meetings for Portuguese workers, TMC members arrived in force to belittle the council's recent conversion to solidarity.[73] When the TMC accused Father Manuel Salvador, pastor of St. John the Baptist, of advising workers to end the strike in his Sunday sermon, Father Salvador denied the charge and Silva was forced to side with the church and apparently against the strikers.[74]

The council crossed the color line to invite African American union leaders to speak at its rallies. Frank Crosswaith, organizer for the Pullman Porters Union, told a meeting in the Bristol Arena that attracted nine hundred listeners by the time he had finished speaking, "In the struggle between these two organized groups race and religion do not count. The manufacturers try to force you to recognize them. They pace French against Portuguese, Polish against English knowing that when they get them divided, they can ride upon beds of ease for centuries to come as the employees remain divided."[75]

To attract Polish members, the council began a new union for all Polish workers regardless of their craft. However, the implications of seven craft unions and a Polish union weren't lost on most Polish mill workers. President

Jan Kisiel of the Polish Textile Workers Union compounded the problem when he hinted that the strike could be settled with a cut of 5 percent instead of 10 percent.[76] Most Polish strikers were in no mood to offer a wage cut, and the organization disappeared.

Special Council meetings for French Canadian workers led by Horace Riviere, a veteran UTW organizer, proved more successful as hundreds of French Canadian workers joined the council's unions. Some became union leaders after the strike.[77] The TMC had much less success recruiting French Canadian workers. In the middle of the strike, Felix Ouillette was named president of the TMC but soon resigned in a dispute over picket line tactics. He took most of his countrymen to the Textile Council with him, saying, "I don't believe there is another Franco-American in the TMC."[78]

But the TMC continued as the main force on the picket lines while the Textile Council preferred to avoid confrontation with the millowners and the law. At the end of the strike's second month, after weeks of Batty's arguing that it already had closed the mills, the Textile Council resumed picketing.[79] The council's picket lines were smaller than the TMC's, however, and usually the TMC maneuvered council pickets into following their lines.

When a few and then hundreds of TMC pickets were arrested, the Textile Council claimed good citizenship for its members in contrast to the TMC's lawlessness. Finally, with the TMC leading the majority of mill workers and even attracting the council's members, the council's leaders had to yield the high ground and get down with the strikers.

By that time, the battle was being fought with a different enemy, however. No longer were the two unions the main antagonists in the strike. The millowners awoke as if from a long sleep and began their assault.

The Textile Council long before had won its place in the city. The council picketed the mills with little police interference and conducted meetings rent-free in public parks, community buildings, and the Bristol Arena. New Bedford's ruling establishment treated the TMC very differently. TMC members were harassed by city officials, arrested by police, and sentenced by the courts. When Mayor Ashley refused the TMC use of the city's parks and other public property, the union held rallies in vacant lots and city streets, always with an eye out for the police. Smaller meetings were held in empty buildings in workers' neighborhoods.

The city's newspapers also favored the Textile Council over the TMC. They carefully reported the council's actions and treated council leaders with respect, describing Batty, Binns, and the others as cool, patient, law-abiding citizens and businesslike professionals. The local press portrayed the TMC leaders as invading strike agitators and romantic adventurers who were "tempestuous, excitable, unsteady, and even weak-chinned." As the strike wore on, the millowners used their control over the legal, media, and civic institutions against both labor organizations and tried to end the strike on their own terms.

The Establishment versus the TMC

At 6:30 a.m. on May 8, police broke into TMC headquarters on Potomska Street. They evicted the fifty people preparing for picket duty, saying the building was not licensed as a meeting place and did not comply with fire and health regulations.[80] Deputy Police Chief Samuel McLeod, who led the raid, threatened to close the TMC's North End quarters in the Madeirense Sporting Club as well. Two weeks later, the club banned the TMC from holding further meetings, declaring that it no longer supported the group and that the TMC hadn't paid its rent.

The TMC's space problems were solved when Oliva Saulnier, former mill worker and IWW member blacklisted from the 1912 Lawrence strike, came to a TMC rally held in the city dump on Cove Street. After the rally, Saulnier offered the TMC free use of a property called Saulnier's lot, located near the mills in the South End, an open space large enough to hold several thousand people, surrounded by buildings and fenced off from the street.

> *My father went over there and told the strikers, "I can't give you any money, but you can meet on my land." Our property was all fenced in. They put their own guards in there, and if you didn't have a card, you couldn't get onto the lot. You had to be a textile worker. Someone had to recognize you, or you had to have a pay envelope or a receipt of some kind to show that you had worked in a mill.*
>
> *We had a right to have meetings on our own property. We had a right to keep the police out as long as there was no disturbance, and the way to prevent a disturbance was to prove that everyone who came in had worked in a mill. They never had any trouble on our property. They met every day, about two or three hundred people, to decide what they were going to do that day, where they were going to picket and so forth. They had everything pretty well organized.*[81]
>
> —*Al Saulnier*

The city's police and courts caused the TMC more serious problems. Although the police often patrolled picket lines and escorted strikebreakers through mill gates during the strike's first month, they seldom interfered with the TMC picket lines. As the crowds grew larger, showing increasing support for the TMC, the police moved in. They made their first arrests on May 10, charging Christina Simores and Angelina Tsoupreas with disturbing the peace, carrying concealed weapons (two feet of gas pipe and a bag of bricks), and attacking a police officer. Tsoupreas had bitten the policeman on the arm when he tried to throw her into the paddy wagon.[82] Judge Milliken found both women guilty and sentenced them to six months in prison. The women appealed to superior court, and all charges except disturbing the peace were thrown out. Each woman was ordered to spend one month in prison.[83]

More arrests quickly followed. At the end of May, the Citizens' Mediation Committee convinced the millowners to meet with the Textile Council to discuss a compromise. Nothing came from the meeting because the millowners continued to insist on the wage cut. But the TMC, excluded from the negotiations, stepped up picketing to convince both the millowners and the council that the strike couldn't be settled without them. The police responded by arresting several picketers, including Beal and Murdoch, for disturbing the peace. They were charged with singing on the picket line and encouraging others to sing. Each was found guilty and sentenced to ninety days in prison by Judge Milliken, who further ruled that using the word "scab" was illegal. The TMC appealed all sentences to superior court.

June proved a busy month for the courts as police increased their vigilance. After he was promoted to police chief upon the sudden death of Chief Cole, McLeod directed all policemen to picket duty, postponed vacations, and ordered double shifts.[84] On June 14, Elizabeth Donnelly, who had dropped out of Boston University to work as a labor organizer and who led children on the picket lines,[85] was arrested for singing, "We'll catch the boss and put him in the sauce and never let him go," to the tune of "A hunting we will go." Several others were arrested that day, including Bessie Katsikaras, for the second time. She replied in court, "God gave me my voice, and God is the only one that can keep me quiet."[86] Augusto Pinto, arrested for the third time in the strike, claimed he wasn't singing but was silently opening and closing his mouth.[87] Milliken gave heavy sentences to all three.

> *I never saw a black cop. Very few Portuguese cops. They were mostly Irish, English, some French Canadians. They were out to break the picket line. There were mass arrests.*[88]
>
> —*Joe Figueiredo*

The rainy summer gave the TMC another weapon besides singing. While leading a large picket line at the Wamsutta Mill, Beal was ordered by police to stop singing and replied, "Go to hell," before a policeman moved in to arrest him. A woman next to Beal hit the policeman with her umbrella, and a brawl began. The strikers used stones and umbrellas and at least one policeman swung his club. Several people were injured, including Beal and a policeman who was bitten just above the elbow. Beal and eight other strikers were arrested and taken away in paddy wagons. Some two hundred picketers followed them on foot, singing and shouting. En route, Katsikaras was arrested again but continued to sing at the top of her lungs. When told to keep still at the station, she replied, "Go to hell. I'll picket tomorrow, and I'd like to see the damned cop who can take me out of the picket line."[89]

On June 22, Murdoch, Beal, and eleven other defendants appeared in superior court on appeal from their district court convictions. The English and French Canadian jury, which probably thought the TMC a nuisance to begin with, first convicted Murdoch. Avery sentenced him to sixty days in jail, and five minutes later Murdoch found himself in prison. The next day, Beal pleaded guilty for a lesser sentence of thirty days in prison. The judge continued the cases of ten other defendants until November. The millowners didn't gain much advantage with Murdoch and Beal in the county jail, however.

Angered by the arrests, more people joined the TMC's picket lines; even Textile Council members joined TMC pickets for the first time. On the day of Murdoch's trial, at the same spot where he had punched Beal in the face two months earlier, Batty joined Beale and the rival unions picketed together at the Wamsutta's gates. The pickets sang and shouted while the police stood quietly on the sidelines and made no arrests.

Later that day, at the trial of Frances Mikolajczyk and Veronica Ogozalak for throwing stones while marching in a Textile Council picket line, New Bedford trial lawyer Jacob Minkin carefully distinguished his defendants from the TMC, referring to the "slander and calumny being heaped upon

New Bedford because of the activities of outsiders." He convinced Special Judge James Doran that the police had no evidence against Mikolajczyk and Doran found her not guilty, the first acquittal of the strike. He found Ogozalak guilty but filed the case and took care to distinguish her from the TMC pickets, saying she "doesn't appear dangerous or in any way undesirable. She was on the scene and was carried away by the excitement."[90]

Changing of the Guard in the TMC

Since the beginning of the strike, leadership had been shifting away from Beal and Murdoch and toward the Passaic group, which was more experienced in leading strikes. Their abrupt transfer from the picket line to the New Bedford House of Correction simply concluded the change in the TMC's leadership. Eli Keller, veteran of the Passaic strike and president of Passaic UTW Local 1618, took Craton's place as head of relief and over the next few weeks assumed control of the TMC. The Passaic group of Keller, Rubenstein, and Ellen Dawson, secretary-treasurer of another Passaic UTW local, along with occasional visits from Weisbord, now held control of the TMC. The new leadership of the TMC moved even closer to the tactics used in Passaic. They planned a massive parade for July 1 and applied for a city permit. Chief McLeod refused on the grounds that the parade was a demonstration. Looking to test the police, the TMC continued with its plans. Thousands of TMC supporters prepared to march in two groups: one in the North End under Rubenstein and the other in the South End under Keller, with a plan to meet in the city's center. McLeod called out every police officer in the city. The police blocked both routes with trucks and paddy wagons and arrested Rubenstein, Keller, and thirty others.[91]

> *Workers gathered, and we started to march. No sooner had we started when the cops came in with clubs. I've never seen clubs like that size before. They were like Indian route sticks. Have you ever seen the pictures? About three-and-a-half to four feet long. You couldn't get near the guy that was swinging it at you. They waded into us and broke it up, and that is when I landed in a pie wagon or a converted truck used as a paddy wagon. I see those clubs in my nightmares.*[92]
>
> —*Jack Rubenstein*

The TMC leaders declared that the arrests violated their constitutional right to peaceful assembly. Mayor Ashley defended Chief McLeod, saying,

"If the recognized unions [the Textile Council] want to hold a parade, I will see that they have a permit. They are a splendid group of citizens, and I know they will do nothing contrary to the law. I do oppose and will continue to oppose any parade sponsored by the group of outsiders, who have come in here since the strike began."[93] Special District Court Judge George Gardiner found all defendants guilty of parading without a permit and sentenced them to six months in prison, which they appealed.[94]

The strategy borrowed from Passaic worked. For ten weeks, picket lines, parades, rallies, and court cases kept the mill workers focused on the strike. Although Textile Council leaders considered mass marches and parades beyond the limits of responsible union behavior, they resumed picketing and even seemed willing to join the TMC on the picket line. Together, at least temporarily, they faced the greatest test of the strike.

The millowners, who had sold off their inventories and were ready to resume production, prepared to open their gates in a direct confrontation with both the council and the TMC.

The Millowners Reopen the Mills

On June 27, the millowners announced they would open the mills on Monday, July 9, with the 10 percent cut in effect. The council was confident that the strikers could again shut down the mills. Batty said, "We welcome the test. We have no fear that it will result in anything except a more convincing demonstration than ever of the determination of the textile operatives of New Bedford to stick it out until they win their strike."[95] Both the TMC and the Textile Council prepared for the opening by building their picket lines. On Monday, the week before the opening, the council held a practice picket. Thousands of mill workers watched large lines from both unions picket the mostly closed mill gates.

Tension mounted as the day for the mill opening approached. Mayor Ashley called in police from other cities and asked for volunteers from the National Guard, offering five dollars per day, roughly the same as mill wages for men. When no one volunteered, Ashley conscripted the guard members to serve at the army rate of one dollar per day.[96] The National Guard readied mounted soldiers, artillery, and live cartridges.

> *The mill owners made efforts to open up the mills, and they called out the National Guard. I was in Battery F. They called out the riot call, and we all went up to the*

state armory. We were all lined up. Now in Battery F most of us had friends or members of our families who were on strike, and some of us were strikers. So that when they called out the batteries, the one battery they didn't call was Battery F. One guy says, "I ain't going to shoot no striker. My mother is on strike." I was already known as being an activist in the strike. So I said, "If they send us out there what are we going to do?" When they were up in front to call out the batteries, they sent out Battery B, the cavalry. But we were kept in the armory. Later on we learned that they had decided that there were too many people in Battery F that they could not rely on.[97]

—*Joe Figueiredo*

On July 9, twenty thousand mill workers picketed the mill gates and watched as almost no one entered the mills. A jubilant Batty declared, "A complete tie-up. We have won for the second time. It is wonderful. Never has there been such a display of solidarity in a textile strike before. The crowds just cheered and applauded when the gates were closed at 7:15. You would have thought it a vaudeville show rather than a strike."[98]

Mayor Ashley and Chief McLeod claimed credit for peace on the picket lines and justified their use of National Guard troops. Ashley, still trying to placate both the millowners and the Textile Council, said, "Our people here are not troublesome and never have been. It was not because of any action on their part that the National Guardsmen were brought into the situation, but there are outsiders here who would cause trouble if they could, and I know it."[99]

Both the TMC and the Textile Council intensified their picket lines after the mill reopened. On July 10, several thousand TMC supporters picketed all night at the Kilburn Mill, which was rumored to be operating with strikebreakers.

It was reported that some scabs had been taken in by some mill owners, and we kept a 24-hour picket line going for a little over two days. The result was that after two-and-a-half days, the owner had to let the scabs out.[100]

—*Eula Mendes*

Both unions ran picket lines, with Batty often leading the council's lines himself. Chief McLeod called out all his men and ordered in some reserves. At times the crowds surged out of control, and on one evening several hundred mill windows were broken. The police and the courts' more permissive stance toward the council began to change. Chief McLeod stood by the arrests of four council members for picketing strikebreakers' homes, saying, "People have an unquestionable right to go to and from their homes and what is further to live in their homes, without being disturbed by anyone."[101] For the first time in the strike, New Bedford's Board of Commerce openly opposed the Textile Council and unanimously voted that, "mass and house picketing and the formation of crowds in the vicinity of industrial plants act against the best interest of the whole community, and the board appeals to the public to discourage the continuance of such practices and to support the authorities in a strict enforcement of the law."[102]

The council, which was a member of the Board of Commerce, sharply disagreed. Batty said, "The Board apparently regards the strike as a picnic, but it is more than that. It is a struggle for existence, an economic right, and we will not yield our legal rights and privileges."[103]

The Millowners versus the Textile Council and the TMC

The week after they failed to reopen the mills, the Cotton Manufacturers' Association changed leaders, and John Sullivan, president of the association and owner of the Taber Mill, took charge. Sullivan immediately claimed that picketing deprived the millowners and workers of their right to reopen the mills.[104] Sullivan saved most of his criticism for the TMC, which he said "constitutes a menace both to the mills and to the established labor organizations. It is directly connected to the communistic and Bolshevik organizations and lives on trouble."[105] Sullivan also declared there were eight hundred "reds" in New Bedford and charged that Quakers, Republican congressmen, and some clergymen had joined the socialists.

Sullivan also blamed the police, Mayor Ashley, and the courts for being too lenient. He advised Mayor Ashley to emulate former governor Calvin Coolidge, who had fired all the striking police in Boston ten years earlier. He also told the court to limit the number of people on picket lines and at other gatherings to the "smallest possible number."[106]

Some millowners decided to take direct action themselves. The same day that Sullivan started his attack, John Burton, owner and general manager at the Nashawena Mill, got out of his car at a picket line and threatened the crowd with his revolver. The police stepped in and convinced him to get back into his car. Burton had said earlier at a public meeting that "he want[ed] every Red run out of town."[107]

A few days after Sullivan requested that the police stop the picketing, both the council and the TMC sent large picket lines to stop strikebreakers from entering the Sharp Mill. Sergeant Augustus Velho told picket leaders to disband their picket lines. When the TMC refused, Velho arrested several picketers, including Augusto Pinto, for parading without a permit. A scuffle ensued because members of both unions liked Pinto, and Velho told Reisch, who was leading the council's picket, to disband her line. She stood her ground, and Velho put her in the police wagon. In a prepared statement, Batty criticized Mayor Ashley and Chief McLeod for the arrests. Batty compared Reisch's arrest for peaceful picketing with the police force's condoning Burton's drawing a gun on the picketers. "This difference in treatment by the police department is due to the existence of an invisible government," he said.[108]

The next day, a police force of more than one hundred was dispatched to the Sharp Mill to break up a crowd of over five thousand picketers from the TMC. When the police moved in to arrest Pinto again, a riot broke out. Several police officers were injured, including Sergeants William H. McCarty, veteran of many a struggle with pickets, and Augustus Velho, who had made most of the arrests in the strike. McCarty was bitten on the arm, hit on the head with a large stone, and pummeled with fists and clubs. McLeod gave the order to read the riot act, which meant that everyone present could be arrested for rioting, and the crowd disbanded. The next afternoon, anticipating more disturbances, McLeod sent to Fall River for police reinforcements. Again, the riot act was read to the throngs of strikers at the Sharp Mill. When the crowd failed to disperse, strikers were herded into awaiting vans. Eighty-two were arrested and charged with rioting. Over the next few weeks, Milliken kept his promise to stop the picketing. He reduced the maximum picket size to ten people and then to one person. He gave harsher sentences and larger fines and increased bail for disturbing the peace to more than a mill worker's yearly salary. TMC members and their supporters continued to pledge cash and property to bail out those arrested, however.[109] Over half a million dollars was raised for bail, mostly from New Bedford's Portuguese community.[110]

> *There were some very vicious battles. For instance, the mill owners got a judge to minimize the picketing. Our committee's answer to that was mass picketing. So I was directed to the Hathaway Mill. We had about one thousand pickets there. That*

day there were about 45 people arrested. And some people were hurt. There was this Portuguese worker. They cracked his head. They took him down to the police station which was about ten blocks away. They had thousands of people around that police station trying to get him out.[111]

—Joe Figueiredo

Altogether, there was something like 888 arrests, and many of them were arrested many times. For example, I was arrested a number of times, I don't know how many times. We sometimes stayed just a few hours, sometimes overnight or sometimes even days or weeks, but we were usually let out on bail. And a few days later maybe we were arrested again.

— Eula Mendes

Although the court's ire was directed mostly at the TMC, the police's heavy hand also fell on the Textile Council for the first time in the strike. Finally, even Batty was arrested for loitering when he walked the picket lines.[112]

While the Textile Council increased its picketing, the TMC continued to lead the mass pickets, facing constant hostility from the police and the courts. When the TMC applied to Mayor Ashley for another parade permit, he again refused and brought in another small army of police and militia. Once again it rained, but this time the TMC backed down and called off the march. On July 30, several police vans pulled up to the Whitman Mill and began arresting people on the picket line. Beal, fresh from his thirty-day prison term, encouraged everyone to climb into the vans.[113] The police, rather than push people into the vans, were busy pulling women and children out.

People were hungry. I remember one time there was a march and the police brought those big moving vans. Everybody jumped into the vans to get arrested just to get a full meal. That was quite a stunt![114]

—Al Saulnier

The final count was 256 people arrested, a record for the strike.[115] More bedlam followed at the police station. Defendants appeared by the score before Milliken, who sentenced Beal, Rubenstein, and the other leaders to six months in jail and the rest to two months.

Meanwhile, a huge crowd of strikers and their families surrounded the police station.[116] McLeod called out the National Guard, which drove back the crowds with fixed bayonets. Several strikers didn't retreat and were thrown into jail with the others. A few people were cut by bayonets or bruised by the crowds. For the next few days, the jails remained full, and hundreds of people crowded around the police station, but the militia backed off and the situation cooled. Eventually, all those arrested were released on bail.

> *I'll never forget that day. The National Guard came down with their bayonets and tried to get the people to go home. I got scared and ran away. I'll never forget for I broke my heel while running. My father got scared when he saw the bayonets. They let people out of jail the next day, and these people went back on the picket line. Nobody got hurt, but the bayonets did scare people.*[117]
>
> —*Mary Alves*

After an unsuccessful attempt to spread the strike to neighboring Fall River,[118] District Court Judge Edward Hanify was particularly harsh with the TMC. When the one hundred or so arrested appeared in court, he gave Rubenstein, James Reid, and the other leaders six months in jail. He offered the rank and file probation, but only if they denounced the TMC.[119] Hanify set bail of about two years' wages for each of the TMC leaders and for those members who didn't denounce the TMC. A few days later, the Fall River strike ended when most workers drifted back to the mills.

The defeat in Fall River didn't weaken support for the TMC among New Bedford mill workers. On August 21, seven thousand people greeted Murdoch on his release from prison. He gave a speech to over five thousand at Saulnier's lot. A few days later, Mayor Ashley was forced to give the TMC a parade permit for Labor Day because he had already given a parade permit to the Textile Council. He listed several conditions, however: the TMC had to march separately from the council, and no children, singing, placards, and banners, "excepting those bearing name of organization," could be part of the parade.[120]

On September 9, five thousand union members marched through the city as several thousand more lined the streets and attended the day's events. Council members and their supporters quietly marched behind their union's insignia, and speakers included politicians and celebrities, led by U.S. Senator David Walsh. But the TMC march was several times larger than the council's and, as usual, more colorful. Many wore traditional Portuguese attire, and scores of marchers carried U.S. flags. To avoid Ashley's prohibition, the TMC had formed organizations such as "the Society of 700 Prisoners," signifying those arrested during the strike, with banners to match.

The next day, the editorial in the *Evening Standard* praised both groups for their decorum. It had the Textile Council firmly in mind, however, when it offered hope "that reason and justice would soon triumph, the essential partnership would be restored, and workers and management would soon unite in operating the industry on which New Bedford's welfare depends.[121]

Works Cited

Asher, Martha Stone. "Recollections of the Passaic Textile Strike of 1926." *Labor's Heritage* 2, no. 2 (1990): 4–23.

Ashley, Mayor Charles S. Scrapbook. 1892–1936. New Bedford Public Library, New Bedford, MA.

Beal, Fred. *Proletarian Journey: New England, Gastonia, Moscow.* New York: Hillman, Curl Inc., 1937.

Blanchard, Paul. "New Bedford Goes on Strike." *New Republic,* May 23, 1928.

Burgy, Herbert J. *The New England Cotton Textile Industry: A Study in Industrial Geography.* Baltimore: Waverly Press, 1932.

Daily Herald. Fall River. Various issues, 1928.

Evening Standard. New Bedford, MA. Various issues, 1897–1932.

Katz, Jamie W. "Opportunity, Exclusion, and the Immigrant: Textile Workers in New Bedford, Massachusetts, 1890–1930." Unpublished honors thesis. Harvard University, 1974.

Lahne, Herbert J. *The Cotton Mill Worker.* New York: Farrar & Rinehart, 1944.

Lauck, W. Jett. "The Cotton-Mill Operatives of New England." *Atlantic Monthly, 1919.*

Lenin, V. I. "Left-Wing Communism—an Infantile Disorder." *Selected Works of V. I. Lenin.* New York: International Publishing, 1967.

Lovett, Robert Morss. "New Bedford's Strike—a Knockout or a Comeback?" *New Republic,* September 12, 1928.

McMullin, Thomas. "Industrialization and Social Change in a Nineteenth-Century Port City: New Bedford, Massachusetts, 1890–1930." PhD diss., University of Wisconsin, 1976.

McMullin, Thomas. "Lost Alternative: The Urban Industrial Utopia of William D. Howland." *New England Quarterly* 55, no. 1 (1982): 25–38. https://doi.org/10.2307/365701.

New Bedford Times. New Bedford, MA. Various issues 1922, 1928, 1929.

Santos, Michael W. "Community and Communism: The 1928 New Bedford Textile Strike." *Labor History* 26 (1985): 230–49.

Saposs, David. *Left Wing Unionism: A Study of Radical Policies.* New York: International Publishing, 1926.

Ware, Caroline. *The Early Cotton Manufacture.* New York. Hart, Schaffner & Marx, 1931.

Whitney, Jessamine S. "Infant Mortality: Results of a Field Study in New Bedford, Massachusetts, Based on Births in One Year." Washington, DC: U.S. Department of Labor, Children's Bureau, 1920.

Wolfbein, Seymour. *The Decline of a Cotton Textile City: A Study of New Bedford.* New York: Columbia University Press, 1944.

Notes

1. This chapter was truncated and edited by Miguel Moniz from Daniel Georgianna with Roberta Hazen Aaronson, The Strike of '28 (New Bedford, MA: Spinner Publications, 1993).

2. Thomas McMullin, "Industrialization and Social Change in a Nineteenth-Century Port City: New Bedford, Massachusetts, 1890–1930" (PhD diss., University of Wisconsin, 1976), 30.

3. McMullin, "Industrialization and Social Change," 34.

4. McMullin, "Industrialization and Social Change," 34–40.

5. McMullin, "Industrialization and Social Change," 66.

6. McMullin, "Industrialization and Social Change," 10.

7. McMullin, "Industrialization and Social Change," 50–55.

8. McMullin, "Industrialization and Social Change," 41–43.

9. Jamie W. Katz, "Opportunity, Exclusion, and the Immigrant: Textile Workers in New Bedford, Massachusetts, 1890–1930" (unpublished honors thesis, Harvard University, 1974), 26, 27.

10. McMullin, "Industrialization and Social Change," 26–27.

11. Joe Figueiredo, New Bedford textile workers strike of 1928 oral history interviews and research collection, MC 9. Southeastern Massachusetts Historical Collections, Claire T. Carney Library Archives and Special Collections, University of Massachusetts Dartmouth, Dartmouth, MA.

12. Herbert J. Lahne, *The Cotton Mill Worker* (New York: Farrar & Rinehart, 1944), 104; Jessamine S. Whitney, "Infant Mortality: Results of a Field Study in New Bedford, Massachusetts, Based on Births in One Year" (Washington, DC: U.S. Department of Labor, Children's Bureau, 1944), 41.

13. Lahne, *The Cotton Mill Worker*, 106

14. Whitney, "Infant Mortality," 37–39.

15. Whitney, "Infant Mortality," 22–25.

16. Katz, "Opportunity, Exclusion, and the Immigrant," 76.

17. Jack Rubenstein, interview with Daniel Georgianna, September 2, 1980, Dumont, NJ; Jack Rubenstein interview with G. Schulz, August 19, 1980, New York, NY. New Bedford textile workers strike of 1928 oral history interviews and research collection, MC 9. Southeastern Massachusetts Historical Collections, Claire T. Carney Library Archives and Special Collections, University of Massachusetts Dartmouth, Dartmouth, MA.

18. Pete Fauteux, interview by D. Bastarache, January 14, 1981, Fairhaven, MA; Pete Fauteux interview by D. Bastarache and Daniel Georgianna, January 29, 1981, Fairhaven, MA. New Bedford textile workers strike of 1928 oral history interviews and research collection, MC 9. Southeastern Massachusetts Historical Collections, Claire T. Carney Library Archives and Special Collections, University of Massachusetts Dartmouth, Dartmouth, MA.

19. Katz, "Opportunity, Exclusion, and the Immigrant," 54.

20. Katz, "Opportunity, Exclusion, and the Immigrant," 54.

21. Katz, "Opportunity, Exclusion, and the Immigrant," 60–64; David Saposs, *Left Wing Unionism: A Study of Radical Policies* (New York: International Publishing, 1926), 98.

22. Lahne, *The Cotton Mill Worker*, 195.

23. Lahne, *The Cotton Mill Worker*, 201; Katz, "Opportunity, Exclusion, and the Immigrant," 62.

24. Seymour Wolfbein, *The Decline of a Cotton Textile City: A Study of New Bedford* (New York: Columbia University Press, 1944), 10, 157.

25. Wolfbein, *The Decline of a Cotton Textile City*, 156–58.

26. Figueiredo interview.

27. Mayor Charles S. Ashley, Scrapbook, 1892–1936, New Bedford Public Library, April 4, 1928, 72.

28. *Evening Standard*, April 9, 1928, 3.

29. *Evening Standard*, April 18, 1928, 7.

30. James F. McKenna, New Bedford textile workers strike of 1928 oral history interviews and research collection, MC 9. Southeastern Massachusetts Historical Collections, Claire T. Carney Library Archives and Special Collections, University of Massachusetts Dartmouth, Dartmouth, MA.

31. *Evening Standard*, April 11, 1928, 2.

32. *Evening Standard*, April 24, 1928, 8.

33. *Evening Standard*, April 24, 1928, 7.

34. Ashley, Scrapbook, April 1928, 153.

35. *Evening Standard*, May 4, 1928, 2.

36. Ashley, Scrapbook, April 1928, 127.

37. *New Bedford Times*, April 18, 1928. p.4.

38. *New Bedford Times*, April 18, 1928. p.4.

39. *Evening Standard*, June 16, 1928, 3.

40. *Evening Standard*, September 4, 1928, 2; August 19, 1928, 21.

41. *Evening Standard*, June 3, 1928, 3.

42. *Evening Standard*, September 19, 1928, 21.

43. *New Bedford Times*, June 15, 1928, 2.

44. *Evening Standard*, October 12, 1928, 1.

45. Beatrice Pacheco, interview by Roberta Hazen Aaronson, October 8, 1980, New Bedford, MA. New Bedford textile workers strike of 1928 oral history interviews and research collection, MC 9. Southeastern Massachusetts Historical Collections, Claire T. Carney Library Archives and Special Collections, University of Massachusetts Dartmouth, Dartmouth, MA.

46. Michael W. Santos, "Community and Communism: The 1928 New Bedford Textile Strike," *Labor History* 26 (1985): 233.

47. Paul Blanchard, "New Bedford Goes on Strike," *New Republic*, May 23, 1928, 10.

48. *Evening Standard*, May 9, 1928, 6.

49. Martha Stone Asher, "Recollections of the Passaic Textile Strike of 1926," *Labor's Heritage* 2, no. 2 (1990): 11.

50. Asher, "Recollections of the Passaic Textile Strike of 1926," 11.

51. Fred Beal, *Proletarian Journey: New England, Gastonia, Moscow* (New York: Hillman, Curl, 1937), 98.

52. Beal, *Proletarian Journey*, 99; Ashley, Scrapbook, April 1928, 64.

53. *Evening Standard*, July 22, 1928, 2.

54. Beal, *Proletarian Journey*, 99; Papandreu interview.

55. *Evening Standard*, May 25, 1928, 2; Rubenstein interview.

56. Eula Mendes, New Bedford textile workers strike of 1928 oral history interviews and research collection, MC 9. Southeastern Massachusetts Historical Collections, Claire T. Carney Library Archives and Special Collections, University of Massachusetts Dartmouth, Dartmouth, MA.

57. Rubenstein interview.

58. *Evening Standard*, May 1, 1928, 13.

59. *Evening Standard*, May 3, 1928, 6.

60. *Evening Standard*, April 18, 1928, 1.

61. Figueiredo interview.

62. *Evening Standard*, May 6, 1928, 2.

63. *Times*, May 7, 1928, 1.

64. *Evening Standard*, May 29, 1928, 2.

65. Al Saulnier, interview by I. Costa and Daniel Georgianna, August 25, 1981, New Bedford, MA. New Bedford textile workers strike of 1928 oral history interviews and research collection, MC 9. Southeastern Massachusetts Historical Collections, Claire T. Carney Library Archives and Special Collections, University of Massachusetts Dartmouth, Dartmouth, MA.

66. *Evening Standard,* April 18, 1928, 2.

67. *Evening Standard,* April 18, 1928, 2.

68. Figueiredo interview.

69. Rubenstein interview.

70. *Evening Standard,* May 1, 1928, 2.

71. Herbert J. Burgy, *The New England Cotton Textile Industry: A Study in Industrial Geography* (Baltimore: Waverly Press, 1932), 170.

72. *Evening Standard,* June 12, 1928, 18.

73. *Evening Standard,* May 24, 1928, 5.

74. *Evening Standard,* June 4, 1928, 1.

75. *Evening Standard,* May 21, 1928, 1.

76. *Evening Standard,* May 16, 1928, 3.

77. Fauteux interview.

78. *Evening Standard,* June 22, 1928, 2.

79. *Evening Standard,* June 16, 1928, 3.

80. *Evening Standard,* April 17, 1928, 1; May 1, 1928, 1; May 6, 1928, 2.

81. Saulnier interview.

82. *Times,* May 10, 1928, 2.

83. *Evening Standard,* June 26, 1928, 1.

84. *Evening Standard,* June 25, 1928, 1.

85. *Evening Standard,* June 14, 1928, 1.

86. *Evening Standard,* June 14, 1928, 9.

87. *Evening Standard,* June 25, 1928, 13.

88. Figueiredo interview.

89. *Evening Standard,* June 20, 1928, 2.

90. *Evening Standard,* June 28, 1928, 15.

91. *Evening Standard,* July 1, 1928, 1; July 13, 1928, 1

92. Rubenstein interview.

93. *Evening Standard,* July 2, 1928, 2.

94. *Evening Standard,* July 13, 1928, 1.

95. *Evening Standard,* June 27, 1928, 1.

96. *Times*, July 7, 1928, 2.

97. Figueiredo interview.

98. *Evening Standard*, July 9, 1928, 1; *Times*, July 9, 1928, 1.

99. *Evening Standard*, July 7, 1928, 2.

100. Eula Mendes. New Bedford textile workers strike of 1928 oral history interviews and research collection, MC 9. Southeastern Massachusetts Historical Collections, Claire T. Carney Library Archives and Special Collections, University of Massachusetts Dartmouth, Dartmouth, MA.

101. *Evening Standard*, July 15, 1928, 2.

102. *Evening Standard*, July 17, 1928, 2.

103. *Evening Standard*, July 17, 1928, 2.

104. *Evening Standard*, July 18, 1928, 4.

105. *Evening Standard*, July 20, 1928, 1.

106. *Evening Standard*, July 19, 1928, 2.

107. *Evening Standard*, June 1, 1928, 1.

108. *Evening Standard*, July 23, 1928, 1.

109. *Evening Standard*, July 25, 1928, 1.

110. Robert Morss Lovett, "New Bedford's Strike—a Knockout or a Comeback?" *New Republic*, September 12, 1928, 91.

111. Figueiredo interview.

112. *Evening Standard*, August 15, 1928, 2.

113. Beal, *Proletarian Journey*, 104.

114. Saulnier interview.

115. *Evening Standard*, July 31, 1928, 1.

116. *Evening Standard*, July 31, 1928, 1.

117. Mary Alves, interview by D Bastarche, August 31, 1981, New Bedford, MA. New Bedford textile workers strike of 1928 oral history interviews and research collection, MC 9. Southeastern Massachusetts Historical Collections, Claire T. Carney Library Archives and Special Collections, University of Massachusetts Dartmouth, Dartmouth, MA.

118. *Daily Herald*, August 9, 1928, 1.

119. *Daily Herald*, August 15, 1928, 2.

120. *Evening Standard*, August 25, 1928, 1.

121. *Evening Standard*, September 10, 1928, 6.

CHAPTER 7

Portuguese Labor Activism in Southeastern Massachusetts

......

PENN REEVE

The history of American immigration is also the history of the American labor movement. Immigrant men, women, and children, under economic and political pressure in their native lands, emigrated to the United States seeking work in the fields and factories. Finding less than ideal wages and working conditions, they began to struggle for greater power over their working lives by organizing and joining labor unions.

Southeastern Massachusetts was one of many centers of early industrialization on the Eastern Seaboard and therefore became a center for labor organizing. Fall River and New Bedford were leading textile mill towns during the late nineteenth and early twentieth century. They experienced significant labor struggles that paralleled those occurring in other towns and cities throughout the nation. In southeastern Massachusetts, the largest group of immigrants during this period was the Portuguese. Their active participation in the labor struggles of the region is the subject of this chapter.[1]

In the first two decades of the twentieth century, over 1.4 million Portuguese immigrants arrived in the United States, settling mostly in California and southeastern Massachusetts.[2] They arrived from the mainland, the Azores, and Madeira. As part of the great influx of the so-called new immigrants to the United States from southern and eastern Europe, they were often disdained by the more established "old immigrants" from England, Scotland, Wales, and Ireland, who had become well entrenched in the skilled factory jobs. The established immigrants also viewed "new immigrants" as culturally and even racially inferior and therefore unworthy of joining their established craft unions. Many chose to believe the Portuguese and other "new immigrants" were reluctant to engage in union activities and would work as "scabs" for low wages.[3]

Some stereotypes of the Portuguese that became commonplace in the early twentieth century have persisted until the present day. The prevailing view at the time was that the Portuguese were "hard working" but best suited for less skilled jobs requiring brute strength and little education.[4] Prejudices toward the newer immigrants from southern and eastern Europe were based on prevailing racist ideas that these were innately inferior immigrants compared with the more established northern and western European immigrants. The fear was that they would work at lower wages and that would depress all workers' wages. They were seen as culturally inferior because of their rural background and lack of formal education. The older immigrants preemptively excluded them from their craft unions.

One still hears some of these views expressed locally despite the current representation of Portuguese immigrants and their descendants at all levels of the region's economic and social life. The primary goal of this chapter will be to demonstrate, contrary to past and present stereotypes, that Portuguese men and women have been actively involved in labor organizations, both as leaders and as rank-and-file participants. By examining secondary sources and the testimony of Portuguese workers and labor organizers at the time, this chapter represents a preliminary attempt as, to date, no other attempt has been made to document their participation.

Women have always been recruited into factory work, often at less skilled jobs, with the factory owner's belief that they could be hired at lower wages and, because of family responsibilities, would be less apt to resist owner demands for long hours and low wages. Although women are sometimes stereotyped in the labor movement as more malleable and docile than males, women were active in the textile labor movement in southeastern Massachusetts as they have been elsewhere. This research indicates that women were represented in all labor organizing activities, and although men held most high-level positions in the labor organizations, some women assumed important leadership roles.

I have chosen to examine the issue of Portuguese labor participation between the 1920s and 1930s because it was during this period that the U.S. labor movement experienced a significant transformation.

In the 1920s, the movement perpetuated an old struggle dating back to the nineteenth century between conservatives and radicals/leftists.[5] Workers in the 1920s continued to be subjected to repressive government and industry actions. Federal, state, and local laws and court actions limited workers' rights to organize unions and improve the harsh conditions of factory life. Factory owners demanded long hours of work for low pay in an extremely unhealthy working environment. During these difficult times, workers fought back in the only effective manner possible, by organizing themselves into unions—organizations that had the legal power to negotiate on their behalf. They demanded healthier working conditions, shorter workdays, and higher pay, goals that are characterized here as part of a more conservative union agenda.

Some organizers incorporated these same goals but added more far-reaching ones, including workers gaining control over factories and using the unions as a political base for pushing society closer to socialism. For southeastern Massachusetts, the New Bedford textile strike of 1928 was the clearest and most dramatic example of these massive organizing efforts that were also occurring throughout the United States. Most workers and their leaders sought the right to be represented by a union and to gain higher pay and better working conditions. But the radical/leftist leaders of the strike and rank-and-file workers who followed them had the more radical goal of eventual worker control over the industry, a labor party, and ultimately a socialist economy. The radicals were most active during the 1920s and 1930s, although, as illustrated in this chapter, their efforts were largely unsuccessful.

By the late 1940s and early 1950s, federal legislation, such as the Taft-Hartley Bill of 1947 and the McCarthyism of the early 1950s, as well as the conservative union leadership's own actions, led to the elimination of radicals/leftists from the leadership of most unions. The year 1955 represents the conclusion of this process of "deradicalization" of the U.S. labor movement because in that year, the once more radical Congress of Industrial Organizations (CIO) joined with its long-time rival, the conservative American Federation of Labor (AFL) to form the largest labor federation in the United States. From 1955 to the present day, the movement's conservative direction has been left virtually unchallenged. With unequivocal support of capitalism at home and abroad, and goals limited to improving wages and working conditions, the American labor movement continued on this more conservative path—one that came to set it apart from labor movements in all other advanced capitalist societies of the world.[6]

Elsewhere, labor organizations as well as distinct labor parties advocated a more left-leaning agenda, including more worker control in the factory and in society, socialized public services, including health care, and a labor party that would offer more power to workers. In the American two-party system, the Republican Party has been aggressively hostile to unions and the Democratic Party, where the movement placed all its hope, turned out to be a weak advocate for labor and strongly antisocialist. All advanced capitalist countries, with the exception of the United States, have a labor party and/or a socialist party that has a significant degree of political influence and has led successful efforts to pass federal laws protecting workers' rights and health.[7]

To summarize, this chapter will attempt to demonstrate (1) that despite stereotypes to the contrary, the Portuguese were active participants in the southeastern Massachusetts labor movement during this period and (2) that the particular character of their participation was shaped by conservative and radical/left political forces within the unions and in the society at large.

Early Portuguese Migration in the Textile Industry

Prior to 1870, few Portuguese emigrated to southern New England. The official U.S. Census of that year reported only 8,971 Portuguese-born individuals living in the United States.[8] In the mid-1800s, the whaling industry attracted a few Portuguese to the East and West Coasts, but it was not until the expansion of the textile industry that Portuguese immigration to southern New England accelerated. By 1900, 17,885 Portuguese were living in Massachusetts alone, and by 1920, the number increased to 50,294. A decade later, Massachusetts was home to more than 62,000 second-generation Portuguese.[9]

In an effort to continue their traditional culture, some Portuguese who settled in Fall River and New Bedford opted for life on small farms, joined the New Bedford fishing fleets, or engaged in traditional trades, such as carpentry or masonry. However, these opportunities were scarce in New England. The primary work was to be found in the textile mills, and that is where the overwhelming majority found jobs. In New Bedford, merchant families had transferred their investments from whaling to the production of fine cotton textiles. By the beginning of the First World War, thirty-two New Bedford cotton manufacturing companies employed thirty thousand people.

During the first thirty years of the twentieth century, the cotton textile industry employed approximately 90 percent of New Bedford's manufacturing workers.[10] New Bedford mills were built along the railroad tracks and river in the north and south ends of the city. To this day, these areas are largely Portuguese American communities.

Fall River, the "Spindle City," was a leading cotton textile manufacturing center in the1800s, but very few Portuguese lived in the city during that time. Of the total Fall River population in1870, only 132 individuals were from southern and eastern Europe, and only 104 were Portuguese immigrants. Over 80 percent of Portuguese mill workers in Fall River arrived after 1901. As late as 1880, all but forty of Fall River's textile employees were either native-born or born in northwestern Europe. The Portuguese and Polish immigrants generally entered mill jobs held by departing English and Irish who had advanced to higher-paid, more skilled factory jobs. By 1900, six thousand of Fall River's immigrants originated from southern and eastern Europe, and that number exceeded ten thousand persons five years later. Azoreans comprised half this total. Almost the entire Portuguese and Polish population was working in the mills by 1910.[11]

Transition to Factory Work

In the early years of the twentieth century, most of the Portuguese who immigrated to southern New England were farmers from the Azores and Madeira and had virtually no industrial work experience. The textile mills in the region could accommodate thousands of unskilled workers, placing them into the least skilled jobs that required only brief on-the-job training. Their typical tasks were tending machines as bobbin boys, doffers, carders, combers, sweepers, and spoolers and in many of the other less-skilled jobs.[12]

The transition from rural agriculture to urban industrial life was a shock for all these immigrants. Textile work had always been difficult. As Cumbler points out, nineteenth-century "textile workers in Fall River rose daily in the early dawn to face exhausting, intensive labor, long hours, and low pay."[13] They endured ten-to-twelve hour shifts, six days a week, at monotonous, tedious tasks, arriving home totally exhausted. Constant, close supervision, speedups, stretch-outs (adding more machines per worker), and dusty, poorly ventilated mills plagued the textile workers. In the early twentieth century, conditions were only somewhat better, and periodic speedups and wage cuts led to great hardships for the workers.[14]

Many Portuguese Americans have vivid memories of working in the mills. In 1931, at age fourteen, Manuel Medeiros left school to work at a Fall River textile plant. He recalls the hazardous health conditions in the plant: "It was rough in the mills where the cotton was processed through the machines. There was a heavy, musty odor. Miners work in the mines and they get all that coal dust. There's no ventilation of any kind. Today they call it black lung. Well, in those days we had the white cotton lung disease. I knew a man that worked in the picking room that died from that, just swallowed too much cotton."[15] In 1924, at age sixteen, Lydia Souza entered the mills to help support her family, which included nine siblings. She remembers when she was a little girl that her father missed lunch to tend machines twelve to fourteen hours a day. Visiting her father in the mills, Lydia was struck by the "deafening noise and the film of cotton in the room."[16] Joe Figueiredo's father was born in Lisbon, and his mother in São Miguel; both worked in the New Bedford mills. Joe was born in Boston in 1920 and started in the mills as a teenager. He later became very active in radical union politics including the 1928 New Bedford textile strike. He remembers visiting his mother, who worked as a spool tender at City Mill in New Bedford: "In those days they did not permit the workers to use the freight elevators to go up to work in some cases four, five or six floors. There was no lunch room or chairs and tables to eat on, and most of the workers gathered around their machines sitting on boxes of bobbins, and even when the machines were shut down for lunch, there was still cotton dust in the air and cotton all over her eyebrows and around her ears and she would wipe it out and the sweat would still hold it."[17]

Like other new immigrants, the Portuguese were subjected to the tyranny of skilled workers and hiring bosses. Skilled loom fixers and menders were often paid extra on the output of the weavers in their sections. These were typically English, Welsh, and Scottish and later French Canadian craft workers who often subcontracted piecework to the new Polish and Portuguese immigrants. Pushed to their limits "women fell ill and asked out that is asked to leave the machine because of illness or exhaustion although often the request was denied. This happened with such frequency that the companies in Fall River kept a crew of stand-by women" to immediately replace their colleagues.[18]

Workers used many workplace strategies to alleviate their difficult conditions. Besides informal means of resistance, such as sabotage, sick-outs, slowdowns, or quitting, many new immigrants joined labor organizations as a necessary means of improving their oppressive work situation. The 1928 New Bedford textile strike demonstrated the willingness of the Portuguese, regardless of their background and experience prior to arrival, to join organized labor actions.

The 1928 New Bedford Textile Strike

Although competition with Southern textile companies intensified in the late 1920s, the fine cotton textile industry located in New Bedford was expanding and profitable. Yet, in 1928, the New Bedford textile manufacturers demanded a 10 percent pay cut, a dramatic reduction in wages at the time. The millowners were making a profit at the time but there was evidently a dip in demand, and they decided to operate at the same rate of profit even though they were not operating at the same rate of production.[19]

Wage cuts and speedups occurred throughout the textile industry's history. In 1898, New Bedford millowner demands had been almost identical to those of 1928. In the earlier strike, owners demanded a 10 percent wage cut, claiming competition from Southern mills forced them to demand the cut. Many workers reacted to the wage cut immediately by walking off the job, and English-dominated craft union leaders espousing a conservative political philosophy and strike goals competed with leftist radicals advocating a more socialist ideology and militant actions for control of the strike.[20]

In 1928, the Textile Committee (TC) representing craft unions did not represent the majority of mill workers, including the less-skilled, mostly Portuguese, Polish, and French Canadian workers, who also walked off their jobs. As happened in 1898, a rival, more militant organization, the Textile Mill Committee (TMC), formed to represent them. The TMC was made up of local workers and outside organizers, including radicals with experience in other labor-organizing efforts, such as the 1912 Lawrence "Bread and Roses"[21] strike and the Passaic strike in 1926. The immediate goals of the TMC were to stop the wage cut and gain legal union representation for unrepresented workers. They did not declare their long-term future goals of having more workers in decision-making and management positions in the factory, except to more politically radicalized workers.[22]

A few Portuguese were already radicalized from prior political experience in the United States and in Portugal. Local members of the Industrial Workers of the World (Wobblies), a radical labor group formed in 1905, for example, advocated all workers be united in one single union, and local anarchosyndicalists, typically from central regions of mainland Portugal, advocated replacing capitalism, private ownership, wages, and the federal government with a society managed by workers via their organizations. Edward Mendes,[23] for example, was blacklisted from millwork in Gouveia, Portugal, for his radical politics, and in 1912, two years after Portugal's monarchy was overthrown, Mendes and many others fled Portugal. He obtained contract work in a cordage factory in Plymouth, Massachusetts, working alongside Bartolomeo Vanzetti, the martyred labor leader.[24] His daughter, Eula, remembers that, throughout her childhood, her father held political meetings in their house, and she became, in part, because of her father's influence—a union activist as well. The family was living in New Bedford at the time of the 1928 textile strike. Eula had been working in the City Mill since age thirteen, and her father told her, "There is a strike. You must go on strike. You must be with the workers." She celebrated her eighteenth birthday walking a picket line.

Since most of the twenty thousand unskilled and semiskilled mill workers were Portuguese, and they were largely excluded from TC strike organizing activities, they found a home in the more militant TMC. Of the nine members of the TMC local leadership, six were of Portuguese extraction.[25] Some Portuguese played an active role in the daily strike activities of the TMC. They helped organize rallies, distribute food to striking workers, translate pamphlets, and attend rallies. Because of the large numbers of Portuguese participating in the strike, leaflets and pamphlets were translated into Portuguese. At the rallies, Joe Figueiredo, Eula Mendes, and other Portuguese leaders gave speeches in Portuguese. Eula Mendes, for example, was a member of the strike committee, translating leaflets and speeches from Portuguese to English and vice versa. She became secretary of the TMC and an active speaker, helping to organize Portuguese workers and maintain their morale.

While the Portuguese from the Azores were typically seen as more conservative and less willing to join the union than mainland Portuguese, the harsh conditions of mill work created an awareness of the need for protection and organization and a readiness to join labor-organized activities. Regardless of whether they were from the islands or mainland, the Portuguese joined the TMC by the thousands. According to Eula Mendes,

> When the strike began, the Portuguese people got involved immediately. . . . They were the most active, not only Portuguese from Portugal, but from the islands, from the Azores, Madeira and from the Cape Verde Islands. The people from the islands were a little more conservative. . . . They had no background of working in factories when they came . . . but they became more active. The strike was pretty solid among the Portuguese people.[26]

Contrary to some claims as to the Portuguese reluctance to join the labor movement, the overwhelming majority participated in the strike.

The six-month strike ended when the TC and millowners worked out an agreement for a 5 instead of 10 percent per hour wage cut. The TMC was excluded from negotiations and the vote. During the strike and after the vote, the authorities attacked the TMC, arresting many leaders and members so they could not participate in the final settlement negotiations. The charges were dropped after the strike.

TMC organizers were accused of being dangerous outside agitators and un-American. The local media "red-baited"[27] the TMC leadership and used the threat of deportation to intimidate radical leaders and discourage noncitizens from joining their cause. Augusto Pinto, one of the strike picket captains, for example, was arrested many times during the strike and convicted twenty-two times. On appeal, Pinto's convictions, like those of most other defendants, were later dismissed. However, in his case—no doubt to make an example of him to the others—the U.S. Immigration Service forcibly placed Pinto on a ship bound for Salazar's Portugal, where labor militants were treated harshly.

He reportedly died under Portuguese military custody en route to prison in Cape Verde, "sending a shudder through New Bedford's Portuguese community." One month after Pinto's deportation, William Murdoch, a key TMC labor leader, was deported to his native Scotland.[28]

Although companies rehired many workers, they refused to rehire those who had been active in the TMC. Some left the area. Eula Mendes got a job for a while in the TMC and in 1929, worked for the newly formed communist-led National Textile Workers Union. A few years later when the

NTWU dissolved, she was hired as a part-time office worker and organizer by the local United Textile Workers (UTW) union office but then was let go because of her membership in the Communist Party. The union feared a "red-baiting" backlash if she remained.

By 1932, the southward movement of the textile industry and the Depression had created mass unemployment in the New Bedford mills. Unemployment rose rapidly, and wages fell. Radicals had been purged, blacklisted, and, in a few cases, deported. Repression of radicals in the local labor movement left a vacuum of militant labor leaders. Portuguese workers were left in the hands of the conservative TC since the AFL craft unions largely excluded them.

The New Deal and the CIO

In response to declining wages during the Depression and the hardships these economic and political shifts caused, there were continuous attempts to organize workers. The labor movement received a big boost from Franklin Delano Roosevelt's New Deal. Section 7(a) of the 1933 National Recovery Act permitted collective bargaining and ostensibly protected union organizing from retribution by employers. The National Recovery Act also called for employers to set more reasonable limits on work hours and to set a minimum wage.[29]

Adding to federal protections for workers, in the spring of 1935 Congress passed the Social Security Act and a sweeping new federal labor law, the National Labor Relations Act, that created the National Labor Relations Board. For the first time, workers had the support of a federal board that protected their right to organize and be legally represented.[30] This was not a total victory for workers since the president appoints the board, and few have strongly supported unions.

Although not taken seriously by industry, these federal protections of workers stimulated the largest union organizing drive in U.S. history. Hundreds of thousands of workers joined unions. The membership in the Textile Workers Union of America (TWUA) rose throughout this period and into the war years. By 1944, the TWUA could count four hundred thousand members, the largest CIO union in the country.[31]

Competition for new members between the older, more conservative AFL and the new, more militant CIO generated great enthusiasm and a rise in the membership of both labor organizations. "The eruption of a socially conscious and broadly inclusive CIO movement attracted a whole new generation of union activists, including Poles, Russians, Lithuanians, Italians, Greeks, and Portuguese workers who had not found a home in the AFL craft unions. Despite the differences between the AFL and the CIO, the charges and the countercharges, a new spirit encompassed the labor movement."[32]

In 1936 and 1937, after breaking with the more conservative craft unions affiliated with AFL, the CIO began to organize based on the principle of industry-wide unions, giving workers much more leverage in collective bargaining. The CIO targeted new immigrant workers in major industries—such as textiles, auto, steel, and mining—who had not been welcomed in the AFL craft unions. In Massachusetts and throughout the country, the CIO often utilized militant tactics on the picket lines, although few entertained a radical labor agenda, such as giving workers more control in the factory or establishing a workers' party, as in most industrialized countries where the party serves as the base for gaining worker political power through the electoral process. The national TWUA, on the other hand, was the epitome of the business union model of unions, narrowly focused on the right to organize, wages, and working conditions.

From its inception, the TWUA was hierarchically arranged and not very democratic. Sidney Hillman and the CIO Textile Workers Organizing Committee intentionally created centralized and hierarchical unions without the possibilities of independent factions emerging within it. When unions merged or amalgamated, it was forced amalgamation from above. As Mariano Bishop told delegates to the 1939 UTWA convention, "We have heard a lot of talk about rank-and-file. There are some in the union who try to spread the impression that they are for the rank-and-file, while the rest of us are not.... The finest thing that the union can do for the rank-and-file is to make the union administration stronger and [more] eficiente [sic]."[33]

Unlike some CIO unions, such as the United Packinghouse Workers Union, the United Auto Workers, and the United Electrical Workers, which had some socialists and communists in them, Hillman, as president of the Textile Workers Organizing Committee (TWOC-CIO), and future presidents of UTWA made no place for them.[34] The UTWA, from which the TWOC-CIO emerged, had always been anticommunist in the 1930s. For instance, during the 1934 national textile strike, when the communists made overtures to join the strike effort, the head of the UTWA national strike committee, Francis J. Gorman warned, "Communist agitators are entering the conflict . . . they would be fought to the limit. We will have to fight not only the employers and their hired thugs, but the Communists who are now trying to take advantage of the situation to promote their own philosophy."[35] Joseph A. Sylvia, regional strike director of New England, blamed communists for riots and deaths of workers in Rhode Island.[36]

During the mid-1950s, hundreds of Portuguese immigrants joined the Fall River and New Bedford labor unions, mostly those affiliated with the CIO. In Fall River, from the 1930s to the 1940s, Mariano Bishop, Manuel Melo, and Mike Botelho—all known labor activists of Portuguese descent—led organizing drives for the UTW locals to join the CIO and signed up many new members. New Bedford also became a stronghold of CIO organizing and successes, paralleling the successes in Fall River. Twenty-four shops made up the Joint Board of New Bedford and included over fifteen thousand union members.[37]

Mariano Bishop was typical of the more conservative UTWA union officials who became organizers for the UTWA-CIO in southeastern Massachusetts in the 1930s and 1940s. Bishop emigrated from the Azores and entered Fall River mills as a doffer at age ten. He lived in the Portuguese South End and socialized at the Liberal Athletic Club. In the 1920s, Mariano became president of the dyers unit of the UTWA. At the time of the 1934 strike, he was serving as organizer, business agent, and president of the New Bedford–Fall River Textile Council affiliated with the UTWA.[38] He and his assistants closed down many plants throughout the region of Fall River and southern Rhode Island.

They deployed pickets and stirred up lively protests. Once Bishop was arrested by state police and then was pulled out of their hands by a group of angry women picketers.[39]

Although the 1934 strike failed to achieve its goals, Bishop continued to build the CIO's Textile Workers Union (UTWA-CIO) in the Fall River area. With Ed Doolan, he brought hundreds of workers into the UTWA-CIO. Eventually, he became executive vice president of the national union. He had long been the protégé of President Emil Rieve and was in line to succeed him as president of the national union. Tragically, in 1953, at the age of forty-six, just before this succession happened, Bishop suffered a massive heart attack and died.[40]

Despite union gains, the 1930s created many economic difficulties for most immigrants in southeastern Massachusetts. The Portuguese took a variety of jobs in the tight labor market. The garment shops hired only a fraction of the workforce that had been employed in the textile mills. Some individuals left for other parts of the country, such as California and New Jersey. Others took whatever jobs were available locally. These included working for clothing, synthetic fibers, rubber, or housewares manufacturers or taking jobs in the trades.

The Taft-Hartley Bill

Although the federal government made efforts to lift the country from its economic doldrums, it was not until World War II that the economy recovered and many people found work. Though unions expanded simply because of job growth and because labor disputes occurred, unions and managers tempered their disputes and labor's militant voice was muted. Conservative labor leaders and management representatives on the National War Labor Board administered settlements.

After accepting frozen wages and long hours during World War II, in its aftermath increasing numbers of workers fought for improved wages and working conditions. Strikes were frequent. In retaliation, companies lobbied Congress for passage of amendments to the Social Security Act of 1935. The amendments were written almost entirely by the National Association of Manufacturers, the most conservative business lobby in the nation. The amendments became known as the Taft-Hartley Bill, or to many in the labor community, the "slave labor bill" and were generally viewed by them as the most repressive federal labor laws of any advanced capitalist society. The bill was passed over Truman's veto with substantial support of the Democratic Party. Neither Truman nor leading democrats fought to defeat the bill.[41]

The 1947 Taft-Hartley Bill weakened labor's power on every front. The amendments allowed states to pass laws forbidding the "closed shop," which permitted workers to not join the union, thereby weakening its unity and power. The acts made unions and union leaders financially liable for losses incurred by businesses that were struck and made unions more vulnerable to court injunctions. Taft-Hartley outlawed secondary boycotts when workers in related plants strike in support of an existing strike. Wildcat strikes or spontaneous walkouts were declared illegal. Strikes had to be announced, voted on, and not contradicted by contract. Strikes by federal workers, a growing part of the workforce, were prohibited. The president was given the power to order workers back to work. Employers could sue workers for breach of contract.[42]

Most important for the radicals of the left and the conservatives on the right were the loyalty oaths. All union officers had to sign an affidavit swearing they were not members of the Communist Party and that they did not advocate the overthrow of the government by force or by any unconstitutional means. The U.S. Supreme Court eventually declared the oaths themselves unconstitutional. The Cold War hysteria that was sweeping the nation precipitated the oaths, as well as the intention of business to kill the power of radicals and, thereby, weaken the labor movement.

The AFL and CIO purged unions with known communists in leadership or any union whose leadership refused to sign the loyalty oaths. The National Labor Relations Board would not certify any union election unless candidates had all signed. Communists and those leaders fearing that label withdrew from leadership or were forced out. Anyone who advocated ideas of worker power and equality was subject to the suspicion of being a communist and losing their standing. Fear spread through the union ranks, squelching democratic debate.[43]

The majority of locals in New Bedford and Fall River supported signing the loyalty oaths. The majority of Portuguese on the board, including at least one communist member, were against signing. Manny Fernandes and others in leadership positions led the effort to get the board to accept signing the oaths. Cold War hysteria that was sweeping the nation established a likely context for business to build into the bill these repressive oaths.[44]

The conservative leadership of the national TWUA made the decision for Fernandes and other local leaders. They interpreted the amendments to mean that if a worker did not sign, he/she could not run for or remain in an official leadership position within the union. Knowing the communists on the board would be purged, they supported mandated signing of the oaths. If Fernandes and others wanted to stay in office or run for future office, they would have to sign. But Fernandes and the majority of the local leadership were not radicals, but patriotic Americans, and did not really object to signing the loyalty oaths. He made the motion to the council in favor of signing the oaths. According to Fernandes, Portuguese labor leaders were actively involved in the "loyalty oath" debate and represented both sides of the issue. He noted that

> The so-called "active Portuguese" were against the signing of the affidavit. The more conservative ones would say well it's the law, I'm gonna sign it. The liberal ones said I don't care if it's the law, I don't have to sign it and I'm not a commie. . . . More Portuguese (members) than any other nationality were against signing the affidavit. We did have a majority of Portuguese on the board but it was primarily (conservative) ones.[45]

The impact of the Taft-Hartley Bill, especially on the grievance procedure, was immediate. As Fernandes observed:

> From now on you just didn't take the so-called procedures of settling a grievance in the old way . . . because under the law if you . . . caused the company some hardship or loss of production . . . then there were damages . . . the union would be liable for damages. So, in my opinion, that made the union leadership cautious in how they settled a grievance. . . . In my opinion, it sort of weakened our grievance procedure.[46]

McCarthyism

Intensification of the Cold War mentality that led to McCarthyism and the political "witch hunts" of the early 1950s targeted many, including foreign-born union leaders who were socialists, anarchists, and communists. Many union members, like most Americans, embraced the anticommunist mood and the purges of radical union leaders that followed. But the repression had a general chilling effect on all union activism.

One tool the government used to sap union militancy was to deport or threaten to deport noncitizens who were active leftists in the labor movement, which caused anyone critical of the current economic and political situation to hesitate to voice their concerns. The tactic has a long history in the United States, and we have already seen how it operated at the end of the 1928 strike to eliminate leftists from the scene.

The Smith Act of 1940 and the Subversive Control Act (McCarran-Walter Act) of 1950 became tools for removing militant labor leaders. Under the 1950 act, at age forty-two, Eula Mendes was arrested at her home in New Bedford as a subversive alien due to her membership in the Communist Party.

She was not a U.S. citizen, having been denied that opportunity because of her arrests during the 1928 strike. She had no ties; her parents were dead, and her husband, also active in the 1928 strike, had recently divorced her. After losing appeals, Mendes was deported in May 1953. "I heard the iron [gate] clang behind me."[47] Portugal was a fascist state—the country Augusto Pinto had been deported to in 1929 and in which he was then allegedly killed by authorities. Mendes feared a similar fate. She thus sought and was granted asylum in Poland, where she lived until her death in 2003.

Mendes reflected on the chilling effect arrest and deportation threats had on the foreign-born workers in the unions at the time:

> The question of picking on foreign-born people was used during the McCarthy days as a pressure against people generally. . . . My arrest had an effect of creating a lot of fear amongst a lot of Portuguese people who were not citizens. And this question of arresting so many at that time all over the country also had an effect of trying to break the progress of the trade union movement.[48]

Despite repression of labor militancy throughout the 1950s, unions continued to organize and fight for wages and better working conditions. However, their militancy was muted by the purge of radical union members. With the merger of the conservative AFL and a "deradicalized" CIO in 1955, the union movement continued on its conservative path. In southeastern Massachusetts, the continued declining economy and dominance by the conservative CIO-affiliated UTWA and its subsequent conservative incarnations (ACTWU-UNITE and HERE-UNITE) that followed this period have meant that a radical reemergence was unlikely to occur.

Conclusion

The purpose of this chapter was to dispel certain stereotypes concerning Portuguese immigrants' historic involvement in the labor movement of southeastern Massachusetts. Arriving with the flood of "new immigrants" in the late 1800s and early 1900s, the Portuguese came primarily from a rural, uneducated, and politically conservative background. They entered the factories of New England. More established "old immigrants" from England, Scotland, Wales, and Ireland looked down on these new arrivals, believing them culturally and racially inferior, lacking knowledge of factory regime, and too politically conservative to join unions.

Yet despite these imagined and real handicaps, the Portuguese, southeastern Massachusetts's largest immigrant group at the time, joined the labor movement by the thousands and were quickly socialized into the hardships of industrial factory life. Often thought to shy away from the risks associated with labor activism, Portuguese women workers, too, joined the labor movement to improve their lives. Some, like Eula Mendes, rose to leadership positions. The active participation of Portuguese men and women was evident during the 1928 New Bedford textile strike and later in the CIO organizing of the 1930s and 1940s.

This chapter has focused on an important era in U.S. labor history, a period of transformation. In the 1920s and 1930s the U.S. labor movement included both a conservative and significant radical/leftist strand. The 1940s and 1950s saw the rise of repressive labor legislation in the Taft-Hartley Bill and Cold War McCarthyism that led to the purging of radicals/leftists from the labor movement. The merging of the once radical CIO with the always-conservative AFL in 1955 signified clear dominance by the conservatives that has continued to this day. David Caute reflects on the long-term impact of the events of this era on the U.S. labor movement: "So from the moment of its conception (1955), the AFL-CIO was and would become during the second half of the century the most conservative and ideologically acquiescent [central labor organization] among capitalist democracies."[49]

This is an initial attempt to document the participation of Portuguese immigrants in the U.S. labor movement. Since their descendants continue to represent the largest ethnic group in the region, it would be useful to build on current research by documenting their participation in labor unions since the 1950s. Reflecting on the Portuguese American contribution to the region's labor movement today, Peter Knowlton, United Electrical Workers Union organizer in New Bedford commented, "I can't think of a single union local in this area that doesn't have at least one person of Portuguese descent in its leadership." Other leaders in the area I talked with confirmed this observation. In order to test this generalization and to analyze the current role of the rank-and-file Portuguese worker in the labor movement, it will be necessary to collect additional oral histories of contemporary Portuguese American workers and labor leaders.[50]

Works Cited

Buhle, Paul. *Taking Care of Business: Samuel Gompers, George Meany, Lane Kirkland and the Tragedy of American Labor.* New York: Monthly Review Press, 1999

Clawson, Dan, and Mary Ann Clawson, "What Has Happened to the US labor Movement?" *Annual Review of Sociology* 25 (1999): 95–119.

Cumbler, John T. *Working-Class Community in Industrial America—Work, Leisure and Struggle in Two Industrial Cities, 1880–1930.* Westport, CT: Greenwood Press, 1979.

Daniel, Clete. *Culture of Misfortune: An Interpretive History of Textile Unionism in the United States.* Ithaca, NY: Cornell University Press, 2001.

Georgianna, Daniel, with Roberta Hazen Aaronson. *The Strike of '28.* New Bedford, MA: Spinner Publications, 1993.

Goldfield, Michael "Union Democracy and the U.S. Labor Bureaucracy." *New Politics* 7, no. 4 (2000): 87.

Gordon, J. "The United Farm Workers and the California Agricultural Cause." In *Cause Lawyers and Social Movements,* edited by Austin Sarat and Stuart A. Scheingold. Stanford, CA: Stanford University Press, 2006.

Green, James R. *The World of the Worker: Labor in Twentieth Century America.* New York: Hill and Wang, 1980.

Huse, Donna. "An American Story." In *Portuguese Spinner: An American Story,* edited by Marsha L. McCabe and Joseph D. Thomas. New Bedford, MA: Spinner Publications, 1998.

Juravitch, Tom, William F. Hartford, and James R. Green, *Commonwealth of Toil: Chapters from the History of Massachusetts Workers and Their Unions.* Amherst: University of Massachusetts Press, 1996.

Kelly, Richard *Nine Lives for Labor.* New York: Praeger, 1956.

Marsha McCabe and Joseph D. Thomas, eds. *Portuguese Spinner: An American Story* (New Bedford, MA: Spinner Publications, 1998).

Montgomery, David. *The Fall of the House of Labor.* Cambridge: Cambridge University Press, 1987.

Silvia, Philip T. "The Position of the 'New' Immigrant in the Fall River Textile Industry." *International Migration Review* 13, no. 1 (1976): 221–32.

Stepan-Norris, Judith, and Maurice Zeitlin, *Left Out: Reds in America's Industrial Unions.* Cambridge: Cambridge University Press, 2002.

Wagner, Steven. "How Did the Taft-Hartley Act Come About?" *History News Network,* October 14, 2002.

Williams, Jerry. *And Yet They Come: Portuguese Immigration from the Azores to the United States.* North Dartmouth, MA: Tagus, 2005.

Zieger, Robert H., and Gilbert Gall, *American Workers, American Unions: The Twentieth Century (The American Moment).* Baltimore: John Hopkins University Press. 2002.

Notes

1. This essay is an adaptation of two earlier articles by the author, "The Portuguese Worker" and "Three Lives for Labor: Eula Mendes, Manny Fernandes and Tina Ponte," *Portuguese Spinner: An American Story,* ed. Marsha McCabe and Joseph D. Thomas (New Bedford, MA: Spinner Publications, 1998), 230–45.

2. Jerry Williams, *And Yet They Come: Portuguese Immigration from the Azores to the United States* (North Dartmouth, MA: Tagus), 2005.

3. Philip T. Silvia, "The Position of the 'New' Immigrant in the Fall River Textile Industry," *International Migration Review* 13, no. 1 (1976): 221–32.

4. Silvia, "The Position."

5. The terms "conservative" and "radical" or "leftist" appear in labor studies literature and are not always clearly defined, nor is there full agreement on their meaning. Yet they are useful terms because they differentiate two broad and divergent strands in the tactics and political agenda of the labor movement. The conservative labor leaders and organizations represented a greater level of worker accommodation to the demands of the owners and support for the capitalist system. In the period under consideration, the dominant representative of this strand is the AFL and various unaffiliated skilled craft unions. They focused on obtaining legal recognition for unions and on improving working conditions, wages, and benefits. The radicals, sometimes referred to as leftists, and here referred to as radical/leftists, were generally inspired by Marxist thought and practice. They also supported the legal right to organize unions and the improvement of working conditions, wages, and benefits, but they had more far-reaching goals. They advocated increasing worker control over running the factories and, depending on which faction one considers, the reformation up to the total abolition of capitalism in favor of socialism, a shift in the structure of U.S. economy from one based on profit motive to one based on the needs of the workers and run by workers. These radical/leftist groups included the Industrial Workers of the World, the Socialist Party, the Communist Party, and others.

6. Judith Stepan-Norris and Maurice Zeitlin, *Left Out: Reds in America's Industrial Unions* (Cambridge: Cambridge University Press, 2002).

7. Scholars have proposed various reasons for the conservative tradition of the U.S. labor movement in contrast to the more leftist character of those in other advanced capitalist countries. These include (1) the unique historical background of U.S. capitalism, which militated against the formation of greater working-class solidarity ("American exceptionalism"); (2) greater opportunities for workers and/or their offspring to achieve upward social and economic mobility; (3) repression by the government and private industry policies and actions; and finally, (4) divisive policies and strategies within the labor movement. See Paul Buhle, *Taking Care of Business: Samuel Gompers, George Meany, Lane Kirkland and the Tragedy of American Labor* (New York: Monthly Review Press, 1999); Dan Clawson and Mary Ann Clawson, "What Has Happened to the US labor Movement?" *Annual Review of Sociology* 25 (1999): 95–119; Michael Goldfield, "Union Democracy and the U.S. Labor Bureaucracy." *New Politics* 7, no. 4 (2000): 87.

8. Williams, *And Yet They Come,* 32.

9. Williams, *And Yet They Come,* 32.

10. Daniel Georgianna, with Roberta Hazen Aaronson, *The Strike of '28* (New Bedford, MA: Spinner Publications, 1993).

11. Silvia, "The Position."

12. Silvia, "The Position."

13. John T. Cumbler, *Working-Class Community in Industrial America—Work, Leisure and Struggle in Two Industrial Cities, 1880–1930* (Westport, CT: Greenwood Press, 1979), 144–45

14. Cumbler, *Working-Class.*

15. Donna Huse, "An American Story," in *Portuguese Spinner: An American Story,* ed. Marsha L. McCabe and Joseph D. Thomas (New Bedford, MA: Spinner Publications, 1998).

16. Huse, "An American Story," 39.

17. Joseph Figueiredo, interview by Robert Shartery, March 14, 1983. Portuguese Oral History Project 1987–92, Ferreira-Mendes Portuguese American Archives, University of Massachusetts Dartmouth, Dartmouth, MA.

18. David Montgomery, *The Fall of the House of Labor* (Cambridge: Cambridge University Press, 1987), 101–2

19. Georgianna, *The Strike,* 50.

20. Georgianna, *The Strike,* 41–43

21. The Bread and Roses strike was a textile workers strike in Lawrence, Massachusetts, in 1912. Mostly women and new immigrants including Lithuanians, Armenians, Poles, Portuguese, and a dozen other nationalities came together for a nine-week strike. Strike meetings were held at ethnic clubs, such as the Portuguese center. The strike was organized by the radical Industrial Workers of the World, usually referred to as the "Wobblies". It was one of the few successful strikes organized by the radicals/leftists during the period. The strike demonstrated the potential for unity and unionizing among "new immigrant" workers. The 1926 textile strike in Passaic, New Jersey, led by Communist Youth ended in failure. Some of the leaders of this twelve-month-long strike traveled to New Bedford, Massachusetts, to help organize the New Bedford textile strike of 1998. See Tom Juravitch, William F. Hartford, and James R. Green, *Commonwealth of Toil: Chapters from the History of Massachusetts Workers and Their Unions* (Amherst: University of Massachusetts Press, 1996), 75–86; Georgianna, *The Strike,* 82–83.

22. Eula Mendes interview by Penn Reeve and Jack Stauder, July 2–3, 1986. Portuguese Oral History Project 1987–92, Ferreira-Mendes Portuguese American Archives, University of Massachusetts Dartmouth, Dartmouth, MA.

23. Mendes interview.

24. Bartolomeo Vanzetti and Nicola Sacco were two Italian anarchists who were accused of robbery and murder in a 1920 Braintree, Massachusetts, holdup. The case became one of the United States' most well-known political trials because, though the evidence was

circumstantial, their political leanings and their militant anticapitalist and prorevolutionary views made them the target of attacks inside and outside of the court system. As the case gained notice around the world, many people from across the political spectrum saw it as the American justice system on trial. In 1927, they were put to death by electrocution.

25. Georgianna, *The Strike*, 127

26. Mendes interview.

27. "Red baiting" means accusing someone of being a communist or "red." It also can refer to accusing any leftist critic of the U.S. political or economic system. Red baiting challenges leftists for their lack of patriotism to discredit their political ideas. The 1920s (First Red Scare) and the early 1950s McCarthy era (Second Red Scare) are the two primary historic examples of red baiting in American history.

28. Georgianna, *The Strike*, 142.

29. Juravitch et al., *Commonwealth of Toil*, 140.

30. Juravitch et al., *Commonwealth of Toil*, 111.

31. Clete Daniel, *Culture of Misfortune: An Interpretive History of Textile Unionism in the United States* (Ithaca, NY: Cornell University Press, 2001), 138.

32. Juravitch et al., *Commonwealth of Toil*, 118

33. Daniel, *Culture of Misfortune*.

34. Stepan-Norris and Zeitlin, *Left Out*, 76

35. "Textile Strike Is Extended to Silk and Rayon: Strike leaders Fight Red Bid for Power," *Standard Times*, September 1, 1934.

36. "U.T.W Blames Reds for Riots: Unions Strike Leaders Advises Workers not to Tolerate Communists," *Standard Times*, September 14, 1934.

37. Mendes interview.

38. Richard Kelly, *Nine Lives of Labor* (New York: Praeger, 1956).

39. "Strikers Fight Warren Police: Fall River Workers Picket Rhode Island Mill," *Standard Times*, September 6, 1934, 6.

40. Daniel, *Culture of Misfortune*, 237.

41. J. Gordon, "The United Farm Workers and the California Agricultural Cause." *Lawyers and Social Movements*, 2006; James R. Green, *The World of the Worker: Labor in Twentieth Century America* (New York: Hill and Wang, 1980); Juravitch et al., *Commonwealth of Toil*; Steven Wagner, "How Did the Taft-Hartley Act Come About?," *History News Network*, October 14, 2002.

42. Robert H. Zieger and Gilbert J. Gall, *American Workers, American Unions: The Twentieth Century (The American Moment)* (Baltimore: John Hopkins University Press, 2002); Green, *The World of the Worker*, 189–90.

43. Stepan-Norris and Zeitlin, *Left Out*; Wagner, "How Did the Taft-Hartley," 271–77, 278–80; Gordon, "The United."

44. Manny Fernandes, interview by Bela Feldman-Bianco and Penn Reeve, May 14, 1987. Portuguese Oral History Project 1987–92, Ferreira Mendes Portuguese American Archives, University of Massachusetts Dartmouth, Dartmouth, MA.

45. Fernandes interview.

46. Fernandes interview.

47. Mendes interview.

48. Mendes interview.

49. Stepan-Norris and Zeitlin, *Left Out*, 274.

50. Peter Knowlton, United Electrical Workers Union organizer, interview with the author, April 14, 1996. The recently established Ferreira Mendes Portuguese American Archives at the University of Massachusetts Dartmouth, the repository containing many of the oral histories cited in this paper, is an excellent resource and location for future documentation of the Portuguese American contributions to the labor movement.

CHAPTER 8

Political Activism and Migrants from Portugal in New England Industrial Mill Communities (Pre-World War II)[1]

Labor Organization and Voluntary Association Collaboration in the "Movement to Americanize the Immigrant"

••••••

MIGUEL MONIZ

Although the political activism of migrants coming to North America in the post-1960s cohort has been well documented, the efforts at political engagement among migrants settling during the industrial period has been less examined and is less recognized. This paper explores how political activities and vocabularies of ethnic distinctiveness emerging in the 1970s were not a novel phenomenon but rather an extension of and reaction to earlier legacies of immigrant political engagement. This chapter documents the key issues shaping immigrant political responses and how competing, often contradictory approaches to the marginalization of racialized industrial laborers would structure latter constructions of Portuguese ethnic identities in the post-1960s context. Migrant participation in industrial labor unionization and socialist and communist organized protests caused a backlash against leftist politics and discourses of Portuguese nonwhite racial and social identities. Reacting to social, political, and racial marginalization as a result of this activism, other migrants took a more institutionalist approach to civic inclusion encapsulated in their widespread participation in the "Movement to Americanize the Immigrant"[2] that emerged in the early decades of the twentieth century.

Background

Migrants from Portugal began settling in New England from the Azores, Madeira, continental Portugal, and Cabo Verde over the nineteenth century, following whaling, shipping, and manufacturing routes. By the end of the nineteenth century, migrant laborers dominated the region's textile mills, industrial farms, and connected industries. Non-English-speaking migrants made up about 40 percent of Lowell's hundred thousand residents, for example, with almost all of this number having come to the city to work in the mills in the previous fifteen to twenty-five years.[3] The bulk of low-hierarchy industrial mill labor in Fall River and New Bedford was undertaken by migrants from Portugal. These mobile laborers also found work on industrial farms in the region along the coastal shoreline of New England from Connecticut to Cape Cod.

Migrant industrial workers were at the bottom of labor hierarchies, earning the lowest wages and working the longest hours. The conditions under which they were expected to toil were often dangerous, made more so by the grinding monotony of doing the repetitive tasks for six days a week and for twelve to fourteen hours a day with only limited breaks. Technological advancements in mechanization made industrial equipment ever more efficient, but the new machines were created with little regard for worker safety. Hands and bodies were unprotected while working with fast-moving, thunderously powerful, and less than reliable equipment. With some of these machines, children were even preferred as a result of their smaller bodies and the lower wages they received compared to adults. Child labor was also commonplace in industrial agriculture. Standard work conditions led to chronic respiratory problems in the poorly ventilated mills as workers breathed in the humid cotton fiber dust that fogged the air above the looms as they prepared thread and spun cloth. In the din of hundreds of banging and spinning machines the incessant fulmination of sound damaged the workers' hearing. Communities of migrant laborers suffered from elevated infant mortality rates and malnutrition. For children, attendance at school was often cut short by local economies and practices that brought children to work in mills and as seasonal farm labor.[4] The migrants were further marginalized by their tenuous residency status and by a language barrier; they were often marked by religious practices and had limited to no political representation in local and state government.[5]

Carter, Green, and Halpern examine the "racialization of migrant labor" in the context of governmental actions and the passage of laws in the 1900–1925 industrial period supporting the marginalized status of labor classes, through which social position and racial categories were fixed "to naturalize differences and normalize exclusions."[6] Relying on the collection of eugenic data and nineteenth-century ethnologist thinking,[7] policy makers and industrial interests used these racialized categories to suppress the civil rights of migrant laborers. Supported in regional newspapers, these discourses were bolstered by academic scientific writing in the social sciences and education and were further adopted by elite reformers. The influential Reports of the U.S. Congress's Immigration Commission (referred to as the Dillingham Commission) in 1911 would have a far-reaching effect on political debates over migration and was part of efforts to pass laws that codified the racial identities of low-level migrant workers.[8]

Struggles to raise low wages and improve dangerous conditions were stymied through an aggregated system of racialized exclusion[9] in the total institution of the mills. Arguments against the migrants' civic participation was based on perceptions of genetics and cultural and educational inferiority, casting the migrant workers unsuitable for citizenship.[10] Hearings and publications of the Dillingham Commission encapsulated and drove debates over the passage of a spate of antimigrant laws, as well as other legislation intended to racialize and restrict migrant political activism.[11] The forty-one-volume reports were intended to represent scholarly deliberations on the topic of migrant labor in U.S. industry and agriculture, presenting data on demographic, economic, and racial characteristics of the migrants in scientific writing and sociological studies. One volume collected the public statements of industry and union officials, academics, and immigrant association officers. The reports were part of a political process that eventually led to significant restrictions on migration from southern/eastern Europe and Asia. Recommendations in the volumes would be adopted in laws requiring literacy tests and further restrictions on entry by ever-changing eligibility rules defining migrants in terms of their presumed genetics, culture, and intellectual acumen (i.e., the Immigration Act of 1917 sponsored by Dillingham Commission member and Massachusetts Senator Henry Cabot Lodge as well as the Emergency Quota Act of 1921 and the Immigration Act of 1924).

As a major industrial region and primary destination for migrant laborers in the United States, the New England textile mills are covered exclusively in one volume, but discussion of the region appears throughout the reports. Demographic data about migrant mill and agricultural laborers from Portugal are collected, and numerous authors consider Portuguese racial identity, basing differences on geographic origins and an author's estimation of assimilability.

The scientific discourses and studies, along with the solicited commentaries, are an example of early twentieth-century xenophobic arguments casting industrial migrant workers as socially, culturally, and genetically inferior. In volume 41, *Statements and Recommendations*,[12] public comments are collected from hundreds, including current and former elected officials, business leaders, lawyers, academics, university presidents, military officers, and representatives and leaders from various professional organizations, scientific and professional societies, and skilled labor unions. The overwhelmingly pro restriction "America First" comments used discourses about the presumed genetic inferiority and racial identities of the industrial labor class to separate migrant workers by contrasting them with white nationalist definitions of civic belonging.[13]

Even many who recognized the difficult position of migrant industrial workers nonetheless favored restriction, using similar presumptions about racial categories to argue against these workers' assimilability and suitability for civic participation. In racialized demagoguery (typical in the collected volume), the statement by the Immigration Restriction League of Boston, Massachusetts, addressed how cheap migrant labor threatened (white) tradesmen and native workers. Writing for the league, John Norton Pomeroy, LLB, held the "racial character" of migrants to be "of the greatest concern," stating, "We frankly admit . . . that our fundamental objection to the present tide of immigration we wish to exclude is racial. . . . It should be frankly acknowledged as the real objection."[14] Other voices spoke to the presumed lack of racial assimilability of the migrant labor class, including Allen G. Braxton, a lawyer from Richmond, Virginia, who wrote, "For years the Atlantic steamship lines have acted as a siphon to draw off, as it were, the sewage from the cesspools of Europe and discharge it into the choice places of America." Lamenting the threat to white blood purity posed by the immigrants, Braxton continued by bemoaning "the introduction into this country of . . . those races which either cannot be assimilated at all with us or else cannot be assimilated without detriment to our own race."[15]

The racial characteristics of migrants from Portugal are examined in various volumes of the report, echoing earlier writing about Portuguese nonwhite, unassimilable racial characteristics by Bushee[16] and others.[17] It should be pointed out that Portuguese in this case included migrants coming from diverse geographies in continental Portugal, the Azores, Madeira, and Cabo Verde and arriving in New England from these locations as well as a result of having circulated as labor from secondary locations in Brazil, the Caribbean, Hawaii, and other parts of North America. This mobility continued after arrival as the laborers moved across the region or left for other places to seek work. Although individuals from these geographies arriving as Portuguese nationals would share unique histories and strategies in relationship to how they contested racialized marginalization, all were cast as nonwhite in the labor hierarchies of the Second Industrial Revolution. The Rev. M. D. Lichliter, chaplain, writing on behalf of the four hundred thousand–member United American Mechanics (UAM) union, expressed an opinion of the racial inferiority of migrants from Portugal, stating, "Our grand Anglo-Saxon character must be preserved and the pure, unmixed blood flowing down from our Aryan progenitors must not be mingled with the Iberic race, composed of the lower types of the race."[18] Other writing treating Portuguese racial classification included taxonomies presented in volume 5, *Dictionary of Races or Peoples,* by Daniel and Eleanor Folkmar.[19] The low-wage migrants' supposed racial inferiority was based on compilations of eugenic data from studies that divided human populations by geographies corresponding to fixed races that were presumed to determine a biological, psychological, and cultural disposition, which were set apart from the Anglo migrant group. Relying on data from Huxley[20] and others, the Folkmars separated northern and western Europeans from the Portuguese and other Iberian migrants whose racial taxonomy was included with North Africans, Arabs, Middle Eastern peoples, and Indo-Afghans.[21] In a glossary of terms defining "Negro, Negroid, African, Black, Ethiopian or Austafrican," "mulatto" populations belonging to the category include those "who come in largest numbers from Portuguese territory, including the Azores and the Cape Verde Islands, off the coast of Africa, which next to the West Indies, send the largest number of negro immigrants."[22]

The presentation of this scholarly data examined Portugal, the Azores, Madeira, and Cabo Verde, as foreign, nonwhite, and non-American. Further, categorical distinctions were made among some Portuguese using different island geographies to argue for different levels of assimilability. In addition to scientific writing and public political discourses, local newspaper articles, editorials, and public letters from the early 1900s likewise reflected debates over racialization and genetic inferiority discourses shaping migrant identities, blunting their political voice, and denying their rights and place as citizens and civic participants in their communities.

During the mill worker period in New England, agricultural and industrial laborers from Portugal negotiated over conditions in the mills. These conditions were directly linked to the racialization of migrant laborer identities and through layered political marginalization. One key area of political activism in the Portuguese industrial communities were efforts to fight back against these conditions through the organized labor movement.

Union Organization and Labor Movement Protests

Characterizations that migrants from Portugal lacked political engagement are often evaluated by their participation in electoral politics.[23] This definition, however, obscures many other ways in which citizen and noncitizen migrants were involved in legislative processes and political influence. Central among these was participation in the organized labor movement of the early twentieth century. Millowners treated the industrial migrant labor force as pliable and expendable, exploited their bodies, and left them in a socially and economically vulnerable position. Adopting an antagonistic relationship to the migrants and other operatives, the millowners exploited laborers' precariousness through layoffs, cutting wages, and speeding up the production line—structural advantages in their control over the terms and conditions of work. Although unions and migrant beneficent association insurance schemes mitigated against the financial losses of striking, sick, or injured workers,[24] laborers protested at great risk to themselves and their families. They lost wages during strikes and suffered retribution after disputes were settled, including layoffs or being blackballed from future work.

The millowners and manufacturing interests gave financial support to sympathetic elected officials in state and local legislatures, who helped them to determine the terms under which laborers worked.[25] At the local level, authorities and governmental institutions intervened on behalf of the owners, using the enforcement of laws and their control of the police and the

Pinkertons to break up strikes, imprison strikers and organizers, and prohibit and spy on meetings, as well as in support of other tactics used to prevent and antagonize labor organization goals.

Labor's political activist movement in New England during the late nineteenth and early twentieth century was organized in its initial stages primarily by craft and trade unions composed almost exclusively of workers in the so-called skilled trades—most of whom had been recruited from the UK and Ireland, or from among their American-born descendants. These were jobs that typically required apprenticeship, or extensive training, making tradesmen historically more difficult to replace. Trade union work was also precarious,[26] however, as trends in machine technology mechanized work previously undertaken by craftsmen. This elite labor class organized to protect the interests of a particular trade, and although a limited number of non-Anglophone migrants did this work, the trade unions favored natives and English-speaking migrants over industrial workers from southern Europe.[27] Presiding over organizations in which membership already depended on one's position in labor and racial hierarchies, officers in the trade unions were vocal public promoters of the racialized marginalization of migrant workers.

The cotton mills of New England were hierarchical institutions in which operators worked machinery in a complex industrial collective. It was not just the machines that were mechanized. Workday schedules and worker responsibilities were part of a rigidly regulated assembly line operation, with certain parts of the line far more arduous and dangerous than others. Tasks for various stages in the weaving of cloth were separated in the mills onto separate floors. Less refined, less finished, and less handcrafted work was completed on lower floors or in separate work areas. In the carding rooms course cotton fibers were spun, pulled, and wound into taffy-like chords in preparation for further refinement into thread or yarn, which was used to weave finished cloth. In New England, work in the carding room was among the dirtiest, most difficult, and poorest paid in the mill system. They were also spaces segregated by racialized and often gendered labor hierarchies. In many New England mills, the carding room was where Portuguese women and migrants from the Azores and Cabo Verde worked.

The tradesmen unions improved their bargaining position by restricting membership into their organizations. Maintaining the interests of a racialized white and elite labor class, they excluded industrial workers and sought advantages in negotiations with manufacturers for a larger share of wages and to protect workers from routine layoffs. Even in favorable years, 20 percent of the workforce was laid off, often for months at a time. In less economically stable times, around 30 percent of workers would be unemployed in New England's industrial cities for an average of four months of the year.[28] Easily replaceable and with limited political organization and bargaining power, industrial migrant laborers were the most vulnerable and struggled to better their conditions.

In the decades prior to 1900, craftsmen's unions in New England had successes in labor negotiations, for example, temporarily gaining a ten-hour workday in Fall River through protests in 1866.[29] From the 1890s, efforts were made to include unaffiliated workers in strikes and walkouts organized by skilled worker unions, even as they still barred those workers from joining their organizations or having a strategic decision-making role. Industrial laborers in New Bedford, for example, paired with tradesmen unions for labor protests in 1898,[30] and the first significant industrial worker participation in a Lowell citywide textile operative strike and lockout took place in 1903. In Lowell, when some workers refused to accept certain concessions required to end a strike, mill agents simply countered by moving Portuguese, Greek, and Polish workers into their jobs.[31] In a 1905 protest walkout against a wage cut in Fall River organized by the United Textile Workers of America, five thousand trade unionists were joined by fifteen thousand unaffiliated laborers.[32] The migrant unskilled labor pool was an integral part of the Lawrence strike of 1912 (known as the Bread and Roses strike). Smaller-scale strikes took place among unaffiliated workers outside of the mills as well, including among rural and agricultural workers.[33]

These moments of migrant labor solidarity, however, did not encourage trade unionists to open their ranks to industrial workers. Like other labor leaders, the AFL's Samuel Gompers contributed to anti-immigrant public political debate, calling for restricted immigration and the civic exclusion of immigrants, with rhetoric that attributed migrants' physical characteristics to racialized mental and cultural shortcomings.[34] Fears of being replaced and unemployed, exacerbated by mechanization, contributed to trade union leaders' anti-immigrant sentiment and "by 1906 the dominant voices in organized labor were openly and energetically in favor of restricted immigration."[35] Professor of economics and political science W. Jett Lauck,[36] author of several contributions to the Dillingham Commission Reports, advocated restrictions on migration himself, writing that he considered increased mechanization a threat to the tradesmen and trade unions, as it allowed unskilled laborers to do the work of a skilled tradesman. The negotiating power of the protective mule-spinners trade union was diminished with the invention of the ring-spinning frame, for example, with Lauck pointing out that "this made it possible for a *woman* or *girl,* or *inexperienced immigrant,* in a few weeks, to become proficient in spinning yarns."[37] Lauck's uses of italics in the quotation underline his assumptions about the inferiority of these kinds of individuals.

In this environment, early 1900s socialist and communist organizations led unionization efforts among New England's migrant industrial laborers. National parties and local associations provided logistics, leadership, manpower, strategy, and other organizing capacities to support labor activism among industrial workers. The trade unions may have excluded migrants, but, in the words of labor leader Ellen Gurley Flynn, socialist labor organizations like the Industrial Workers of the World (IWW) "championed 'the poorest, the most exploited, the most oppressed workers.'"[38] Narratives of a unified subaltern labor class antagonistic to manufacturing interests are complicated by millowners and craft unions, which triangulated in their negotiations against migrant industrial workers in the total institution of the mills.[39] Workers from England, Scotland, Ireland, and more recent arrivals from French Canada used the racialization of the industrial migrant class as an argument to advance their own racialized assimilability.[40] Indeed, trade union leaders across the country were vocal supporters of the racialization and political discourses that sought to limit the rights of the migrants to work, live in the United States, and ultimately to organize for better conditions.[41]

Rejected from national and local tradesmen's unions and federations, migrant industrial and agricultural workers from Portugal were supported through community-founded social, cultural, beneficent, and civic associations that attended to their social welfare. The migrant associations or fraternal societies provided social welfare assistance, loaned money for business development, and offered other forms of material assistance. The earliest associations established were the widespread insurance (and burial) schemes. The associations were increasingly important during strike actions and were an essential social and political resource helping migrants engage their place in labor hierarchies and racialization discourses. They brought migrant worker communities together outside of the factories and fields in protected spaces that were legally sanctioned for the purposes of public community gatherings. The association halls hosted union organization meetings, candidates' nights, and other community economic and political activities.

Although organization efforts among many islander Portuguese was at first slow, increasing numbers of migrant industrial workers joined strikes and national socialist and communist labor organizations. Indeed, many of the textile workers coming from continental Portugal already had previous experience in the syndicalist movement. National and regional communist, socialist, and syndicalist affiliated leadership applied a model of industrial worker labor organization[42] in New England and other mills in the United States based on principles of communitarianism and socialist principles. These organizations created structures that encouraged leaders to emerge from among the rank and file and relied on migrants—many whose languages were not spoken at an organization's national level. Migrants were necessary to translate documents and work as liaisons with national leaders, and some became leaders themselves, working with other migrants to organize their own communities. Industrial labor organization was indeed seen as "the key to successful opposition to corporate practices."[43] Migrants and migrant women also had avenues to become leaders through their participation, and some emerged in ensuing strikes and walkouts as labor leaders and key organizers.[44]

Socialist leaders represented a more radical approach to labor action, expressing that the political system and the existing legal framework were themselves part of the problem confronting workers who were trying to attain their goals, with some leaders arguing against even signing contracts.[45] Despite joint participation in labor actions, the trade labor leaders remained broadly antagonistic to the migrant industrial workers, with animus directed at the specific labor organizations that supported their goals. The AFL and other trade unions in New England had disputes with the IWW expressed through conflicts over broader political aims (debates that also existed to a lesser degree within the Wobblies' leadership ranks). The AFL was "strongly opposed [to] the political activity of various socialist parties."[46] For their part, socialists "sought broader goals for a unified working class, including higher income, better working conditions for all, and ultimately workers' control of mills and factories."[47] Wertheimer argues the skilled trade unions were pursuing central policies with the owners because they shared a joint interest in negotiating within the system as opposed to the more radical approaches of the socialists.[48]

The success of socialist- and communist-affiliated leaders working with migrant industrial laborers was turned against the workers civic legitimacy as laws during the first Red Scare period criminalized the organizations and migrant industrial worker activism.[49] Demagoguery over racial difference and genetic inferiority was part of the manufacturers' and tradesmen's unions strategies to limit the rights and power of the unaffiliated industrial workers. Conflations of anti-immigrant sentiment, antileftist labor politics, and the imposition of marginalized racial identities constrained the rights of the industrial laborers and intimidated and complicated migrant labor activism efforts. Prohibited from organizing by the law, migrant workers were exhorted to avoid the strike and mass labor movement as it reinforced one's non-American status. In the Dillingham Reports and other writing about the "immigrant question," writers linked the nonwhite identities, genetic shortcomings, and political affiliation of the laborers to reinforce notions of their lack of assimilability.[50]

Socialist- and communist-affiliated industrial labor movement activists faced routine arrests and imprisonment. Strike captain Agusto Pinto was deported for his work during the New Bedford textile worker strike of 1928, and shortly after his repatriation he would disappear under nebulous circumstances on route to the notorious Estado Novo political prison Tarrafal on Cabo Verde—presumed dead after having been a vocal critic of Portuguese dictator António Salazar.[51] Joe Figueredo also tangled with the legal and political system over crackdowns on labor movement activism. A U.S. citizen, he was nonetheless harassed for his migrant labor activism and communist party organization and was called to testify at the House Committee on Un-American Activities hearings. Eula Mendes (who was married to Figueredo) began working as a labor activist during the New Bedford textile workers strike of 1928 and would continue to organize labor as a union secretary and through the Communist Party until she was deported in 1953 because of Taft-Hartley Act loyalty oath requirements. The pro–industrial manufacturer legislation criminalized migrant protest and thwarted activities of leaders but also affected the rank and file. Mendes understood why migrant industrial workers would be cowed. When politicians, the press, and millowners claimed the communist and socialist organizations were "trying to destroy the country . . . that had an effect. Many of those workers were not American born, they were not American citizens, and it was a powerful thing to frighten them."[52] Migrant participation in the labor movement was a community-wide affair, implicating not only the workers but also the community social and economic systems that supported them. The fight for labor rights was quite directly a fight for migrant civic rights.

There were migrants who were dedicated socialists and communists, both in leadership positions in the ranks of unions and the leftist parties. Rank-and-file workers took part in labor protests. Migrants also participated in other social causes, as well, including antifascist marches. Their association with socialist labor organizations caused the migrants to be perceived as a threat to American safety and well-being.[53] The Rev. Lichliter of the Junior Order United American Mechanics encapsulated the sentiment of conflated antagonism toward migrant laborers calling them "the illiterate, the unclean, morally and physically, the un-American, the criminally inclined, yeah, the lower classes of aliens form the dangerous portion of our municipalities . . . are becoming a menace to our institutions."[54]

Mill interests had political and police support and paid private security firms to break up strikes, arresting and perpetrating violence on those speaking out for labor (including beating women and children, as in the 1912 Bread and Roses strike). Although the millowners and newspapers sympathetic to them condemned individual acts, the activities of the strikebreakers were perceived to be upholding the law, while the violent actions on the part of some in the radical labor movement were condemned. Those committing violence against strikers were represented as protecting American values of institutional order, while anarchist violence was used to discredit the broader socialist labor movement, its leaders, and the goals of the migrant workers to improve their situation. These discourses were exacerbated both by the Bolshevik uprising and violence in Europe in 1919, provoking fears of a global socialist movement in the United States. In Rhode Island, for example, the Italian American Galleanistas—an insurrectionary labor group, "defended individual violence against tyrants" to overturn the labor system. These kinds of tactics colored police responses that "arouse race prejudice"[55] and conflated migrant racial or ethnic identity with class and their position in the mills.[56] Violence against protesting migrant laborers was part of broader trends of white nationalist and white supremacist terrorism, including the lynching and imprisonment of Black Americans in the first decades of the 1900s.

The beginning of World War I—and the fear this engendered in white Americans over the loyalty of European migrant industrial workers' and so-called hyphenated Americans to the U.S. cause—would further exacerbate these tensions. Socialist organizations were largely against the war, seeing it as another example of labor exploitation. The National Office of the Socialist Party, for example, released a public statement citing an official party convention vote against the U.S. entry into the war, which the party declared was, like other "modern wars," the result of factionalism among capitalist interests in the belligerent nations and fought with the blood of the poor and working underclass. Even the minority stance of the members of the Socialist Party who were not against the United States' entry into the war, per se, were nonetheless still calling for dialogue with socialists among the United States' enemy combatants, demanding the internationalization of all manufacturing and distribution of food production to alleviate the plight of the global worker on both sides.[57] The anti–World War I stance taken to protect unskilled migrant laborers from exploitation was seen as an affront to traditional American civic duty and used to brand the socialists and migrants as dangerous and unpatriotic.

The economic and political threat of the labor movement led over the decade to growing restrictions on migration, beginning with legislation cutting off migrants from Asia and culminating in the 1920s with laws targeting migrants from southern and eastern Europe that further tightened strictures on Asian and Middle Eastern migration. The political process fomenting these restrictions both criminalized the labor protests and used presumptions about the migrants' inferior racial characteristics to justify their exclusion. Communist and socialist organizations offered a viable alternative for industrial laborers' collective mobilization. With anticommunist laws in force, however, Portuguese migrant workers joining or taking leadership roles in the labor movement through such organizations were vilified by politicians, millowners, and tradesmen alike for seeking an apocalyptic end to the "American" way of life.[58] The costs of confronting their labor position through this kind of organization could be extortionate. Organizing for a voice over their wages and work conditions, protesting Portuguese industrial laborers lost jobs, were barred from future employment, and were beaten, imprisoned, and deported. The police also raided and harassed them for other activities.[59] Migrant workers' political and civic exclusion was advanced through laws that legitimized authoritarian measures ostensibly against "communists" but were used ultimately to thwart industrial migrant labor movement organization.[60] Presumptions about racialized categories of (un)suitability as a result of political affiliation and labor movement activism were part of efforts to deny migrant industrial workers' civic participation. Representing the political activity of a racialized labor class as dangerous and un-American further reinforced perceptions against their assimilability. When considering the so-called apathy of migrant Portuguese who eschewed involvement in labor activism, it is important to recognize that the cause was less characteristic of apathy than a legitimate fear of reprisal. In any event there would be less risky avenues for migrant political participation even as these competing strategies would result in reactionary and racist capitulation to white nationalist power processes.

The "Movement to Americanize the Immigrant"

In a direct response to the marginalization, criminalization, and racialization of migrant labor political activism, elites, officers, and members of various voluntary social organizations would take a different approach to political activism. Intended to counteract the impression of Portuguese leftist political identities and racialized marginalization, older Portuguese associations joined and newer civic organizations were formed to participate in the widespread "movement to Americanize the immigrant" of the first decades in the 1900s. The collaboration of Portuguese voluntary organizations in the movement is an unexamined and largely ignored example of political activism, including the effect it had on early twentieth-century Portuguese migrant community electoral forays. This early activism created a form of political engagement that yet guides Portuguese placemaking in New England as elites and organizations in Portuguese migrant communities continued to develop Americanization goals long after the national organizations had lost their impetus. Through the movement, the Portuguese voluntary organizations undertook racial and social mobility strategies engaging white nationalist power politics.[61]

The U.S. population increased more than 20 percent over 1890–1915 as 25 million migrants came to the United States to work as industrial laborers. The mills transformed cities[62] with the arrival of industrial workers, making them and their families an even greater percentage of the local population of urban centers. Similar transformations took place in some New England rural areas.[63] An elite group of progressive and politically and academically connected intellectuals composed of social scientists, public education advocates, reform-minded community organizers, religious groups, and policy makers at the highest levels of state and federal government challenged anti-immigrant sentiments, policies, and laws. The writers gave public lectures, created social programs, and enacted policies to "assimilate" immigrants and Black Americans. These Americanization principles predated the Dillingham Commission—which was really part of the debate itself—and grew over the subsequent decade. In the context of increasing labor and civil rights activism among communities of migrant industrial workers (as well as U.S.-born Black Americans), antimigrant fear mongering and xenophobic discourses questioned the loyalties of "hyphenated Americans."[64] Guided by sociological scientific studies, educational philosophy, and reformist writing,[65] the educational and cultural programs enacted collaborations between progressivist elites and communities of migrant laborers.[66] The political movement opposed much of the "America First" agenda, although there was overlap among the ideas of proponents of these competing political and philosophical positions. Those advocating for Americanization[67] saw it as an answer to what some called the "immigrant question," a euphemism referring to conditions of poverty among communities of migrant mill laborers caused by labor exploitation. Ohio State University sociologist and Fisk University president Fayette Avery McKenzie in 1912 epitomized the Americanization movement's progressive intent, asking, "Is culture a product of biology and blood, or one of psychology and tradition?"[68] Americanization authors challenged eugenicist ethnologist theories about migrant workers and Black Americans "natural" abilities, to examine differences among people that "belong to the psychic characteristics of the social orders, not to the inherent and unchanging psychic natures of the peoples . . . these assimilative processes are social rather than biological," as Americanization proponent Sidney Gulick wrote in 1914.[69] Donald Taft's controversial 1923 *Two Portuguese Communities in New England* was a latecomer to the debates but drew directly from and engaged with Americanization theories and models.

The Americanization movement promulgated upward mobility from poverty and residential blight and sought improvements to industrial migrant workers' health and welfare through programs that taught literacy, English language education, and civic training/access, challenging the restrictionists who relied on racialized narratives of presumed genetic unsuitability, while also engaging the public arguments of the restrictionists to advocate for a softer, progressive version of the "America First" migration policy.

Portuguese Associations, Americanization, and Protomulticulturalism

Some of the lofty ideas of the Americanization movement were difficult to realize given the practicalities of implementation, including financial constraints, political pressures, and organizational obstacles. Reformers, immigrant assistance centers, libraries, health and welfare institutions, and labor movement organizers had experience collaborating with migrant communities. These connections would make migrant leaders and migrant community associations fundamental to the implementation of the reform movement's program. Americanization movement elites enlisted existing migrant associations and provided an impetus for the founding of new civic organizations among communities of mobile labor communities.

Many immigrant associations in Portuguese communities adopted Americanization rhetoric and took on the movement's goals as part of a broader response to the racialization of migrant labor. Their activities demonstrate how the associations wrestled with definitions of Portuguese assimilability, along with acceptance of white nationalist hierarchies in their political rejection of the labor movement's protest strategy. The Portuguese confronted semiotic categories constructed by earlier ethnologist definitions of their identities. Reinforced by early twentieth-century sociological writing[70] on immigration, these racialized categories aligned the Portuguese and other low wage immigrant laborers as inferior and unassimilable.

The tenuousness of Portuguese assimilability required the migrants to devise strategies to transform their racialized marginalization. In this, the civic and cultural associations were a key vehicle of political activism. In an era of robust voluntary associativism in New England and the United States—not only among Portuguese immigrants—progressive elites founded national civic organizations that were designed to collaborate with and spearhead outreach in migrant industrial labor communities. This included organizations such as the North American Civic League (NACL) founded in Boston in 1907 and other city-based immigrant protection civic associations that promoted national patriotic day celebrations and helped organize educational and civics training in migrant industrial worker communities. The organizations carried out their objectives with the financial and political support of state governmental commissions. They lobbied for legislation protecting immigrants and for the government to take a lead role in immigration assistance.[71] Their collaborative arrangements with local migrant associations promoted "the ultimate assimilative capabilities of the immigrant and of his eventual transformation into a patriotic, loyal and intelligent supporter of the great body of principles and practices which the leaders of the movement considered to be 'America's priceless heritage.'"[72]

The state immigration commission in New York working with the NACL presented its joint goals:

> [The] characteristics and problems concerning the immigration question could be met best through a five point program . . . first *assimilation*—or the alternative to restriction—second *education*, elementary, industrial civic, and English—or a change in American standards and ideals; third *distribution*—or congestion, maladjustment, and unemployment with all their attending evils; fourth *naturalization* and direct and permanent contact with American institutions and standards—or constantly increasing colonies and camps, isolation, the establishment of 'race' communities within cities and persistent racial prejudices; and fifth *protection*—or exploitation industrially, financially, and socially which caused aliens to become penniless, diseased or exhausted members of the community within a few years after they had been admitted.[73]

New England, especially Boston (where the NACL headquarters were located), was an "experimental center of the new movement."[74] The NACL worked with local public education and immigrant associations to sponsor adult education classes and engage other issues of immigrant welfare. The state even budgeted $10,000 for Americanization initiatives. In neighboring Rhode Island, a Providence commission established in 1914 attempted "to obtain information for the enactment of such laws as would bring non-English-speaking foreigners into sympathetic relations with American institutions and customs."[75] The New England Industrial Committee of fifteen prominent New England industrialists sought to bring "the immigrants into the 'right relations' with the American people and American Institutions."[76]

Of primary concern to the New England Industrialist Committee, was the status of "un-Americanized foreigners" and the radical labor movement that had led industrial workers to collectively organize with communist and socialist organizations. Americanization efforts in this context were a means to combat "the growth of that type of socialism which is synonymous with treason."[77] With the U.S. military entry into World War I, Americanization movement activities accelerated among immigrants, especially those from countries fighting the United States, who used their participation to publicly express loyalty to their country of residence. The NACL codeveloped a program called the Committee for Immigrants in America, a national campaign brought to hundreds of cities and towns and planning committees. Under the NACL umbrella, 54 organizing institutions representing migrant and other associations from across the nation collaborated on a joint program to celebrate the 1915 Fourth of July national holiday. The agenda was intended to promulgate "a great nationalistic expression of unity and faith in America."[78] The patriotic celebrations of America in which migrant associations participated helped communities negotiate their assimilability through a collaborative performance of white nationalist discourses of political and civic belonging. In so doing, they were able to provide a counternarrative to their racialized labor class marginalization and mute demagoguery delineating them as un-American based on industrial migrant laborer affiliation with socialist and communist organizations.

By 1917, there were over one hundred Americanization programs active throughout the country including in Boston, Brockton, Fall River, Lowell, and Taunton in Massachusetts, and in Providence, Rhode Island, that directly engaged with "295 national, racial, patriotic, immigrant and philanthropic societies, 50 national religious societies and organizations, and 1071 foreign newspapers."[79] Similar programs would spread in subsequent decades to other Portuguese migrant communities. Nationwide, 1,754 centers carried out the Bureau of Naturalization program, which included syllabi and "racial advisors" assigned to do outreach to foreign associations "holding conferences among their people, speaking in their lodges and in public gatherings, translating material for publication in their foreign language papers, and a host of other duties."[80]

Due to social networks, churches, and migrant-owned presses and news organizations, the Americanization movement fell short of goals to mute non-English languages, however, they had success with the children of immigrants. Although the presses were treated as a necessary ally of the movement, in theory, foreign languages and the immigrant press were seen as detrimental to immigrants' rapid acquisition of English, which movement proponents felt left them in danger of communist and socialist influence. Turning American-born children away from immigrant languages was intended to bring about an end to "colonization" as a result of industrial workers living in closed-off social enclaves around the mills. In practice, however, Americanization ideals had to be communicated to migrant communities that did not speak English, so there was little other recourse but to rely upon collaborations with institutions that would perpetuate and promulgate foreign languages.[81] This also meant that the movement would need to rely upon an elite group of migrant organizers who would be responsible for carrying out the programs in their own communities. Americanization proponent and fellow at Chicago's McCormick Theological Seminary Archibald McClure used the term "immigrant leader." In *Leadership of the New America,*[82] McClure provides examples of associational collaborations in local communities, including newspapers and religious outreach. Reporting his firsthand experiences conducting religious training with immigrants in Chicago, McClure emphasized the importance of migrant community leaders in successful missionizing and Americanization programs. In its own way, Americanization was a form of missionary work[83] proselytizing a gospel of white nationalist structured civic religion.

Studies on U.S. labor organization have chronicled political and culturally relevant voices driving migration debates and labor activism; however, migrant laborer agencies in their own organization are a less examined theme.[84] Industrial migrant workers from Portugal have relied upon the organizational structure of their many chartered socioreligious, cultural, and economic associations[85] as a vehicle for migrant agency and political activism,[86] to shape narratives over their civic belonging,[87] and to advocate for their social, economic, and intellectual welfare.[88]

The economic, political, and civic engagement activities of the Portuguese Fraternity stand out during the first decades of the 1900s, but many other social, religious, and cultural associations also participated. Founded in Cambridge in 1897 and begun as an insurance scheme, there would eventually be more than thirty Portuguese Fraternity branches spread throughout industrial and rural migrant communities into the 1930s. The organization also promoted citizenship and naturalization drives intended to create a Portuguese community–centered voting bloc. Portuguese Fraternity branches were active in multiple communities, with local press noting the efforts of the society in Hudson, Nantucket, East Boston, Falmouth, and Cambridge. The Fraternity also had political connections to the Portuguese Republic, when New Bedford native Charles Serpa, the American-born director of the supreme lodge, was appointed as vice consul of New Bedford in 1915.

Early twentieth-century organizations like the Portuguese Fraternity and later the Portuguese American Civic League engaged migrant assimilability and Portuguese racialization questions through collaboration with national civic organizations like the NACL and the Committee for Immigrants[89] and developed their own Americanization movement educational goals. The organizations sent delegates from Portuguese communities to meetings of the national civic leagues and formed their own local chapters. The Commonwealth of Massachusetts Report of the Commission on Immigration outlined a twelve-point plan promoting the Americanization of immigrants including the maintenance of neighborhood centers in public schools and in "foreign districts" as part of outreach that would offer substitutes to "dangerous commercialized recreation" through "fellowship, as well as assistance" to combat national and municipal problems.[90] Such programs for Portuguese immigrant communities were common in both urban and rural spaces (in New Bedford and Falmouth, for example), with immigrant associations sponsoring adult education programs and speeches by national advocates and local immigrant leaders. Their work with local school committees prompted early forays into electoral politics as the organizations also sponsored candidates for offices and debate nights to promote their preferred choices, which, by the 1930s frequently came from the Portuguese immigrant communities themselves.[91]

Between 1909 and 1959 in the state of Rhode Island alone there were some 150 associations incorporated by Portuguese migrants dedicated to providing access to civic belonging through educational initiatives, including classes in citizenship and naturalization and English language proficiency, and other forms of direct political mobilization.[92] Through the associations, migrant industrial workers participated in patriotic and American national celebrations including Fourth of July celebrations, Pilgrim commemorations, and other civic events such as fundraisers for World War I bond drives[93] and commemorations for American soldiers who served and were killed in the war. The dedication of monuments and public citywide municipal events created pageants for recursive expressions of presumed patriotism, civic virtue, and hardworking industriousness,[94] all positive qualities about the group that were reported in the press. Such public demonstrations—often accompanying other migrant and non-migrant associations in New England's industrial cities and towns—shaped public narratives of belonging that could rebut the anti-immigrant and white nationalist political arguments over the migrants' lack of assimilability. In the 1920s, the kinds of associations chartered by Portuguese migrants increasingly began to counter antimigrant fervor and legislative setbacks, including the criminalization of migrant laborer protest activities and exclusionary migration policies.

Indeed, the largest number of new organizations founded in Portuguese communities from the 1930s to the 1950s (the period after the restrictive anti-immigrant laws were passed) were those explicitly chartered as civic associations intended to promote "citizenship," the inculcation of "American values," and "devotion to American principles," and so on.[95] They operated as community-based institutions to "better understand our civic and political duties as American Citizens in order to better serve our city, state and nation," which they hoped would "elevate the standing of Portuguese-American Citizens . . . specially dedicated to Portuguese American youth striving for better education, better civic and social interests, better recognition, to which full citizenship entitles it."[96]

Conclusions

These nuanced public Anglo-conformity performances, however, existed alongside the associations' role as cultural and social hubs to produce migrant material culture and the Portuguese language. Rather than muting public displays of migrant material culture, Americanization activities assisted such expressions to be recontextualized as American or argued that Portuguese national heroes should be seen as American heroes.[97]

For example, associations promoted the betterment of the "Portuguese-American Race" by instilling "American" civic ideals through Americanization efforts, while simultaneously celebrating and promoting Portuguese material culture production and encouraging versions of Portuguese history that best suited arguments over their racialized assimilability.[98]

Over subsequent decades, the Americanization movement led many associations with Portuguese names to change them in state filings to English, often rewriting charters and bylaws, including some of the first founded in New England. Associations promoting Americanization and civic league activism in Newport, for example, included the Portuguese-American Civic Women's League (1934), which was formed "to keep alive the heroic deeds of the Portuguese Race; to inculcate the spirit of Americanism and to promote respect and esteem for the American Flag and the high ideals and institutions for which it stands"; and the Portuguese-American Republican Club (1940), which was concerned with the "Americanization of the citizens of Portuguese descent." The club's goal—to Americanize those who were *already* citizens—demonstrates Portuguese efforts to gain citizenship rights by signaling assimilability and points out the persistent nature of Portuguese nonwhite social exclusion. In 1952, when two of the oldest Portuguese migrant associations in Newport merged and anglicized their name to the Vasco Da Gama Holy Ghost Society, the new organization's bylaws were rewritten to limit membership to Portuguese of the "white race,"[99] challenging assimilability narratives through explicit participation in white nationalist identity politics of exclusion.

Americanization mobilities were facilitated by adopting these oppressive, racialized categories of difference to reconstruct industrial migrant Portuguese identities as white, American, assimilable, and deserving of civic participation.

Interestingly, the associations likewise negotiated space for language, socio-religious practices, and community cultural lifeways in a way that protected the migrants from having their cultural production politicized as disqualifying. These migrant-centered advocacy efforts make the associations key institutions that helped to create the public cultural wherewithal for later transformations of multiculturalism as a model of civic engagement.

Migrant industrial worker assimilability through the Americanization program—and its promise of social mobility (social well-being and civic participation)[100]—failed, however, to fundamentally challenge industrial capitalism's necessity for a class of low-wage labor migrants in racialized social categories of exploitation and exclusion. Americanization was in this regard less about turning the "Portuguese" into "Americans" than about mediating the boundaries of social exclusion and civic inclusion. Stated another way, social mobility is examined not through a discussion of migrant "assimilation" but rather through how the group engaged political power processes around their assimilability—actions intended to address social and racial marginalization.

Works Cited

Archives

Boott Cotton Mill, U.S. National Park Service, Lowell, MA.

Falmouth Enterprise, Falmouth Public Library Digital Archive, Falmouth, MA.

Falmouth Historical Society Archives, Falmouth, MA.

Faunce, William. The Spirit of America or Teaching Democracy. 1916–1924. The Meaning of America (five versions), box 6, folder 2, A108. Hay Library, Special Collections, Brown University, Providence, RI.

Ferreira-Mendes Portuguese-American Archives, University of Massachusetts Dartmouth, Dartmouth, MA.

Figueredo, Joseph. Oral History Interview at Tamiment Library and Robert F. Wagner Labor Archives. 1983. Collection call no: OH.002 Location: Box: 15, CD: Figueredo 1-4, CD: Figueredo 1-4, Box: 3, Cassette: 86 A-D, Cassette: 86 A-D, Box: 7, Folder: 31, Folder: 31

Lowell History Center, University of Massachusetts, Lowell, MA.

Lowell Sun, Lowell Public Library Archive, Lowell, MA. Massachusetts.

Massachusetts Secretary of State Archives, Boston, MA.

Mendes, Eula. Oral history interviews, New Bedford Textile Worker's Strike of 1928 Oral History Interviews and Research Collection, University of Massachusetts Dartmouth, Claire T. Carney Library Archives and Special Collections. Interviews by Daniel Georgianna, 1985, MC9 box 8, tape 56, 57, 58; interviews by Penn Reeve, 1987, MC9 box 1, 16. Dartmouth, MA.

New Bedford Strike of 1928 archive, Claire T. Carney Library Special Collections Archives, University of Massachusetts Dartmouth, Dartmouth, MA.

Portuguese Consul file, New Bedford Whaling Museum Special Collections. New Bedford, MA.

Rhode Island Secretary of State Archives. Providence, RI.

Woods Hole Historical Museum, Woods Hole, MA.

Works Cited

Abbott, Grace. "The Immigrant and Internationalism." In *The Immigrant and the Community*, 267–81. New York: Century, 1917.

Allen, Theodore W. *The Origin of Racial Oppression in Anglo-America.* Vol. 2 of *The Invention of the White Race.* London, New York: Verso, 1994.

Allen, Theodore W. *Racial Oppression and Social Control.* Vol. 1 of *The Invention of the White Race.* London: Verso, 1994.

Azevedo, Rui Vitorino. "Not Quite White: The Ethno-Racial Identity of a Portagee." *Op. Cit.* 12 (2010): 19–34.

Barker, Jean E. "Cape Verdean-Americans: A Historical Perspective of Ethnicity and Race." *Trotter Review* 10, no. 1 (1996): 17–20.

Barrow, Clyde. *Portuguese-Americans and Contemporary Civic Culture in Massachusetts.* North Dartmouth, MA: Tagus Press, 2002.

Bastos, Cristiana. "Migrants, Inequalities and Social Research in the 1920s: The Story of *Two Portuguese Communities in New England." History and Anthropology* 29, no. 2 (2018): 163–83.

Bastos, Cristiana. "Portuguese in the Cane: The Racialization of Labour in Hawaiian Plantations. In *Ambiguous Inclusions: Inside Out, Outside In, vol. 1 of Changing Societies: Legacies and Challenges*, edited by Sofia Aboim, Paula Granjo, and Alice Ramos, 65–96. Lisboa: Imprensa de Ciências Sociais, 2018.

Beckert, Sven. *Empire of Cotton.* New York: Alfred A. Knopf, 2014.

Benton-Cohen, Katherine. *Inventing the Immigration Problem: The Dillingham Commission and Its Legacy.* Cambridge, MA: Harvard University Press, 2018.

Bradley, Joseph. *Voluntary Associations in Tsarist Russia.* Cambridge, MA: Harvard University Press, 2009.

Brauer, David. *Nellie Stone Johnson: The Life of an Activist.* St. Paul, MN: Ruminator Books, 2001.

Brown, Fidelia O. "Decline and Fall: The End of the Dream," In *Cotton Was King: A History of Lowell, Massachusetts*, edited by Arthur L. Eno Jr, 141–58. Somersworth: New Hampshire Publishing Co. 1976.

Boas, Franz. *Changes in Bodily Form of Descendants of Immigrants.* Vol. 38 of *Reports of the Immigration Commission [Dillingham Commission Reports].* Washington, DC: U.S. Congress, 1911.

Buhle, Paul, *Marxism in the USA: from 1870 to the Present Day.* London: Verso, 1987.

Bushee, Frederick A. *Ethnic Factors in the Population of Boston.* New York: Macmillan Company for the American Economic Association, 1903. Reprint by American Immigration Experience Series. New York: Arno Press and *New York Times*, 1970.

Cance, Alexander. *Recent Immigrants in Agriculture.* Vol. 24 of *Reports of the Immigration Commission [Dillingham Commission Reports].* Washington, DC: U.S. Congress, 1911.

Carter, Bob, Marcie Green, and Rick Halpern. "Immigration Policy and the Racialization of Migrant Labour: The Construction of National Identities in the USA and Britain." *Ethnic and Racial Studies* 19, no. 1 (January 1996): 135–57.

Casid, Jill H. *Sowing Empire.* Minneapolis: University of Minnesota Press, 2005.

Chatterton, Fenimore. "Exhibit 31." In *Statements and Recommendations Submitted by Societies and Organizations Interested in the Subject of Immigration.* Vol. 41 of *Reports of the Immigration Commission [Dillingham Commission Reports]*, 124–25. Washington, DC: U.S. Congress, 1911.

Cimino, Eric. "The Traveler's Aid Society: Moral Reform and Social Work in New York City, 1907–1916." *Faculty Works: History and Political Science* 3 (2016): 48. https://digitalcommons.molloy.edu/hps_fac/3.

Creel, George. "The Hopes of the Hyphenated." *Century Magazine* 91, no. 3 (January 1916): 350–63.

Dewey, John, and Evelyn Dewey. "Democracy and Education." *Schools of To-Morrow*, 287–316. New York: E. P. Dutton and Co., 1915.

Dominguez, Virginia. *White by Definition: Social Classification in Creole Louisiana.* New Brunswick, NJ: Rutgers University Press, 1986.

Du Bois, W. E. Burghardt. "The Negro in the United States." In *The Negro,* 183–231. New York. Henry Holt and Company, 1915.

Dunbar Olivia Howard. "Teaching Immigrant Women." *Harper's Bazaar* 47 (June 1913): 277–78.

Elliott, E. N., ed. *Cotton Is King, and Pro-Slavery Arguments: Comprising the Writings of Hammond, Harper, Christy, Stringfellow, Hodge, Bledsoe, and Cartwright, on This Important Subject.* Augusta, GA: Pritchard, Abbott & Loomis, 1860.

Eno, Arthur L. Jr., ed. *Cotton Was King: A History of Lowell, Massachusetts.* Somersworth: New Hampshire Publishing Company, 1976.

Errington, Sara. "The Language Question: Nativism, Politics, and Ethnicity in Rhode Island, 1919–1925." In *New England Disharmony: The Consequences of the Industrial Revolution,* edited by Douglas Reynolds and Katheryn Viens, 92–111. Kingston: Rhode Island Labor History Society and the Labor Research Center, University of Rhode Island, 1993.

Estep, Gerald A. "Portuguese Assimilation in Hawaii and California." *Sociology and Social Research* 26, no. 1 (September 1941): 61–69.

Fernandes, Gilberto. "'Oh, Famous Race!' Imperial Heritage and Diasporic Memory in the Portuguese American Narrative of North America." *Public Historian* 38, no. 1 (February 2016): 18–47.

Fernandes, Gilberto. *This Pilgrim Nation: The Making of the Portuguese Diaspora in Postwar North America.* Toronto: University of Toronto Press, 2020.

Festas do Espírito Santo. "Ritual, Etnicidade, Transnacionalismo: As Festas do Espírito Santo na América do Norte." http://festasdoespiritosanto.pt/.

Folkmar Daniel, assisted by Elnora Folkmar. *Dictionary of Races or People.* Vol. 5 of *Reports of the Immigration Commission [Dillingham Commission Reports].* Washington, DC: U.S. Congress, 1911.

Forbes, Francis B. "Notes on the Fraternal Beneficiary Corporations Doing Business in Massachusetts." *Publications of the American Statistical Association* 8, no. 57 (March 1902).

Georgianna, Daniel, with Roberta Hazen Aaronson. *The Strike of '28.* New Bedford, MA: Spinner Publications, 1993.

Goldberg, David Theo. *Racist Culture: Philosophy and the Politics of Meaning.* London: Blackwell, 1993.

Grant, Madison. *The Conquest of a Continent; or, The Expansion of Races in America.* New York: C. Scribner's Sons, 1933.

Gross, Ariela Julie. *What Blood Won't Tell: A History of Race on Trial in America.* Cambridge, MA: Harvard University Press, 2008.

Gulick, Sidney L. "Are Japanese Assimilable?" In *The American Japanese Problem: A Study of the Racial Relations of the East and the West,* 118–68. New York: Charles Scribner's Sons, 1914.

Halter, Marilyn. *Between Race and Ethnicity: Cape Verdean Immigrants 1860–1965.* Champaign: University of Illinois Press, 1993.

Haney-Lopez, Ian F. *White by Law: The Legal Construction of Race.* New York: New York University Press, 1996.

Harney, Robert F. "'Portygees and Other Caucasians': Portuguese Migrants and the Racialism of the English-Speaking World." In *Portuguese Migration in Global Perspective,* edited by David Higgs, 113–35. Toronto: Multicultural History Society of Ontario, 1990.

Hartmann, Edward George. *The Movement to Americanize the Immigrant.* New York: AMS Press, 1967. First published in 1948.

Heath, Kingston William. *The Patina of Place.* Knoxville: University of Tennessee Press, 2001.

Hicks, George L. *Experimental Americans: Celo and Utopian Community in the Twentieth Century.* Champaign-Urbana: University of Illinois Press, 2001.

Higgs, David, ed. *Portuguese Migration in Global Perspective.* Toronto: Multicultural History Society of Ontario, 1990.

Higham, John. *Strangers in the Land: Patterns of American Nativism 1860–1925.* New Brunswick, NJ: Rutgers University Press, 1994.

Huebner, Grover G. "The Americanization of the Immigrant." *Annals of the American Academy of Political and Social Science* 27, no. 3 (May 1906): 191–213.

Hunter, Douglas. *The Place of Stone: Dighton Rock and the Erasure of America's Indigenous Past.* Chapel Hill: University of North Carolina Press, 2017.

Huxley, Thomas Henry. "On the Geographical Distribution of the Chief Modifications of Mankind." *Journal of the Ethnological Society of London* 2, no. 4 (1870): 404–12.

Ignatiev, Noel. *How the Irish Became White.* New York: Routledge, 1995.

Jackson, K. David. *Adverse Genres in Fernando Pessoa.* New York: Oxford University Press, 2010.

Jenks, Jeremiah Whipple, and William Jett Lauck. *The Immigration Problem.* New York: Funk and Wagnalls Company, 1913.

Kellor, Francis. "By-products of Americanization Day." *Immigrants in America Review* 1, no. 3 (September 1915): 16–17.

Kenngott, George, *The Record of a City: A Social Survey of Lowell, Massachusetts.* New York: Macmillan, 1912.

Keyssar, Alexander. "Unemployment and the Labor Movement in Massachusetts, 1870–1916." In *The New England Working Class and the New Labor History,* edited by Herbert G. Gutman and Donald H. Bell, 233–50. Chicago: University of Illinois Press, 1987.

Kornweibel, Theodore. *'Seeing Red': Federal Campaigns against Black Militancy 1919–1925.* Bloomington: Indiana University Press, 1998.

Lang, Henry R. "The Portuguese Element in New England." *Journal of American Folklore* 5, no. 16 (1892): 9–18.

Lauck, W. Jett. *Cotton Goods Manufacturing in the North Atlantic States; Woolen and Worsted Goods Manufacturing.* Vol. 10 of *Reports of the Immigration Commission [Dillingham Commission Reports.]* Washington, DC: U.S. Congress, 1911.

Lauck, W. Jett. "The Cotton Mill Operatives of New England." *Atlantic Monthly* 109 (May 1912): 706–13.

Leal, João. *Azorean Identity in Brazil and the United States: Arguments about History, Culture and Transnational Connections.* North Dartmouth, MA: Tagus Press, 2011.

Leal, João. "Festivals, Group Making, Remaking and Unmaking." *Ethnos* 81, no. 4 (2016): 584–99.

Leal, João. "Migrant Cosmopolitanism: Ritual and Cultural Innovation among Azorean Immigrants in the USA." In *European Expansion and Indigenous Response,* edited by Francisco Bethencourt. Cosmopolitanism in the Portuguese-Speaking World 27. Leiden: Brill, 2017.

Leal, João. "What's (Not) in a Parade? Nationhood, Ethnicity and Regionalism in a Diasporic Context." *Nations and Nationalism* 20, no. 2 (2014): 200–217.

Leis, Philip E. "Ethnicity and the Fourth of July Committee." In *Ethnic Encounters: Identities and Contexts,* edited by George L. Hicks and Philip E. Leis, 239–58. North Scituate, MA: Duxbury Press, 1977.

McClure, Archibald. *Leadership of the New America: Racial and Religious.* New York: George H. Doran Company, 1906.

McKenzie, Fayette Avery. "The American Indian of Today and Tomorrow." *Journal of Race Development* 3, no. 2 (October 1912): 135–55.

Melo, Daniel, and Eduardo Caetano da Silva, eds. *Construção da Nação e Associativismo na Emigração Portuguesa.* Lisboa: Imprensa de Ciências Sociais, 2009.

Miles, Robert. *Capitalism and Unfree Labour.* London: Tavistock, 1987.

Miles, Robert. *Racism after "Race Relations."* London: Routledge, 1993.

Miles, Robert. *Racism and Migrant Labour.* London: Routledge, 1982.

Moniz, Miguel. "The Day of Portugal and Portuguese Heritage, Social Exclusion, and Imagined Mobilities: Legacies of Racialized Migrant Industrial Labor in Contemporary New England." Special issue, *Ocean Crossings,* edited by André Novoa, *Portuguese Literary and Cultural Studies* 33 (2021): 95–153.

Moniz, Miguel. "The Shadow Minority." In *Community, Culture and the Makings of Identity,* edited by Andrea Klimt and Kim Holton, 409–30. North Dartmouth, MA: Tagus Press, 2009.

Pap, Leo, *The Portuguese-Americans.* Boston: Twayne Publishers, 1981.

Piascik, Andy. "Bread and Roses a Hundred Years On." *Industrial Worker,* March 2012. https://www.iww.org/content/bread-and-roses-hundred-years.

Radecki, Henry. *Ethnic Organizational Dynamics: The Polish Group in Canada.* Waterloo, ON: Wilfrid Laurier University Press, 1979.

Rector Lizzie C. "Workers Class for Adult Illiterates." In *Adult Illiteracy,* edited by Winthrop Talbot, 44–48. An issue of the *Bulletin of the Department of Interior Bureau of Education* 35 (1916).

Reeve, Penn. "Portuguese Labor Activism in Southeastern Massachusetts." In *Community, Culture and the Makings of Identity,* edited by Andrea Klimt and Kim Holton, 337–56. North Dartmouth, MA: Tagus Press, 2009.

Reeve, Penn. "Three Lives for Labor." In *Portuguese Spinner: An American Story.* Edited by Joe Thomas and Marsha McCabe, 236–45. New Bedford, MA: Spinner Publications, 1998.

Reports of the Immigration Commission [Dillingham Commission Reports]. Vols. 1–41. Washington, DC: U.S. Congress, 1911.

Roberts, Peter. "The Library and the Foreign-Speaking Man." *Library Journal* 36 (October 1911): 196–99.

Roediger, David R. *Towards the Abolition of Whiteness: Essays on Race Politics and Working-Class History.* London: Verso, 1994.

Roediger, David R. *Working toward Whiteness; How America's Immigrants Became White.* London, New York: Basic Books, 2018.

Ross, Edward A. *The Old World in the New: The Significance of Past and Present Immigration to the American People.* New York: Century, 1914.

Sardinha, João. *Immigrant Associations, Integration and Identity: Angolan, Brazilian and Eastern European Communities in Portugal.* Amsterdam: University Press, 2009.

Schmidt, Regin. *Red Scare: FBI and the Origins of Anti-Communism in the United States, 1919–1943.* Copenhagen: Museum Tusculanem Press, 2000.

Shimazu, Naoko. *Japan, Race and Equality: The Racial Equality Proposal of 1919.* Nissan Institute Japanese Studies Series. New York: Routledge, 1998.

Silvia, Philip T. Jr. "The Position of 'New' Immigrants in the Fall River Textile Industry." *International Migration Review* 10, no. 2 (Summer 1976): 221–32.

Smith, Raymond. "Social Stratification, Cultural Pluralism and Integration in West Indian Societies." In *Caribbean Integration Papers on Social, Political and Economic Integration,* edited by S. Lewis and T. G. Mathews, 226–58. Puerto Rice: Institute of Caribbean Studies, University of Puerto Rico, 1966.

Statements and Recommendations Submitted by Societies and Organizations Interested in the Subject of Immigration. Vol. 41 of *Reports of the Immigration Commission [Dillingham Commission Reports].* Washington, DC: U.S. Congress, 1911.

Taft, Donald. *Two Portuguese Communities in New England: Studies in History, Economics and Public Law,* edited by Columbia University Political Science Faculty. New York: Longman's, Green & Co. 1923.

Talbot, Winthrop. *Americanization: Principles of Americanism, Essentials of Americanization, Technic of Race-Assimilation.* New York: H. W. Wilson, 1917.

Talbot, Winthrop. "The Workers Class." *Adult Illiteracy Bulletin* 35 (1916): 38–50.

Vapnek, Lara. *Elizabeth Gurley Flynn: Modern American Revolutionary.* Boulder, CO. Westview Press, 2015.

Walker-McWilliams, Marcia. *Reverend Addie Wyatt Faith and the Fight for Labor, Gender and Racial Equality.* Champaign: University of Illinois Press, 2016.

Wertheimer, Barbara Mayer. *We Were There: The Story of Working Women in America.* New York: Pantheon Books, 1977.

Williams, Jerry. *And Yet They Come: Portuguese Immigration from the Azores to the United States.* New York: Center for Migration Studies, 1982.

Zaroulis, Nancy. "Daughters of Freemen: The Female Operatives and the Beginning of the Labor Movement." In *Cotton Was King: A History of Lowell, Massachusetts,* edited by Arthur L. Eno Jr., 105–26. Somersworth: New Hampshire Publishing, 1976.

Notes

1. I submitted this paper as a Research Fellow of the ERC Advanced Grant Project Colour of Labour: the racialized lives of migrants—PI Cristiana Bastos (Universidade de Lisboa, ICS; ERC-2015-AdG-695573, 2016–2021; http://colour.ics.ulisboa.pt). Framed and supported by the Colour of Labour project, the research included broad archival work on the civic engagement and political and economic marginalization of migrant labor in New England, in an attempt to understand racialization processes among Portuguese industrial and agricultural workers. Longitudinal participant observation in New England on Portuguese migrant racialization and marginalization includes a paper presented at the Race, Culture, Nation Conference (April 6–8, 2001, University of Massachusetts Dartmouth and Brown University), which was developed for publication through the FCT Post-Doc grant "Migration, Identity and the State." Field and archival research on the formation and role of migrant associations in racialization processes was also supported through the FCT project Ritual, Etnicidade, Transnacionalismo—PI João Leal, CRIA-Universidade Nova de Lisboa (PTDC/CS-ANT/100037/2008), which examines socioreligious associations. I am grateful for the financial and intellectual support of the Portuguese Studies units at the University of Massachusetts Dartmouth, the Center for Portuguese Studies and Culture, where I was a visiting scholar in April 2018, and at the Ferreira Mendes Portuguese-American Archives and Tagus Press; UMass Lowell, the Saab Center for Portuguese Studies and the Lowell Center for History; the Boott Cotton Mills Museum; and Meg Costello and the Falmouth Historical Society Archive. A special thanks to the Portuguese and Brazilian Studies Department at Brown University and the Luso-American Foundation (FLAD), which supported me as the Michael Teague Brown/FLAD Visiting Professor in Portuguese Studies in Fall 2019. I would also like to acknowledge Daniel Georgianna, UMass Dartmouth, Professor Robert Forrant, UMass Lowell, and Professor Philip T. Silvia, Bridgewater State, for their influential research and personal insights

assembling the story of migrant industrial labor in New England to which this paper is indebted.

2. Taken from Edward George Hartmann, *The Movement to Americanize the Immigrant* (New York: AMS Press, [1948] 1967).

3. George Kenngott, *The Record of a City: a Social Survey of Lowell, Massachusetts* (New York: Macmillan Company, 1912), 24–44.

4. W. Jett Lauck, *Cotton Goods Manufacturing in the North Atlantic States; Woolen and Worsted Goods Manufacturing,* vol. 10 of *Reports of the Immigration Commission [Dillingham Commission Reports]* (Washington, DC: U.S. Congress, 1911); W. Jett Lauck, "The Cotton Mill Operatives of New England," *Atlantic Monthly* 109 (May 1912): 706–13; Kenngott, *The Record of a City,* 138–71; Donald Taft, *Two Portuguese Communities in New England: Studies in History, Economics and Public Law* (New York: Longman's, Green & Co., 1923).

5. Local agencies were supported by residential patterns of migrant communities settled around the mills, creating a residential structure for the promotion of mobility and economic benefit. Kingston Wm Heath, *The Patina of Place* (Knoxville: University of Tennessee Press, 2001); Rose P. Rodrigues, this volume; Paula Celeste Gomes Noversa, this volume; M. Glória de Sá, this volume.

6. Bob Carter, Marcie Green, and Rick Halpern, "Immigration Policy and the Racialization of Migrant Labour: The Construction of National Identities in the USA and Britain," *Ethnic and Racial Studies* (January 1996): 135–57. See also early work on constructions of whiteness by Robert Miles, *Racism and Migrant Labour* (London: Routledge, 1982); *Capitalism and Unfree Labour* (London: Tavistock, 1987); *Racism after "Race Relations"* (London: Routledge, 1993); Virginia Dominguez, *White by Definition: Social Classification in Creole Louisiana* (New Brunswick, NJ: Rutgers University Press, 1986); Ian Haney-Lopez, *White by Law: The Legal Construction of Race* (New York: New York University Press, 1996); Naoko Shimazu, *Japan, Race and Equality: The Racial Equality Proposal of 1919,* Nissan Institute Japanese Studies Series (New York: Routledge, 1998), 77–78. Ariela Julie Gross, *What Blood Won't Tell: A History of Race on Trial in America* (Cambridge, MA: Harvard University Press, 2008) examines these processes in reference to Portuguese legal categories.

7. E. N. Elliott, ed., *Cotton Is King, and Pro-Slavery Arguments: Comprising the Writings of Hammond, Harper, Christy, Stringfellow, Hodge, Bledsoe, and Cartwright, on This Important Subject* (Augusta, GA: Pritchard, Abbott & Loomis, 1860).

8. These exclusions are embedded in the "policing and refurbishment" of racialized labor classes that limit mobility by controlling "assimilability . . . the reconstitution of national identities . . . articulated through concepts of 'race' in which, amongst other things, colour, country of origin and religion, came to operate as key signifiers of difference. Through immigration and nationality laws, governments and administrations ranked human populations into hierarchies of assimilability." Carter et al., "Immigration Policy," 135–57.

9. See historical interviews with communist labor organizer Eula Mendes, New Bedford Textile Worker Strike of 1928 Oral History Interviews and Research Collection MC9 box 8, tape 56, 57, 58, interview with Daniel Georgianna, 1985; New Bedford Textile Worker

Strike of 1928 Oral History Interviews and Research Collection, MC9 box 1, 16, interview by Penn Reeve; Figueiredo, Joseph. Oral History Interview at Tamiment Library and Robert F. Wagner Labor Archives, https://digitaltamiment.hosting.nyu.edu/s/cpoh/item/3944, 2017. Implicit intersections of racial categories and political organization are referenced in Philip T. Silvia Jr., "The Position of 'New' Immigrants in the Fall River Textile Industry," *International Migration Review* 10, no. 2 (Summer 1976): 221–32; Daniel Georgianna with Roberta Hazen Aaronson, *The Strike of '28* (New Bedford, MA: Spinner Publications, 1993); Penn Reeve, "Portuguese Labor Activism in Southeastern Massachusetts," in *Community, Culture and the Makings of Identity,* ed. Andrea Klimt and Kim Holton, 337–56 (North Dartmouth, MA: Tagus Press, 2009); Marcia Walker-McWilliams, *Reverend Addie Wyatt Faith and the Fight for Labor, Gender and Racial Equality* (Champaign: University of Illinois Press, 2016).

10. This is explored in Portuguese communities in industrial New England in Miguel Moniz, "The Day of Portugal and Portuguese Heritage, Social Exclusion, and Imagined Mobilities: Legacies of Racialized Migrant Industrial Labor in Contemporary New England, special issue *Ocean Crossings,* ed. André Novoa, *Portuguese Literary and Cultural Studies* 33 (2021): 97–98.

11. Benton-Cohen argues that Jerimiah W. Jenks, the Cornell University Social Scientist appointed by Roosevelt to the Dillingham Commission who "shaped its priorities and methods" and oversaw the commission's work, held that certain racial backgrounds and immigrant statuses were not compatible with participation in democracy. Katherine Benton-Cohen, *Inventing the Immigration Problem: The Dillingham Commission and Its Legacy* (Boston: Harvard University Press, 2018), 22, 35.

12. *Statements and Recommendations Submitted by Societies and Organizations Interested in the Subject of Immigration,* Vol. 41 of *Reports of the Immigration Commission [Dillingham Commission Reports]* (Washington, DC: U.S. Congress, 1911).

13. The political and scientific discourses relied upon racialized categories to exclude certain classes of migrant workers from both civic and human rights—a justification used by ethnologist writers for the violence inflicted during the global slave trade as well, relying on arguments that held that those working as slave labor were genetically inferior and unequipped for citizenship. See David Theo Goldberg, *Racist Culture: Philosophy and the Politics of Meaning* (London: Blackwell, 1993); David R. Roediger, *Towards the Abolition of Whiteness: Essays on Race Politics and Working Class History* (London: Verso, 1994); Theodore W. Allen, *Racial Oppression and Social Control, vol. 1 of The Invention of the White Race; and* Theodore W. Allen *The Origin of Racial Oppression in Anglo-America, vol. 2 of The Invention of the White Race* (New York: Verso, 2012); Noel Ignatiev, *How the Irish Became White* (New York: Routledge, 1995).

14. *Statements and Recommendations,* 127.

15. *Statements and Recommendations,* 124.

16. Frederick A. Bushee, *Ethnic Factors in the Population of Boston* (New York: Macmillan Company for the American Economic Association, 1903).

17. See literature reviews, examples, and studies on racialization of Portuguese non-white and contested identities in Henry R. Lang, "The Portuguese Element in New England," *Journal of American folklore* 5, no. 16 (1892): 9–18; Alexander Cance, *Recent Immigrants in Agriculture,* vol. 24 of *Reports of the Immigration Commission [Dillingham Commission Reports]* (Washington, DC: U.S. Congress, 1911); Edward A. Ross, *The Old World in the New: The Significance of Past and Present Immigration to the American People* (New York: Century, 1914); Madison Grant, *The Conquest of a Continent; or, The Expansion of Races in America* (New York: C. Scribner's Sons, 1933); Gerald Estep, "Portuguese Assimilation in Hawaii and California," *Sociology and Social Research* 26, no. 1 (September 1941): 61–69; Leo Pap, *The Portuguese-Americans* (Boston: Twayne Publishers, 1981), 160; Robert F. Harney, "'Portygees and Other Caucasians': Portuguese Migrants and the Racialism of the English Speaking world," 113–35, in *Portuguese Migration in Global Perspective,* ed. David Higgs (Toronto: Multicultural History Society of Ontario, 1990); Georgianna, *Strike of '28,* 77; Marilyn Halter, "Identity Matters," in *Between Race and Ethnicity: Cape Verdean Immigrants 1860–1965,* 163–78, (Champaign: University of Illinois Press, 1993); Jean E. Barker, "Cape Verdean-Americans: A Historical Perspective of Ethnicity and Race," *Trotter Review* 10, no. 1 (1996): 17–20. Gina Sánchez Gibau, "Contested Identities: Narratives of Race and Ethnicity in the Cape Verdean Diaspora," *Identities* 12, no. 3 (2005): 405–38; Gross, *What Blood Won't Tell;* Miguel Moniz, "The Shadow Minority," in *Community, Culture and Makings of Identity,* ed. Andrea Klimt and Kim Holton, 409–30 (North Dartmouth, MA: Tagus Press, 2009); Rui Vitorino Azevedo, "Not Quite White: The Ethno-Racial Identity of a Portagee," *Op. Cit.* 12 (2010): 19–34; Cristiana Bastos, "Migrants, Inequalities and Social Research in the 1920s: The Story of *Two Portuguese Communities in New England," History and Anthropology* 29, no. 2 (2018): 163–83; Cristiana Bastos, "Portuguese in the Cane: The Racialization of Labour in Hawaiian Plantations," in *Changing Societies: Legacies and Challenges,* ed. Sofia Aboim, Paula Granjo, Alice Ramos, 65–96 (Lisboa: Imprensa de Ciências Sociais, 2018); Graça Índias Cordeiro, this volume.

18. *Statements and Recommendations,* 24. In his comparatively lengthy (ten pages) statement, Lichliter draws a line from migrant workers presumed genetic makeup, low moral character, and cultural practices to reasons for their restriction, declaring them unassimilable in negative comparisons with white Americans. *Statements and Recommendations,* 18.

19. Daniel Folkmar assisted by Eleanor Folkmar, *Dictionary of Races or Peoples,* vol. 5 of *Reports of the Immigration Commission [Dillingham Commission Reports]* (Washington, DC: U.S. Congress, 1911).

20. Thomas Henry Huxley, "On the Geographical Distribution of the Chief Modifications of Mankind," *Journal of the Ethnological Society of London* 2, no. 4 (1870): 404–12.

21. Folkmar, *Dictionary,* 6.

22. Folkmar, *Dictionary,* 101.

23. For example, Clyde Barrow, *Portuguese-Americans and Contemporary Civic Culture in Massachusetts* (North Dartmouth, MA: Tagus Press, 2002). See also Gilberto Fernandes, *This Pilgrim Nation: The Making of the Portuguese Diaspora in Postwar North America*

(Toronto: University of Toronto Press, 2020), who recognizes the failings in this approach but downplays the importance of the prewar labor movement or radical activity as evidence of migrant politicization.

24. See data collected on the organizations in Francis B. Forbes, "Notes on the Fraternal Beneficiary Corporations Doing Business in Massachusetts," *Publications of the American Statistical Association* 8, no. 57 (March 1902): 1–29.

25. Sven Beckert, "Building War Capitalism," in *Empire of Cotton: A Global History*, 29–55 (New York: Alfred A. Knopf, 2014); Georgianna *Strike of '28;* Silvia Jr., "The Position of 'New' Immigrants," 232; Nancy Zaroulis, "Daughters of Freemen: The Female Operatives and the Beginning of the Labor Movement," in *Cotton was King: A History of Lowell, Massachusetts*, ed. Arthur L. Eno Jr., 105–26 (Somersworth: New Hampshire Publishing Company, 1976).

26. Alexander Keyssar, "Unemployment and the Labor Movement in Massachusetts, 1870–1916," in *The New England Working Class and the New Labor History*, ed. Herbert G. Gutman and Donald H. Bell, 233–50, (Chicago: University of Illinois Press, 1987), 235.

27. Silvia Jr. "The Position of 'New' Immigrants," 226, 228; Georgianna, *Strike of '28*, 29; Lauck, *Cotton Goods*, 706–13.

28. Keyssar, "Unemployment and the Labor Movement." 233–36.

29. Georgianna *Strike of '28*, 30–31.

30. Georgianna, *Strike of '28*, 35.

31. Fidelia O. Brown, "Decline and Fall: The End of the Dream," 141–58, in *Cotton Was King: A History of Lowell, Massachusetts*, ed. Arthur L. Eno Jr., 149–50 (Somersworth: New Hampshire Publishing Co., 1976). This was likewise the case in Fall River, where newer mobile workers from Portugal and Poland were placed into what had previously been French Canadian jobs.

32. Silvia, Jr. "The Position of 'New' Immigrants," 222.

33. *Falmouth Enterprise*, January 10, 1920, 5.

34. See examples from the *Reports of the Dillingham Commission*; Silvia Jr. "The Position of 'New' Immigrants," 226; Barbara Mayer Wertheimer, *We Were There: The Story of Working Women in America* (New York: Pantheon Books, 1977), 199; Paul Buhle, *Marxism in the USA: From 1870 to the Present Day* (London: Verso, 1987), 271; John Higham, *Strangers in the Land: Patterns of American Nativism 1860–1925* (New Brunswick, NJ: Rutgers University Press, 1994); David Brauer, *Nellie Stone Johnson: The Life of an Activist* (St. Paul, MN: Ruminator Books, 2001).

35. Keyssar, *Out of Work*, 243.

36. Author of multiple volumes in the *Dillingham Commission Reports*, Lauck was a researcher for government statistical agencies and would eventually become a union economist.

37. Lauck, "The Cotton Mill Operatives of New England," 710.

38. Lara Vapnek, *Elizabeth Gurley Flynn: Modern American Revolutionary* (Boulder, CO: Westview Press, 2015), 24.

39. In this regard, the mills—including the legal system and the economic and political power dynamic among the mill-ownership group and different factions of racialized, marginalized low-hierarchy workers—operates as a total institution in the way a plantation system does. See Raymond Smith, "Social Stratification, Cultural Pluralism and Integration in West Indian Societies," in *Caribbean Integration Papers on Social, Political and Economic Integration,* ed. S. Lewis and T. G. Mathews, 226–58 (Puerto Rico: Institute of Caribbean Studies, University of Puerto Rico, 1966); Jill H. Casid, *Sowing Empire* (Minneapolis: University of Minnesota Press, 2005).

40. Restrictionist voices also targeted migrants in general, even though these English-speaking migrants were seen as more compatible with white America. See, e.g., Fenimore Chatterton's statement in "Exhibit 31" in *Statements and Recommendations,* 124–25.

41. *Statements and Recommendations.*

42. Andy Piascik, "Bread and Roses a Hundred Years On," *Industrial Worker,* March 2012, https://www.iww.org/content/bread-and-roses-hundred-years; Vapnek, *Elizabeth Gurley Flynn.*

43. Brown, "Decline and Fall," 153.

44. Penn Reeve, "Portuguese Labor Activism," 337–56; Eula Mendes interviews (1985, 1987).

45. A statement from the IWW Industrial Union Manifesto, issued in 1905 for a Chicago conference assesses: "This system offers only a perpetual struggle for slight relief from wage slavery. It is blind to the possibility of establishing an industrial democracy, wherein there shall be no wage slavery, but where the workers will own the tools which they operate, and the product of which they alone should enjoy."

46. Georgianna, *Strike of '28,* 37.

47. Georgianna, *Strike of '28,* 37.

48. Wertheimer, *We Were There,* 199.

49. Theodore Kornweibel, *'Seeing Red': Federal Campaigns against Black Militancy 1919–1925* (Bloomington: Indiana University Press, 1998); Regin Schmidt, *Red Scare, FBI and the Origins of Anti-Communism in the United States, 1919–1943* (Copenhagen: Museum Tusculanem Press, 2000).

50. *Statements and Recommendations,* 124–25.

51. Penn Reeve, "Three Lives for Labor," in *Portuguese Spinner: An American Story,* ed. Joe Thomas and Marsha McCabe, 236–45 (New Bedford, MA: Spinner Publications, 1998).

52. Eula Mendes interviews (1985, 1987).

53. Lauck, *Cotton Goods Manufacturing,* 125.

54. *Statements and Recommendations,* 18.

55. Buhle, *Marxism,* 273; 280.

56. Buhle, *Marxism*, 284.

57. National Office Socialist Party, Anti-War Proclamation 1917.

58. See the Eula Mendes (1985, 1987) and Joe Figueredo interviews (1983).

59. For example, in Falmouth, police almost exclusively targeted Portuguese (who made wine and *aguardente* for home consumption) in prohibition raids, *Falmouth Enterprise*, Saturday, May 31, 1924, 3; the New Bedford Strike of 1928 oral history file Claire T. Carney Archives, UMass Dartmouth, also details police and national guard violence against Portuguese communities.

60. Mendes interviews (1985, 1987); Figueredo interview (1983).

61. Moniz, "The Day of Portugal."

62. Heath, *The Patina of Place*; Rose P. Rodrigues, this volume; Paula Celeste Gomes Noversa, this volume.

63. In the two decades around the turn of the century, e.g., the Portuguese-born population of agricultural Falmouth rapidly grew to 40 percent of the total.

64. See, e.g., Grover G. Huebner, "The Americanization of the Immigrant," *Annals of the American Academy of Political and Social Science* 27, no. 3 (May 1906): 191–213; Peter Roberts "The Library and the Foreign-Speaking Man," *Library Journal* 36 (October 1911): 196–99; Fayette Avery McKenzie, "The American Indian of Today and Tomorrow," *Journal of Race Development* 3, no. 2 (October 1912): 135–55; Jeremiah W. Jenckes and William J. Lauck, *The Immigration Problem* (New York: Funk and Wagnalls Company, 1913), 317–18; Olivia Howard Dunbar "Teaching Immigrant Women," *Harper's Bazaar,* 47 (June 1913): 277–78; Sidney L. Gulick, "Are Japanese Assimilable," in *The American Japanese Problem: a Study of the Racial Relations of the East and the West,* 118–68 (New York: Charles Scribner's Sons, 1914). John Dewey and Evelyn Dewey, "Democracy and Education," in *Schools of To-Morrow*, 287–316 (New York: E. P. Dutton and Co., 1915), 313; W. E. B. Du Bois, "The Negro in the United States," in *The Negro,* 183–231 (New York: Henry Holt and Company, 1915), 224; George Creel, "The Hopes of the Hyphenated," *Century Magazine* 91, no. 3 (January 1916): 350–63. Winthrop Talbot, "The Workers Class," *Adult Illiteracy Bulletin* 35 (1916): 38–50; Lizzie C. Rector, "Workers Class for Adult Illiterates," in *Adult Illiteracy*, ed. Winthrop Talbot, 44–48. An issue of the *Bulletin of the Department of Interior Bureau of Education* 35 (1916); Grace Abbott. "The Immigrant and Internationalism," in *The Immigrant and the Community* (New York: Century, 1917), 271. There are many examples in Talbot's excerpted volume: Winthrop Talbot: *Americanization* (New York: H. W. Wilson Company, 1917).

65. In notes and public talks from 1916–24, for example, Brown University president William Faunce lectured throughout the industrial northeast about core tenets of Americanization principles as a remedy to social problems in industrial worker neighborhoods.

66. For a history of the movement written midcentury see Hartmann, *The Movement to Americanize,* and Talbot, *Americanization.*

67. Sara Errington, "The Language Question: Nativism, Politics, and Ethnicity in Rhode Island, 1919–1925," in *New England Disharmony: The Consequences of the Industrial*

Revolution, ed. Douglas Reynolds and Katheryn Viens, 92–111 (Kingston, RI: Rhode Island Labor History Society and the Labor Research Center, URI, 1993).

68. McKenzie, "The American Indian," 140.

69. Gulick. "Are Japanese Assimilable." Anthropologist Franz Boas made exactly this argument in the Dillingham Commission volume he wrote, *Changes in Bodily Form of Descendants of Immigrants* (vol. 38).

70. See Bastos, "Migrants, Inequalities," for a discussion of reactions of Portuguese in New England to Taft's *Two Portuguese Communities;* Graça Índias Cordeiro, this volume.

71. Eric Cimino, "The Traveler's Aid Society: Moral Reform and Social Work in New York City, 1907–1916," *Faculty Works: History and Political Science* 3 (2016): 48, https://digitalcommons.molloy.edu/hps_fac/3

72. Hartmann. *The Movement to Americanize,* 7. Hartmann's extensive discussion of the Americanization movement is analyzed by Errington, "The Language Question."

73. New York–New Jersey Committee of the North American Civic League for Immigrants, December 1909–March 1911, 5–6 (title of the leagues report for the period). See also, page 11 of this report. Cited in Hartmann, *The Movement to Americanize,* 57.

74. Hartmann, *The Movement to Americanize,* 43.

75. Hartmann, *The Movement to Americanize,* 87.

76. Hartmann, *The Movement to Americanize,* 87.

77. Hartmann, *The Movement to Americanize,* 90–91.

78. Hartmann, *The Movement to Americanize,* 112.

79. Hartmann, *The Movement to Americanize,* 196–97.

80. Hartmann, *The Movement to Americanize,* 178.

81. See Countryman, "Shall Public Libraries," 229–31.

82. Archibald McClure, *Leadership of the New America: Racial and Religious* (New York: George H Doran Company, 1906).

83. As evident in Americanization texts by Gulick, "Are Japanese Assimilable," 118–16; and Peter Roberts "The Library and the Foreign-Speaking Man."

84. Sources about the Portuguese community include Silvia Jr. "The Position of 'New' Immigrants"; Georgianna, *Strike of '28;* Reeve, "Portuguese Labor Activism"; and the strike of 1928 oral history archives collected by Georgiana Penn and others (Claire T. Carney Library, UMass Dartmouth) as well as other area oral history archival projects including the UMass Lowell Center for History and Falmouth Historical Society archives.

85. Most studies examine associative processes among recently founded rather than industrial era activities, which remain a lacuna in Portuguese historiography, with Fernandes, *This Pilgrim Nation,* a notable exception. For studies of more contemporary associativism see João Sardinha, *Immigrant Associations, Integration and Identity: Angolan, Brazilian and Eastern European Communities in Portugal* (Amsterdam: University Press,

2009); Daniel Melo and Eduardo Caetano da Silva, eds., *Construção da Nação e Associativismo na Emigração Portuguesa* (Lisboa: Imprensa de Ciências Sociais, 2009); João Leal, *Azorean Identity in Brazil and the United States: Arguments about History, Culture and Transnational Connections* (North Dartmouth, MA: Tagus Press, 2011); João Leal, "Festivals, Group Making, Remaking and Unmaking," *Ethnos* 81, no. 4 (2016): 584–99. João Leal, "Migrant Cosmopolitanism: Ritual and Cultural Innovation among Azorean Immigrants in the USA," in *European Expansion and Indigenous Response*, ed. Francisco Bethencourt, 233–49, Cosmopolitanism in the Portuguese-Speaking World 27 (Leiden: Brill, 2017). Outside of the Portuguese community see Henry Radecki, *Ethnic Organizational Dynamics: The Polish Group in Canada* (Waterloo, ON: Wilfrid Laurier University Press, 1979); Joseph Bradley, *Voluntary Associations in Tsarist Russia* (Cambridge, MA: Harvard University Press, 2009).

86. In Rhode Island, e.g., with substantially fewer numbers of migrants from Portugal than Massachusetts, there were around 350 of these associations chartered with the Rhode Island secretary of state in the period from the late 1800s until after World War II.

87. Hartmann, *The Movement to Americanize.*

88. Leal, *Azorean Identity;* Leal "Festivals"; Melo and da Silva, *Construção da Nação e Associativismo.*

89. Francis Kellor, "By-products of Americanization Day," *Immigrants in America Review* 1, no. 3 (September 1915): 16–17. See discussion in Hartmann, *The Movement to Americanize,* 122.

90. Hartmann, *The Movement to Americanize,* 74.

91. I.e., the Cape Verdean Citizens Political Club, which ran a 1935 candidate's night in support of Falmouth School Board candidate John DeMello.

92. Rhode Island Secretary of State Archives, charter documents (nonbusiness associations).

93. Hartmann, *The Movement to Americanize.*

94. Philip E. Leis, "Ethnicity and the Fourth of July Committee," in *Ethnic Encounters: Identities and Contexts,* ed. George L. Hicks and Philip E. Leis, 239–58 (North Scituate, MA: Duxbury Press, 1977).

95. Rhode Island Secretary of State Archives.

96. Rhode Island Secretary of State Archives, charter documents of Portuguese American Political Club of Pawtucket and Portuguese American Civic League.

97. I.e., Dighton Rock, the Miguel Corte Real myth. See Moniz, "The Day of Portugal"; Douglas Hunter "American Place-Making: Dighton Rock as a Portuguese Relic," in *The Place of Stone: Dighton Rock and the Erasure of America's Indigenous Past,* 215–39 (Chapel Hill: University of North Carolina Press, 2017); Gilberto Fernandes, "'Oh, Famous Race!' Imperial Heritage and Diasporic Memory in the Portuguese American Narrative of North America," *Public Historian* 38, no. 1 (February 2016): 18–47.

98. I.e., União Portuguesa Beneficiente (Cumberland, RI) 1928; The Gremio of the Daughters of Portugal (Bristol, RI) 1937 in Rhode Island Secretary of State Archives.

99. Bylaws, "Vasco da Gama Holy Ghost Society," 1952, University of Massachusetts Dartmouth Archives and Special Collections Ferreira-Mendes Portuguese-American Archives: MC 95/PAA.

100. Faunce, "Papers," 1916–24; Errington, "The Language Question."

CHAPTER 9

At the Portuguese Feast

......

NELSON H. VIEIRA

Pushing my way through the jostling crowds
Where Lusitanian ancestry strikes me in every face,
I celebrate my annual sensation of pride and discomfort
Knowing I shall never resolve the tug-of-war that is my fate.
Surging through to soak up the fond memories of a skinny little boy.
Of a young adult not always filled with ethnic pride,
I feel this older me emerge as I look down upon all those Portagees.
How difficult to be both me and them,
How simple to be just one.
But that can never be with a vowel-ending name.
Though born American, assimilating is unending as forever.
For purposes of consolation, tho,
This varied self I am is never one but many!
—I am my pride. I am my shame, I am myself,
Secretly realizing only parts and combinations are all I'll ever know.

(First published in *Gavea-Brown*, vol. 3, March 1982.)

SECTION 3

Memories of Life and Work

CHAPTER 10

Negotiating Place and the Ethnic Experience

Joseph Conforti's *Another City upon a Hill* (2013)

CARMEN RAMOS VILLAR

Joseph Conforti's memoir, *Another City upon a Hill* (2013), is a text where the memories of growing up as a member of two immigrant groups, Portuguese and Italian, intermingle with the aim of representing the contribution of those immigrant groups in Fall River, a city, as the blurb in the cover tells us, "where ethnic heritages matter."[1] This multilayered account is where Conforti, as a historian, textually negotiates his impulse to educate the reader about how the cotton mills conditioned the life of the immigrant community around them, with the other impulse of telling the reader about growing up in that immigrant community. The epilogue provides the reason for writing the memoir: after a tour with Fall River's Historical Society, Conforti had not recognized the portrait of the city aimed toward tourists, in particular its lack of reference to the ethnic contribution to the city. With this in mind, the starting point for this memoir is Fall River's history as a textile city, whose economic rise and fall affected the many immigrant groups who came to work on the mills. Against this backdrop, Conforti describes his family, centering on the rocky relationship between his father, a second-generation Italian American, and his mother, also a second-generation immigrant, this time Azorean American. Conforti then moves on to examine his childhood, reflecting on the unconscious negotiations between the different immigrant groups in Fall River as he describes the schools he attended and the different neighborhoods he grew up in. Conforti's description of his academic success as a historian of New England is couched in terms of how education in particular was a route toward assimilation into the mainstream, thus enabling him to transcend the markers of class and ethnicity. In this way, Conforti's memoir explores the drive for assimilation and interethnic tensions within Fall River, in a controlled text that straddles the boundaries of being both a historical account and a piece of life writing.

As Sidonie Smith and Julia Watson observe, "Memory is contextual. . . . Acts of remembering take place at particular sites and in particular circumstances,"[2] noting that "autobiographical narratives . . . signal and invite reading in terms of larger cultural issues and may also be productively read against the ideological grain."[3] The context for remembering in Conforti's text is both Fall River as a place and the place of the ethnic subject within this space. In bringing the ethnic character of Fall River into view, Conforti is also reading against the grain, to use Smith and Watson's words, and uncovering the processes whereby a particular ideology made the ethnic character slowly recede from view in the mainstream discourse of Fall River as a city. The textual construction of the ethnic self and the immigrant community in Conforti's text underlies an impulse to correct and protect the image of the ethnic subject that is conditioned by the specific experience of an immigrant community in Fall River. Looking at Conforti's examination of the ethnic subject within Fall River aims to extend Cristian Aguiar's analysis of how Conforti and other Portuguese American life writers "challenge the universalization of the working class subject . . . by emphasizing their positions as individuals marked by class, race, ethnicity and, crucially, space. Asserting their individuality through discrete economic and cultural practices, they challenge their own objectification"[4] and "resist dominant narratives that reduce them to uncommunicative 'subjects.'"[5] By looking at how Conforti reads the ethnic subject into Fall River, this essay also aims to extend my previous analysis of Portuguese American autobiographies as texts in which the self evolves to echo the shifts in the national discourses of the United States, from assimilation to ethnic affirmation.[6] In this essay, the aim is to examine how Conforti's text also responds to regional attitudes about the Portuguese American community in the context of New England, and specifically Fall River. I argue that, by couching the depiction and contribution of the immigrant community to Fall River in the academic perspective of the historical account, and then including his own experience of growing up as a member of that immigrant community, Conforti's text uncovers how discourses about the ethnic self are shaped by, and respond to, a combination of social, political, and personal factors.

Miguel Moniz comments that "the perceptions by Portuguese immigrants and their descendants of their own racial and ethnic identity and how they have been identified by others have depended upon broader historical, political, and economic circumstances that have shifted over the past century, causing Portuguese racial and ethnic identity to shift as well."[7] This idea of a shifting identity is echoed by Cristiana Bastos in her analysis of the publication of Donald Taft's *Two Portuguese Communities in New England,*[8] which examines the factors behind the high infant mortality rates in Fall River and Portsmouth.[9] Bastos highlights that Taft's study echoed negative perceptions of recently arrived immigrant groups in an ethnically divided city whereby "immigrant groups entered the mills of New England in the lower positions and eventually moved into better jobs; historically, they also moved from racialized positions as non-white to ethnic white and, eventually, mainstream white."[10]

According to Bastos, the move in racial categorization could only happen when another wave of immigrants came, adding that "in Fall River's industrial economy in the 1920s, the Azorean Portuguese were the late arrivals. When Taft conducted his research, they were stuck in the lower strata and appeared as a homogenous group."[11] Bastos's analysis is contextualized within the wider social discourses that led to the 1924 U.S. Immigration Act, the positive academic reception the study achieved, and, crucially for the present essay, the negative response Taft's publication received from the Portuguese American community in neighboring New Bedford, which had a longer historical presence as an immigrant group in the United States. According to Bastos, the Portuguese American community in New Bedford raised objections to Taft's depiction of Portuguese Americans in New England because "race was a very sensitive issue for the Portuguese Americans in New England. It was not simply that their classification in an unwanted position in the racial hierarchies of the day was like adding insult to the injuries endured in the past and the present . . . it also threatened their future as migrant communities . . . [and] of the Portuguese as a worthy 'race' that deserved a better place in the symbolic hierarchies."[12]

This negative portrayal and perception of the Portuguese American community was still present in the 1980s. When analyzing how the Big Dan's rape trial was reported in the English and Portuguese American press, Mia Michael comments that prejudice was a reality that confronted Portuguese Americans throughout their long history of settlement in the region. Viewed as nonwhite, they were subject to employment and housing discrimination and even segregated in movie theaters in early twentieth century. Portuguese Americans continued to experience social exclusion and discrimination in New Bedford and Fall River at the time of the rape.[13]

Michael goes on to examine how the Portuguese American community reacted to the reporting of the rape case, the first to be fully televised in the United States, commenting that the community "decried the disproportionate media attention they believed the case and their community was receiving as well as the once 'buried' xenophobic attitudes this attention resurrected"[14] and that the reporting of the case caused divisions "within a community that had long endured anti-immigrant prejudice and class discrimination."[15] Both Bastos and Michael, therefore, highlight the stigma attached to the Portuguese American community in Fall River which, as will be examined below, perhaps explains why Conforti highlights that the ethnic history of Fall River is hidden in plain sight.

In attempting to redress how Fall River is being portrayed to tourists, Conforti's description of the city outlines the contribution made by the ethnicities in shaping it, providing an alternative history of this city as well as enabling Conforti to conduct a textual examination of his ethnic self. The approach taken by Conforti to highlight the ethnic contribution in Fall River echoes Michael's observations on how the objections of the Portuguese American community to the way the media portrayed them during the Big Dan's rape case also centered on "why their positive contributions to the region did not receive the same amount of exposure as the crime."[16] In a way, Conforti should be seen as one of the many voices seeking to give visibility to the ethnic contribution in New England, be it Portuguese American or otherwise. The memoir becomes a textual journey of finding the ethnic. In the prologue, Conforti comments that his "academic specialization on Puritanism and colonial America represented a search for the 'real' New England and an escape from the ethnic Catholicism of my youth in Fall River."[17] This statement suggests an incomplete image of New England as a place, where the ethnic experience of the immigrant groups that arrived at a later stage in its history has been left out. To complete the portrait of Fall River, Conforti first turns his attention to religion, specifically Catholicism. For Conforti, the presence of Catholicism in Fall River explains certain behaviors, particularly within an environment described as being dominated by Irish Catholicism where, in public, competition within the different Catholic immigrant groups spilled over from the Church into the workplace.[18] Catholicism and national origins are described as entwining to create what Conforti terms as cultural Catholicism;[19] Conforti outlines how faith becomes practiced in an ethnic way through, for instance, each immigrant group worshipping their own image of the Virgin Mary or participating in processions whose route reaffirmed the boundaries of the parish and, by extension, the immigrant group. Conforti concludes that "public devotion on Fall River served as a marker of ethnicity, not just Catholicism."[20] In other words, what could be seen as a private matter of individual choice, religion, becomes projected into the public sphere of practicing ethnicity in a specific place, where the dynamic conflicts between the different immigrant groups play out in Fall River.

Conforti's description of Fall River's ethnic Catholicism is described as an influencing factor for the life choices and behavior of many inhabitants in Fall River. Ethnic Catholicism is also a connecting thread between the private story of Conforti's life and the public story of the city. Against this background, Conforti emerges as the product of conflicting immigrant groups, and conflicting approaches to the embodiment of the ethnic stereotypes assigned to these groups in public. On the one hand, his family is described as "devout ghetto Catholics. That is, they boarded up their minds and nailed them shut to any religious ideas and influences that did not stem from Catholicism."[21] On the other, Conforti's parents differ in their approach to Catholicism, perhaps as a reflection of their own immigrant origins. For instance, Conforti's father is described as giving up cigarettes for Lent, yet, in Conforti's words, when he came home, he would retrieve "his tobacco pipe from a bureau drawer where it had gathered dust for a year. The pipe supplied his daily nicotine until Easter Sunday."[22] In effect, his father projected a set of behaviors in public that marked him as Catholic, yet he behaved differently in the private space of the home, where he was not under public surveillance. Conforti's mother, on the other hand, emerges in the text as a more devout Catholic, but hers is a Catholicism that is practiced in private and does not have a public projection that would mark her out as a Portuguese American. As Conforti comments: "My mother was a faithful observer of the festa [for St. Anthony] rather than a participant, even though she had been one of the founding members of a women's sodality. I think she saw the procession as a little too public and Portagee for her refined social tastes, what with its promiscuous mingling of immigrants and second-generation Azoreans."[23]

Conforti also comments on how his mother resented the influence that her mother-in-law had on her husband, presenting the marriage as a daily embodiment of cultural negotiation between the two. This extended to masking the immigrant origins of her husband's family, who, in Conforti's words, "resembled the insufficiently scrubbed, often darker Azoreans from whom she remained aloof, even as she cherished her Portuguese heritage and identity."[24] Conforti's description of her might go some way to explain why she behaved in this way: "My fair complexioned mother also confronted the second generation dilemma of coming to terms with her ethnic heritage while proving to others that she was not just another Fall River 'Portagee.' This common ethnic slur, a kind of Portuguese equivalent of 'Wop' or 'Dago,' usually referred to lower-class, poorly educated immigrants and their children. For some it served as an alternative to the more cutting 'black Portagee.'"[25]

Conforti's depiction of his mother's intention to leave her ethnic markers behind highlights the context in which studies on the Portuguese immigrant group emerged, echoing the racialized and ethnically hierarchical society outlined by Bastos.[26] Both parents attempted to overcome the signs that would single them out as ethnics. This echoes Aguiar's observation that the life narratives of authors like Conforti show the connections between different ethnicities in the same place and space to outline a "complexity of multigenerational migrant communities."[27] Added to this, Conforti's mother, who was born in 1910,[28] is likely to have been aware of the Portuguese American community's objections to how they had come across in Taft's study after its publication. Even if she did not know the specific details, it is clear that she was conscious of the negative image of the ethnic, particularly of the Portuguese American community, at a time when there was a strong drive for assimilation.

It is not surprising to read how Conforti's mother was seeking to minimize anything that marked her or her family as ethnic, nor is it surprising to read how Conforti, who was born in 1945, experienced the effects of his family's ethnic masking firsthand. Conforti's mother, then, is used as an example in the text of how the socially inherited images of ethnic markers informed the behavior of the ethnic subject. This is clearly seen in how she takes steps to avoid her sons becoming too ethnically marked[29] so that it would not "reflect on her, frustrating the Bento family quest for American social respectability."[30] This observation is reminiscent of what Camille Canti terms as ethnic passing, that is, how the immigrant consciously takes steps to erase ethnicity in public by adopting certain behaviors that diffuse or hide ethnic origins so as to assimilate.[31] The choice of what Conforti describes as "more 'American' names" for her children[32] or how Conforti describes his mother only speaking Portuguese as a private language with her sister at home could be seen as a strategy that enabled ethnic passing toward achieving assimilation. However, assimilation is exposed as difficult and elusive for the Conforti family, uncovering the conflict between the private and the public spaces that immigrant groups negotiated; the food they ate at home was a mix of Portuguese and American food,[33] the clothes worn by the children in the family singled them out as different,[34] and the images the family watched on TV showed an idealized, alternative America that contrasted with their own working-class family.[35] The description of how Conforti's mother treated the newly arrived Azorean immigrants at the start of the 1960s shows how her public projection of assimilation was precarious: "In many respects, she faced a generational dilemma. Extending charity to an immigrant cousin's family represented one thing. Engaging 'greenhorn' relatives on level ground disrupted her identity as an assimilated Azorean-American woman. . . . The new immigrants exposed the fault lines in Fall River's Portuguese community."[36]

Here, Conforti highlights the confrontation of cultural practices with the need to keep up appearances in an ethnically stratified environment where assimilation is the ideal to be achieved, particularly if assimilation enables sidestepping the rivalry between immigrant groups. It also shows how the publicly projected image of masking ethnicity was a problematic negotiation of cultural expectations; the carefully cultivated image of assimilation could be easily destabilized by following the cultural kinship ties expected of the Portuguese in the United States when welcoming newly arrived family members. Conforti, in writing about this aspect, uncovers this confrontation and rescues the hidden, private ethnic experience for the reader who might not be aware of the daily negotiations required in the pursuit of seeming to have assimilated to American culture and society and how the tensions of the public and private space could destabilize the desire to bypass ethnic markers.

For Conforti, the need to conform to expected social behaviors would result in a desire to mask his ethnic origins in public. The focus on sports, and the advancement through education, particularly his training as a historian of New England's history, becomes a means to an end. Education enables him to transcend his ethnicity markers to become, in his words, "protestanized," so that he "would become a free agent,"[37] or a CWASP, that is, a Catholic that is highly educated and assimilated to the United States.[38] His comments about how his teaching career could have been helped by his family's connections in Fall River's unofficial network of calling in favors[39] show that he deliberately turned his back on the ethnic aspect of his self, which, as he acknowledged in the text, made his life harder. However, as the essay has been arguing, Conforti is a product of his specific childhood environment, and of a wider social attitude toward ethnic difference. Conforti recognizes that "without that education I could never have written this memoir, never viewed myself as distinct from, and more than, the sum of socioreligious attributes that composed my narrative of origins and identity."[40] By explaining why his ethnicity was masked in public, it is not so much a case of Conforti writing himself back into the community as much as it is an explanation of why people like him would choose to engage in ethnic passing, masking their ethnicity in a space where showing it in public was a disadvantage.

Conforti's unease with speaking about the private sphere is a conscious constraint in his writing and another way in which attitudes toward the ethnic condition how the private self is presented in public. Conforti's emphasis on Catholicism projects a carefully cultivated public persona, but it also outlines how this self is presented. In the prologue, Conforti comments how "it proved a challenge to wean my writing away from what I was taught growing up: you don't speak about family and especially yourself in public."[41] However, there is more at play here. As Smith and Watson observe, "When life narrators write to chronicle an event, to explore a certain time period, or to enshrine a community, they are making 'history' in a sense. But they are also performing several rhetorical acts: justifying their own perceptions, upholding their reputations, disputing the accounts of others, settling scores, conveying cultural information, and inventing desired futures among others."[42] Conforti's memoir is an account where the author tries to steer a path not only between the public and the private spaces, between two immigrant groups within his family, between the perceived socially accepted ethnic self in public with the hidden private ethnic self, but also between two traditions; the trained historian struggles to put forward the personal account, and the personal account interferes with the historian's training of achieving objectivity. This makes Conforti's memoir a problematic example of life writing. His account is multilayered but is also constructed in a very controlled way.

As this essay argues, Conforti, as a historian, textually negotiates his impulse to educate the reader about how the cotton mills conditioned the life of the immigrant community around them as well as the other impulse of telling the reader about growing up in an immigrant community and how that experience shaped the ethnic subject within an immigrant community to behave in certain ways both in public and in private. As Aguiar notes, this multifaceted analysis means that the approach taken by Conforti blends the academic and the autobiographical, choosing "to speak only for himself and to couch other judgements in the terms of academic analysis."[43] It is almost as if Conforti's text is a biography of the ethnic side of Fall River, or a sociological study of that city, alongside the biography of his parents. As the essay explores below, the autobiographical self emerges as hidden and constrained by the bigger discourse of Fall River as a place. For example, in the first chapter, we find sections on the story of Fall River charting the decline of the mill industry, and the concomitant effect on the population. At the same time, Conforti tells us about how he crossed the river either to go to school or to work in the mills, to pay for his tuition, without fully being aware of his surroundings. The idea given by Conforti is that history is alive everywhere but that the passage of time erases the memory of that history so that what remains are traces, like names or buildings, whose context and background are forgotten.

Conforti's training as a historian comes through in many places in the text,[44] particularly in the two pages of references that point to what he has used for the more historical sections of his memoir[45] and in the "notes" section in which he specifically clarifies which texts inform the historical background given in the memoir.[46] Conforti even goes as far as describing and interpreting the photographs provided in the text. This results in a textual negotiation between two traditions, the historical on the one side and the autobiographical on the other, which create a text that is carefully controlled by its author. The process of making the place of the ethnic invisible, therefore, is shown to be caused as a result of either the passing of time or how certain perceptions of a place become entrenched and their context is lost, be it consciously or not.

As Smith and Watson note, "We might want to think about how particular sites of narration perform cultural work, how they organize the personal storytelling upon which they rely. And we might want to think about what kinds of narratives seem 'credible' and 'real' at particular sites of narration."[47] In Conforti's text, the tension between representation and representability is being played out not only in the tension between the text being both a historical and a life writing account but also in the fact that the self that Conforti presents to the reader makes him an exception that arose from an ethnic group. Commenting on this aspect within the wider context of Portuguese American life writing, Aguiar explains how, on the one hand, the writers' educational backgrounds and life trajectories cast their lives, and their parents lives, as exceptional, which would place them outside of the community they write about,[48] but, on the other, "it is through the process of remembering parents, place, and work that each of those authors is able to re-assert important ties to those communities. . . . They each conclude with a return "home" to the community."[49] Aguiar also remarks that "if [Conforti] is going to write a memoir of Fall River, and particularly if he is going to write one of working-class Azorean-American Fall River, he has to prove that he is from there . . . in the form of a remembered narrative from the position of relative power."[50] The relative power Aguiar refers to is that of the ethnic who left the immigrant community, who trained as a historian, and who now seeks to be recognized as being part of that immigrant community. It is also an immigrant subject that can write the ethnic story back into a place that has masked, even forgotten, the ethnic presence in that place and space. As such, the text shows this as a process that engages in a precarious balance of representability.

The careful negotiation between historical account and life writing in Conforti's text, the careful control of how the self and the ethnic are perceived, comes at a price. If, on the one hand, this control gives credibility to Conforti's sociohistorical portrayal of Fall River, and provides evidence for his book to be taken as a serious study, on the other, as was already noted, the personal side of his life writing suffers. Although Conforti provides the reader with the story of his life and of his family, it is carefully framed within the overall aim of providing a portrait of the ethnic presence in Fall River. Aguiar observes that "Conforti is content to remember his city as a fully-formed, fully-grasped social and physical entity throughout the entirety of his text."[51] This implies that the personal side is somewhat in flux, not fully formed, something that, perhaps, Conforti refers to in his preface when he reports that, after reading a draft of his memoir, Frank X. Gaspar had "pointed out that the personal narrative was too often in the background to the story about Fall River."[52] Framing his personal story within an overall ethnic portrait of Fall River, itself also framed in academic terms, might explain Conforti's reticence in not giving away too many details about himself. For instance, Conforti gives scant details of the story of how he met his Italian American wife, who was a nun at the time of meeting, explaining this as being out of respect and that he could not do the story full justice in words.[53] Instead, he reframes it within the parameters of ethnicity and religion: "I had fallen in love with an individual—a woman I found attractive, intelligent, warm, outgoing, and a pillar of integrity. But my marriage to former Sister Josetta would represent a kind of reaffirmation of or return to my background, at the same time as I was struggling to gain social and intellectual distance from it. Negotiating that tension, the stress I often kept to myself would sometimes surface as a strain in our marriage."[54] This is the closest Conforti comes to providing us with an emotional and personal description of himself in the narrative, and uncovering the strain between the projection of a public and private persona. Looking at the relationship with his wife within the parameters of ethnicity and religion is familiar ground; it echoes the description of ethnic Catholicism examined above. Even here, in what is a private story of a marriage, the overall effect achieved is to uphold Conforti's intention of showing that ethnicity matters, and that it should not be overlooked when seeing the effect of ethnic passing discussed earlier. In a way, his personal experiences are pared down so that they become synonymous with the experiences of the other inhabitants in Fall River in their negotiation of the public and private, of the individual and the collective, of how ethnicity matters.

Neither a historical study nor an example of life writing, this text straddles both categories, creating a hybrid text that succeeds in rescuing the ethnic subject from being misunderstood, even forgotten, in the overall history of Fall River. It is also a text that straddles the journey that the ethnic self has taken from assimilation to ethnic affirmation, even pride at recognizing ethnic origins. It is a text that is located within the regional constraints that immigrant groups come under in the space of Fall River as a city, New England as a region, and the United States as a nation, uncovering why assimilating within the idealized melting pot and the erasure of ethnic markers might have been desired. Using his family as an example, as a representative portrait, enables Conforti to outline not only how the Fall River inhabitants navigated the different immigrant group boundaries but also how they took steps to control the projection of their private and public selves in an ethnically challenging environment. In a sense, Conforti is engaging in "mimetic politics, [where] the ethnic subject identifies with the host [society] and is thus accepted in American culture, while the ethnic factor often remains prepolitical, apolitical, or simply a private matter."[55] In highlighting the lack of awareness of his surroundings when he was growing up, Conforti shows himself as part of the collusion in not portraying Fall River as a city made up of many ethnicities, and of not recognizing the ethnic contribution to the history of Fall River. Conforti's text goes some way to make amendments to this oversight by showing that ethnicities have always been present in Fall River. In doing so, Conforti's text highlights not only willful ethnic blindness in mainstream discourses but also the complicity of the immigrant community, or communities, in contributing to that blindness, albeit in an environment where ethnic projection was difficult.

By way of conclusion, it is worth noting that Conforti's text is an unusual example where the discursive arc from invisibility to visibility and affirmation of an immigrant community can be found. This narrative arc is evidenced both in the self that is presented to the reader and in the text's aim of making the ethnic visible in the history of Fall River. Conforti, therefore, fulfills Smith and Watson's observation that "since discourses are historically specific, what counts as experience changes over time with broader cultural transformations of collective history."[56] Just as Conforti's text would not have been possible without the specific ethnic experience of his immigrant background in Fall River, it would have also been impossible had there not been a shift in valuing the ethnic experience within the American mainstream or had there not been a move to valuing the place and presence of the Portuguese American community in Fall River, in New England, and in the United States. The combination of the local, regional, and national seen through the lens of the ethnic subject is, to use William Boelhower's words, "a dialogical production . . . a poetics of continuity through the current act of interrogating the world."[57] What starts as an exercise in uncovering the dynamics behind the silencing of the ethnic contribution in Fall River by Conforti, an exercise in putting the city's historical ethnic heritage back into focus, ends up also acknowledging the role of all the social players in this place (and beyond) in the making of history in any place. In so doing, Conforti fulfills the potential of the role of memory as "a means of 'passing on,' of sharing a social past that may have been 'obscured,' in order to activate its potential for reshaping its future of and for other subjects . . . [whereby] acts of personal remembering are fundamentally social and collective."[58] Conforti's text shows how the voice of the ethnic was not heard due to regional as well as national constraints. It also explains how the stereotype of the Portuguese American community as an invisible minority might have arisen.[59] Like Conforti, the Portuguese American community colluded in shaping this stereotype by reinforcing the idea of its positive contribution to society, but in an understated way.[60] This is an image of the Portuguese American community that Conforti also echoes in his text. Ultimately, through the act of writing, Conforti makes a strong claim for the Portuguese American community to be acknowledged, seen as present, of having a voice.

Conforti's personal account highlights that the Portuguese American and Italian American immigrant communities were visible to those who lived in Fall River. Just like his parents, Conforti cannot hide his ethnic self, even if the attempt is made at ethnic passing. His text, therefore, gives voice to an experience of the negotiation inherent in assimilating to the mainstream, and uncovers the racialized and discriminatory narratives that obscured this experience in mainstream accounts of a place and space. As such, Conforti's text is one of the many voices that have risen from the Portuguese American community in recent years through the medium of life writing. These Portuguese American life writing texts raise the profile of this community, but they are not isolated instances of voicing the Portuguese American immigrant experience. Both Bastos and Michael show that the Portuguese American community has spoken against the perceived image that the mainstream has of it as an immigrant group. The conclusion to be drawn is that the Portuguese American community is not so much an invisible minority or a minority among many that are being silenced in places like Fall River, but, as Conforti shows in the text, it is a community that exercises self-censorship to fit within a mainstream discourse that erases difference in a "society that cultivated white supremacy"[61] for a community that, to repeat an earlier quote "had long endured anti-immigrant prejudice and class discrimination."[62] Bastos, Michael, and Leo Pap[63] all point to the Portuguese American community being active in Fall River, to its voicing concerns and making itself visible when it mattered. Conforti's text, then, stands as one of the many examples about the Portuguese American immigrant experience, albeit within the socially accepted parameters of life writing as a channel for the voice of the ethnic experience in the United States to be heard. After all, life writing has a long tradition in the United States as a mode for communicating the self, and for communicating the ethnic experience.[64] If anything, the publication of

Portuguese American life writing accounts shows a desire to speak about the Portuguese American experience after making a conscious choice to *speak,* knowing there might be those who are willing to listen and to recognize the place and space in which they are speaking from.

Works Cited

Printed sources:

Bastos, Cristiana. "Migrants, Inequalities and Social Research in the 1920s: The Story of *Two Portuguese Communities in New England.*" *History and Anthropology* 29, no. 2 (2018): 163–83.

Boelhower, William. *Immigrant Autobiography in the United States (Four Versions of the Italian American Self).* Venezia: Essedue Edizioni, 1982.

———. *Through a Glass Darkly: Ethnic Semiosis in American Literature.* New York: Oxford University Press, 1984.

Browder, Laura. *Slippery Characters: Ethnic Impersonators and American Identities.* Chapel Hill: University of North Carolina Press, 2000.

Canti, Camille. "'Pass the Identity, Please': Culinary Passing in America." In *A Tavola: Food, Tradition and Community among Italian Americans,* edited by Edvige Giunta and Samuel J. Patti, 10–19. Staten Island, NY: American Italian Society, 1998.

Conforti, Joseph. *Another City upon a Hill (a New England Memoir).* North Dartmouth, MA: Tagus Press, 2013.

Fagundes, Francisco Cota. "Portuguese Immigrant Experience in America in Autobiography." *Hispania* 88, no. 4 (2005): 701–12.

Feldman-Bianco, Bela. "Saudade, Imigração e a Construção de uma Nação (Portuguesa) Desterritorializada." *Revista Brasileira de Estudos Populares* 9, no. 1 (1992): 35–49.

———. "Multiple Layers of Time and Space: The Construction of Class, Ethnicity, and Nationalism Among Portuguese Immigrants." In *Community, Culture and the Makings of Identity,* edited by Kimberly Da Costa Holton and Andrea Klimt, 51–94. North Dartmouth, MA: Tagus Press, 2009.

Michael, Mia. "New Bedford's Infamous 1983 Rape Case: Defending the Portuguese-American Community." *Historical Journal of Massachusetts* 46, no. 1 (2018): 79–113.

Moniz, Miguel. "The Shadow Minority: An Ethnohistory of Portuguese and Lusophone Racial and Ethnic Identity in New England." In *Community, Culture and the Makings of Identity,* edited by Kimberly Da Costa Holton and Andrea Klimt, 409–30. North Dartmouth, MA: Tagus Press, 2009.

Pap, Leo. *The Portuguese-Americans.* Boston: Portuguese Continental Union of the U.S.A., 1992. First published 1981.

Ramos Villar. "Janus and the Portuguese Emigrant: The Autobiographies of Portuguese Immigrants in the United States." *Luso-Brazilian Review* 49, no. 2 (2012): 232–50.

Silva, Reinaldo. *Representations of the Portuguese in American Literature.* North Dartmouth, MA: Tagus Press, 2008.

Smith, Sidonie, and Julia Watson. *Reading Autobiography: A Guide for Interpreting Life Narratives.* Minneapolis: University of Minnesota Press, 2001.

Taft, Donald. *Two Portuguese Communities in New England.* New York: Arno Press and the *New York Times,* 1967 (1923).

Web sources:

Aguiar, Christian. "The New England Lusophone Archipelago: A New Reading of Azorean-, Cape Verdean– and Portuguese-American Literature." MA thesis, Georgetown University, 2015. https://repository.library.georgetown.edu/bitstream/handle/10822/760843/Aguiar_georgetown_0076M_12981.pdf;sequence=1

Notes

1. Joseph Conforti, *Another City upon a Hill (a New England Memoir)* (North Dartmouth, MA: Tagus Press, 2013).

2. Sidonie Smith and Julia Watson, *Reading Autobiography: A Guide for Interpreting Life Narratives* (Minneapolis: University of Minnesota Press, 2018), 18.

3. Smith and Watson, *Reading Autobiography,* 19.

4. Cristian Aguiar, "The New England Lusophone Archipelago: A New Reading of Azorean-, Cape Verdean– and Portuguese-American Literature," MA thesis, Georgetown University, https://repository.library.georgetown.edu/bitstream/handle/10822/760843/Aguiar_georgetown_0076M_12981.pdf;sequence=1: 20.

5. Aguiar, "The New England Lusophone Archipelago," 31.

6. Carmen Ramos Villar, "Janus and the Portuguese Emigrant: The Autobiographies of Portuguese Immigrants in the United States," *Luso-Brazilian Review* 49, no. 2 (2012): 232–50.

7. Miguel Moniz, "The Shadow Minority: An Ethnohistory of Portuguese and Lusophone Racial and Ethnic Identity in New England," in *Community, Culture and the Makings of Identity,* ed. Kimberly Da Costa Holton and Andrea Klimt, 409–30 (North Dartmouth, MA: Tagus Press, 2009), 412.

8. Donald Taft, *Two Portuguese Communities in New England* (New York: Arno Press and the *New York Times, 1923).*

9. Cristiana Bastos, "Migrants, Inequalities and Social Research in the 1920s: the Story of *Two Portuguese Communities in New England,*" *History and Anthropology* 29, no. 2 (2018): 1–21.

10. Bastos, "Migrants, Inequalities and Social Research," 2.

11. Bastos, "Migrants, Inequalities and Social Research," 11–12

12. Bastos, "Migrants, Inequalities and Social Research," 14.

13. Mia Michael, "New Bedford's Infamous 1983 Rape Case: Defending the Portuguese-American Community," *Historical Journal of Massachusetts* 46, no. 1 (2018): 82. See also Moniz, "The Shadow Minority," 419.

14. Michael, "New Bedford's Infamous 1983 Rape Case," 89.

15. Michael, "New Bedford's Infamous 1983 Rape Case," 104–5.

16. Michael, "New Bedford's Infamous 1983 Rape Case," 105.

17. Conforti, *Another City upon a Hill*, 5.

18. Conforti, *Another City upon a Hill*, 18.

19. Conforti, *Another City upon a Hill*, 124.

20. Conforti, *Another City upon a Hill*, 109. In this passage, Conforti also describes the Portuguese community's ethnic Catholicism as encompassing the worship of the image of Fátima, the *festa* for St. Anthony, and the placement of the statue of the Virgin Mary in front of the house.

21. Conforti, *Another City upon a Hill*, 102.

22. Conforti, *Another City upon a Hill*, 103.

23. Conforti, *Another City upon a Hill*, 108–9.

24. Conforti, *Another City upon a Hill*, 52.

25. Conforti, *Another City upon a Hill*, 39.

26. Bastos, "Migrants, Inequalities and Social Research."

27. Aguiar, "The New England Lusophone Archipelago," 14.

28. Conforti, *Another City upon a Hill*, 38.

29. Conforti, *Another City upon a Hill*, 54.

30. Conforti, *Another City upon a Hill*, 55.

31. Camille Canti, "'Pass the Identity, Please': Culinary Passing in America," in *A Tavola: Food, Tradition and Community Among Italian Americans*, ed. Edvige Giunta and Samuel J. Patti, 10–19 (Staten Island, NY: American Italian Society, 1998).

32. Conforti, *Another City upon a Hill*, 51.

33. Conforti, *Another City upon a Hill*, 64.

34. Conforti, *Another City upon a Hill*, 57.

35. Conforti, *Another City upon a Hill*, 67, 85.

36. Conforti, *Another City upon a Hill*, 94–95.

37. Conforti, *Another City upon a Hill*, 123.

38. Conforti, *Another City upon a Hill*, 89.

39. Conforti, *Another City upon a Hill*, 168–69.

40. Conforti, *Another City upon a Hill*, 123.

41. Conforti, *Another City upon a Hill*, xi.

42. Smith and Watson, *Reading Autobiography*, 10.

43. Aguiar, "The New England Lusophone Archipelago," 39.

44. These range from his quoting of scholarly works to fill in the story of Fall River (see p. 15), to his brother's documentation of his parents' life through interviews, notes, and documents to reconstruct the family history (see p. 30)—a letter and book of accounts within them, which he reproduces as an example of his father's tenacity (see p. 44), even referring to his brother's MA thesis on the Italian community in Fall River (see p. 32).

45. Conforti, *Another City upon a Hill*, 199–200.

46. Conforti, *Another City upon a Hill*, 201–2.

47. Smith and Watson, *Reading Autobiography*, 56.

48. Aguiar, "The New England Lusophone Archipelago," 49.

49. Aguiar, "The New England Lusophone Archipelago," 50.

50. Aguiar, "The New England Lusophone Archipelago," 74.

51. Aguiar, "The New England Lusophone Archipelago," 43.

52. Conforti, *Another City upon a Hill*, xi.

53. Conforti, *Another City upon a Hill*, 159.

54. Conforti, *Another City upon a Hill*, 161.

55. William Boelhower. *Through a Glass Darkly: Ethnic Semiosis in American Literature* (New York: Oxford University Press, 1984), 138–39.

56. Smith and Watson, *Reading Autobiography*, 26.

57. Boelhower, *Through a Glass Darkly*, 108.

58. Smith and Watson, *Reading Autobiography*, 20–21.

59. Reinaldo Silva. *Representations of the Portuguese in American Literature* (North Dartmouth, MA: Tagus Press, 2008).

60. See Bastos, "Migrants, Inequalities and Social Research"; Michael, "New Bedford's Infamous 1983 Rape Case"; Moniz, "The Shadow Minority"; Bela Feldman-Bianco. "Saudade, Imigração e a Construção de uma Nação (Portuguesa) Desterritorializada," *Revista Brasileira de Estudos Populares* 9, no. 1 (1992): 35–49; and Bela Feldman-Bianco, "Multiple Layers of Time and Space: The Construction of Class, Ethnicity, and Nationalism Among Portuguese Immigrants," in *Community, Culture and the Makings of Identity*, ed. Kimberly Da Costa Holton and Andrea Klimt, 51–94 (North Dartmouth, MA: Tagus Press, 2009).

61. Bastos, "Migrants, Inequalities and Social Research," 14.

62. Michael, "New Bedford's Infamous 1983 Rape Case," 104–5.

63. Leo Pap, *The Portuguese-Americans* (Boston: Portuguese Continental Union of the U.S.A. 1992 [1981]), 233.

64. See William Boelhower, *Immigrant Autobiography in the United States (Four Versions of the Italian American Self)* (Venezia: Essedue Edizioni, 1982); Laura Browder, *Slippery Characters: Ethnic Impersonators and American Identities* (Chapel Hill: University of North Carolina Press, 2000); Francisco Cota Fagundes, "Portuguese Immigrant Experience in America in Autobiography," *Hispania* 88, no. 4 (2005): 701–12.

CHAPTER 11

From the Portuguese Islands to the Mill City

Social Activism and the Emergence of Community in the Twentieth Century

......

KADY PHELPS-EL MERNISSI

This study of the Portuguese population in Lowell, Massachusetts, begins in the late nineteenth century and analyzes how two distinct periods of immigration patterns affected the city. The first wave brought migrant workers to the area who found employment in the city's cotton mills. The second wave of Portuguese individuals came as a direct result of the Azorean Refugee Act of 1958, introduced in American Congress by then senator, and eventually president John F. Kennedy (D, MA) and Senator John Pastore (D, RI) after the Capelinhos Volcano eruption in Faial, Azores, displaced six thousand people. Furthermore, the Hart-Celler Act in 1965 repealed a broad-based national immigration restriction law in effect since 1925. The ensuing study argues that each cohort of Portuguese immigrants shaped Lowellian culture and that the people who settled here established institutions, practiced traditions, and developed a new culture within the community resulting from the power of organizing.[1]

Lowell, Massachusetts, the birthplace of the Industrial Revolution, needed workers. Periods of immigration brought thousands of laborers to Lowell, nicknamed "the mill city," located on the perimeter of the Merrimack River. The area became incorporated in 1826 and subsequently became a city in 1836. Its landscape became gradually altered by the emergence of textile mills and newly constructed canals. Early industrial producers recruited New

England's women to work in their mills, but upon global recognition of economic opportunity originating from these factories, many migrants arrived seeking employment. Half of the population in Lowell identified as foreign-born by 1900.[2] Migrant workers became the primary source of the region's labor until the 1920s. An influx of Portuguese arrived in Lowell and found employment in the city's cotton mills beginning in the 1890s. "Not coincidentally," says sociologist Jessica Sperling, "it was during this decade that an American consulate was established in the Azores, an area of high Portuguese migration to the United States."[3] The Portuguese migration story is one part of this complex tapestry.[4]

Life in the textile industry provided opportunities, but not without sacrifice. Working in the mills was arduous and compensated poorly. Hazardous factories put the lives of workers at risk, many of whom died from inadequate safety measures. Various maladies spread quickly because of the proximity workers encountered in the mills. The tenements that housed textile workers did not boast any additional amenities; most of the time the homes of workers were shared by numerous families. Although mill workers earned a living wage, most of the wealth accrued from the factories stayed in the hands of mill overseers, who never hesitated to cut the wages of their employees when textile competition emerged throughout Maine and New Hampshire. Mill overseers ensured their profits by cutting production costs heavily and forced their employees to work harder, but without compensation. Lowell historian Mary Blewett stated that "mill agents began to increase the speed of machinery, while giving workers responsibility for third looms and extra spinning frames."[5] Still, workers came and endured the hazardous conditions in exchange for the slightest bit of financial stability. Consequently, a Portuguese community developed in Lowell, as Madeirans and Azoreans brought cultural practices and influenced the city through traditions. During the late nineteenth and early twentieth century, Lowell's Portuguese population consisted of Madeirans and Azoreans, with continental Portuguese not represented among the city's population.[6] This chapter argues that a distinct Portuguese community evolved throughout the twentieth century, developing gradually as more immigrants settled in the region and established several generations of people who shared common migration trajectories and work patterns and engaged in similar interests, philosophies, and community welfare goals.

Personal stories from Portuguese families display how the lives of the Portuguese in Lowell revolved around activism and social engagement. Henry Pestana's narrative portrays how mill work had a generational impact on the workers. Firmo Correa's actions exhibit a Portuguese community that did not hold back in its mutual assistance for its transatlantic and transnational families in the wake of the Capelinhos Volcano eruption in Faial, Azores. Deolinda Mello dedicated her life to teaching immigrants English and assisted them with the immigration process. Finally, Nomesia Iria led unionized movements against unjust conditions at the Prince Macaroni facility. These stories highlight how Portuguese migrants in Lowell valued unrelenting support for the social welfare of the broader community.

Portuguese Beginnings in Lowell: 1890–World War II

The first Portuguese migrants to the United States—beginning as early as the 1700s to the early 1880s and in relation to whaling—came mostly from Faial, Pico, Flores, Corvo, and São Jorge. Over the period from 1890 to 1920, one million Portuguese migrated from their homeland, mostly to Brazil, while 160,000 settled in the United States, many finding their way to New England's burgeoning industrial centers.[7] The first wave of Lowell's Portuguese migration began arriving in the late nineteenth century. Portuguese settling in surrounding coastal towns during the period worked in the whaling industry, which was responsible for migrant employment at the time. The 1890s was a time of transition for Lowell, Massachusetts; the city's textile mills needed new workers due to low employment rates during the American Civil War. New technologies, such as public transportation, allowed individuals to live in established ethnic neighborhoods rather than crowded mill tenements. Before the development of streetcars in Lowell, people in the city walked as their primary method of transportation. In 1889, the Lowell & Suburban Street Railway Company introduced electric streetcar lines with direct routes from downtown into outside neighborhoods. The trolleys stopped throughout downtown Lowell at almost every block, which eased congested sidewalks and made the city more accessible to textile employees. The trolley system revolutionized transportation and made it easier to work in surrounding towns. The Newmarket Mills, located about fifty miles away from Lowell, ran a line between the towns, which allowed Lowell's mill managers to send any surplus employees to Newmarket, New Hampshire, to work whenever Lowell mills did not need them to run production.

By George Kenngott's account in *The Record of a City* (1912), "A large foreign, non-English speaking population has come to Lowell almost entirely during the last twenty-five years."[8] Compared to other areas in Massachusetts with a significant Portuguese population, Lowell was unique. In Fall River and New Bedford, the immigrant population was predominantly Portuguese. In Lowell, however, the city consisted of a wide array of ethnic groups. According to Kenngott, in the early 1900s, there were 20,000 native-born in Lowell, 20,000 French Canadians, 8,000 Greeks, 2,500 Portuguese, 2,500 Jews, 2,000 Poles, 500 Germans, 200 Armenians, 200 Belgians, 200 Syrians, and a few Russians, Lithuanians, and Chinese.[9] Upon moving to Lowell, Portuguese migrants adjusted to living among several populations with each with their own distinct cultural practices.

In 1900, the 17,885 foreign-born Portuguese in Massachusetts were concentrated in six counties, with 63.5 percent in Bristol County (Fall River and New Bedford) and 9.7 percent in Middlesex County (Lowell). By 1920, just over 50,000 foreign-born Portuguese resided in the Commonwealth of Massachusetts, with the highest concentrations in the same two counties. Restrictive legislation enacted by Congress in 1917, 1921 and 1924, dramatically slowed Portuguese arrivals in the United States. For the decade of the 1930s, just 3,329 Portuguese immigrants entered the country. By the 1940s, the number was 7,423, less than 750 people a year.[10]

The first Portuguese immigrants settled in a few distinct neighborhoods in Lowell, primarily Back Central, but also Chapel Hill and the City Hall District. The Portuguese migrating to Lowell during this time were from the Atlantic islands, either from Madeira or the Azores. These individuals typically had agrarian backgrounds, so mill work was quite different from the work to which they were previously accustomed. Although the Portuguese lived in a concentrated area, they were located only minutes away from the Polish, Greek, Jewish, and French districts. As industrialization in New England developed, so did the Portuguese community in Lowell. Mill workers faced horrendous conditions at the factories but had to persevere through the work to afford their homes. Those who saved enough money eventually moved out of tenement housing and into less populous areas. Typically, ethnic groups relocated to part of the city called Centralville, which is located north of downtown and across the Merrimack River. Those who could not

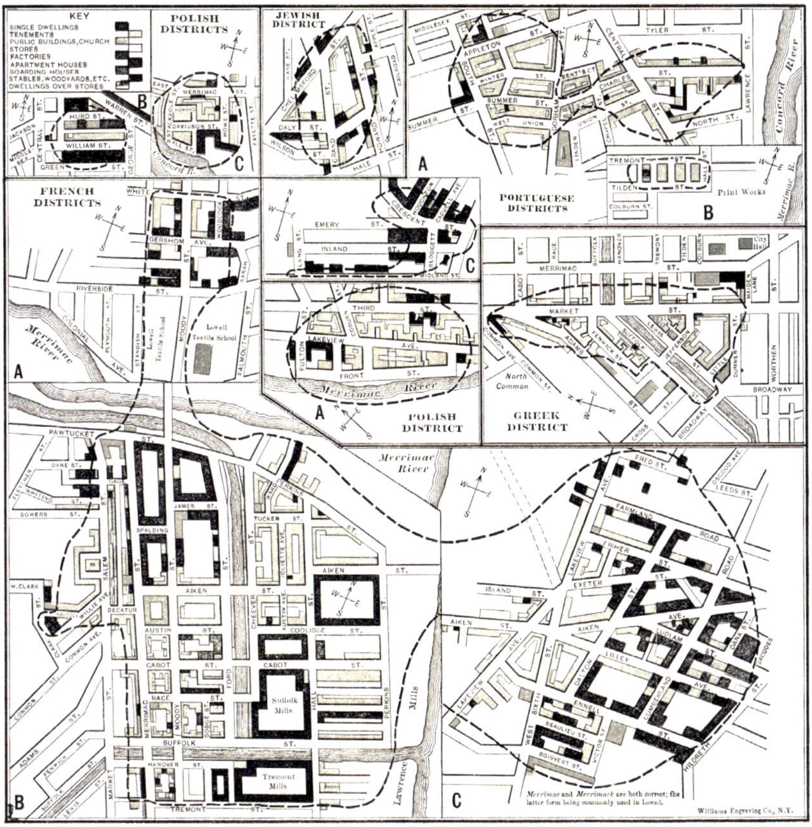

Figure 1. Ethnic Districts, 1912 from "Record of a city" by George F. Kenngott. Collection of the Lowell Historical Society.

afford nicer housing lived in tenements and eventually moved into housing projects.

The money earned from mill work gave some the opportunity to build a different life in the city. Kenngott remarked that he noticed Portuguese immigrants established homes throughout the city and made Portuguese districts through the patterns of these settlements. He noted that some areas of the community were "old and dilapidated" but others had "neat and attractive homes, which are reminders of their native homes in the beautiful Azores."[11] Kenngott had a favorable perception of the Portuguese and recognized that any of the negative aspects of the Portuguese community arose from overcrowded tenements and overworked people.

Cultural practices and institutions of the Azorean and Madeirense mill workers of Lowell took root in the city in the early twentieth century. Like Irish migrants who had earlier established St. Patrick's parish in the Acre neighborhood, a Portuguese Catholic Parish was founded in Back Central. A cohort of nine hundred Portuguese individuals visited Reverend Anthony J. Pimentel in East Cambridge, Massachusetts, to seek guidance on creating a center of worship in Lowell in 1901. With his guidance, the Portuguese Lowellians purchased a small church from the Methodists and used the building for mass. Azorean Reverend Joaquim V. Rosa became the church's first pastor. However, the church could not accommodate the rapidly increasing number of Portuguese individuals who desired to practice Catholicism. As more people settled in Lowell, fundraising for a larger building commenced through the donations of prominent Portuguese individuals. Laborers had built St. Anthony of Padua on Lowell's Central Street, where by 1907 it had become a focal point for the Portuguese Catholics in the community. The church opened on May 30, 1908, and remains the city's largest ethnic parish. The church served as a place to not only worship God; it also helped bring people together in the city. Every year, the church celebrates the Feast of the Holy Ghost with a lively procession among the streets in Back Central. The socioreligious festival also serves as a secular way to congregate within the Portuguese community. As Jerry R. Williams described:

> The celebration of the Feast of the Holy Ghost, the major celebration in Azorean communities, usually lasted for several days and provided ample opportunities to dance the chamarrita, and other traditional dances, to listen to the singing contests between extemporaneous composers, to renew old acquaintances, and to strengthen family ties. The festa concluded on Sunday, with a procession through the streets of the city. Led by a band, the procession included groups of men carrying the statues of saints from the church, followed by members of the various religious fraternities. The parade terminated at the church where a High Mass was conducted in Portuguese for the participants and other members of the community. The festa concluded with the serving of a traditional meal of meat and bread to the entire community.[12]

These and other Portuguese community association festivals provided abundant opportunities to meet with friends and family, bond over music and food, and escape from the toils of mill work.

From 1919 through 1922, a regular column about the Portuguese community in Lowell titled "Ecos de Lowell" appeared in *A Alvorada Diária*, a Portuguese American daily newspaper, providing a glimpse of Portuguese cultural activities. Associations and societies included the Funchalense Club e Musica, the Club Perola do Atlantico, the Lisbon Social Club, the Club Lusitano, the Sociedade D. Maria Amélia (a woman's club), the Sociedade São João Baptista, the Sociedade São José, and the Sociedade Beneficente de Santo Antônio. These institutions allowed Portuguese individuals to meet others with similar backgrounds as themselves.[13]

The International Institute of Lowell helped immigrant families adjust to life in Massachusetts by providing assistive services and organizing community events. Those who went to the International Institute of Lowell for assistance received guidance on adjusting to life in the city. This organization, founded in 1919, helped immigrant families adjust to life in Massachusetts, organizing community events and promoting services that helped newcomers in the city in their transition to their new city. The International Institute offered language and naturalization classes to help immigrants obtain U.S. citizenship. It also provided cooking classes, featuring recipes from different ethnic groups from all over Lowell. These activities gave Portuguese women the chance to meet other women, forging friendships over food at the institute. From 1958 to 1980 Deolinda Mello, whose parents migrated to work in Lowell, served as the executive director of the International Institute, having a direct hand in assisting Portuguese and other migrant groups in Lowell during an expanded period of the settlement.

Mello studied library science at the University of Rhode Island and Lowell State Teachers College, working as a librarian at the Lowell General Hospital School of Nursing while teaching English in an adult literacy program. The English classes Mello taught helped Portuguese speakers learn English, allowing them to communicate with other existing populations in Lowell, a skill especially important to business owners.[14]

Immigrants opened various businesses throughout the Portuguese district, including Silva & Barreiro's Fish Market, Joao Rocha's general store, Agência de Livros Alvorada Bookstore, Jose Ferreira's shoe shop, Antonio Silva's cord wood delivery, and the Lisbon Barber Shop. The Portuguese created a district that allowed one to carry out daily tasks without the need to venture out into other areas of Lowell. However, most Portuguese Lowellians learned English through classes offered at the International Institute or from working alongside English speakers. Interactions among migrants from other parts of the globe were common. This is seen in the life of Manuel Pestana, who lived in the Portuguese district but opened businesses in the French section of Lowell.

In March 1911, Manuel and Hilda Alves Pestana boarded the Italian ship SS *Sannio* from their home in Funchal, Madeira, to go to Boston, Massachusetts, for their honeymoon, but they ended up remaining and settling in Lowell where they had family,[15] living in the Back Central neighborhood nicknamed "Portuguese Broadway" because of the large Portuguese population. Before settling in Lowell, Manuel Pestana had worked on an English ship, which allowed him to learn multiple languages. Henry Pestana, Manuel and Hilda's eldest son, claimed that his father was "the only one at that time that provided insurance to the Portuguese people in Lowell. And where he spoke four or five different languages, he even had the Italians and the French insured."[16] Henry Pestana's perceptions were based on childhood experiences; he vividly remembered traveling around town with his father at Christmas time to hand out Metropolitan Life Insurance–sponsored calendars as advertisements around the city. He felt impressed that his father could speak so many languages and could talk to most of the ethnic groups who lived in Lowell. Manuel Pestana worked for Metropolitan Life Insurance for twelve years before opening Pestana's Luncheon on Charles Street. Before opening Pestana's Luncheon, Manuel Pestana owned a small restaurant in the French district, which he named Bon Ami ("good friend" in French) Lunch, although business did not do well there. Manuel Pestana never worked in the textile industry; however, his wife, Hilda Alves Pestana, worked in New Hampshire at the Newmarket Mills. She left that job as soon as the Pestana family felt financially stable, not too long after settling in Lowell, which proved necessary, since she had to take care of her ten children that she had over the course of a decade.[17] When the Pestana children were old enough, they too, worked in the mills.

Strikes, protests, and demonstrations historically resulted in positive social change throughout American history. The formation of labor unions had a profound effect on the lives of Portuguese mill workers and served as a vital tool to advocate for labor rights. Many workers in the Portuguese community joined the Industrial Workers of the World (IWW) Local Union 436 and organized labor strikes. Strikes in surrounding mill towns often occurred concurrently, like in the case of the 1912 Bread and Roses strike in Lawrence,

Figure 2. "Law and Order in Lawrence," *Collier's Weekly,* March 9, 1912

which influenced the subsequent textile strike in Lowell shortly afterward, and other subsequent industrial strikes throughout the region, such as the 1928 New Bedford textile workers strike and the 1933 Lowell shoe strike.[18] The strikes proved that civil conflicts could help workers obtain their goals when unified. With help from Elizabeth Gurley Flynn, an organizer from the IWW, the workers had the guidance that helped obtain a settlement.

Elizabeth Gurley Flynn proudly advocated for free speech and workers' rights; in 1909, she chained herself to a lamppost to elongate her protest and deter police from arresting her. Flynn traveled throughout the country to participate in protests of labor workers, despite constant criticism and sexism regarding her beliefs. Much of the public did not approve of her protests because of the universal belief that women's work should be primarily domestic. Flynn described the reactions of the public concerning the advancement of women's rights: "Suffragist speakers on street corners were invariably told: 'Go home and wash your dishes,' or, regardless of their age: 'Who's taking care of your children?'"[19] Despite the lack of support for her lifestyle, Flynn devoted her life to activism. She gained approval by soliciting the crowd's interest because she spoke with intelligence and charisma. Flynn went to Lawrence in January 1912 to assist and encourage workers of the textile mills to protest the dishonest practices of the industry.

Figure 3. The Pestana family: Henry, Eric, Beverly, Karen, and Norbert, November 1957. Courtesy of the Pestana Family Collection.

The 1912 Bread and Roses strike, which included Portuguese mill workers, abruptly began on January 11 when textile laborers discovered they had received faulty paychecks. Lawrence mill employees were angry with a new law that decreased the standard fifty-six-hour workweek to fifty-four hours as it reduced their pay. Although the law forbade mills from cutting their employees' weekly salary, workers discovered that an average deduction of $0.32 had come out from their pay. Previously, workers earned $8.76 for fifty-six hours of work; the wages were low, considering the long hours and high mortality rate for employees.[20] The workers demanded that they receive a 15 percent increase in wages and increased pay for overtime.[21]

The city of Lawrence did not support the strike. Mayor Michael Scanlon responded to the protest by sending militia to the streets. The harsh conditions of frigid January weather created difficulty for the strikers; the situation worsened when millowners sprayed the protesters with fire hoses. In response, the strikers threw glass shards at the plants, breaking the windows. Mayor Michael Scanlon could not handle the protesters, stating, "We will either break this strike or break the strikers' heads."[22]

Flynn helped devise a plan that made the strike a success by gaining national attention. The IWW sent hungry children of protesters to wealthy families who supported the strike throughout the upper Northeast. The tactic worked because it generated sympathy and reduced costs for protesting mill parents. She also established services by obtaining volunteers to help arrange necessities and funds to sustain the protestors, including food and medical care. The IWW collected nationwide funding to send more children to New York and Philadelphia; however, the police blocked the attempt. Police attacked the women and children waiting to go to their temporary homes at the train station. Law enforcement violently arrested thirty-five women and children, beating them until they could not fight back any longer. Enraged strikers filled the police station in protest. The police department charged the women with neglect.[23]

Flynn stated: "It was a day without parallel in American labor history. A reign of terror prevailed in Lawrence, which literally shook America."[24] This is a great example of how immigration has been a no-win situation in the lengthy history of the American labor movement.

Elizabeth Gurley Flynn's declaration was correct; the press, already attracted to the storyline of the children's exodus, documented the brutality extensively in the media, gaining the attention of first lady Helen Herron Taft. The House of Representatives and the Senate immediately began an intense investigation of the strike.[25] The city of Lawrence faced national embarrassment. Newspapers ran stories describing the disheartening scene that occurred at the train station. *Collier's Weekly's* political cartoon gained the attention of newspaper readers with cartoonist Art Young's illustration, called "Law and Order in Lawrence," that depicted a police officer brutally hitting a group of women and children with a bloody club. Young labeled the illustration "The hunger city. Dividends for millowners—starvation wages for workers." Although the children never made it to their temporary homes to continue Flynn's style of protest, the media's attention instigated public concern for the mill workers in Lawrence.

The national attention led to victory; millowners responded to the negative press by giving in to the demands of strikers. Millowners increased the weekly wage 15 percent, adjusted the workforce to decrease stress on the workers, agreed to avoid discrimination of strikers, and ended premium systems, an unjust practice limiting wages depending on one's attendance and production of textiles. Other mills throughout New England followed suit because of the threat of counterstrikes.[26] The protest officially ended March 14, 1912, lasting through the most brutal months of winter.

The 1912 Bread and Roses strike in Lawrence had a profound effect on the Portuguese and played a critical role in building the twentieth-century labor movement. Upon seeing the victory that had occurred just a few towns over, Portuguese Lowellians had organized their own strike to demand higher salaries and improved working conditions. Flynn traveled to Lowell upon hearing about the strike and wrote that "the leaders of the strike were Portuguese."[27] Flynn planned to speak at the local IWW hall to help guide protesters. When she arrived at the hall, the IWW chairman asked Flynn what languages she spoke. When she replied that she only spoke English, "He looked disappointed, and said: 'They won't understand,'' meaning that since many Portuguese individuals had not yet learned English, there may be a communication issue, especially since the Portuguese were the ones who led the movement.[28] The Portuguese did not need Flynn's assistance to unionize. Flynn noted that the Portuguese had taken to the streets to run a picket line, where they played musical instruments such as flutes, violins, and the triangle to gain the public's attention while they shouted their own slogans. Flynn claimed that the addition of music to the picket line was in part due to the belief that it brings good fortune to the textile strikers and bad luck to their bosses.[29] The strikers obtained a 10 percent raise, and although they felt upset that they had not received 15 percent, the mill workers in Lowell settled, hoping that the strike had impacted millowners and that they would eventually be more lucrative with wages. The early textile strikes of the twentieth century set a precedent for Portuguese Lowellians, who practice civic activism to this day. The 1912 Lowell textile strike marked the beginning of a trend fueled by Portuguese workers of Lowell to be part of a broader social process and helped facilitate the act of mutual assistance among local institutions.

The textile industry remained a powerful Industry over the next two decades, and mill work remained a reliable job for those seeking employment even among workers born in Lowell to migrant parents like the Pestana's son Henry, who obtained a job at the Newmarket Mills in New Hampshire. Pestana worked as a filling hand and learned how to appreciate the intricacies of textile production. Despite the difficulty of mill work and hazardous conditions in the factory. Pestana found the entire process fascinating and appreciated that his job provided him with experience necessary to work well in other positions.

Pestana stated, "Working in the weave department did teach me a lot about efficiency, how to work among machines and things, cause I wound up working places where you had to have efficiency."[30] Pestana believed that the mill operations were impressive because he saw that the combined efforts of employees resulted in greater production.[31]

Pestana's fascination with mill work and the textile industry was nevertheless accompanied by frustration with the millowners and management, as became evident when the United States joined World War II and industrial mill work in Lowell declined.

The labor of global migrants that had made Lowell the center of industrialization soon abated. During the mid-nineteenth century, Lowell had more cotton spindles in the city alone than the entire Confederacy.[32] The textile industry in Lowell declined greatly during 1920–30, disappearing altogether by the mid-twentieth century. Southern textile mills had opened and found greater success because cotton did not have to be transported to the factories where farmers grew the fiber locally. In addition, labor unions had not developed as significantly in the area, influencing mill operators to move their facilities south to avoid having to deal with unionized employees. The Great Depression and World War II had a profound effect on Lowell.

The once industrious city that attracted thousands of migrant workers no longer operated as a manufacturing epicenter. In the early 1930s, Louis Adamic, a reporter from *Harper's Monthly Magazine,* came to Lowell to work on a project about mill towns. Regarding Lowell he wrote, "I had a creepy feeling as I walked through some of the streets. . . . I saw broken window panes pasted over with paper, the residents, apparently, being too poor to replace them."[33]

Between 1919 and 1939, Massachusetts lost 45 percent of its textile jobs. The demand for servicemen seized mill workers from their jobs, with many of them drafted to serve in World War II. Most of these servicemen did not reenter the textile industry because it did not offer the same opportunities as it previously had. Many of the cotton mills had either ceased operations entirely or changed business models. To compensate, during the war effort, many factories focused on parachute production. Life in Lowell changed dramatically during this period because of mill closures, which forced immigrants to reconsider employment and community life in the city. In the period of global economic depression in the 1920s–30s, Portuguese immigration to the United States slowed to a trickle. In addition, Portuguese Lowellians faced the prospect of threatened livelihoods as a result of factory closures.

Henry Pestana stopped working in the mills in the early 1940s when he entered the United States Navy to serve during World War II. Upon leaving the textile industry, his boss promised that he would save his job for when he returned after the war. Upon his arrival back in Lowell, however, Pestana said, "My job was promised. When I came back out they had eliminated my job and they had tied it into a loom fixer's job. So the loom fixer was doing two jobs under the 'patriotic system,' they called it."[34] Pestana's boss offered him a position for less salary than he had made before he served, which influenced him to quit. A mill career that spanned from the days of Lowell's first large-scale Azorean and Madeiran migration had come to an end alongside the Industrial Era in Lowell. Upon leaving the textile industry, Pestana found employment through General Electric Wiring, an electronics company. He noticed the undeniable differences between textile production and working at General Electric: "Where production was tops, you had to produce. Today, people have jobs but they don't really produce. They know things, but when it comes to producing production, I don't see how they do it. Electronics and all that has a different way of producing what you don't see; it isn't visible like it is when you're producing cloth."[35]

The Second Wave of Portuguese Immigration: Post–World War II to 2000

Over 1957 and 1958, the Capelinhos Volcano erupted in Faial, Azores, Portugal, leading to two hundred subsequent earthquakes that brought great devastation to the island and other parts of the archipelago. The destruction ruined the economy and businesses of the residents as the harsh effects of the lava and ensuing volcanic plume halted food production on the island and led to widespread suffering. The eruptions buried businesses, farmland, and homes under tons of ash. With unusable farmland, little food supply, and a dangerous environment, the number of incoming visitors declined, further damaging the economy. Residents were forced to abandon their homes and look elsewhere to make a living and to provide for themselves and their families.

In the wake of the Capelinhos volcanic eruption, migrants and their children from the islands who lived in Lowell advocated locally to assist friends and family back in the Azores. Lowell resident Firmo Correa, for example, wrote to then Massachusetts senator John F. Kennedy and asked for assistance for Azoreans after the natural disaster. In his letter, Correa asked Kennedy to use political pressure to declare the Azorean residents refugees and allow them to enter the United States unencumbered by restrictive migration quotas for migrants from Portugal. Correa told Kennedy: "These poor people are in a terrible state at the present time and need help immediately."[36] In their subsequent correspondence, an at-first skeptical Kennedy asked for evidence of the conditions that transpired because of the volcanic eruption, prompting Correa to educate the senator about the situation by sending him Azorean newspaper articles. In a June Senate floor statement Kennedy claimed, "Everywhere within a four-mile radius the lava and ash spread fear and destruction," urging fellow politicians to pass the bill. The passage of this legislation was a beginning to the eventual end to harsh quotas that had been in effect since 1924, when the federal Immigration Act of 1924 dramatically slowed the entry of new immigrants to the country. The law's quota system made it particularly hard for immigrants from eastern and southern Europe, including Portugal, to enter the United States.[37]

The first significant upsurge in new Portuguese arrivals in the United States came after the 1957 and 1958 Faial Island volcano eruptions ruined the island's economy. Senator John F. Kennedy (D, MA), and John O. Pastore (D, RI), along with others in Congress drafted the 1958 and 1960 Azorean Refugee Acts, permitting the admission of Azoreans in excess of existing federal immigration quotas. This marked what many called the second stage of Portuguese migration to the United States. The Azorean Refugee Act initiated the migration of 175,000 Azoreans to the United States within a twenty-year period.[38]

The first family to arrive in Lowell because of the legislature passed was Antonio Mello and his family. They came to Lowell in early June, sponsored by Mrs. Jose Boldeia, Mello's sister, who lived in the city already. Lowell residents volunteered to bring eight families over from the island. Upon arrival, Mello quickly became employed, with the *Lowell Sun* reporting, "Although accustomed to farming, raising and selling corn, Mr. Mello has already started assembly line work at the Wakefield Industries, Inc."[39] Economic conditions improved in the United States during the 1950s; however, they deteriorated in that period in the Azores. In the 1960s, as the Portuguese government attempted to redirect the movement of labor migration from the United States to Europe "webs of kinship made way for the continuous arrival of new Portuguese contingents (mostly from the Azores and, to a lesser degree, Portuguese mainland) to the United States."[40] Between the 1960s and 1980s, American governmental policies enabled many families to reunite in New England.

After serving out President Kennedy's first term, Lyndon B. Johnson began looking into passing some of the migration laws that JFK had previously in his agenda, ending with the passage of the Hart-Celler Act in 1965, a milestone that abolished national origins quotas and expanded the number of migrants by way of making it easier for family reunification to occur.[41]

As a result of the restrictive migration quotas passed earlier in the century, about 70 percent of the available legal migration slots were designated for those from the United Kingdom, Germany, and Ireland, meaning that on top of the small number of immigrants that were allowed into the country at any given time, the majority of the legal entries went to predominantly white, English-speaking nations.

One of the objectives of the Hart-Celler Act was to transform the rules from favoring migrants from a particular country, making a fairer system based on family reunification and a call for skilled laborers and addressing discrimination against migrants from the largest new migrant groups to have come to in the industrial mill worker period, including the Portuguese.

When signing the Hart-Celler Act of 1965, LBJ swore the bill "will not restructure the shape of our daily lives." Abolishing the quota system in place since the Immigration Act of 1921, however, changed everything for the millions of previously excluded applicants hoping to migrate to the United States. To this day, the bill is still the basis for modern U.S. migration law.[42]

The act facilitated even more Portuguese to migrate to the United States. With an established community in Lowell, New Bedford, and throughout southeastern New England, many of these second-wave migrants came to settle with previously established families in the city.

Working Lives and Civic Activism

The second movement of Portuguese Atlantic Islander immigration that occurred in the 1950s and early 1960s period settled in the Back Central neighborhood of Lowell and in other localities of previous Portuguese migrant generations. Earlier Portuguese migrant laborers originated from Madeira and the Azores, but the second significant migration consisted almost entirely of Azoreans escaping the natural disaster that occurred in the islands in 1957–58. This period found Lowell in the midst of a massive economic and social transformation. Many of the existing neighborhoods had declined and required a significant amount of repair from years of abandonment and lack of upkeep. Beginning in the mid-1960s, Lowell city officials, political elites, wealthy individuals, and the *Lowell Sun* newspaper proposed urban renewal projects for neighborhoods in economic decline, including the Portuguese neighborhood in Back Central.

One of the primary projects proposed included the expansion of a local highway called the Lowell Connector to alleviate traffic congestion inbound and outbound of downtown. The city proposed the removal of numerous commercial and residential buildings throughout South Lowell, including completely removing a portion of Back Central. The expansion of the Lowell Connector would result in an absolute upheaval of the Portuguese community, forcing many to move.[43] Similar highway projects in Fall River, New Bedford, and Providence cut through older Portuguese residential industrial mill communities with disastrous effects.[44]

Organized opposition against the expansion quickly developed in response from the Portuguese community. Most of the individuals who advocated against the Lowell Connector's expansion had lived in the city for decades and had established familiarity with local politics. Newer immigrants did not usually own homes, so most of them did not participate in organized opposition. Leaders of the opposition group included Father John Silva, pastor at St. Anthony's Church, and long-time residents Gladys Picanso, Edward Santos, and Manuel Figueira. Father John Silva informed the neighborhood residents of Back Central of the city's plans of destruction; he urged people to reach out to other ethnic groups in Lowell for support. Seventeen-year-old Azorean immigrant Dimas Espinola, influenced by Father John Silva's requests, served as a language interpreter in the Portuguese community and helped those in need of translation services. The Connector opponents held rallies and formed alliances with community officials and successfully defeated the Lowell Connector expansion project. The alliances the Connector opponents formed greatly influenced the outcome of their actions. Manuel Figueira believed that the combined efforts of people working together is the main reason why their campaign succeeded. He stated, "That's why I say it took the people, the good people [all] over the city to help us!"[45] They organized opposition from the Portuguese community and enforced Portuguese group identities, an important part of collective activism.

Portuguese civic activism increased over the next few decades through the efforts of a group of Portuguese organizers. Joseph Mello Jr., who had advocated against the Lowell Connector Expansion, continued his activist efforts through a campaign that aimed to improve housing conditions in Lowell. Mello, the son of migrants from Portugal, expressed frustration concerning the state of rental housing and pushed for a rent-control program to protect residents. Mello, who served as secretary of the Lowell Central Labor Council, and other rent-control activists faced the strong opposition of Lowell's landlords, businesses, and city officials, who believed that the group's proposed measures were akin to socialist practices. In 1974, the rent control proposal went to the city council but was defeated by a 5–4 vote. The city council, however, soon created a housing review board to assess tenants' complaints and implement resolutions depending on the grievance.[46]

As part of the Lowell urban renewal project the National Park Service recognized the Boott Mills, a former textile mill turned into an industrial history museum, as a historical landmark in 1978. Pestana visited to see how they had reconstructed mills as he remembered working in them. Upon entering the large room full of looms, he noticed that they were not turned on and he asked a park ranger why they were not on. When Pestana learned that no one at the museum actually knew how to operate the looms, he both taught employees how to run them and also made mechanical fixes to the machinery, bringing to life in the museum the deafening sounds of textile production. Pestana volunteered for a few years in the mills and shared his memory of mill work to those willing to listen, collaborating with Lowell historians to provide his account of life during the first half of the twentieth century. Pestana remained passionate about the preservation of the history of the mills and Portuguese community until his death in August 1988.[47]

Like the textile workers before them, post–World War II migrants who settled in Lowell found employment in factories manufacturing clothing, shoes, food, or electronics. Although mill operations in the city have ceased, the grueling nature of work in other kinds of manufacturing persisted. Workers endured extreme conditions in the factories, coping with noisy machinery, strong odors from oils and various chemicals, and lack of temperature control in the buildings, meaning that no heat existed in the winter and no air conditioning in the summer. Supervisors watched employees closely while they performed repetitive tasks. Portuguese workers earned little compensation for their efforts, occupying among the lowest-paid jobs in the factories, receiving pay either at or only slightly above minimum wage.

Most of the laborers in Lowell's manufacturing factories relied on one another to withstand the unforgiving environment of industrial work, especially since little to no unionization occurred in these industries. One of the most prolific companies in Lowell, Prince Macaroni Manufacturing Company, employed over four hundred workers, most of them Portuguese migrants and Lowell-born generations from Portuguese migrant communities. Prince Macaroni had operated in the North End of Boston before beginning its operations in Lowell in 1939, maintaining a significant industrial and cultural presence in the city through the twentieth century. During the Great Depression demand for cheap food staples like pasta caused the business to expand, and the factory moved to Lowell in order to increase production. The company achieved even more success with a highly successful advertising campaign in the early 1950s intended to broaden the pasta market to non-Italians. The slogan "Wednesday Is Prince Spaghetti Day" quickly became a regional cultural phenomenon, encouraging the consumption of pasta as part of New England's popular culture.

The south Lowell site of the factory earned the neighborhood the name Spaghettiville, and the company was an important part of the economic survival of Lowell. Although factory work at Prince Macaroni required persistence and its employees faced arduous conditions, the business became an institution that fostered relationships and networking opportunities for the Portuguese in Lowell. The Pellegrino family, owners of Prince Macaroni, had the reputation of being kind employers because they provided fair wages to those who came to the company with little to no qualifications. Prince Spaghetti pasta worker and Azorean immigrant Nomesia Iria stated, "We come to this place [Lowell], and what we find is work. We find friendship. We find family. The first words of English I learn here. Here is where I become part of America." The factory became synonymous with many Portuguese Lowellians' experience during their first years in America.

The operation of Prince Macaroni changed drastically when New England's chief pasta manufacturer was sold by the Pellegrino family to the Ohio-based Borden Corporation in 1987. The factory workers were left unprotected by the provisions of the Pellegrino's sale of their company, and the new management angered Prince Spaghetti workers when they cut employee benefits and established a twelve-hour workday without the opportunity of overtime compensation. Nomesia Iria initiated a successful unionization effort in response. The machine operator led a movement within the company that united workers together so they could negotiate their working conditions. The Borden Corporation signed a contract with the union, improving wages, health benefits, and the overall working environment within the company. However, within three years of negotiation, Borden declared that it planned on permanently closing the pasta plant in Lowell. This devastated Iria and her coworkers in the plant who campaigned for Prince to remain in the city. Massachusetts Senators John Kerry (D) and Edward Kennedy (D) intervened and attempted to find an outside company to purchase the plant. Boston Macaroni, a company formed by prior managers, investors, and unionized workers of Prince, offered to buy the Lowell company; however, the deal was dismantled when the Borden Corporation refused to sell the Prince name. Prince Macaroni Manufacturing ceased its operations in Lowell in 1997. Iria stated, "It's very sad to see a brand that belonged to Lowell be made someplace else like Montreal or Ohio . . . to me, it's sad—that blue box belongs to Lowell." When Iria learned that the company would close in Lowell, she asked if she could purchase one of the last boxes of pasta manufactured in the plant as a keepsake, believing that it would be "part of history."

This study touches upon three important contributions; through the power of organizing immigrants were welcomed into the ranks of labor, validating their struggle for equality and unity.

It shows how Portuguese immigrants played a critical role as part of the American labor movement, by the same token revealing how immigration has been a no-win situation in the history of the American labor movement. Last but not least, it shows how social cohesion and social activism helped give Portuguese immigrants a voice through the processes of social justice.

Throughout the twentieth century, Lowell's Portuguese population cultivated a distinct community; they unified based on similar identities and affinities. The Portuguese naturally convened together because they shared similar experiences. The first cohort of Portuguese migrants came from either the Azores or Madeira and endured the transition from agrarian work to industrialized life in Lowell. The Portuguese set a precedent in 1912 during the Lowell textile mill strike and began a social activist trend among the ethnic group that lasted throughout the twentieth century. After the collapse of the textile industry, the Portuguese found jobs in new trades, such as General Electric Wiring and Prince Spaghetti pasta manufacturing. A new cohort of Portuguese came as the result of the Azorean Refugee Act of 1958, bringing an entirely new group of Portuguese migrants to the city. The Hart-Celler Act of 1965 widened the parameters for immigration and made Lowell appealing to Portuguese residents from the mainland. This new group settled among an existing Portuguese community and had access to its established institutions. Portuguese mainlanders had experience with labor movements, which encouraged some of them to participate in labor movements in Lowell, such as the Lowell Connector strike. Each wave of Portuguese immigration molded Lowellian culture; the migrants who established their lives in the city formed new institutions, practiced traditions, and developed a new culture within the community as a result.

Works Cited

Adamic, Louis. "Tragic Towns of New England." *Harper's Monthly Magazine*, May 1931.

Blewett, Mary. *The Last Generation: Work and Life in the Textile Mills of Lowell, Massachusetts, 1910–1960.* Amherst: University of Massachusetts Press, 1990.

City Development Authority. Memorandum, "Lowell Community Renewal Program: Action Program," 1972. no. 2003, 045. John Mullen Collection. Lowell Historical Society, Lowell, MA.

Correa, Firmo. Letter to John F. Kennedy, n.d., John F. Kennedy Presidential Library and Museum.

Doyle, Michael. "House Resolution Commemorates 1958 Azorean Refugee Act." *McClatchy (Washington DC)*, August 12, 2008. Accessed February 26, 2019. https://www.mcclatchydc.com/news/politics-government/article24495382.html.

Flynn, Elizabeth Gurley. *The Rebel Girl: An Autobiography, My First Life (1906–1926).* New York: International Publishers, 1974.

Forrant, Robert, and Susan Grabski. *Lawrence and the 1912 Bread and Roses Strike.* Charleston, SC: Arcadia Publishing, 2013.

Forrant, Robert, and Christoph Stobel. *Ethnicity in Lowell: Lowell National Historical Park Ethnographic Overview and Assessment.* Boston: Northeast Region Ethnography Program, National Park Service, U.S. Department of the Interior, 2011.

Georgianna, Daniel, and Roberta Hazen Aaronson. *The Strike of '28.* New Bedford, MA: Spinner Publications, 1993.

Goldfarb, Stephen J. "A Note on Limits to Growth of the Cotton-Textile Industry in the Old South." *Journal of Southern History* 48 (1982).

Green, Judi. "Volcanic Eruption Brings Family to the U.S." *Lowell Sun,* June 16, 1959.

Holton, Kimberly DaCosta, and Andrea Klimt, eds. *Community, Culture and the Making of Identity: Portuguese-Americans along the Eastern Seaboard.* Portuguese in the Americas Series. North Dartmouth, MA: Center for Portuguese Studies, 2009.

Kengott, George F. *The Record of a City: A Social Survey of Lowell, Massachusetts.* New York: Macmillan Company, 1912.

"The Legacy of the 1965 Immigration Act: Three Decades of Mass Immigration." Center for Immigration Studies. Last modified September 1, 1995. Accessed March 1, 2019. https://cis.org/Report/Legacy-1965-Immigration-Act.

Mahoney, Molly, Kady Phelps, Robert Forrant, Frank Sousa, and Gray Fitzsimons. *From the Atlantic Islands to Lowell, MA: Continuity and Change in the Mill City's Portuguese Community.* Lowell, MA: Saab Center for Portuguese Studies, 2018.

Marcos, Daniel. *The Capelinhos Eruption: Window of Opportunity for Azorean Emigration.* Providence, RI: Gávea-Brown, 2008.

Marion, Paul. "Timeline of Lowell History from 1600s to 2009." *Yankee Magazine,* November 2009.

Moniz, Miguel. "Change and Tradition in Fox Point: Echoes of the Past in the Spirit of Community." In *Portuguese Spinner: An American Story,* edited by Marsha McCabe and Joseph Thomas, 178–85. New Bedford, MA: Spinner Publications, 1998.

Moran, William. *The Belles of New England: The Women of the Textile Mills and the Families Whose Wealth They Wove.* New York: St. Martin's Press, 2002.

Phelps, Karen Pestana. Interview with the author. Dracut, MA. October 1, 2018.

Rocha, Edward. "The Lowell Shoe Strike in 1933." In *Surviving Hard Times,* edited by Mary Blewett. Lowell, MA: Lowell Museum, 1982.

Sperling, Jessica. "Portuguese and Portuguese Americans, 1870–1940." In *Immigrants in American History: Arrival, Adaptation, and Integration,* edited by Elliot R. Barkin, 563–74. Santa Barbara, CA: ABC-CLIO, 2013.

University of Massachusetts Lowell. "Portuguese Record Images." Library Guides: Center for Lowell History. Accessed February 24, 2019. https://libguides.uml.edu/c.php?g=492497&p=3447082.

U.S. Congress. Report on Strike of Textile Workers in Lawrence, Mass in 1912, H.R. Rep. No. 62nd, 2d Sess.

Watson, Bruce. *Bread and Roses: Mills, Migrants, and the Struggle for American Dream.* New York: Penguin Books, 2005.

Williams, Jerry R. *And Yet They Come: Portuguese Immigration from the Azores to the United States.* New York: Center for Migration Studies, 1982.

Notes

1. Personal stories from the Portuguese community from Henry Pestana, Firmo Correa, Deolinda Mello, and Nomesia Iria display how Portuguese life evolved in Lowell. The individual accounts provide insight into how ethnic districts impacted life in the city while simultaneously fostering a new group identity. This study is an important contribution, because it serves as a testimony on how social cohesion and social activism helped give the Portuguese immigrants a voice through the processes of social justice. I first explored these ideas in an exhibition I coauthored entitled "From the Atlantic Islands to Lowell, MA: Continuity and Change in the Mill City's Portuguese Community" for the Saab Center for Portuguese Studies. Portions of this chapter come from the exhibition, which is now part of the Saab Center for Portuguese Studies of Lowell's permanent archive. The personal stories from Henry Pestana, Firmo Correa, Deolinda Mello, and Nomesia Iria arose during the research completed for the exhibition. I am grateful for my research team for that project that made this chapter possible, notably, Robert Forrant, Frank Sousa, Molly Mahoney, and Gray Fitzsimmons. Furthermore, thank you to Henrique Amaral for help with Portuguese-English translation.

2. Paul Marion, "Timeline of Lowell History From the 1600s to 2009," *Yankee Magazine*, November 2009.

3. Jessica Sperling, "Portuguese and Portuguese-Americans, 1870–1940," in *Immigrants in American History: Arrival, Adaptation, and Integration*, ed. Elliot R. Barkin (Santa Barbara: ABC-CLIO, 2013), 563.

4. For more information about ethnography in Lowell, Massachusetts, see University of Massachusetts Lowell History Department (Robert Forrant and Christoph Strobel), *Ethnicity in Lowell: Lowell National Historical Park Ethnographic Overview and Assessment* (Boston: Northeast Region Ethnography Program, National Park Service, U.S. Department of the Interior, 2011).

5. Mary Blewett, *The Last Generation: Work and Life in the Textile Mills of Lowell, Massachusetts, 1910–1960* (Amherst: University of Massachusetts Press, 1990), 4.

6. For more about Portuguese demographic data in the late nineteenth and early twentieth century, see the Center for Lowell History's collection of immigration documents, University of Massachusetts Lowell, "Portuguese Record Images," Library Guides, Center for Lowell History. Accessed February 24, 2019. https://libguides.uml.edu/c.php?g=492497&p=3447082.

7. Molly Mahoney et al., *From the Atlantic Islands to Lowell, MA: Continuity and Change in the Mill City's Portuguese Community* (Lowell, MA: Saab Center for Portuguese Studies, 2018).

8. George F. Kenngott, *The Record of a City: A Social Survey of Lowell, Massachusetts* (New York: Macmillan Company, 1912), 28.

9. Kengott, *The Record of a City*, 28.

10. Jerry R. Williams, *And Yet They Come: Portuguese Immigration from the Azores to the United States* (New York: Center for Migration Studies, 1982), 115–16.

11. Kenngott, *The Record of a City*, 53.

12. Williams, *And Yet They Come*, 20.

13. Mahoney et al., *From the Atlantic Islands to Lowell.*

14. Mahoney et al., *From the Atlantic Islands to Lowell.*

15. For an oral history account of the Pestana family's history, see Blewett, *The Last Generation*, 192–200.

16. Blewett, *The Last Generation*, 192–200.

17. Olga Pestana and Angelina Pestana died in 1918 as toddlers.

18. The inspiration for the name of the movement originated from a speech by Rose Schneiderman. Schneiderman stated, "The worker must have bread, but she must have roses, too." Schneiderman's declaration emphasized the nature of the strike, making it the perfect name for the movement. For more information about the New Bedford textile strike of 1928, see Daniel Georgianna and Roberta Hazen Aaronson, *The Strike of '28* (New Bedford: Spinner Publications, 1993). For more information about the 1933 Lowell shoe strike, see Edward Rocha, "The Lowell Shoe Strike in 1933," in *Surviving Hard Times*, ed. Mary Blewett (Lowell, MA: Lowell Museum, 1982), 115.

19. Elizabeth Gurley Flynn, *The Rebel Girl: An Autobiography, My First Life (1906–1926)* (New York: International Publishers, 1974), 57.

20. William Moran, *The Belles of New England: The Women of the Textile Mills and the Families Whose Wealth They Wove* (New York: St. Martin's Press, 2002), 183.

21. Bruce Watson, *Bread and Roses: Mills, Migrants, and the Struggle for the American Dream* (New York: Penguin Books, 2005), 71.

22. Robert Forrant and Susan Grabski, *Lawrence and the 1912 Bread and Roses Strike* (Charleston, SC: Arcadia Publishing, 2013), 44.

23. Flynn, *The Rebel Girl*, 138.

24. Flynn, *The Rebel Girl*, 138.

25. U.S. Congress, Senate, Report on Strike of Textile Workers in Lawrence, Mass in 1912, report prepared by Chas. P. Neill, 62nd Cong., 2d sess., 1912, Government Print, 19.

26. Forrant and Grabski, *Lawrence and the 1912 Bread and Roses Strike*, 95.

27. Flynn, *The Rebel Girl*, 145.

28. Flynn, *The Rebel Girl*, 145.

29. Flynn, *The Rebel Girl*, 145.

30. Blewett, *The Last Generation*, 200.

31. Historian Mary Blewett described Pestana's responsibilities in *The Last Generation*: working in the drawing-in-room deepened Pestana's appreciation of the process of production. His job as a warp rigger was to place beams wound with warp threads into

the backs of empty looms and draw the warp through the harnesses. His partner ran an automatic knot-tying machine, technology that largely eliminated the relatively well-paid work of drawing-in girls.

32. Stephen J. Goldfarb, "A Note on Limits to Growth of the Cotton-Textile Industry in the Old South," *Journal of Southern History* 48 (1982): 545.

33. Louis Adamic, "Tragic Towns of New England," *Harper's Monthly Magazine,* May 1931, 751.

34. Blewett, *The Last Generation,* 199.

35. Blewett, *The Last Generation,* 200.

36. Firmo Correa to John F. Kennedy, n.d., John F. Kennedy Presidential Library and Museum.

37. See Daniel Marcos, *The Capelinhos Eruption: Window of Opportunity for Azorean Emigration* (Providence, RI: Gávea-Brown, 2008); Michael Doyle, "House Resolution Commemorates 1958 Azorean Refugee Act," *McClatchy (Washington DC),* August 12, 2008. Accessed February 26, 2019, https://www.mcclatchydc.com/news/politics-government/article24495382.html.

38. Doyle, "House Resolution."

39. Judi Green, "Volcanic Eruption Brings Family to the U.S.," *Lowell Sun,* June 16, 1959, 2.

40. Kimberly DaCosta Holton and Andrea Klimt, eds., *Community, Culture and the Making of Identity: Portuguese-Americans along the Eastern Seaboard,* Portuguese in the Americas Series (North Dartmouth, MA: Center for Portuguese Studies, 2009), 51.

41. "The Legacy of the 1965 Immigration Act: Three Decades of Mass Immigration," Center for Immigration Studies. Last modified September 1, 1995; accessed March 1, 2019, https://cis.org/Report/Legacy-1965-Immigration-Act.

42. Marcos, *The Capelinhos Eruption.*

43. Memorandum by The City Development Authority, "Lowell Community Renewal Program: Action Program," 1972, no. 2003, 045, John Mullen Collection, Lowell Historical Society, Lowell, MA.

44. Miguel Moniz, "Change and Tradition in Fox Point: Echoes of the Past in the Spirit of Community," in *Portuguese Spinner: An American Story,* ed. Marsha McCabe and Joseph Thomas, 178–85 (New Bedford, MA: Spinner Publications, 1998).

45. Mahoney et al., *From the Atlantic Islands to Lowell.*

46. Mahoney et al., *From the Atlantic Islands to Lowell.*

47. Mahoney et al., *From the Atlantic Islands to Lowell.*

CHAPTER 12

A Tale of Two Worlds

A Portrait of Portuguese Immigrant Labor

• • • • • •

CAMILO VIVEIROS JR.

I came to America because I heard the streets were paved with gold. When I got here, I found out three things: first, the streets weren't paved with gold; second, they weren't paved at all; and third, I was expected to pave them.

—*Old Italian story*[1]

When Did the Largest Portuguese Migration Flow Occur in the United States?

In 1957–58, a volcanic eruption paved the way for humanitarian relief for the Azorean islands and significantly reshaped U.S. immigration policy. The island of Fayal was overwhelmed with a catastrophic natural event, which provided the opportunity for humanitarian concerns to finally intervene in the restrictive immigration policies that had been in place since the 1920s. Finally, after decades of depression, the American economy had prospered from its position in the post–World War II global economy, giving economic rationale for increasing the significant influx of immigrant workers into U.S. industries for the first time since the early 1900s. These are the stories of Americo Almeida, Antone Pacheco, and Camilo Viveiros (Sr.), three Portuguese immigrants who found their way across the Atlantic. Each of their life paths have different patterns, but all shared a common city and occupational experiences.[2]

When Does the (Immigration) Story Begin?

Americo immigrated to the United States with his family when he was three years old, in 1967. Antone and Camilo came to the United States within a year of each other, but with nearly a ten-year age difference. Antone was nine when he immigrated in 1949, and Camilo was eighteen when he crossed the ocean in 1950. Americo and Antone immigrated because of their parents' decisions, while Camilo, who was older, came without his parents but with his siblings.

What Were the Reasons for Immigrating?

Under the *minifundia* system of agriculture in the Azores, as families expanded, their plots of land were subdivided into smaller and smaller parcels that eventually could not support them. This system of agriculture, which harkens back to feudal times, was still in place in the Azores when Mac, Antone, and Camilo immigrated to the United States. Adding to the challenges of subsistence farming, a colonial war waged by the corporatist dictator Salazar threatened to enlist young men in a life-endangering war abroad. Camilo explained that if he had remained in Portugal for another six months, he would have been forced into military service. While the colonial war no doubt influenced the timing of his decision, his immigration and his siblings' immigration also had to be arranged in order or to be synchronized with a policy that required migration for family members under twenty.

Although none of their families knew each other in the Azores, they shared a common place of destination. Southeastern Massachusetts had long been part of a chain migration pattern for the Atlantic islanders who inhabited the Azorean archipelago. Southern Massachusetts had also been a destination from the whaling period, when Yankee captains took their Azorean crews along, to the tidal wave of the Industrial Revolution, which created a labor demand for industrial workers in the United States.

What Was Life as a Laborer in America?

Once in the United States, Camilo worked for one day in a textile factory and then chose construction work. While working as a laborer he met Manuel Pacheco, another Portuguese immigrant. He eventually married Manuel's daughter Mary Gilda. Antone or "Tony" is Mary's younger brother. Mary

Gilda and Camilo raised five children. Theresa Marie was their oldest. While in high school, Theresa met Americo "Mac" Almeida, and after high school they married. Thus, these three men who had not had common familial bonds in the Azores became family. Tony became Camilo's brother-in-law, and Mac became his son-in-law. But their stories entwined not only through their relationships to one another but also through common work experiences, shaped by the larger structural material forces of the global economy, immigration policies, and the U.S. labor movement.

History, Cycles, and Gender in the Division of Labor

In the United States the three men worked in factories and as construction workers and laborers. However, in the small-scale agricultural setting of the Azores, the family unit prevailed as the economic model. This fact had clearly demarcated the sexual division of labor. Men worked the fields and the ocean, whaling, fishing, harvesting, planting, and supervising livestock. Women tended to children and the family's clothing, prepared meals, and often fed livestock as well as assisted with the storage and preservation of food. In southeastern Massachusetts, the majority of Portuguese American laborers worked in the manufacturing industry, where the rhythmic noise of machinery and foremen overlooking their shoulders became a constant in their lives, replacing the cyclical seasons of the year and the agricultural activities from the world they had left behind.

Although there was not much of an opportunity to change jobs for the Portuguese immigrants from the "old country," there is a parallel to be drawn from this gendered division of labor. A lot of men, like Camilo, tried working in the factory but eventually decided that they preferred the harsh climate of the outdoors. Similar to Camilo, Tony started working in the factories and then moved onto construction. Tony explained, "I went straight to Arrow Manufacturing. I started the day after I was interviewed." The fact that men worked outdoors and women worked indoors in the garment industry mirrored the traditional division of labor in the Azores.

What Is the Story of Labor in Your Family?

Multiple generations of Portuguese women in Camilo's family worked in the factories and experienced the "double-shift" of industrial and domestic indoor work. Although I had assumed that Camilo was the first in his family to migrate to the United States, his parents actually immigrated first. His mother came as a child and returned to the Azores during the Great Depression, shortly before Camilo was born. When Camilo and his siblings migrated to the United States, she originally refused to return. She "hated this country" because she had all the normal duties of motherhood (childcare, housework, food preparation) and in addition had to work in the factory. In the United States the work burden was doubled.

In explaining his mother's story, Camilo cited the display of Lewis Hine's photos at the Heritage State Park in Fall River. He explained that he had looked for his mother's image in those famous portraits, which were dedicated to reforming child labor policy in the United States. Lewis Hine's "The Portuguese Spinner" is the most iconic image of the Portuguese working class. Yet Camilo's mother might have been in one of those photos. His family history was captured in these images, for Camilo's mother and his aunt worked in the factories beginning at age nine and age ten, respectively.

Camilo did not romanticize the working conditions that his mother faced. He commented that people were "treated like slaves in the shops." He knew that children worked twelve-hour days. With this fact he acknowledges the conditions that his mother faced that led him to believe that there must not have been unions. He stated, "That's why I say there were no unions then. It was next to slavery." His comments indicate that the push that spurred people to come from Portugal to the United States probably played a greater role than the pull of factory life in the United States.

His second wife, Maria, described her experience in the factories during this same period. Most factories worked through a piecemeal structure. You were paid by the amount that you produced, so even if ethnic competition was hampered, individual competition was promoted. Each person had a particular specialization. Maria stitched sleeves. Camilo's first wife Mary Gilda (1936–99) stitched labels. Mary Gilda's mother stitched collars. According to Maria, about five women would work on each item of clothing. Maria explained, "When it comes to me, it already got the collars. After me, it went to those who put the cuff. The machines were in lines. All the girls were like this." The conditions in the shop were unpleasant. According to Maria, "It was hot. The windows were the only air conditioners. The wind would come over and pull out the thread on the machine, so we tried to keep the windows closed." Because the wind was bad for the sewing process, the women had no ventilation.

There were two unions for women who worked in the sewing factories. Whether you made clothes for men or clothes for women determined which union you were in. Those who made women's clothing were in the International Ladies Garment Union (ILGWU). Those who made men's clothes were in the Amalgamated Clothing and Textile Union. According to Maria, workers in both unions were paid about the same. Mary Gilda, Maria, and Beatrice worked for the International Ladies Garment Workers Union. Thus, the lives of both men and women were shaped by their working conditions and unions, despite the differences in their gendered division of labor.

The Labor Patterns of Exclusion and Discrimination

While there were jobs for immigrants like Mac, Camilo, and Tony, ethnic chauvinism kept the recent newer immigrant populations from higher-paying work. This pattern emerged from a long history of union discrimination. For example, historians Georgianna and Aaronson explained that "fifty years before the 1928 strike, when English weavers, spinners, loom fixers, and other skilled craft people" had their own unions, "the majority of mill workers" of French Canadian, Portuguese, and Polish immigrants "were not union members by discrimination, choice, or because they were working jobs not covered by craft union."[3] This trend continued into the twentieth century. Penn Reeve in his essay "The Portuguese Worker" further documents this trend in stating how the Dillingham Commission Report of 1911,[4] which was openly biased against new immigrants, pointed out that management still preferred to hire old immigrants: English, Welsh, Irish, and French Canadians.[5] By 1928, "although over one half of mill workers were Portuguese or Cape Verdean they held less than 10 percent of skilled jobs."[6] Indeed, even as "the number of mill will workers doubled," mostly due to Portuguese immigration, "the English mill workers maintained their tight hold on union leadership."[7]

The Time of Labor Strikes: How Did the Disunion of Unions Work?

Despite these practices of exclusion exclusionary practices, the Portuguese did try to join unions and sometimes took radical labor actions. During the events that led up to the strike of 1928, "the lower paid workers, mostly Portuguese, Cape Verdean and Polish workers were not willing and refused to quietly follow the forefront lead of the craft unions that had long excluded them."[8] Instead they flooded to the more militant textile mill committees. Similarly, the Portuguese of Fall River who were excluded from the craft unions were attracted to the Congress of Industrial Organizations during the strike of 1934.[9] According to a March 4, 1984, *Providence Journal* article by Paul R. Carrier[10] entitled "Workers Challenged Shop and Win; Union Becomes a Way of Life in Fall River," it was March 19, 1934, that the ILGWU recruited women workers at the Little Dorothy factory who were out on strike. According to Carrier, "Cynical observers who described the workers as young and frivolous predicted that the strike would fail." But six weeks later they were back on the job and the ILGWU had a new local. In 1941, the union signed up two thousand workers at Har-Lee Manufacturing. All of the names of the rank-and-file workers were Portuguese. This is to say that despite these obstacles, the Portuguese did organize and did join unions.

Yet their success in joining unions and waging strikes should not be understood as removing discrimination. In particular, favoritism remained rampant. According to Georgianna and Aaronson, "Mill owners probably treated workers of their nationality better than they did other immigrants."[11] Even though Mac, Camilo, and Tony were not aware of any formal exclusionary practices of labor, they saw these forms of favoritism at play in their own work sites. Tony explained, "I can tell you that when we came over there wasn't too much love for us greenhorns."[12]

Similarly, when asked about discrimination, Camilo answered, "In the sweatshops people were treated more or less the same. This area was more or less immigrant people, and there was no discrimination with people because they were like sweatshops, and you worked like slaves." He later continued "Any Portuguese, Spanish, English, whatever you were, most people would say they were French and the boss were French. There was only a minority of Portuguese. They didn't look down on you, but they didn't treat you as good as your people. They did not discriminate against you, but they favor their own people." Obviously, this is a nice way of saying that discrimination did exist through favoritism.

Given this long history of exclusion, and the strong history of favoritism, we must ask how much of the rhetoric was reality when ILGWU president Louis Stulberg in 1969 wrote in *Workers Challenge*: "In our Union there are no Jewish members or Portuguese members or French Canadian members. There are only ILGWU members."

How Was Ethnicity Used as a Structural Measure of Exclusion from Business Unionism?

Camilo, Mac, and Tony all belonged to unions and are pro-union. They are quick to point out the benefits of union contracts and benefits. These contracts and benefits helped them acquire more economic stability for their families. Yet Mac, Tony, and Camilo's experiences in these unions represented business unionism that was built off a past from practices of exclusion. Although unions were open to Portuguese by the time they immigrated, the unions were still not based on movement model of fostering broader interracial and multiethnic social movements.

The cultural heritage of these three men is exhibited in their strong religious vows. Keep in mind that often xenophobic ethnic chauvinism has been used to portray ethnic groups as unorganizable because of religious and cultural differences. They adhere to different religious or cultural norms. The Portuguese are not the first to be considered unfriendly to union membership by those who held power in unions. Similar narratives were used to exclude French Canadians, Irish, African Americans, Asian Americans, and new waves of immigrants. In *The Encyclopedia of the American Left,* Daniel Georgianna, characterizes the Portuguese as a "generally conservative ethnic group."[13] Although this may be true when judging the Portuguese by their religious beliefs, it largely disregards labor activity in ongoing labor organizing. It also does not take into account the cultural and political norms of the United States, which assimilated Portuguese Americans into a mostly conservative labor methodology.

The period in which Tony, Mac, and Camilo became active with unions in the United States followed the McCarthy-era purges of the unions of their more radical elements. The changes and adaptations to the purges of militant and communist labor organizers strengthened the liberal and conservative approaches to labor. It derailed the potential of labor to direct itself toward building broader social movements rather than addressing narrow bread-and-butter concerns. Historian Nelson Lichtenstein refers to the unions who came out on the top in the 1950s and 1960s as "big labor."[14] In the 1950s and 1960s, caution, bureaucracy, and self-interest replaced solidarity and social transformation. Furthermore, he asserts that in addition to the purges, labor's conservatism was affected by "the birth of new unions under a New Deal" and "forced draft quest for production and social peace during World War

II."[15] The lack of independent politics in New Deal unionism turned quickly into machines of bureaucracy and of corruption.

Life Experience: How Was Tony, Mac, and Camilo's Union Experience?

After a short episode of factory work, Tony then worked as a member of the Laborers Union. He explained, "I went into a union job with your father [Camilo] which was Dimarios Construction and I worked there about a year and a half."[16] Yet his main job as a union member was with the United Auto Workers. He stated, "Then I went onto General Motors and that was a union job. And I was there from 1960 until I retired in 1989."[17] Tony worked on the assembly line in the former Framingham-based auto manufacturing plant Fisher Body.[18] He explained that "the money was good" at General Motors, even considering the commute from Fall River to Framingham.[19] He described the plant: "We had two shifts going and there were 4,000 workers there. The line itself went for 21 miles throughout the whole plant. It would weave and loop."[20]

Tony described in detail the practical benefits that the union won through strikes and work stoppages targeting Chrysler, Ford, and General Motors. He explained, "The UAW [United Autoworkers Union] would say 'this one will be General Motors' turn' and then a few years later it would be Ford's turn and three years later it would be Chrysler's turn and twelve years they'd go back to General Motors."[21] According to Tony, the UAW had to fight for every benefit and wage increase they ever won. He exclaimed, "Let me tell you, General Motors never gave us anything."[22]

Tony points to cost-of-living increases and benefits along with wage increases that resulted from the UAW's nationally coordinated strikes. Yet during these prolonged strikes Tony would go into debt, making it difficult to maintain family finances even with union support.[23] He stated, "One time we were out about nine weeks in the 1970s."[24] The UAW's campaign to increase benefits and wages during contract expirations resulted in tangible benefits for Tony. After the auto manufacturers built another assembly line in Tennessee, Tony's plant closed. Although Tony appreciates his union benefits and describes himself as pro-union, he also had some critiques of unions and pro-union laborers. He felt that sometimes "lazy" workers would take advantage of union support to protect their unethical behavior.

Mac was involved in a variety of union campaigns and unions. Early in his work career, at age eighteen, he worked as a mechanic at a leather tannery in Taunton. The factory, named Reuping, manufactured Stride Right shoes and Kenney's shoes, along with other major sneaker brands such as Nike.[25] Although there was a union, a campaign was underway to revitalize the union. "We were already unionized. But they wanted a better union in there."[26] Mac was one of the few bilingual employees. He was able to communicate with both Portuguese- and English-speaking workers and was quickly appointed shop steward. As Mac explained, "I spoke Portuguese and English and probably 75–85 percent of the population was strictly Portuguese."[27] His role as a shop steward in this brief drive to build a stronger union was the highest position he has held in a union.

Amid this campaign to improve working conditions at the factory, the shop closed. According to a May 11, 1984, *Boston Globe* article, the company proclaimed that it notified the workers union the day before layoffs began.[28] The plant manager Charles L. Letourneau told the paper, "We notified the Taunton leather workers union, yesterday. . . . We'll start laying off workers Friday (today) and they will continue to be laid off on a staggered basis up to June 30. The plant will be put in mothballs then." Mac explained, "Yeah, they just heard about it (the union organizing campaign), and boom, nobody knew. Nobody expected it. I mean, we just had started talks and all of a sudden, shut down."[29] The shock of the abrupt factory closing to Mac was even more dramatic to long-term workers, like Mac's father. Mac's father worked at that factory for seventeen or eighteen years, since "he got into this country."[30]

As a young person, freshly out of high school, Mac found himself speaking to the media about the actual reasons behind the plant closing. Although the owners pointed to competitive global forces, Mac expressed skepticism about their professed rationale. Instead, he highlighted how they were about to form a new union there. When asked if owners closed it because of the union organizing, Mac replied, "You know the way it works around here. They will never say it's because of the union. They'll say it was because of cost and this and that and the other thing. It wasn't like this place was slack. We were always booming. We always had work. We barely ever had any layoffs."[31]

Mac went on to work union and nonunion jobs. At another union job site in Rhode Island, he worked in a shipyard, where workers belonged to the International Steelworkers Union. There he participated in a dynamic campaign where the bosses attempted to bring in scabs while Mac and his coworkers were locked out from the shipyard. Mac described the situation: "We ended up having a meeting about whether to go on strike or not. Before the meeting was even done, before the contract was up, he locked the gates."[32] Because of this lockout, they were out on strike for a few months. Mac explained, "It was like the entire summer we were out. We would be out on the picket line every day. It was probably about three months."[33] Mac described the armored personnel carrier that was used to bring in scabs as resembling a vehicle in the Clint Eastwood movie *The Gauntlet.* It has "wire mesh on the windows and the wheels are all covered in steel." When we knew the scabs were coming in we used to have big turnouts."[34] Mac explained that employee replacements faced sometimes violent repercussions from his fellow union members: "The scabs that crossed the line and were still in there. It was hell for them in there. . . . A lot of scabs were getting hurt."[35]

According to Mac, "It ended up being an illegal lockout. . . . We ended up going back. We got our jobs back."[36] He continued, "That's why we ended up going to court. That's why it's considered a lockout, he locked us out before the contract was done. That's why we were able to collect unemployment, because if you strike you don't collect unemployment."[37] Because Mac was able to collect unemployment, he did not face the same level of financial distress during the Steelworkers strike that Tony faced during UAW strikes.

Mac displays an unwavering commitment to the union ethic. At points in his life where he was employed at nonunion jobs, he had to work multiple jobs to make ends meet because of the lower pay. For example, when Mac worked at Carter Electric, a nonunion job, he worked two other jobs including "delivering pizzas at night . . . working at the car auction on weekends."[38] Generally, he was paid more in his union positions.

Camilo's work life was shaped by his experience in one union. According to Camilo, in the field of construction unions were less participatory than in the garment industry. Camilo attributed this to differences in the history and structure of unions. Construction unions had a more top-down approach and focused on a more dispersed workforce, which was not as concentrated in one location. It was further shaped by the established relationships between company bosses, contractors, and union officials. At one point in his career, Camilo was offered a position as an assistant to a superintendent. Camilo refused the position and maintained his membership in the laborers' union. Although this new position would have offered increased financial benefits, Camilo explained that superintendents often made choices that cut costs at the expense of the quality of work. Rather than gaining financially and compromising his values, Camilo remained a union member in a lower-paid position. Camilo recognizes the significant impact that unions have had on his family in the scopes of both women's and men's work from the factory to the construction site.

How Did Portuguese Immigrants Experience Harmony and Dissonance at Work in the United States?

One major issue was deindustrialization. Although jobs were available, there were clear limitations to the types of employment that Mac, Camilo, and Tony were able to look toward. Mac worked in the trades because "back then, you take a trade, get a job, that was about it. I mean, most of the people had expectations of maybe living their own place or maybe just hooking up with a good job."[39] Yet those good jobs that all three men relied on have been in decline for some time. According to Tony, "Going back in the '70s, the UAW had 400,000 union workers. Now they are down to 74,000. So you can imagine how they are there using robots, automatic machinery. . . . Everything is upgraded to where they are using less and less manpower."[40]

During the 1980s, southeastern Massachusetts lost over half of its manufacturing jobs, in an area in which manufacturing has been the primary economic engine. According to the article "Economic Boom for Whom?" in *WorkingUSA*, "Mirroring the restructuring of the U.S. economy, over the past three decades, Massachusetts' economy shifted from manufacturing to services. The manufacturing base has been declining during that time, but unlike the rest of the country, Massachusetts manufacturing decrease became intensified in the 1990s. The commonwealth's manufacturing dropped from more than 30 percent of all jobs in 1969 to 13 percent in 1999. Between 1992 and 1997, while total U.S. manufacturing rose 4 percent, Massachusetts lost 131,359 manufacturing jobs."[41]

In the most recent period jobs shifted from those that had been relocated from the North to the U.S. South to the Global South. As Camilo explained, "They want to make a profit, so they move wherever they can make a profit.

That's what happened with Quaker and Cotton Mills." A widespread story that explains the flight of Northern factories to the South puts the blame on unions, obscuring the economic control and moral decisions of factory owners. For example, despite a general sympathetic portrayal of industrial workers, the orientation film for the Lowell National Historic Park contends that the supervisors moved south because of unions. One can say that owners went south in an effort to escape the wage standards and concessions maintained by unions. Highlighting unions as a cause for plant closings rather than owners' unscrupulous desire to create profits at any costs misleads the public into thinking that if unions had not existed then industrial jobs would have remained. This is still a strong argumentative tool for supervisors who want to break union membership.

The role of unions has shifted with the deindustrialization of the economy. According to Camilo, during the early years "the union was always more important for workers. The unions looked after their own people. The unions go against the owners. Even if they made more money without unions, there was no one to fight for them [in the nonunion shops]." It makes sense that people's attitudes about the union would correlate to their economic ability to have union jobs. The generation of working-class people who were loyal union members can be better understood by recognizing the direct economic benefits they were able to receive in an era when labor could successfully maintain and foster increased concessions (although often meager) for their members.

Additionally, there were clear economic self-interested benefits that were awarded for long-term union membership. For example, in order to collect a pension, it was beneficial to remain at union jobs for long periods. The economic incentives as well as the past power of unions to directly impact workers' lives help explain the pro-union stance of generations past. This is unfortunately almost a bygone period of widespread pro-unionism.[42]

Unions are increasingly seen as irrelevant. Indeed, actual union membership is on the decline. According to the U.S. Department of Labor, union membership rates steadily declined from 20.9 percent in 1983 to 12 percent in 2006. The number of persons belonging to a union fell by 36,000 in 2006 alone to 15.4 million. Whereas Mac, Tony, and Camilo's generation of immigrant workers held union jobs for decades, youth entering the workforce today might have difficulty finding union jobs.

Portuguese Immigration and the History of the American Labor Movement

Each man—Tony, Mac, and Camilo—labored in the American economy, which typically viewed the Portuguese as a source of manual labor. Early on in Tony's work life he worked as a laborer in construction sites. Camilo's experience as a laborer spans decades from his teenage years to retirement. Mac, currently in his forties, after job site closings that were the sites of union struggles, at a leather factory and a shipyard, went on to work as a union construction laborer. All three of these men have adapted to a new country, have learned a second language, and have assimilated into an American cultural milieu. With flexibility and adaptability, they learned skills and life ways necessary to accommodate life in the New World. As individuals they have transitioned from the Old World of Portugal to the modern climate of American society, and the jobs they have relied on are part of a dwindling labor force. The jobs they were trained to do no longer exist in growing numbers.

Conclusion

Capitalism as a historical system has integrated a variety of labor forms within a functioning division of labor. The shifting of industrial production from overseas, the growth offshore manufacturing, and the expansion of the service sector created a bifurcated labor market with strong demands at the upper and lower levels but not in the middle.

Both Mac and Tony participated in carpools that took them to their work sites. Mac took a fifteen-passenger van: "We had a little 'Portegee' bus."[43] Tony also participated in carpools to job sites.[44] New organizing methodologies developed out of the challenges of organizing undocumented workers could be applied to build the union movements in communities such as Fall River. For example, day laborers organizing in workers centers have successfully organized mobile workforces whose commutes are not dissimilar to the carpools that Mac and Tony experienced. New styles of labor organizing that are not formalized as unions also bypass the restrictions implemented by the Taft-Hartley legislation. With the creativity and multiethnic unity fostered by increased organizing emphasis on new immigrants, the labor movement may bear more fruit. But old prejudices most first give way to working-class alliances.

Works Cited

Associated Press. "Tannery to Close, 146 Will Lose Jobs." *Boston Globe,* May 11, 1984.

Buhle, Paul. *Marxism in the USA: from 1870 to the Present Day.* London: Verso, 1987.

Carrier, Paul. "Workers Challenge Shop and Win; Union Becomes a Way of Life in Fall River." *Providence Journal,* March 4, 1984.

Connelly, Mary Jo, Peter Knowlton, Peter Capano, and Harneen Chernow. "Economic Boom for Whom?," *WorkingUSA 5,* no. 3 (Winter 2001–2): 135–36.

Georgianna, Daniel, "Portuguese Americans." In *The Encyclopedia of the American Left,* edited by Mary Jo Buhle, Paul Buhle, and Dan Georgakas, 630–31. Oxford: Oxford University Press, 1998.

Georgianna, Daniel with Roberta Hazen Aaronson. *The Strike of '28.* New Bedford, MA: Spinner Publications, 1993.

Juravich, Tom, James Green, and William Hartford. *Commonwealth of Toil: Chapters from the History of Massachusetts.* Amherst: University of Massachusetts Press, 1996.

Green, James R. *The World of the Worker: Labor in Twentieth Century America.* New York. Hill and Wang, 1980.

Lichenstein, Nelson. *State of the Union: A Century of American Labor.* Revised and expanded edition. Princeton, NJ: Princeton University Press, 2013.

United States Immigration Commission. *Reports of the Immigration Commission [Dillingham Commission Reports].* 41 vols. Washington, DC: U.S. Congress, 1911.

Wagner, Steven. "How Did the Taft-Hartley Act Come About?" *History News Network,* October 14, 2002.

Williams, Jerry. *And Yet They Come: Portuguese Immigration from the Azores to the United States.* North Dartmouth, MA: Tagus, 2005.

Notes

1. https://patsalmonhistory.com/i-was-expected-to-pave-them/.

2. Interviews were conducted by the author in person over the course of a year, 2008. The author transcribed the recordings and tied the workers experiences together from the three different generations of Portuguese workers' experiences, all migrating from San Miguel in Acores to Fall River, Massachusetts.

3. Daniel Georgianna with Roberta Hazen Aaronson, *The Strike of '28* (New Bedford, MA: Spinner Publications, 1993), 29.

4. United States Immigration Commission, *Reports of the Immigration Commission [Dillingham Commission Reports]*, 41 vols. (Washington, DC: U.S. Congress, 1911).

5. See Penn Reeve, this volume.

6. Georgianna, *The Strike*, 40.

7. Georgianna, *The Strike*, 40.

8. Georgianna, *The Strike*, 75.

9. James Green, *The World of the Worker: Labor in Twentieth Century America* (New York: Hill & Wang, 1980).

10. Paul Carrier, "Workers Challenge Shop and Win; Union Becomes a Way of Life in Fall River," *Providence Journal*, March 4, 1984.

11. Georgianna, *The Strike*, 29.

12. Tony interview, 1.

13. Daniel Georgianna, "Portuguese Americans," in *The Encyclopedia of the American Left*, ed. Mary Jo Buhle, Paul Buhle and Dan Georgakas, 630–31 (Oxford: Oxford University Press, 1998).

14. Nelson Lichenstein, *State of the Union: A Century of American Labor*, rev. ed. (Princeton, NJ: Princeton University Press, 2003), 142.

15. Lichenstein, *State*, 142.

16. Tony Interview, 2.

17. Tony Interview, 3.

18. Tony Interview, 12.

19. Tony Interview, 3.

20. Tony Interview, 5.

21. Tony Interview, 3.

22. Tony Interview, 6.

23. Tony Interview, 4.

24. Tony Interview, 3.

25. Mac Interview, 1, 4.

26. Mac Interview, 1, 4.

27. Mac Interview, 1, 4.

28. *Associated Press*, "Tannery to Close, 146 Will Lose Jobs," *Boston Globe*, May 11, 1984.

29. Mac Interview, 1, 5.

30. Mac Interview, 1, 7.

31. Mac Interview, 1, 5.

32. Mac Interview, 1, 12.

33. Mac Interview, 1, 11.

34. Mac Interview, 1, 13.

35. Mac Interview, 1, 14.

36. Mac Interview, 1, 11.

37. Mac Interview, 1, 12.

38. Mac Interview, 1, 18.

39. Mac Interview, 1, 8.

40. Tony Interview, 4.

41. Mary Jo Connelly, Peter Knowlton, Peter Capano, and Harneen Chernow, "Economic Boom for Whom?," *WorkingUSA* 5, no. 3 (Winter 2001–2): 135–36.

42. Since this was written, we are currently (2024) seeing the largest increase in pro-union sentiment in the U.S. society in decades, especially among young workers under 30.

43. Mac Interview, 1, 7.

44. Tony Interview, 9.

CHAPTER 13

Adriano(s)

ONÉSIMO T. ALMEIDA

Translated by David Brookshaw

Do you know Adriano? A pair of shifty, penetrating eyes in a restlessly energetic eleven-year-old body, five of which still bear traces of Terceira the few times he speaks Portuguese.

The first time I saw him was when he was carrying a huge bundle of newspapers next to College Travel, on the corner of Waterman and Thayer Streets. The delivery truck belonging to the *Providence Journal* had deposited that Himalayan mountain right there a few minutes before, and he, recently arrived back from school, took a pair of wire cutters from his back pocket and cut through the thick wire. The wind was gusting round the Science Library, and the temperature on the thermometer next to it read twenty-eight degrees Fahrenheit, but folk only notice the effect when it reaches the equivalent of minus two degrees centigrade. He grabbed a sack he had with him, stuffed the newspapers into it and set off, his body bent double and his right arm at an angle of forty-five degrees, while the other arm valiantly sought to balance the weight. He relieved himself of his load by leaving copies at Barus and Holley, the Department of Linguistics, Applied Mathematics, and the Informatics Laboratory.

I followed that little bundle of energy and determination. I engaged him in conversation by the Department of Anthropology. He said he didn't have much time because he had to stick to his timetable and his clients were waiting for their evening paper. But he would pass by the department on the following day. He only had school until midday.

He turned up as promised. He sat himself down in the chair opposite as if we were colleagues of long standing. He spoke English all the time, although he knew I was Portuguese because he'd heard me speak it in the street. He opened up in front of me and told me of his world. He's a businessman. That's all he wants to be. Apart from newspapers, he has other business interests. He sells seeds for flowers, for example. And postcards. He receives orders through the post. In translation, the poetic side of his speech is lost, in this case the prosaic, businesslike language of the great American world in the skinny little body of a Portuguese islander.

"I want to be a businessman. That's all I'm interested in. It's because I love, I adore money."

He had come from Terceira six years before and that was why he was more American than Portuguese. In fact, he wants to forget the little that he remembers of the islands. How he'd bashed his head against a wall, how he'd broken a leg . . . *a hill here, some flat land over there, the ugly grey sea, cows . . . ah!, milking them with a basin and the cow stepping in the milk . . .*

"But all that's to be forgotten. I hate the Portuguese. I don't like being Portuguese. I'd like to have been born here. The Portuguese are stupid. I'm American by blood now. The best business I do is with stupid Portuguese. . . . I wish I didn't know Portuguese. In fact I'm really trying to forget it. But all the businessmen I talk to tell me that it's good for business here if you know Portuguese. It's true, but . . . annoying! . . . I'm Portuguese. What can I do? But I detest it. I hate being Portuguese. I don't like people to call me Portuguese. And it's not as if I'm ashamed. It's out of hate! So at this point, let's stop the questions. There's nothing more to answer. I don't like talking about all this nonsense . . .

Ah! Thank God I'm from Terceira and not São Miguel. I hate people from São Miguel. At my school, almost everyone's from São Miguel. I'd never heard of São Miguel before I came to America. It was only here that I learnt those sons of bitches existed, along with Asia and California. But California's good! It's somewhere I'd even like to live. Having a house in Beverly Hills and being a film producer in Hollywood! . . . Great . . . dreams! . . .

When it comes to people from São Miguel, I only like to listen to them arguing. The way they talk is funny. It sounds bad, but it's comical. And I love to laugh. They say the same words as the rest of us, but they do something inside their mouths that makes those strange sounds. I'm not the only one who doesn't like them. My father doesn't either. He doesn't like blacks or *san-michaels*...

But I do business with them. Not only them, of course! With Americans too. And with students from Brown. Many of them are my friends. They buy the paper from me and other things too that I sell. I've already told some of them that if I see that they're buying stuff just because they pity me, I'll throw the money in their face. . . . I sell books. . . . I get 10 cents for each one. I've got two bank accounts. I opened one all by myself without anyone knowing. How? That's a secret! The other one was with my father. I've got four hundred and twenty-five dollars and eighty cents in one, my own secret one. A hundred and seven and a half in the other, in the Old Stone Bank . . .

I gamble with money. I do anything I have to so as to earn a few coppers. I never take it out of the bank. I could if I wanted, but when I do it'll be for a really big business deal. One day, I'll get some really big business. I'll sit there in my office like a gent and all the deals will be done over the phone or on the computer. The money will flow. A big house. Swimming pool, a summer house in Cape Cod and a winter house in Vermont. And blond chicks by my side. . . . Vermont's really beautiful. There are cows there, but they don't shit on the road like they do in the Azores. They've got class.

Television? I watch 'Charlie's Angels.' Because of Farrah Fawcett's tits. Beautiful! I like Elton John, the Beatles, and Elvis. He died from drugs, did you know that? He didn't find out what the secret was: you only need a little bit to make you feel good . . . otherwise, say goodbye to business . . .

What else is there on television? I see everything. Did you see that program yesterday where the father raped his daughter? What a dirty great son-of-a-bitch. You need to be really greedy to do a thing like that . . . Watch loads of television. My parents can't understand. They don't know what's going on. They ask me and I pretend I don't hear them, or I give them some nonsense by way of an answer. It's too much for them.

What do they know about the world? The only place they go to is East Providence! My mother . . . she'd faint. But they almost never watch television. All my mother does is clean. She's always cleaning. When she finishes, she begins all over again. All my father does is work. When he leaves the factory, he works downtown from six till ten cleaning two banks. At the weekend, he cleans a factory in Warren. If he could live without sleeping, he'd get himself another job as well. For the hours I work, I almost put away more money in the bank than he does. Business, that's what pays. He does the work of a slave. A Portugee's work. On Sundays, he doesn't work. He's already beaten me three times with a rope. I've got the marks on my back. Do you want to see? He's almost got divorced various times. I know everything that goes on. They ought to hide certain things from me, but they don't. But I think that even if they did, it wouldn't make any difference. I'm aware of all that goes on between them. What do you expect? I'm the same flesh and blood. It's as if they think I can't see . . . or can't understand. And if I want to find something out, it only takes a couple of seconds. I'm a detective. But at home, there are some things I'd rather not know. Sometimes I arrive really late so as not to see what's happening. If I was an adult, I'd run away from home. I wish I could leave. It's as if they don't love me.

My sister got married early because of my father. He's as hard as nails. He's the one who's the boss. The one who pays the bills is my mother, but it's all in his name. At the bank, he signed some bits of paper so that I couldn't take any money out of my account without his permission. But over here in this country, he's blind . . . you know? I've already got used to living without having to think about them. It's only at night that they get on my nerves. But I'm never there, even when I am. In the summer, they go to the beach and my mother doesn't even take her dress off. And they take food from home with them. They're so tightfisted. Me, no. I like money but not the way they do. I love to enjoy life."

I interrupted that bubbling current, stream, torrent, cascade, cataract, inviting him to come and have something to eat with me.

"Why not? As I don't pay taxes, I can't call it a business lunch and claim it back at the end of the year." I pretended not to hear. And so off we went to Spats. He already knew it. That and all the other restaurants on Thayer Street and elsewhere. He'd gone in to suss the place out. In some restaurants, he'd been thrown out for being underage, but he had time to take it all in, so as to know what it was like and then be able to tell others about it. One time he actually got into quite a chic restaurant in Newport, where rich people go by yacht and the poor go by car. He went by yacht with some posh folk from East Side.

My parents have never been to a restaurant. Not even to McDonald's. As far as they're concerned, the Baltimore Hotel could be a creature from Africa. I've already eaten there. For free. Like a rich guy. . . . My mother, apart from East Providence, is now going to get to know the road to Boston again.

She's going to the islands to *pagar uma promessa* (pay a promise?) to the Holy Spirit. Apparently, the Holy Spirit plays for Terceira, and Santo Cristo for São Miguel. When I was born, I was at death's door, and she said that if I lived, she'd . . . I don't know how to say this in English . . . I only know in Portuguese: *pagar uma promessa.* There are things I can only say in English, and others I only know in Portuguese. But the Portuguese things I don't know how to say in English. How do you say it . . . sound funny, they seem silly.

I didn't die. All the better. If it had been to stick around back there in the islands, my feet full of cow shit, I wouldn't have minded kicking the bucket; but as I came here, she might as well go back there in peace in order to pay her promise. It's always good to make sure, just in case."

***

"Ah! You know my son, Adriano, sir? That little rascal, may God forgive me? I don't know what to do about him. I made a mistake coming to this country."

I listened in silence to the depiction by Adriano's father of his son, the lad I had met just a few weeks before. I was in the middle of buying some Portuguese products in the supermarket and mall simultaneously translated into Northeastern Portuguese, the Family Market, just off Wickenden Street.

"His mother's fed up with him. He refuses to speak Portuguese, and when he does, it's to tell us we don't understand anything. We dress him and feed him. We work like dogs, night and day, and even at weekends. All for nothing. He doesn't care about us at all. He's involved in all sorts of little business deals, buying and selling things. He goes out with students from that big high school up there and gets up to all sorts of mischief with them. I'm told he goes into bars and is already known to the police. I was told he's friendly with some boys who sell drugs over in Fox Point.

I came to this country to get a better life and I've ruined the boy's. He's beyond salvation. I don't know what can be done about him. He'll do business with the devil if he has to. Even if I decided to leave this place, he wouldn't come. I've given him a good hiding from time to time, but it hasn't produced results. Maybe I haven't given him enough. What am I to do? I'm trapped in this country. He's beyond the pale. He doesn't want anything to do with his parents, or with the church, or with our customs, the things we've got which are truly ours . . ."

***

"Oh! You know Adriano too, do you?" Steve, who's a fourth-year medical student asked me a few days ago in the Graduate Center Bar.

Yes, of course. It goes without saying. To which Steve replied: "What a great kid! Smart, intelligent, full of life. He understands everything. He grasps it all. Even out of thin air. What an awareness he has of things. And of the world! He's a spirit of free enterprise. Everyone knows him in the dormitory. He walks down the corridors and goes into everyone's room. He talks, asks questions. He answers without any inhibitions. He's got friends all over the university. He went to spend the weekend in Vermont with my colleague Dave and learned to ski. Dave told me he threw himself down the slopes like a madman. . . . But he's well mannered. He comes out aggressive when we tread on his feet even if only to test him, but he's incredibly sensitive. He's got a very mature view on the world and on life generally. He's got human feelings that are far too profound for his age. We took him to New York last weekend to watch a basketball game with Columbia University. We spent the afternoon in Manhattan, and he wanted to see everything. If we'd let him, he would have got to know it all in no time. He says New York is his type of jungle. Challenging. It's the sort of place where you feel like getting ahead. You could really grow big there and set up a business the size of one of those skyscrapers.

The first time I met him was when I was working part time in the Science Library. A security guard told me a small boy had got into the hall and had disappeared among a crowd of students in the elevator. We went and found him on the fourteenth floor, admiring the view. When the guard told him he wasn't allowed in there, he told him he knew that only too well, but that was precisely why he had given them the run around. It didn't matter anymore now because he's seen what the view was like from up here so he wouldn't feel the same craving every time he walked past the building.

He squeezed himself into the back seat of one of the coaches of the Brown football team to go and see a game against Harvard at Cambridge. He isn't big enough physically to play football, but he doesn't like soccer. He says it's a game played by greenhorns and Portugee. He's going through the stage of rejecting his culture, but he could turn into a big man—why not?—a big entrepreneur, which is what he dreams of being. The lad's a prodigy, he's brilliant. Full of qualities. A genius. If he keeps going like this, he's got his future guaranteed. A great future. A big Adriano, that's what he's going to be, because he's already a little big man."

***

"'Do you know Adriano? A wee lad from Terceira who's in my parish, who spends a lot of time around the university and who sells the school newspapers?"

"Yes, of course. But why do you ask, Father?"

"You know, a number of people have spoken to me about the boy to see if something can be done about him. From what people say, I don't think that's going to be possible, because the boy must be wallowing in vice by now. Keeping such bad company. . . . They say he goes with the students to ski up in the mountains, to New York, to jazz concerts in Newport, and to that rubbish they call punk at the Civic Center. They say he smokes marijuana and makes money to buy drugs by selling this and that. He's not interested in the church and only came to see me once at the rectory to ask permission to sell Christmas cards at a dance in the hall.

They say he frequents bars (and the police don't say anything!) and shouts rude remarks at girls he passes in the street. In the procession for Our Lady of Health, he stood on the sidewalk insulting the Communion children and crossed the cortege to take a photo of the lad dressed as Saint John the Baptist, which he now goes around showing everyone and calling the boy a sissy.

His father doesn't care, and his mother is oblivious to what's happening. The Sodality of Our Lady of Rosario was willing to pay part of the expenses if he went to a house of correction. He got himself involved with American ruffians, and now he's just like them or worse. Could you find a way of speaking to someone who could call him to order and make him behave responsibly? He has a lot of influence over many boys, even older than him, and some of them no longer come to catechism on Saturdays because of him. And what's worse, he's turned them into a gang under his leadership. So young still, and he's sold his soul to the devil."

***

"Do you know Adriano? He is Portuguese! What a kid!" The director of the distribution department at the *Providence Journal* said to me last week.

If I was Portuguese, I must know him. He wasn't anything like the other Portuguese children, who were passive and timid. He was forthright. He had the aggression required of a businessman. He's courageous. He doesn't have any complexes. He's got presence of mind. A sense of responsibility. He's a hard worker. He works really hard like a good Portuguese, but he's got the determination and aggressive spirit that the Portuguese lack. And he's a tough competitor. He wins all the prizes as best newspaper vendor. He's already contacted a number of companies that advertise for vendors. He gets the goods through the mail and then takes care of things. He's even got a prize for best retailer in the area. He fixed himself up with a P.O. Box at the post office with his name on it, and I'm told he's always getting merchandise there. If Portugal had a few more like him, there'd be no need for so many of their folk to emigrate over here. You people lack that type of temperament. If he wants to stay here a few more years, he'll have plenty of opportunities in the company. Not just in the newspaper. With his talent and some schooling, he'll go far. He may even end up heading a multinational.

***

"Do you know the creature? Adriano? The devil incarnate," commented Mrs. Olinda Ferreira joining her hand and raising her eyes to the heavens, while Mr. Machado was wrapping up some sweet bread baked in the manner of the islands and Adriano came, dropped a bundle of newspapers, and left in a flash. Olinda had witnessed the brief *hi!* that the two had exchanged in the few seconds Adriano stopped in Machado's Portuguese Sweet Bread Bakery.

"The devil he is, God help me! And his parents know, but they don't care. He says he's got a bank account and his father can only withdraw money from it with his permission. He takes drugs. He leaves home and only gets back late, if he gets back at all. He's already going around with women and he doesn't want to know about religion. He says the Portuguese are all greenhorns and dumb, but he's Portuguese too. In flesh and blood like we all are. Every bit of him made there, to God's order. Unless it was the devil's, so help me! My! That one probably owes him money already! The things I hear he does, Holy Father. He's a disgrace to all the Portuguese, for we've always been well brought up and respectful of the customs in this country. What will the Americans say? That the Portuguese don't bring their children up well and let them do what they want. It looks bad and it gives our Portuguese community a bad name . . ."

***

"Oh! Do you know Adriano? I guess everybody knows him," the teacher commented one day between sips of coffee after some meeting or other. "He's very intelligent. Or rather, he's smart but doesn't apply himself very hard. He's always amusing in what he says and does. Sometimes they're really quite incredible things. A few days ago, he was teasing a little girl who didn't know Portuguese. He was calling her *my girl,* and then he turned to his friends who know Portuguese and joked: *My dear girl, my dear gal . . . inha.* Another time, he heard one female teacher say to another, concerning a gentleman she'd never been introduced to—*I was never introduced*—and joined in the conversation with an impertinent question: "No one's ever introduced himself into you?"

He got a cuff round the ear, but then they split their sides laughing in the staff room.

Once, in my class, he kept looking behind him at the girls. *Look to the front, at this picture, Adriano,* I told him. And he, quick as a flash: *There's a picture behind me, and the scenery's prettier!*

It's a pity he doesn't study a bit harder. He's not a bad kid. Apparently, he's got problems at home. But he never talks about them. I only remember talking to him about his father once. He picked up a book by Manuel Ferreira—coincidentally his father's name—in the classroom of a Cape Verdean teacher and began to show it to his colleagues, saying it had been written by his father. When he'd got everyone to believe him, he burst out laughing and just said, My father already died.

He doesn't like taking work to do at home. He does his homework during the break. Apparently, his parents force him to work so that he can help them pay for the house. Like so many immigrants do, in fact. But it'll be a pity if they oblige him to leave school at sixteen.

Apart from that, he's like the other kids. He watches soaps on television late at night and grasps everything. He knows one of the characters is homosexual and the other a transvestite and that Danny and Helen had to get married in a hurry, but who's the boy of his age who doesn't know that and much more? He's got the most beautiful pair of lively eyes. He doesn't offend people when he's being cheeky. Even though he's sometimes really cheeky. But there's a gentleness about him, maybe that Portuguese gentility that the islands leave in people. He's a tiny volcano that's emerged from all that peace and quiet, but his fire doesn't burn, and if it does, then it doesn't hurt. *I love him.*"

***

"Ah! Do you know Adriano? . . . you know something? He's a . . ."

SECTION 4

The Making of an Academic Field

CHAPTER 14

Interview with Nelson Vieira

......

CRISTIANA BASTOS AND BELA FELDMAN-BIANCO

Nelson Vieira, now Emeritus Professor of Portuguese and Brazilian Studies at Brown University, was born in New Bedford, Massachusetts, in 1939, of Madeira-born parents. He graduated in 1961 from the University of Wisconsin–Madison and earned his doctorate from Harvard University in 1969. As a young scholar, he played a crucial role in the creation of the Center for Portuguese and Brazilian studies at Brown University. The center had both an important connection with the community, via the training of bilingual and ESL teachers, and a notable academic impact on the Brown academic community, ultimately leading to the creation of the Department of Portuguese and Brazilian Studies. This department has been a key player in the shaping of the Luso-Brazilian academic field, a point of reference across the United States and beyond, and a pivotal place for international scholars working on Portuguese, Brazilian, Portuguese-speaking African, Portuguese American, and related issues.

In an online interview with Bela Feldman-Bianco and Cristiana Bastos, Nelson Vieira kindly shared some of his insights and memories about that experience and its process.

Q: Nelson, can you tell us a bit on what led you to this field? Was your family background influential? What was your educational trajectory, and how did it become a central role in the creation of the Portuguese and Brazilian Studies Department?

Nelson: Let us start when I was in grade school and my parents wanted me to enroll in the Escola Oficial Portuguesa, a school that was funded by the Portuguese government as an educational and cultural outreach to the Portuguese-speaking communities around the world. I went twice a week after my regular public school to study Portuguese. Besides speaking Portuguese at home, the EOP was the beginning of my formal educational exposure to Portuguese. I also studied Portuguese in high school because my school also offered Portuguese classes, so the Portuguese element was always with me. And to make the Portuguese trajectory even more developmental, I was awarded a year-long Fulbright fellowship to study in Portugal, then followed by my very first professional teaching position at New Bedford High School teaching Portuguese and French, beginning in 1962. So you can say that the Portuguese has been with me all along in terms of education. Therefore, it was natural for me to pursue this field of study, which had already been sparked during my junior year abroad in Brazil, where I studied at the Federal University of Bahia in Salvador, Brazil.

While Portuguese had always been with me, it was the Brazilian experience as an undergraduate that sealed it all. Brazil made a lasting impression on me. Later, after three years of teaching in high school, I applied to Harvard and received a fellowship to study for a master's degree in French and a PhD in Portuguese. And after four years of graduate study I received my first full-time teaching job at Brown University where my goal was to teach Portuguese as an assistant professor but also to work with the Portuguese community in terms of training teachers in bilingual education. At that time, in the late sixties there were more bilingual schools beginning to emerge in different foreign languages in public school systems across the country. While at Brown, I became a Portuguese resource to train local public school teachers in the Providence area in bilingual materials and methodology. Part of this first position centered upon foreign language pedagogy, and that experience became very important because this focus offered me a unique perspective on cognition/content in teaching Portuguese as a first and foreign language. Since I was expected to train teachers in a bilingual format, I received funding to study the Spanish bilingual public schools in Miami, Florida. Pedagogy became very important in my development as a trainer and as a college professor. These pedagogical skills eventually strengthened and characterized one of the curricular features of teaching Portuguese as a foreign language at Brown. While the university goals were very research oriented, because of my bilingual training experience, a focused foreign language pedagogical element became an integral component of teaching Portuguese as part of a university curriculum. Eventually that element was passed on to our colleagues, teaching undergraduates, which in turn gave us a good head start in terms of innovative foreign language teaching being recognized at the university. In this vein, we offered the latest trends, methods, and materials in foreign language teaching. Consequently, it was not just going from Harvard to a research position at Brown, but the position also turned into a broad mission of teaching Portuguese language and pedagogical training, in addition to teaching and conducting research in Portuguese and Brazilian literatures.

During my second year of teaching at Brown, I met Professor George Monteiro when he had just returned from Brazil where he was a Fulbright scholar teaching American literature at the University of São Paulo. As a professor in Brown's English Department and a Luso-American, George became very interested in what we were doing in Portuguese and he became very supportive. At his suggestion we formed an ad hoc committee, identifying different faculty across disciplines in various departments at the university who were conducting research in Portuguese, Portugal, Brazil, Portuguese Africa, and Portuguese America. By the way, at that point, I was in the Hispanic and Italian Studies Department (Portuguese didn't even figure in the title). To make a long story short, George and I discussed the future of Portuguese as a discipline. Having George as an established English professor was very helpful, because he knew the ins and outs of university administrations. Above all, and fortunately, George was interested in developing his own research interests in Portuguese, which I believed had been stimulated in São Paulo. While he was teaching and mentoring English graduate students studying American literature at Brown, he simultaneously began to cultivate his own research interests in Portuguese and Brazilian literatures. In other words, Portuguese at

Brown became a second research mission for George even though we were a very small program. Whenever we wanted to make advances or if we wanted to make ourselves more viable to the university, George became a guiding light. Since he already had an established cachet as a veteran scholar at the university, he would often be the spokesperson for us with the administration. We all dealt with university administrators and deans, but George gave us credibility, so to speak, and in this fashion he became for us a mentor par excellence. George was already a tenured professor in English. He continued to teach English literature but slowly, as we began to expand and grow over the years, he would teach, for instance, a seminar on the Portuguese modernist poet Fernando Pessoa in the Portuguese program.

We grew slowly . . . this took years, it wasn't just overnight, we argued steadily for every single curricular development, faculty position, and budgetary assistance for our program. I think one of the overall structural and feasible factors for growth, to give Brown credit, rested with Brown's creation in the mid-seventies of an expanded structure to the undergraduate curriculum, toward more diverse and internationalized learning, categorized by the new rubrics of centers, institutes, and programs. So, seeking to be a more stable structure, we applied to be a new center and became one of the first to be awarded, which thereby enabled us to become an official academic unit at Brown University. We received a small budget and had stationery printed.

That was in 1975, but soon after we added to our curriculum a Masters Bilingual Program to train public school teachers at the university through a federal grant from the U.S. Office of Education. That grant represented an important step because it helped us solidify even more our newly established structure. In fact, in the eyes of the university, we also became more recognized because we were bringing in all this federal tuition money from the United States government.

Q: Was Adeline Becker on board already? And the other founding scholars?

Nelson: Adeline Becker started to be involved in our program via the bilingual project and its English as a second language (ESL) component. She had been an English reading teacher in the Providence public schools who then provided ESL methodology for the Portuguese bilingual program at Brown. All the above factors sharpened the focus upon language and teaching, while we all continued with our respective publications, research, and study projects. Interestingly, Adeline Becker was admitted to Brown's Anthropology Department to study for a PhD with a specialization on the anthropology of education as she continued to work with our center. However, prior to Adeline Becker's involvement, Onésimo Teotónio de Almeida, a central figure in our historical development at Brown, had come on board earlier as a community resource leader in our bilingual program while he was a doctoral candidate in Brown's Department of Philosophy. He energized the program with his indefatigable and dedicated community work by also acquiring educational grants from Portugal, affording us funding not only for Portuguese books, cultural events, lecture series, and symposia but also for a regular Portuguese lecturer teaching position initially funded primarily by the Portuguese government and later with grants to bring visiting professors from Portugal.

So to be very frank, one of the reasons that we became developmentally successful as a center stemmed from the activity of our grantsmanship, that is, bringing tuition, research, and teaching funds from the outside (federal, international, and local), which the university appreciated. This financial strategy afforded us credibility and educational ammunition to defend ourselves with the university administration. Eventually we established in the early eighties another MA program, specializing in Brazilian Studies, and after more growth a PhD program in the early nineties. During the seventies and eighties we had already attracted junior Brown faculty, rising scholars like the sociologist Peter Evans, whose research and teaching focused upon the sociopolitical dynamics of the Brazilian reality. A significant junior faculty member in Afro-American Studies was Anani Dzidzienyo from Ghana who also taught Afro-Brazilian courses in our Portuguese program.

But this process took years, actually decades, for our program to develop fully. In the meantime, during the summers we conducted a special Bilingual Institute to train public school teachers with the assistance of other colleagues to teach or work with local educators. We continued the summer Brown Bilingual Institute for ten years in the seventies and eighties, forging a reputation as an educational bilingual and second language resource in southeastern New England, resulting in the training of over five hundred teachers, some of whom also received MA degrees in Bilingual/ESL and Cross-Cultural Studies at Brown.

So, all this educational activity at Brown University and the local communities contributed to making our development more feasible and multidimensional. With George, myself, and Onésimo, Luiz (Luiz Fernando Valente) also became an integral part of our faculty. After Onésimo received his PhD degree, he became full-time faculty, but he had already been teaching steadily with us while he was a graduate student. Luiz had been teaching at Providence College after he had earned his PhD from Brown (in comparative literature). Later he was hired to teach language and literature in our program. Consequently, we were able to expand our faculty over the years by justifying to Brown our ever-growing nationally and internationally recognized program, which also necessitated more full-time faculty with the increase in student enrollments on the undergraduate and graduate levels.

I don't know if we could achieve all these developments today, because then we were a lot younger, had a lot of energy, cultivated multiple teaching and research interests, all of which enabled us to strengthen our team of George, myself, Onésimo, Luiz, and Anani Dzidzienyo (from African American Studies). Besides our inherent camaraderie, we were constantly expanding our interests in Portugal and Brazil as well as in Portuguese Africa, which infused us with a cohesive spirit of committed cooperation that was enriched by vibrant intellectual dialogues on teaching, research, and scholarship, plus a strong proclivity toward capacity building.

Moreover, I do not believe we would have been able to make strong arguments on program development without proving to the university that the field of Portuguese and Brazilian Studies warranted serious intellectual attention. As the Luso-Brazilian field gained more prominence on the national and international levels, with more professional journals and books being published as well as more professional national and international meetings increasing, to say nothing of our own initial departmental symposia and periodicals like *Gávea-Brown* and *Brasil/Brazil,* the Brown administration did appreciate that we were a professionally productive and committed university unit.

There had been a longtime collaboration between Portuguese and Brazilian Studies and the Department of History since the 1970s, and especially going back to the development of a joint strategy in the mid-1980s to enable Brown to bring the most prominent historian of Brazil in the English-speaking world, Thomas E. Skidmore, whose appointment in 1988 to the Carlos Manuel de Céspedes Chair added a new dimension and scholarly value to both the History Department and the Portuguese program.

Today we have, just as an aside, the provost of Brown University, Richard Locke, an American political scientist from MIT who speaks fluent Portuguese. It just happened, irrespective of our Portuguese program, and so, what I'm implying is that we sort of had an invisible guardian angel helping us all along, but in fact we were generously nourishing that guardian angel.

I think what's particularly interesting, once we got to the graduate and PhD level, in the early nineties, was the proposal for a department, which meant going for approval from the whole university, the Undergraduate Curriculum Committee, and the Graduate Council. But since we were admitting more graduate students on the MA level, plus a growing outside interest in graduate Portuguese Studies at Brown, as teacher-scholars we were able to justify a PhD level in 1992. Graduate students in the MA bilingual program continued to be funded by outside money, coordinated by POBS [Portuguese and Brazilian Studies] and the Educational Alliance, directed by Dr. Adeline Becker in addition to a new cohort teacher-training program coordinated by Dr. Maria Pacheco, both appointed as adjunct faculty in POBS. Today, graduate students in our doctoral program are primarily funded by the Brown Graduate School. Most of our financial support of doctoral graduate student fellowships derives from the university, but sometimes with outside funding from Portugal and Brazil.

Also, I wish to reiterate that the bilingual component continues, that is, the training of public school teachers under the tutelage of Dr. Maria Pacheco. Interestingly, in 2020 we regrettably celebrated Maria Pacheco's retirement. In addition, her important role within the Educational Alliance became notable since Dr. Pacheco headed the Center for Diversity and Equality in Education. Up until 2021, we still have public school teachers enrolled in the MA degree program in ESL and

Cross-Cultural Studies at Brown. Even though as scholars we prioritize research and scholarship, that is not simply the case, because all faculty participated in one way or another in the training or teaching of Portuguese language and culture on all levels of the curriculum.

In other words, while our graduate program is interdisciplinary, multidisciplinary, it also is one that has links to these two different aspects of learning—formal literary/cultural research and foreign language teaching. Furthermore, we became multidisciplinary or interdisciplinary on the undergraduate and graduate levels, because we discovered that there were many academic resources scattered across Brown via researchers, professors, trainers in other departments who were working on Portugal and Brazil—so why not bring them together. This collaborative action also led us into the social sciences, even into the sciences. For example, we had medical students enrolled in Portuguese because they wanted to conduct research in Brazil on infectious diseases, etc.

I think the other big step for us was spreading out and making ultimately joint appointments. For instance, Anani Dzidzienyo was in his home Department of Afro-American Studies and soon joined Portuguese and Brazilian Studies, where he taught two courses in POBS and two courses in Afro-American. After Thomas Skidmore in history retired, James Green was hired, offering two courses in history and two courses in Brazilian history. Those connections were significant for affording us a notable presence at the university. In other words, POBS was not just a small foreign language and literature department; instead it had broader goals, manifested as we collaborated with other faculty in different departments and programs, such as Judaic Studies, where I [Professor Vieira] was a fellow. While we were theoretically driven in terms of literature and culture, we also incorporated social sciences and history as part of our undergraduate and graduate curricula.

I believe everybody felt very passionate about our respective fields but also as a collaborative team. We had our differences, but we truly worked together. It was not serendipity because we functioned willingly and strategically as a team.

Q: In sum, you had a very unique trajectory, much entangled with the institutionalization of Portuguese and Brazilian Studies at Brown. In

1975 you left the Hispanic and Italian Studies Department, where there was not much room for the study of Portuguese, and almost single-handedly created a center, which ultimately led to the department. The center was quite unique in its interfaces with language pedagogy, research interests, and openness to interdisciplinarity and partnerships; the center attracted other scholars, who brought in further research interests and external funding, visibility with the administration, and achievements such as an undergraduate program even before there was a formal department, one that once founded became a high-profile department at the university. How do you look back at this? How does it compare with other centers and departments?

Nelson: We were able to branch out and be multidisciplinary because of the center's flexibility and the fact that the university was expanding in international and interdisciplinary arenas. We also became the first center to offer an undergraduate degree. In general, centers were devised to just bring people together, while POBS was working practically as a department. As stated above, our higher status became officially established when we were approved as a department in the early nineties. The department replaced the center. For about fifteen-plus years we were a center, but when we became a department the center disappeared. So in a sense the center had been a prestructure for the department.

Q: How did you compare, and compete, with other places in the U.S. where there were Portuguese Studies initiatives, like Santa Barbara or Harvard?

Nelson: Our connections with other universities were more on the graduate and scholarly levels, especially as we offered graduate courses and later when the PhD was instituted. We have had some graduate student exchange due to Brown's participation in a special program where selected graduate students can apply and spend a semester at Santa Barbara or at Brown or at Harvard. For instance, since the Portuguese graduate curriculum at Harvard had not been extensive at the time, Harvard graduate students would come down to Providence to enroll in our graduate seminars. Moreover, these other universities, except for UMass Dartmouth, didn't have an extensive foreign language component and outreach that Brown offered, to say nothing of our array of diverse graduate literature and culture seminars with their interdisciplinary focus. Also, outstanding graduate students from Portugal and Brazil were also applying to our doctoral program and were admitted. Plus, the interaction stimulated by our conferences, the Gávea-Brown Press, and the publication of our research journals contributed to our reputation as a multidimensional program. Collaboration across universities was also manifested by individual scholars working on joint research programs and symposia.

Q: You say you had a community component. How did that work?

Nelson: Our connection with the training of public school teachers either via workshops or on the master's level for the most part was strengthened by the local bilingual realities in addition to our cultural programs and lecture series open to the Luso-Brazilian communities. Our colleague Onésimo stimulated these mutual interests and served as a significant cultural liaison with the Portuguese communities. He discovered and brought to the university featured Portuguese artists, poets, and novelists from the community to participate in our cultural programs. Educational and cultural activities underscored the importance of the language not just as an academic resource but as an ongoing dialogue with the local communities, which took the form of educational workshops, special cultural programs including lecture series. Many community members were regulars, particularly those who spoke Portuguese, at our events. The community recognized us as a resource and, for instance, by helping teachers receive state credentials to teach Portuguese as well as providing foreign language exams for certification, as an evaluation tool to attest to one's command of the Portuguese. So all these ties solidified our linkages with the local communities, and I believe that if we hadn't demonstrated our interest in the community, it would have been a program without that invaluable dialogue. Furthermore, the *apoio,* assistance from the outside in terms of local interests, community support, and especially U.S. government and international funding all contributed to fostering a viable program.

Q: One way to describe your contribution to the field is the making of a transnational, cosmopolitan approach to Portuguese and Lusophone connections, including Brazil, Portuguese-speaking Africa, etc. How do you feel about it?

Nelson: We felt very strongly about making those connections, but our colleague Anani Dzidzienyo, who offered Afro-Brazilain courses on Brazilian race relations, was a pioneer in Black Studies. Later, he formulated a popular course on the Portuguese-Brazilian-African triangle, and that triangle was really important for us to connect more with Portuguese Africa and go beyond the straight Lusophone or more traditional Lusophone development. That kind of connection was truly significant because it opened us to more possibilities with Portuguese-speaking Africa. Today there are students who are in literature and work with Portuguese-speaking Africa on their dissertation. So I think that we felt very strongly about this because we envisioned the potential in establishing such connections. And I believe Anani represented a major educational impact and ultimately the curriculum stemmed from his influence. While we still do not have a full-time Africanist, our colleague Distinguished Senior Lecturer Leonor Simas-Almeida in Portuguese literature expanded her curricular offerings to include courses on Lusophone African literature. Interestingly, our other distinguished senior lecturer, Dr. Patricia Sobral, POBS's Portuguese language undergraduate coordinator, who teaches Portuguese via theater art methodology, was hired in 2002. Recently, she conducted a research project on Portuguese-speaking families around the globe and traveled to Mozambique, utilizing connections established by POBS.

Bela: It is very interesting because, at some point, you have these very strong local connections so you could initiate a good beginning because you had the community, and also I think that you trained teachers from the community and even engaged in cultural events local poets and artists. But the fact that you were grounded in the community and received resources because of the community made you also very much transnational—it's a very interesting story.

Q: Last question, addressed to Nelson Vieira as a researcher: What are your current interests? Is there something you would like to share?

Nelson: One of my strong research interests lies with Brazilian fiction and particularly narratology and its ability to provide critical perspectives on life. There are two books or collections edited by other scholars that are forthcoming, one out of Hebrew University in Jerusalem and one out of Oxford University, in which I participated with two essays on Clarice Lispector. She has been one of my specialties throughout my career, and I was one of the early scholars to recognize a Jewish trace in Clarice Lispector's writing. That is, readers can discover a Jewish voice in her writing that is not overtly or referentially Jewish. My work on Clarice is ongoing. I gave a keynote in Israel, in Jerusalem, for a conference on her oeuvre, focusing upon the fact that being a child of an immigrant family, she possessed an outlier perspective that was always looking toward the other, because she herself was an(other), her family was other, so I argue that her sense of alterity seeps in throughout her work but not necessarily referentially, although her *crônicas* show some of these traces more overtly. I think that in the seventies—she died in 1977—she was already operating on a global level, in terms of reaching readers by having them break out of their perspective in order to really "see" the other; and I believe her novella, *A Hora da Estrela/The Hour of the Star,* is a perfect example of this view, because she strives to create a poor woman without being condescending, without a high literary voice. And she accomplishes this successfully because she forces the reader, without the reader initially knowing, to break out of a staid reader's mold and to inhabit the precarious existence of the main character, a poor and undereducated girl. So I see that alterity very strongly in her work, and I think the readers love her because she is always speaking to somebody with her intimate style, not in a feminist way like "oh I've been a victim of patriarchy" and all those threadbare clichés. Indeed, she was really trying to get into a female voice expressing much more sensitively the world around her; that's what I believe to be one of her great contributions. I've been focusing upon that perspective with these two forthcoming articles.

My other very strong interest lies with a short story writer from the State of Curitiba, Brazil, Dalton Trevisan, who is over ninety years old, actually ninety-five, and he keeps producing. His stories stem from the 1940s up to the present. I am struggling to write a book on his narratives from more than forty collections which indicate his prolific style and provide keen insight into the lower to lower-middle classes, or actually marginalized souls. Trevisan creates a human comedy in a scathing style that appears to sensationalize the pornographic. However, I argue that he has been misread all along, because while his subject matter is often very erotic and even graphic, his stories are not written for vicarious pleasure. For my book I have a possible title "Reading the Unregarded"—that is, Trevisan's "performance-writing" about neglected souls who are passed over socioeconomically, people who live in the psychological shadowlands of Brazil. Trevisan is calling attention, in a Chekovian manner, to their mishaps, flaws and survival given their limited resources. I believe he is the best contemporary short story writer in Latin America, and I just hope he continues to live and to write so I can finish my book!

CHAPTER 15

Interview with Frank F. Sousa

......

BELA FELDMAN-BIANCO

Dear Frank, I remember we first met in 1990, just after you were hired as an assistant professor of Portuguese at the (then) Southeastern Massachusetts University (SMU), where I was at that time the (visiting) University Professor of Portuguese Studies. In that period, Southeastern Massachusetts was still under the impact of the negative repercussions of the New Bedford's ill-famed 1983 Big Dan gang rape. Faced with the increasing demands of influential Portuguese American political and economic leadership, the SMU administration was eager to invest and expand Portuguese studies and activities at its North Dartmouth campus.

In this regard, as the (visiting) University Professor of Portuguese Studies, I had the mission to involve faculty and students in research activities on the Portuguese of southeastern Massachusetts. Also, your arrival as a new faculty member signaled the renewal of the Portuguese language and literature area studies as your colleagues were already retiring. This happened at a historical conjuncture, when SMU was in the process of merging into the University of Massachusetts system. In fact, in 1991, the North Dartmouth campus, renamed as University of Massachusetts Dartmouth or UMass Dartmouth, became one of the five campuses of the University of Massachusetts, a move much celebrated by both administration and faculty and elected officials and institutions in the region.

Against this background, I guess you must have confronted many challenges, when you started to teach at the North Dartmouth campus. Your trajectory was quite diverse from those of your much older colleagues, such as Antone Felix, Gregory Rocha, and Maria Vermette, who were third-generation Portuguese Americans born in New England. As far as I remember, you were born on the island of São Jorge, Azores, and were still a child when you migrated, together with your mother and nine brothers and sisters, to California, where you were raised and pursued your studies.

So, I have a few starting questions.

How was it to leave your big family behind in California and settle in New England? What were the main differences between the two environments? How did you experience being a Portuguese person in each of them? Did the "Portagee" stigma linger? Did it ever affect your family and friends?

Since I had gone away to college at Santa Clara University and then graduate school at the University of California, and had undertaken studies abroad at the Universidade de Coimbra and the Universidad Complutense de Madrid, the idea of moving far away, to the East Coast, was not exactly foreign to me. Indeed, I welcomed it, in good measure because I would be teaching and living near a Portuguese community, as had been the case in my years in California. The immediate difference that I felt in southeastern Massachusetts—particularly in New Bedford, where I lived for nearly six years, and Fall River, which I visited regularly—was the considerable concentration of Portuguese in urban neighborhoods, which contrasted with my experience growing up Portuguese in a rural, farming town in California. The presence of the Portuguese in New England was reflected in the names of the businesses and streets, many Portuguese "national" Catholic churches, and the existence of Portuguese television (the Portuguese Channel) and multiple radio stations. It appeared to me that UMass Dartmouth, situated halfway between New Bedford and Fall River, offered extraordinary opportunities for program building. It seemed like the Portuguese were "more" Portuguese, that is, more connected to the Old Country, the second generation more fluent in the language, which was not unexpected, given their location closer to Portugal. I would regularly have students who were third- and fourth-generation Portuguese and yet still connected to the insular Portuguese neighborhoods on both sides of their family. Surprisingly, sometimes these very American generations still spoke some Portuguese. In addition, I quickly perceived a negative attitude toward the Portuguese that I had rarely witnessed in California. Given my relative mastery of the English language (perhaps because I arrived here at the age of nine, that is, three years earlier than the age when one usually maintains a foreign accent), my colleagues at the University of Massachusetts Dartmouth and friends off campus would momentarily forget that I was Portuguese and proceed to speak of the community in ways that were condescending. I attributed this different attitude toward the Portuguese in southeastern Massachusetts partly to the fact that they were, in economic and educational terms, near the bottom of the social ladder, as a result, at least in part, of having been, for about one hundred years, the last immigrant group to arrive in the region. Maybe as a reaction to being perceived negatively, the derogatory term "Portagee" seemed to trigger a much stronger reaction in the community here than in California, where the term was used sometimes as a joke among the Portuguese and didn't seem to have such a negative connotation. To this day, friends of mine in this region who have read Charles Reis Felix's memoir *Through a Portagee Gate* remark on how offended they had felt by the fact that I, as editor of that great memoir, had accepted the author's deliberate decision to include the pejorative term in the title of the book. Years later, when I moved to UMass Lowell, I could use the term playfully with friends there, in a way that I wouldn't have felt comfortable doing in Fall River, for example. In Portsmouth, Rhode Island, where I live with my family, never once have I felt stigmatized for being Portuguese or having a classic Portuguese last name, and never have my kids been belittled for their Portuguese heritage in a town where the Portuguese were 40 percent of the population in 1920, according to Donald Taft's *Two Portuguese Communities in New England,* a study of the Portuguese in Fall River, Massachusetts, and Portsmouth, Rhode Island. Curiously, Portuguese language and culture have a certain cachet here, as reflected in the fact that Portuguese is offered at the middle school and high school, and the Portuguese-American Citizens Club, founded in 1927, is a local institution that has among its members both Portuguese and non-Portuguese. These Portuguese Americans, whose culture was not revitalized with new immigration in the 1960s and through the eighties, have names like White (Branco) and Smith (Ferreira) and encourage their children to study Portuguese.

What made you pursue a PhD in Portuguese language and literature?

Portuguese was the language used at home in Modesto and then Turlock, California, and my mother, Deolinda Fontes de Sousa, had a staunch respect for Portuguese language and culture to the point that she would dictate texts to us and have us write Portuguese as lessons in the language. Beyond the importance given to Portuguese in my own home, including by the Portuguese radio programs that were on for hours, my love of things Portuguese in the late 1960s and early 1970s was reinforced in the insular, tight-knit community of Turlock, California, first at Sacred Heart Church, where I was an altar boy, and then at the Centro Cultural Português, founded by two missionary priests who had come from East Timor, which was soon converted into a "national" and then "personal" Portuguese parish, Our Lady of the Assumption Church. Without these community and religious experiences in the Portuguese language, including the impressive sermons by Fr. José Carlos, it is difficult to imagine that I would have pursued a PhD in Portuguese, after completing a BS in psychology. A scholarship from the Luso-American Education Foundation, of California, which allowed me to study at the Universidade de Coimbra with Professor Carlos Reis, in the summer of 1980, also played a major role in my decision.

Have your siblings also pursued graduate studies? Are they still living in California?

Though I am the only PhD in the family, five of the ten of us have completed a master's degree and a sixth came one course short of a BS, an unusual expression of dedication to education in our immigrant community. In spite of the fact that she never became minimally fluent in English, my mother was proud of our commitment to education, and possibly lived vicariously through us, as her own ambition had been to become a teacher, not easily attained back in the village. My nine brothers and sisters still live in California, and continue very much connected to Our Lady of the Assumption Church. Indeed, one of my brothers, Fr. Manuel, has been the pastor of the church since 1987, and it remains our actual or emotional religious parish, no matter that half of us now live outside of Turlock, California. I should add that those who did not undertake and complete college degrees have been quite successful in banking, real estate, and dairy farming.

You arrived in New England, just six or seven years after the Big Dan drama. Have you taken this fact into account in the (re)creation of an area and a Center of Portuguese Studies and Culture at UMass Dartmouth?

I was a student at the University of California Santa Barbara during the Big Dan's trial, which I followed in the *New York Times.* I was surprised by some of the things I read, but I never felt the shame or deep insecurity that I came to witness among the members of the community in New England, when I moved here in 1990. I have to admit that part of my motivation for developing a series of projects with my colleagues at Southeastern Massachusetts University/UMass Dartmouth was to counter the negative perception of the Portuguese in the region and to provide the community with positive visibility. I was astonished to learn very quickly that newspapers like the *New Bedford Standard Times* and the *Fall River Herald News* barely covered the community, though the Portuguese were nearly or even over 50 percent of the population in these cities. The Portuguese seemed very much like "the Invisible Minority" described by the sociologist Esthellie Smith in her seminal essay from 1974. The creation of a separate Department of Portuguese in 1999–2000, the first endowed chair at the university in 2001 (Hélio and Amélia Pedroso/Luso-American Foundation Endowed Chair in Portuguese Studies), and the Ferreira-Mendes Portuguese-American Archives in 2009 were intended, in part, to give prestige to Portuguese language and culture and academic and social status to the Portuguese American experience.

Throughout your 23.5 years at UMass Dartmouth you were able to build, among other projects, a Portuguese Summer Program, a new Center for Portuguese Studies and Culture, which replaced the extinct Center for the Portuguese Speaking World, an excellent Department of Portuguese, which offers a bachelor's degree in Portuguese, a Master's degree in Portuguese studies, and a PhD in Luso-Afro-Brazilian Studies and Theory. What were the major challenges you confronted in the process of implementing these and other projects? Have you had any help from the Portuguese and Azorean governments or foundations/enterprises? And what about USA grants?

I arrived at SMU/UMass Dartmouth in 1990, when the Portuguese were beginning to affirm themselves in the region and at the university itself. There had already been a center, involving the names you referred to above, namely, Gregory Rocha, Antone Felix, and Mary Vermette, to which one could add the names of Fred Gifun, professor of Brazilian history, Penn Reeve and Donna Reeves of sociology, and Daniel Georgianna of economics, all of whom had undertaken research on things Portuguese, Brazilian, and Portuguese American. And, more importantly, given that the Center for the Portuguese-Speaking World was no longer in operation, was your work, as Visiting Professor in Portuguese Studies, including the documentary *Saudade,* on the local Portuguese community, to which I contributed as the narrator. This excellent project, which garnered support from the likes of the Massachusetts Cultural Council, showed that it was possible to raise funds for first-rate initiatives related to things Portuguese and Portuguese American at UMass Dartmouth. Once I began the Summer Program in Portuguese in 1994, with support from a local businessman, Mr. Frank B. (Bernardo) Sousa, and grants from the Gulbenkian Foundation and the Luso-American Foundation, it became even more evident that both the university and the local community were ready and willing to finance relevant and consequential initiatives that could have an impact within and outside of the university. This all coincided with the hire of a new chancellor at the university, Peter H. Cressy, a retired admiral who saw the (Portuguese) demographics of the region as an opportunity, both in fundraising and for increasing enrollment. Through Mr. Sousa ("the real Frank Sousa," I used to call him), I was able to meet political leaders, such as State Representative Robert Correia, who wanted to help with new Portuguese projects in the region's only university. (Frank himself and Rep. Correia both shared stories about how the Portuguese had been and continued to be discriminated against in the region.) Rep. Correia proposed and secured a state earmark in the amount of $250,000 for the new Center, beginning in Fiscal Year 1996–97, against the express wishes of the chancellor, who, with some justification, interpreted this largesse as a form of meddling in the university. But his reticence was overcome when the Center for Portuguese Studies and Culture began to fundraise at a level never seen in the humanities at the university, beginning with a five-year, $575,000 grant from the Luso-American

Foundation (FLAD). What became readily apparent, in an American university where fundraising helps define the success or failure of a chancellor, was that Portuguese studies would thrive as long as there were worthy projects and support from individual donors, government agencies (Commonwealth of Massachusetts, the Foreign Ministry of Portugal, and the Government of the Autonomous of the Azores), and foundations like FLAD and the Gulbenkian. This support was always matched by the university, in various ways, including, very importantly, the hire of support staff and faculty (six tenured or tenure-track faculty in the department, the largest number of any program in the country; a faculty director of the archives and a Portuguese-speaking archivist). Nonetheless, some at the university would at times express resistance, as Portuguese grew rapidly and began to cast a shadow over other programs, including other foreign languages. This is why it became imperative to found a stand-alone Department of Portuguese, so that we, the faculty in Portuguese, could tread a different path, including the development of an MA and PhD, efforts headed by Anna M. Klobucka and Victor K. Mendes. When a chair or the dean of the college would not support a new initiative, we could always count on the provost and the chancellor, who, prodded by the demographics of the region and Portuguese American elected officials, would make sure Portuguese studies developed into one of the signature programs of the university. Another source of influence of the center across the campus was that over time and until 2013 the executive board was comprised of eighteen faculty members from *four* different colleges.

How were you able to create a Portuguese Department? And what were the major hindrances you confronted against this endeavor?

To add to what I wrote above, the creation of a department initially encountered resistance from the Department of Foreign Languages and Literature, as would be expected, and from faculty across the university who did not identify Portuguese as an important area of academic study. Indeed, the Portuguese were certainly hardworking, some might say, and appreciated as excellent and dependable builders and gardeners but they were not often associated with high culture and university education. To ensure the success of this new venture, I approached Dr. Rui Machete, president of FLAD, about guaranteeing an endowment of $200,000 to the department, should it come to pass, then canvassed colleagues from across campus, often ones with whom I had served on committees, to secure their vote for the creation of a new department on campus. The objective was to establish an independent academic unit that would guarantee the future success of Portuguese studies. The Department of Portuguese became part of the academic structure of the university, ensuring the independence and self-determination of the enterprise within the College of Arts and Sciences.

Have you received any support from colleagues from other universities on behalf of your projects? What about from members of the Portuguese communities surrounding the university or Portuguese politicians?

As I wrote above, the support of members of the local community and elected officials played a critical role in the development of every project at the university. To the list of politicians above, I would like to add Senators Marc Pacheco and Michael Rodrigues and Representative António Cabral and the mayors of New Bedford and Fall River, who, along with non-Portuguese elected officials, regularly attended events organized by the center, including its annual holiday dinner and regular press conferences. Regarding colleagues elsewhere, they were invited to teach in the Summer Program in Portuguese, with the request that they strongly encourage their own students to come to Dartmouth during the summer. The Hélio and Amélia Pedroso/FLAD Endowed Chair in Portuguese Studies also brought colleagues to the campus, who were not only invited to teach graduate courses in the program developed by Anna M. Klobucka and Victor K. Mendes and directed by the latter but were also asked to contribute to the publications of Tagus Press. This is in part why by 2013 more than fifty volumes had been published by Tagus Press, the publishing arm of the Center for Portuguese Studies and Culture. Among the contributing visiting faculty were João Cezar de Castro Rocha of the Universidade do Estado do Rio de Janeiro, who edited multiple volumes in the journal *Portuguese Literary and Cultural Studies* and several collections of books; and Rui Zink, who supervised the publication in Portuguese (in Lisbon) of volumes originally published in the Portuguese in the Americas Series. I cannot fail to mention my indebtedness to the late and beloved George Monteiro of Brown, who regularly provided helpful advice during my years at UMass Dartmouth and again at Lowell, where he gave brilliant lectures on Camões, Shakespeare, and Pessoa at the invitation of the Saab Center, the English Department, and the Kerouac Center for the Public Humanities.

What are the favorite projects you had implemented at UMass Dartmouth and why? Were there any projects you could not implement? Could you explain?

It is difficult to consider one project more important than another, as each helped strengthen other programs. For example, the Summer Program in Portuguese eventually played an important role in attracting students to the graduate programs and providing summer employment for these same students. Nonetheless, I am particularly proud of the Center for Portuguese Studies and Culture, about which I have already said much, and the Department of Portuguese. The latter played a fundamental role in allowing us to develop an academic program on a national scale, while signaling to the campus community and the region that Portuguese language and Lusophone cultures, comprised of over 260 million people in four continents and eight countries, were worthy of study at the highest level at a university that was now embedded in the UMass system. I could add the archives, dedicated to documenting the history and culture of an underrepresented, underdocumented group, the Portuguese Americans, that is. The work of this unit within the university library has the potential to become an enduring legacy of the work of so many people, many more than I have enumerated here. There was, nonetheless, one project we were not able to implement, and that was RTP [Radio-Televisão Portuguesa] América, the brainchild of Pedro Bicudo, who was then the correspondent for RTP in the U.S. In 1998–99, he proposed to the center and the university the conversion of the television studios located in the university library into the home of RTP América. This project actually got to the point of the very beginning of local television production, but then RTP reneged, for good financial reasons, no doubt, on the agreement that had been signed with fanfare at the university and then in Lisbon. But this failure, which lingered for three to four years, was actually a blessing in disguise, as it kept the studios occupied and allowed us to develop, in the meantime, the proposal for the Ferreira-Mendes Portuguese-American Archives. The proposal was submitted in 2004 and led to a press conference in 2005 announcing the $1.5 million Ferreira-Mendes Portuguese-American Archives Endowment, with Otíla Ferreira, daughter of Ferreira Mendes, one of the founders of Portuguese American radio, making the lead gift. This gift, joined by considerable donations from seven other local Portuguese Americans, triggered a major capital project to convert the old television studios into a state-of-the-art, climate-controlled archival space, which had a public opening in 2009, covered by the local Portuguese and mainstream media. The development of the endowment also allowed for (was conditioned on) the hire of a full-time archivist and a faculty director. This is yet another project, along with the Portuguese American Digital Newspaper Collections launched in the same year, that was made possible by the demographics of the region, financial support from Portuguese Americans, and the continuing financial support of the Commonwealth of Massachusetts via the yearly earmark mentioned above and the leadership of Chancellor Cressy's successor, Chancellor Jean F. MacCormack. And, yet again, the Luso-American Foundation made a decisive contribution. The digitization of the sixteen Portuguese newspapers published in the U.S. before 1930, i.e., the Portuguese American Digital Newspaper Collections mentioned above, was made possible by material support (newspaper collection at the Freitas Library at the União Portuguesa do Estado da Califórnia [UPEC]) and financial support from Elisia and Mark Saab of Lowell, Massachusetts, and the Government of the Autonomous Region of the Azores.

Why have you and your colleagues decided for a Luso-Afro-Brazilian PhD program instead of just a Portuguese studies program? Are there other Luso-Afro-Brazilian graduate programs in the USA?

At the moment that Victor K. Mendes and Anna M. Klobucka launched the PhD in Luso-Afro-Brazilian Studies in 2007, this was the only program with the more encompassing and inclusive title in the U.S. Since then, other programs and/or conference panels have sometimes adopted this moniker.

And how do you compare your present experiences at the University of Lowell and those at the University of Massachusetts Dartmouth. How do the Portuguese communities of these New England localities differ?

The demographics of greater Lowell are quite different from those in southeastern Massachusetts, both in terms of population and political representation. Therefore, the objectives cannot be the same, though opportunities abound. One thing is certain, the university administration in Lowell is every bit as committed to ensuring the success of the endeavor as UMass Dartmouth had been, and Portuguese Americans, like Elisia Saab and her family, including daughter Analise, are fully devoted to the academic program, center, and new archive. This is why there is now a minor area of studies, with a good number of students enrolled, and we are planning to submit a proposal for a major in the next couple of years. The Greater Boston Portuguese-American Digital Archive (PADA) was awarded a three-year, $300,000 grant from the William M. Wood Foundation in 2020, allowing University Libraries to hire a full-time archivist, complemented by a part-time project director hired by the Saab Center. PADA aims to document the Portuguese American experience in the region, except for the South Coast, which is already covered by the archives at UMass Dartmouth. The Saab Center for Portuguese Studies has received other grants from foundations and government agencies in the state, including Mass Humanities (NEH-stateside) for an exhibition on the Portuguese in Lowell in the first quarter of the twentieth century, and the Lowell Cultural Council, the local affiliate of the Massachusetts Cultural Council, has, on three occasions, sponsored cultural initiatives of the center, including two exhibitions. In addition, the center has been able to partner with major local institutions, including the Lowell National Historical Park (two exhibitions, two colloquia, and community events). Like Fall River, Lowell was an industrial city, specifically *the* first American industrial city, and similarly evolved into a postindustrial city, with all the challenges implied by the designation, but with the good fortune of having had Senator Paul Tsongas, a Lowellian who championed Lowell in Washington. Lowell has had two waves of Portuguese immigration, and the Portuguese were associated with work in the mills and factories. But the origin of Portuguese immigration is somewhat different: Lowell was first settled by Madeirans and Azoreans (first wave) and Azoreans (second wave), mostly from Graciosa. There are illuminating stories about Portuguese political and social activism in Lowell. For example, in the late 1960s and early 1970s, city officials, in partnership with the financial and political elites, undertook a series of urban renewal projects, one of which was to build an extension of a highway into downtown in order to improve traffic. However, this project would require the razing of dozens of homes and businesses in Back Central, the major Portuguese neighborhood in the city, resulting in the division of the area into two isolated neighborhoods. The Portuguese community quickly opposed the plan and organized under the leadership of the pastor of Saint Anthony's Church (behind the scenes) and several lifelong residents from the first wave of immigration, along with the support of a few from the second wave, including Dimas Espínola, who would go on to become a major radio personality. Their efforts, including rallies and alliances with other ethnic communities and their clergy and some members of the city council, culminated in the defeat of the highway project and the preservation of the cultural identity and social fabric of Back Central, one of the city's oldest neighborhoods. Another example of social and cultural activism was the community's participation in a year-long project in 1987, conducted by the Folklife Division of the Library of Congress and the Smithsonian, to document ethnic culture among the city's communities. This project resulted in considerable documentary material, including oral histories and photography. In this instance, immigrants from the second wave, now young professionals, such as Maria Cunha (sister of Dimas Espínola) and Luís Pedroso, played a lead role. This experience in social activism brought a group together, including Elisia "Lisa" Teles Saab, that eventually led to the creation of the Saab-Pedroso Center for Portuguese Culture and Research, now the Saab Center for Portuguese Studies.

Given your cumulative experiences, is there anything you would have done differently?

More than any regrets, I feel immense gratitude toward UMass Dartmouth and UMass Lowell for the professional opportunities these institutions have afforded me. I am also ever grateful for the many people who participated in the heavy lifting required to build new programs and academic units. Of particular note is the work of Victor K. Mendes at UMass Dartmouth, who contributed to the Summer Program in Portuguese and Department of Portuguese and, particularly, to Tagus Press (beyond leading the graduate program). His work at the press led to some thirty volumes being published from 1998 to 2013 (and many more since then). I am also grateful to Dean Joseph Deck, who first hired me as an ABD and motivated me to complete my dissertation by threatening to fire me if I did not. Dean William Hogan was also instrumental in securing support for the center at Dartmouth, including the hire of the full-time managing editor of the press, Mario Pereira, in 2011, who helped professionalize and streamline its publications. Tagus Press remains in many ways the crown jewel of Portuguese studies at UMass Dartmouth. At UMass Lowell I have had the unflagging and generous support of Dean Luís M. Falcón, Chancellor Jacqueline Moloney, and my colleagues in the Department of World Languages and Cultures, chair Maria Matz and former chair Carol Salmon. One can always do better and there is no sense in trying to change the past, but, if I could, I would have reserved more time to dedicate to my own research. This is the reason why I have returned to (finally) completing the critical edition of Eça de Queirós's *A cidade e as serras* in a series directed by Carlos Reis of the Universidade de Coimbra at Imprensa Nacional-Casa da Moeda, and why I have another book on Eça de Queirós under contract with a press in São Paulo, Brazil.

SECTION 5

Changing Positionings of Portuguese Migrants and Portuguese-Americans Through Times: Gender, Race and Class

CHAPTER 16

The Occupational Structure of Portuguese Women in the United States in the Twentieth Century

......

M. GLORIA DE SÁ

Introduction

During the first decade of the twentieth century, 8.8 million immigrants entered the United States—the highest number in the history of the country.[1] A large proportion of these "new immigrants" originated in Southern, Eastern and Central European countries and settled into the fast-growing, industrial cities of the Northeast, rapidly changing the ethnic composition of American society. Among these newcomers were over sixty-nine thousand Portuguese.

Being primarily non-English-speaking Catholics and Jews, the "new immigrants" were believed to belong to distinctive and inferior races.[2] Their numbers and characteristics were perceived as a threat to the ideal composition of American society, which was based on "old-stock" northwestern European Protestant cultural patterns. As a result, they frequently met with considerable prejudice. In reference to Italians, for example, Richard Alba reports that a "fair number considered them to be racially inferior to the country's old-stock inhabitants."[3] These prejudices were common even in the so-called scientific literature of the first quarter of the twentieth century,[4] and the Portuguese received their fair share of this type of "scientific" attention. A prominent example of this was the investigation of the high rates of infant mortality among the Portuguese in Fall River, Massachusetts, and Portsmouth, Rhode Island, in the early 1920s, by Columbia University–trained sociologist Donald Taft, who speculated that the phenomenon might be related to "the infusion of negro blood"[5] into the veins of the Portuguese. Unable to come up with a definitive answer to why Portuguese infants were dying at about twice the rate of other children of white parents, he pointed out as possible explanations the "ignorance and illiteracy" of the Portuguese as well as their "lack of interest and meager attainment in education, low wages and economic exploitation, superstition and fatalism, cheap amusements and unrestrained fecundity."[6]

This perspective was so ingrained in the "scientific" thinking of the time, that even when clear evidence against the racial and ethnic inferiority hypothesis was encountered, it was often ignored or, worse, interpreted as positive proof of the very phenomenon it challenged. For instance, a doctor investigating the incidence of tuberculosis among various national groups had this to say about the surprisingly low mortality of Italians from the disease: "They are exceedingly dirty, and they are said to be much underfed. Moreover, being ignorant and superstitious people, and no doubt fearing often the imaginary terrors connoted by registration, they are given to concealing their cases, so that by no means all are reported."[7]

These perceptions were part of a process that led to the restrictive immigration quotas that went into effect in the 1920s, which, allied with the Great Depression and the economic and political consequences of World War II,[8] succeeded in reducing the flow of these groups to a trickle and allowed successive generations to adapt to the American way. Although it wasn't until after 1945 that these "dark Caucasoids" became "white ethnics,"[9] as we entered the third quarter of the twentieth century, scholars were pointing out that an "ethnic miracle"[10] had occurred and that the descendants of these once-labeled "hirsute, low-browed, big-faced persons of obviously low mentality"[11] were doing relatively well. "By all accounts, their education, occupations, and incomes are presently close to—or even in excess of—white Americans from earlier Northwestern European sources," reported Stanley Lieberson[12] in reference to the descendants of the "new immigrants." Later on, by analyzing data from the 1980 U.S. Census, he and Mary Waters concluded that white ethnic groups had become "for all intents and purposes, indistinguishable from one another on some dimension."[13] The argument was that the immigration hiatus of the mid-1920s to the mid-1960s prevented the ethnic distinctiveness of these groups from being renovated through the influx of new arrivals and allowed the second generation to move up the educational and occupational ladders.[14] Even groups, such as Italians, who initially displayed great difficulty in attaining parity in terms of education and entry into the professions and who had been viewed with a considerable amount of prejudice,[15] appeared to have caught up. By the late 1970s Italians had entered what Alba called the "twilight of ethnicity," and differences between them and other Americans of European ancestry, besides being "very mild," had "little meaning for everyday existence."[16]

How about the Portuguese, a group that has much in common with Italians? Like Italians, the Portuguese were primarily Roman Catholics of rural origin who arrived in the United States with very low levels of education and, like them, were considered by the likes of eugenicist Madison Grant to belong to a "lesser" type of European—the Mediterranean subspecies.[17] Did they too enter the "twilight of ethnicity" at the turn of the twenty-first century? Have they followed the European model and become incorporated into European America, or have they remained distinctive?

One of the distinctive traits of the Portuguese at the beginning of the twentieth century was that a large proportion of Portuguese women were in the paid labor force.[18] While their higher-than-average labor force participation may have been an effective strategy to increase family income, it was also associated with negative outcomes, such as high infant mortality. In 1915, for instance, the New Bedford Board of Health attributed the group's high rates of infant mortality to "the neglect of mothers who . . . boarded their offspring with incompetent persons so that they availed themselves of the opportunity to earn the 'big' wages which were paid in the different mills of the city."[19] Investigating the same connection in 1920s Fall River, Donald Taft concluded that although there was no conclusive evidence "as to the extent to which this employment actually affected the lives of the children," there was no doubt that "Portuguese mothers [were] employed in Fall River to a larger degree than other nationalities."[20] Moreover, both Donald Taft and Leo Pap presented evidence that in the first quarter of the twentieth century, the Portuguese worked chiefly in unskilled and semiskilled occupations in the manufacturing and agricultural sectors. Was this still the case at the turn of the twenty-first century or have their occupational characteristics changed?

This chapter attempts to provide some answers to these questions by examining the occupational structure of women of Portuguese origin during the twentieth century. Using U.S. Census data from 1900 to 2000, the chapter outlines the occupational trajectory of the group and compares it to that of other women of European ancestry, attempting to identify whether they followed or deviated from the general European American model and providing possible explanations for the similarities or differences encountered.

Data

The longitudinal data for the study come from the Integrated Public Use Microdata Series (or IPUMS), which consists of a series of high-precision samples of the American population, drawn from fourteen federal censuses spanning from 1850 to 2010. This study uses data from census years 1900 to 2000 but omits 1930, which has not been made available. Overall, census data are judged to be of good quality for three reasons: the expertise of the personnel involved, the sophistication of the technology and the processes used to collect and process the data, and the fact that respondents are under legal obligation to answer census surveys. Nevertheless, the data are still subject to sampling error and non-sampling error, which can be introduced during the collecting and processing procedures, such as editing and coding of responses. Additionally, the data contain some limitations. In this particular study, a major limitation is the small number of cases available. This is particularly true for Portuguese Americans in 1900 and 1910.

The three groups being compared are operationalized as follows:

1. *Portuguese Immigrants*: persons born in Portugal.
2. *Portuguese Americans*: persons born in the United States whose mother or father was born in Portugal (1880–1970) or persons born in the United States who identified their first ancestry as Portuguese (1980–2000).
3. *European Americans*: white persons born in the United States whose parents were also born in the United States (1880 to 1970) or white persons born in the United States who identified their first ancestry as European but not Portuguese (1980–2000).

Portuguese Immigration to the United States: An Overview

To provide a contextual background for this analysis, we begin with an overview of Portuguese immigration to the United States and the presentation of

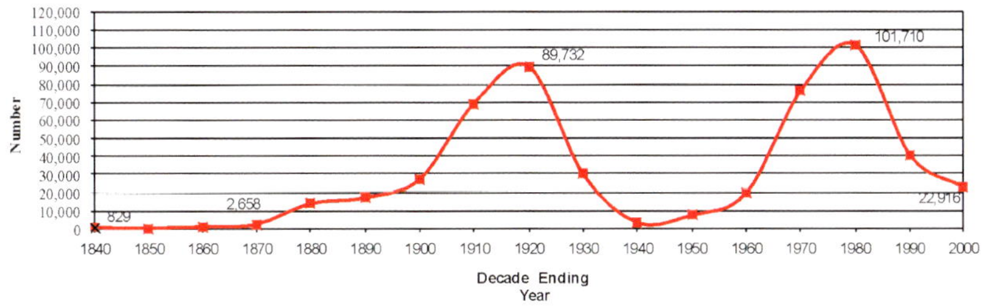

Figure 1. Portuguese immigration by decade: 1840–2000. Source: U.S. Census Bureau

some of the group's socioeconomic characteristics at the end of the twentieth century.

As can be seen from figure 1, Portuguese immigration to the United States occurred in primarily two waves: the first peaked around 1920 and the second during the 1970s. Prior to 1860, the flow of immigrants from Portugal was very low, numbering fewer than a thousand persons per decade. Following the discovery of gold in California in 1849 and the rise of industrialization in New England, however, the number rose sharply, averaging almost eight thousand per year during the first two decades of the twentieth century. Then it dropped drastically, in response to the national origin quotas legislation of the 1920s, so that during the 1930–40 decade it was almost at the same level as the 1860–70 period. By 1960, it was still below the 1900 levels, but in the following decades, with the passage of the Immigration and Nationality Act of 1965, it registered a tremendous surge that culminated in over one hundred thousand persons from 1971 to 1980. Most of the newcomers (about 75 percent) settled in communities of earlier Portuguese immigration along the Eastern Seaboard, especially in New Bedford, Fall River, Providence, Newark, and Greater Boston. At the time of this settlement, these were areas characterized by the presence Portuguese ethnic enclaves with a large degree of institutional completeness, such as Portuguese churches, media, and businesses. They were also areas characterized by a general lack of occupational and educational opportunities.[21]

Since the 1980s, however, Portuguese immigration to the United States has been declining steadily, and in the year 2000 only 1,402 Portuguese immigrants entered the United States. In that year, according to the U.S. Census, there were 1,176,615 persons of Portuguese origin living in the United States, 240,780 of whom, or 20.5 percent, were immigrants (table 1).

Table 1. Selected Characteristics of the Portuguese and U.S. Population: 2000

Demographic Characteristics	**Portuguese Population**	**Total U.S. Population**
Total population	1,176,615	281,421,906
Male	49.1%	49.0%
Female	50.9%	51.0%
Foreign born	20.5%	11.1%
Median age (years)	35	35
Average household size	3	3
Average family size	3	3
Social and Economic Characteristics		
Bachelor's degree or higher (population 25 years and over)	19.1%	30.4%
Speak a language other than English at home (population 5 years and over)	30.2%	17.9%
Median household income in 1999 (dollars)	48,300	41,994
Individuals below poverty level	8.0%	12.1%

Source: U.S. Census Bureau, Summary File 4 (SF 4)

Despite their noted disadvantages at the beginning of the twentieth century, by the year 2000, as shown by table 1, persons of Portuguese ancestry living in the United States were not significantly different from the rest of the U.S. population on many of the characteristics measured by the census. But some disadvantages were still evident. Beginning with the similarities, we see that their sex ratio was basically the same as that of the country as a whole and, despite their noteworthy "unrestrained fecundity"[22] at the beginning of the century, by the century's end their household and family size was the same as that of the general population—three persons. Economically, they were doing better than average. Their median household income was more than $6,000 over the national figure ($48,300 vs. $41,994) and the percentage of individuals living in poverty was only two-thirds of that for the country as a whole (8.0% vs. 12.1%). Educationally and linguistically, however, they were still clearly handicapped. For example, of those age 25 and over, only 19.1 percent had college degrees, compared to 30.4 percent of the total population, and 30 percent spoke a language other than English at home, compared to only 18 percent of all residents, which might be interpreted as a lack of ability to speak English. To the extent that formal education and English language ability represent stocks of human and cultural capital, they appear to indicate barriers to socioeconomic integration as well as continued patterns of ethnic distinction.

As pointed out by Maria Mulcahy,[23] Dorothy Gilbert,[24] and de Sá and David Borges,[25] these advantages and disadvantages are intimately related to the occupational structure, in particular to the group's concentration in blue-collar work, especially manufacturing, and the high rates of labor force participation by women. Concentration in well-paid blue-collar occupations and having a large number of family members in the paid labor force afforded the Portuguese a relatively high degree of economic success, despite their low levels of human capital, as measured by formal education and English language ability. However, this same economic success and the availability of relatively well-paid blue-collar occupations in major areas of Portuguese settlement throughout the twentieth century may have acted as a disincentive to pursue higher levels of education and more skilled and prestigious occupations.[26]

General Occupational Distribution

Portuguese Immigrants

The upper section of table 2 shows the occupational distribution of foreign-born Portuguese females ages 16–70 during the twentieth century. The first thing one may observe about the table is that before 1920 many of the cells are empty, which might lead to the conclusion that there were no Portuguese immigrant women in these particular occupations. To a large degree, however, this may not have been the case. One reason for this pattern is that only women with a valid occupational entry were included in this tabulation, leaving out those who were not classified as being in the formal labor force. In the case of Portuguese immigrant women, until 1920, most of the women in the sample fell into the general category of "unpaid house and family worker," which excluded them from the official occupational categories. Another reason for empty cells is the low number of Portuguese immigrant women in the total sample. These limitations make it difficult to say much about the occupational structure of Portuguese immigrant women during the

Table 2. Occupational distribution of women ages 17 to 70 by year and group: 1900–2000

Year	Professional	Farm owners/ Managers	Managers	Clerical	Sales	Craftsmen	Operatives	Services	Farm Laborers	Laborers
Portuguese Immigrants										
1900	0.00	0.00	0.00	0.00	0.00	0.00	28.57	71.43	0.00	0.00
1910	0.00	0.00	0.00	0.00	0.00	0.00	65.38	26.92	3.85	3.85
1920	0.00	1.52	1.52	1.52	0.00	0.00	90.91	1.52	1.52	1.52
1940	1.87	3.74	0.00	7.48	3.74	0.93	72.90	7.48	0.93	0.93
1950	2.15	0.00	5.38	4.30	1.08	1.08	76.34	7.53	1.08	1.08
1960	1.32	0.00	1.97	4.61	5.92	1.97	67.11	15.13	1.32	0.66
1970	1.20	0.30	0.30	7.81	3.30	2.40	72.37	11.41	0.00	0.90
1980	3.78	0.00	1.51	14.67	2.12	5.60	58.25	11.04	0.45	2.57
1990	7.41	0.00	4.34	17.48	4.48	3.92	40.56	18.74	0.42	2.66
2000	11.93	0.25	5.04	21.40	5.04	5.17	25.58	23.37	0.62	1.60
Average										
1900-1970	0.93	0.79	1.31	3.67	2.01	0.91	67.65	20.20	1.24	1.28
1980-2000	7.71	0.08	3.63	17.85	3.88	4.90	41.46	17.72	0.50	2.28

Table 2. Continued

Portuguese Americans										
Year	Professional	Farm owners/ Managers	Managers	Clerical	Sales	Craftsmen	Operatives	Services	Farm Laborers	Laborers
1900	0.00	0.00	0.00	50.00	0.00	0.00	25.00	0.00	0.00	25.00
1910	0.00	0.00	0.00	7.14	7.14	7.14	50.00	21.43	7.14	0.00
1920	4.00	0.00	0.00	28.00	8.00	8.00	40.00	4.00	0.00	8.00
1940	4.41	2.94	1.47	10.29	5.88	4.41	48.53	19.12	1.47	1.47
1950	3.26	0.00	0.00	21.74	7.61	1.09	57.67	5.43	1.09	2.17
1960	4.07	0.33	0.81	23.90	7.48	1.95	46.18	13.33	0.65	1.30
1970	7.79	0.18	2.54	28.08	7.97	2.36	29.89	19.75	0.72	0.72
1980	12.49	0.26	5.53	35.91	8.20	2.41	13.92	19.45	0.59	1.24
1990	16.15	0.38	11.18	33.72	7.09	1.96	8.29	19.04	0.16	2.02
2000	26.21	0.34	8.51	33.86	7.12	1.01	4.57	17.22	0.19	0.96
Average										
1900-1970	3.36	0.49	0.69	24.16	6.30	3.56	42.47	11.87	1.58	5.52
1980-2000	18.28	0.33	8.41	34.50	7.47	1.79	8.93	18.57	0.31	1.41

Table 2. Continued

European-Americans										
Year	Professional	Farm owners/ Managers	Managers	Clerical	Sales	Craftsmen	Operatives	Services	Farm Laborers	Laborers
1900	13.78	10.32	3.49	5.64	4.01	1.59	21.79	33.74	4.09	1.55
1910	16.53	5.23	1.87	12.68	6.03	1.17	21.57	22.37	11.30	1.26
1920	17.91	3.99	2.43	25.13	8.05	1.57	18.32	16.27	4.00	2.34
1940	19.69	1.30	4.87	25.04	7.77	1.28	16.56	21.71	0.95	0.82
1950	14.45	0.65	4.32	31.41	10.07	1.49	17.75	15.70	3.53	0.63
1960	12.88	0.46	3.29	35.34	10.96	1.23	15.96	17.77	1.53	0.57
1970	15.60	0.25	3.03	36.40	9.08	1.76	13.94	18.17	0.77	1.00
1980	18.48	0.44	6.31	35.19	8.06	2.01	9.50	18.01	0.66	1.34
1990	22.75	0.50	9.96	31.69	7.45	1.91	6.83	16.88	0.49	1.54
2000	29.65	0.39	9.62	30.16	7.12	1.62	5.02	15.27	0.29	0.87
Average										
1900-1970	15.83	3.17	3.33	24.52	8.00	1.44	17.98	20.82	3.74	1.17
1980-2000	23.63	0.44	8.63	32.35	7.54	1.85	7.12	16.72	0.48	1.25

first two decades of the twentieth century, except to note that it adumbrates the overall pattern that takes shape in later years—great occupational concentration in factory work (operatives). In 1920, for example, about 91 percent of Portuguese immigrant females held this type of occupation. In contrast, only 18 percent of European American women worked in factories at this time (table 2, bottom panel). Although this degree of concentration was not to occur again, from 1900 to 1970, the majority (about two-thirds) of Portuguese immigrant women worked as operatives or factory workers.

The year 1920 was the heyday of the cotton mills in the major areas of settlement of Portuguese immigration, such as New Bedford and Fall River in Massachusetts. At the end of that decade, however, a large proportion of the mills moved their looms south,[27] and by 1940 the percentage of Portuguese who were factory workers had declined to 73 percent. But by the end of World War II, the empty mill floors of New England were being filled with sewing machines, which continued to provide factory employment to the majority of Portuguese immigrant women. After having dropped to about 67 percent in 1960, by the time the second wave of immigration was peaking in 1970, the percentage of factory workers among Portuguese immigrant women had risen to 72. By contrast, in the same year, only about 14 percent of European American women worked in factories. From 1900 to 1970, on average, about 68 percent of Portuguese immigrant women worked as operatives in comparison to 18 percent of white native women of native parentage (bottom of table 2). In the late seventies, however, the sewing machines went the way of the looms, and by 1980, the proportion of Portuguese immigrant females classified as operatives had declined to 58 percent. As the process of deindustrialization accelerated, more and more Portuguese immigrant women left the factories, so that by 2000 only about one-quarter of them did this type of work. Nevertheless, that proportion was still five times as high as that of European Americans in general (5%).

As the percentage of operatives declined, the proportion in other types of occupations increased. The occupational category that seems to have been most closely related to fluctuations in the proportion employed in factory work was that of nonprofessional service occupations—a category that includes such jobs as cleaners, and child and elder caregivers. For example, in 1920, when almost 91 percent of Portuguese immigrant women were employed as factory workers, only 1.5 percent worked in nonprofessional services, but by 1960 the proportion in this type of occupation had risen to 15.1 percent, while that in factory work had declined to 67 percent. By 1970, however, the figure had declined to about 11 percent and remained at that level until 1980, even though by this time the proportion of factory workers among Portuguese immigrant women had declined to 58 percent. A possible explanation for the relatively low proportion of nonprofessional service workers among Portuguese immigrant women during these two decades may be the fact that the new immigrants that were coming in at this time could not enter the sector due to human, cultural, and physical capital deficits. Service occupations require English language skills, knowledge of the host culture, and, for those who seek to establish their own businesses, considerable amounts of money. These forms of capital increase with duration of residence in the host country and this may have been one of the reasons why twenty years later, in 2000, the proportion in this type of occupations had risen to over 23 percent, a figure that was actually higher than that of the comparison group, that is, native white women, of whom only 15 percent worked in this type of occupations. Nevertheless, while the gains in human, cultural and physical capital associated with longer duration of residence in the United States may have facilitated the movement of Portuguese immigrant women into nonprofessional service jobs, the major factor was the process of deindustrialization, which took away their traditional occupational niche as factory workers.

Another occupational category that appears to have picked up some of the women displaced from the "operatives" classification was clerical and kindred work. In 1920, only 1.5 percent of Portuguese immigrant women worked in clerical positions. By 1940 the proportion had risen to 7.5 percent, perhaps as a result of the lack of immigration during the 1930s. With no influx of newcomers, the proportion of immigrants who had grown up in America and acquired the education and other types of capital necessary to do this type of work increased, allowing them to move into this occupational category. The percentage of clerical workers then declined for the next two decades, but began to increase again in 1970, and by 2000 it had reached 21.4 percent. Despite the increase, at the end of the century, the proportion of clerical workers among Portuguese immigrants was still much smaller than among European Americans (30.1%), for whom it was the number one occupation.

As for the other positions requiring higher educational and English skills, such as managerial and professional occupations, the numbers were very low for the whole period under observation, although there was a significant increase after 1970. While in 1970 only 1.2 percent of Portuguese immigrant women were found in these occupations, by 2000 almost 12 percent were so classified. Still, this was only one-third of the rate for native women of other European ancestries.

Over the whole twentieth century, other occupational categories have accounted for only a negligible portion of Portuguese immigrant women's occupations. Even by century's end, neither one of them accounted for much more than 5 percent of the total number of workers. Nevertheless, it is perhaps worth mentioning that from 1980 to 2000 there was a relatively high increase in the proportion of "sales workers" and of "managers, officials and proprietors," which went from about 2 to 5 percent. Still, both categories were quite lower than for white natives of European origin. In the case of "managers, officials and proprietors," for example, the figure was only slightly more than half of that of other white natives of European origin (5.0% vs. 9.6%).

Overall, the occupational pattern for Portuguese immigrant women is characterized by a high concentration in factory work throughout the twentieth century. Although this concentration has been diminishing over time, with more women moving into the service, clerical, and, to a smaller degree, professional and managerial occupations, at the turn of the twenty-first century their occupational structure was still considerably distinctive from that of non-Portuguese, native white women.

Portuguese Americans

Over the same period, as expected, Portuguese American women (see the middle of table 2) were less occupationally concentrated than their immigrant counterparts, that is, they were found in a wider range of occupations. In fact, over time, their occupational distribution came to resemble more that of other native women of European origin than of Portuguese immigrants. Nevertheless, they maintained some of the characteristics of their Portuguese immigrant mothers. As was the case with immigrants, until 1970, the category of "operatives" accounted for the largest proportion of workers among them (an average of 43 percent). After 1970, however, "clerical and kindred work" became their modal occupational category, with an average of 34.5 percent of all workers. This was also the modal category for other European Americans (32.4%).

These longitudinal changes appear to be related not only to the transformation of the economic structure of the United States but also to changes in the flows of Portuguese immigration. As shown in the middle of table 2, in 1920, 40 percent of Portuguese American women were factory workers. This was a much smaller proportion than immigrants (91%) but a much greater percentage than other European Americans (18%). Additionally, while in the following decades the proportion of factory workers decreased steadily for other European Americans, for Portuguese Americans it continued to increase until 1950, when it reached 58 percent. It appears that, as with their male counterparts (Mulcahy 2003), during this period of low immigration, Portuguese American women were being recruited into factory work to compensate for the low supply of immigrant labor. After 1960, with the increase in immigration, the proportion of operatives among Portuguese Americans decreased steadily, dropping to only 4.5 percent in 2000. This figure, besides being much lower than that for Portuguese immigrant women (25.6%), is also slightly lower than that of other European American females in general (5.0%). As reported by de Sá it appears that in communities of high Portuguese concentration, factory work had become so stigmatized that Portuguese American women began to leave the factories even when jobs in this sector were still plentiful and better paying than other types of low-skill jobs, such as those in the service sector.[28]

In the first half of the twentieth century, the percentage of Portuguese American women in service occupations fluctuated considerably. From their almost complete absence in this type of work in 1900, it reached about 21 percent in 1920 only to drop again to a mere 5 percent in 1950. After 1950, the proportion of Portuguese American women in this occupational category rose rapidly, reaching almost 20 percent in 1970, and then declined to 17 percent in 2000.

To some degree, these fluctuations, especially in the earlier part of the century, are due to small sample sizes, but they also seem to be related to immigrant flows. The data show that during times of high Portuguese immigration, like around 1920 and 1970, the proportion of Portuguese American women in service occupations rose. In contrast, it dipped when the number of immigrants went down, such as in the 1940s. This pattern supports the hypothesis that during periods when few Portuguese immigrants were coming in, Portuguese Americans were recruited into jobs traditionally associated with their immigrant ancestors, such as factory work, causing a decline in other occupations, such as service jobs.

When compared with other native white women of European origin, prior to 1960, Portuguese American women seem to have been considerably less likely to work in nonprofessional service occupations, but since then they do not seem very different either in terms of changes over time or the overall proportion employed in this type of occupations, although by 2000 the Portuguese had a slightly higher percentage of workers in the category (17% vs. 15%).

As with nonprofessional services, the data about clerical jobs for the early part of the century suffer from the deficiencies of small sample sizes and may, therefore, be inaccurate. It is highly unlikely, for example, that 50 percent of all Portuguese American women were clerical workers in 1900. In the later part of the century, however, figures are much more likely to be reliable, showing a rising flow into this type of occupation. For example, from 10 percent in 1940 the proportion of clerical workers rose to 36 percent in 1980. Although that proportion declined slightly after that year, at the end of the observation period, the majority of American-born women of Portuguese ancestry worked in clerical positions, just like other European Americans. In 2000, over one-third (33.9%) were found in this occupational category, having surpassed the figure for their other European American counterparts (30.2%). Hence, at the turn of the twenty-first century, the typical Portuguese American woman was an office worker, just like her other European American counterparts. They also resembled them in terms of their distribution into other, more prestigious occupations requiring higher degrees of various forms of capital,[29] such as "managers, officials and proprietors" and "professional and technical occupations." But for them, just like for their non-Portuguese sisters, significant movement into these occupations did not arrive until the last quarter of the twentieth century.

Until 1980, the proportion of women working as managers, officials and proprietors was negligible. This was true not just for Portuguese American women but also for other European Americans. In 1970, for example, among the Portuguese, the figure was around 3 percent for native women and less than 1 percent for immigrants. By 2000, however, the proportion had risen to 8.5 percent for Portuguese Americans, a figure that was only one percentage point lower than for other European Americans (9.6%).

A similar pattern characterizes professional and technical occupations, with the variant that prior to 1980, the advantage of other European Americans was much stronger than for managerial occupations. Until 1970, the average proportion of Portuguese American women classified as professional and technical workers was less than 3 percent, a much smaller proportion than for other European Americans (16%). After 1970, however, the proportion went up substantially, and in 2000, 26.2 percent of all Portuguese American women held professional or technical jobs. This was a much higher proportion than immigrant women (12%) and very close to that of other native women of European ancestry (29.7%).

Overall, for most of the twentieth century, the occupational pattern for Portuguese American women is characterized by a high concentration in semiskilled occupations, like factory work and nonprofessional services. The concentration in factory work diminished toward the end of the period, with more women moving into the clerical, professional, and service occupations.

By 2000, in terms of overall occupational structure, Portuguese American women had become more like other European Americans than Portuguese immigrants as can be seen from the rankings of occupational categories shown in table 3. Although the specific percentages differed slightly, like other native white women of European ancestry, about one-third worked in clerical occupations, followed by professional, service, managerial, sales, and factory work. In contrast, Portuguese immigrant women, despite considerable movement into more prestigious occupations, ended the century pretty much as they began it—with about one-fourth working in factories.

Table 3. Ranking of occupational categories by group: 2000

Occupational ranking	Portuguese immigrants	Portuguese Americans	European Americans
1	Operatives	Clerical	Clerical
2	Services	Professional	Professional
3	Clerical	Services	Services
4	Professional	Managers	Managers
5	Managers	Sales	Sales
6	Sales	Operatives	Operatives

Discussion

Why these particular patterns? Why did Portuguese women remain factory workers for such a long period of their history in the United States? Why did it take them so long to catch up with other European Americans?

Until the middle of the twentieth century, the dominant theory of immigrant incorporation into American society was assimilation theory. Assimilation theory did not propose that ethnic or racial minorities would achieve the same characteristics as native whites of Anglo-Saxon descent.[30] Rather, it asserted that the competitive nature of the economy and the democratic characteristics of political institutions in modern urban societies would work toward the elimination of ethnic ties and put an increasing emphasis on achievement rather than ascription. A corollary of the assimilation framework is the so-called human capital theory, which predicts that differences between groups are the result of different stocks of marketable skills, such as education, experience, and language proficiency.

The view that stocks of human capital, such as education, English proficiency, and technical skills are important in the process of integrating various groups, including immigrants, into American society is not a question of great debate. Overall, research done under the human capital approach supports the expectations of assimilation theory, showing that exposure to the host society, as measured in terms of duration of residence and English-language acquisition,[31] for example, moves immigrants toward parity with natives and that groups who are successful in acquiring adequate stocks of human capital, such as Asians, have been successful in reaching or surpassing the socioeconomic achievement of native whites.[32] The question of what makes some groups successful in obtaining this capital while others lag behind for generations, however, cannot be answered by assimilation theory. Why is it, for instance, as George Borjas put it, that levels of literacy in a group's country of origin in 1910 continue to be correlated with the same group's socioeconomic position in the United States almost a century later?[33]

As previously mentioned, a possible explanation is that the concept of human capital, in the economic sense of marketable skills like education and technical know-how, does not capture the full range of the attributes needed for full integration. At the micro level, the incorporation of immigrants and ethnic groups is a function of various forms of capital that also include cultural knowledge and social connections.[34] Those possessing education, specialized skills, and knowledge of the language and culture of the United States will be able to compete for jobs in the open market on parity with members of the dominant group, in this case European Americans. But immigrants arriving with low stocks of human and cultural capital will have to depend disproportionately on ethnic social capital, that is, networks of personal connections, in order to find employment. Hence, the types of occupations available to them will be intimately related to the occupational traditions of their ethnic group, and, therefore, labor market competition occurs primarily between groups of immigrants of the same origin arriving at different points in time, or between generations of the same group. For groups that have developed strong ethnic economies based on entrepreneurship, incorporation usually means becoming a small business owner. This was the pattern followed by Greeks, who, in terms of human capital, were similar to the Portuguese.[35] For those with a tradition of manual work, like the Portuguese, however, the utilization of personal networks leads to factory jobs, especially for those who settled in New England.[36] Once established, these patterns tend to perpetuate themselves over time and will require significant structural transformations in order to change. In the case of the Portuguese, that restructuring did not occur until the last quarter of the twentieth century, with the process of deindustrialization. In 1985, for example, manufacturing still accounted for about 43 percent of total employment in Fall River and New Bedford.[37]

Another related factor contributing to the higher prevalence of factory work among the Portuguese has to do with the timing of their settlement in the United States relative to other European groups. When, at the beginning of the twentieth century, they began to settle in the industrial towns of New England, such as New Bedford, Fall River, and Lowell, most of the mill workers were French Canadians who had replaced earlier groups like the English and the Irish, who had moved into other occupations or out of the area.[38] In the next two decades, as Canadian immigration began to dwindle, newly arrived Portuguese immigrants replaced Canadians in the mills, entering at the bottom of the occupational ladder. By 1920, as Taft pointed out, the Portuguese had become a "permanent element" of New England's workforce and "if they should leave, a substitute labor supply would have to be found."[39] Shortly after Taft came to this conclusion, however, the demise of the textile industry and the passage of the National Origins Act of 1924 ensured that new supplies of immigrant labor were neither needed nor desired until about forty years later. Without new immigrants to push them up the occupational ladder, the children of early Portuguese settlers replaced their parents in the surviving factories and the group remained where it had started—working in factories.[40] The fact that the proportion of operatives among Portuguese American women seemed to increase during times of low Portuguese immigration lends credence to this explanation.

Other possible explanations for the distinctive occupational pattern of Portuguese women is provided by ethnic antagonism and split labor market theories.[41] According to this view, ethnic groups composed of higher-priced workers with more political power contrive to keep lower-priced workers with less political power out of the better-paid occupations. If they succeed, the result is a caste-like system, where lower-priced workers are restricted to specific occupations. Research on the role of trade unions during the first quarter of the twentieth century[42] seems to support the view that members of earlier European arrival groups did try to keep the Portuguese out of certain occupations. But perhaps more significant than these formal strategies were the informal ways in which the Portuguese were discouraged from seeking nonfactory jobs, especially those that required higher levels of education. Personal accounts of myriad Portuguese recount how they were dissuaded from pursuing education beyond the age when they could legally begin to work. Taft himself, in his study of the Portuguese of Fall River, shows that he was aware of this reality when he wrote, "So far as recent school reports show the educational policy of recent years, there seems to be a curious conflict between a desire to keep the children in school longer, and a fear lest what they learn shall make them dissatisfied with the life of a mill operative. . . . Is the educational problem of Fall River to make 'educated' people love to tend looms? Or is it to make them dissatisfied with the cotton mill, and if so, who is to tend the looms?"[43]

This quote also suggests that the persistence of factory work among Portuguese women may be related to the labor needs of the places where they settled. It was not in the interest of those who controlled the economic fate of industrial towns to provide residents with opportunities to seek other types of employment. As a result, residents of these communities were prevented from improving their educational achievement not only by the lack of information, schools, and role models but also by the lack of good-paying jobs for those who were educated. In her study of economic and educational achievement among the Portuguese of Fall River in the early 1970s, Gilbert, for instance, emphasizes the bounded rationality of the Portuguese in choosing blue-collar work over education: "There are jobs available for those without a high school diploma, and there is no guarantee that a diploma will ensure a better job in Fall River. Individuals who go to college run the risk of educating themselves out of the city's capacity to employ them."[44]

Indeed, getting an education and competing with more established groups for so-called middle-class occupations put the Portuguese at higher risk not only of unemployment but also of wage discrimination. As pointed out by Maria Pereira,[45] Mulcahy,[46] and de Sá and Borges,[47] persons of Portuguese ancestry with low levels of education seemed to have an advantage over persons of other groups when it came to income. Those with college educations, however, earned less than members of other groups. Hence, when success is measured by income, it seems reasonable to choose well-paid blue-collar work over lower-paid white-collar jobs with low returns to educational investments. This seems to have been the logic followed by women of Portuguese descent in the United States for most of the twentieth century.

Regardless of the explanations for their concentration in these kinds of occupations, it appears that factory work has been both a gateway and a trap for Portuguese women in the United States. On the one hand, concentration in this type of work provided them with the opportunity to reach a high degree of economic success despite low levels of education. On the other, it may have denied them both the opportunity and the incentive to acquire the educational credentials required for entrance into more prestigious occupations. Nevertheless, by the end of the twentieth century, while Portuguese immigrant women continued to be primarily factory workers, American-born women of Portuguese descent had moved away from the century-old tradition of industrial production work and become virtually indistinguishable from their European American counterparts in terms of occupational structure.

Works Cited

Alba, Richard D. *Italian Americans into the Twilight of Ethnicity.* Englewood Cliffs, NJ: Prentice Hall, 1985.

Alba, Richard, and Victor Nee. "Rethinking Assimilation Theory for a New Era of Immigration." In *The Handbook of International Migration: The American Experience,* edited by Charles Hirschman, Philip Kasnitz, and Josh DeWind, 137–60. New York: Russell Sage Foundation, 1999.

Baganha, Maria I. "The Social Mobility of Portuguese Immigrants at the Turn of the Nineteenth Century." *International Migration Review* 25 (1991): 277–302.

Bonacich, Edna. "A Theory of Ethnic Antagonism: The Split Labor Market." *American Sociological Review* 37, no. 5 (1972): 547–59.

Bourdieu P. "The Forms of Capital." In *Handbook of Theory and Research for the Sociology of Education*, edited by J. Richardson, 46–58. New York: Greenwood, 1986.

de Sá, Maria Glória. "Mobility Ladder or Economic Lifeboat? Self-Employment among Portuguese Immigrant Women in the U.S. from 1970–2006." In *A Mulher e o Trabalho nos Açores e nas Comunidades/ Women and Work in the Azores and the Immigrant Communities*, vol. 5, edited by Rosa Neves Simas, 1271–88. Ponta Delgada: UMAR-Açores, 2008.

de Sá, Maria Glória and David Borges. "Context or Culture: Portuguese-Americans and Social Mobility." In *Building Ethnic Communities: Portuguese-Americans along the Eastern Seaboard*, edited by Kim Holton and Andrea Klimt, 265–90. North Dartmouth, MA: Center for Portuguese Studies and Culture, University of Massachusetts Dartmouth 2009.

Gilbert, Dorothy A. *Recent Portuguese Immigrants to Fall River, Massachusetts: An Analysis of Relative Economic Success.* New York: AMS Press, 1989.

Glazer, Nathan, and Daniel Patrick Moynihan. *Beyond the Melting Pot: The Negros, Puerto Ricans, Jews, Italians and Irish of New York City.* Cambridge, MA: Harvard University Press, 1970.

Grant, Madison. *The Passing of a Great Race: The Racial Basis of European History.* New edition. New York: Charles Scribner's Sons, 1918.

Greeley, Andrew. "The Ethnic Miracle." *Public Interest* 45 (Fall 1976): 20–36.

Hirschman, Charles. "America's Melting Pot Reconsidered." *Annual Review of Sociology* 9 (1983): 397–423.

Huber, John Bessner. *Consumption, Its Relation to Man and His Civilization; Its Prevention and Cure, by John Bessner Huber.* Philadelphia and London: Lippincott, 1906.

Lieberson, Stanley. *A Piece of the Pie: Blacks and White Immigrants Since 1880.* Berkeley: University of California Press, 1980.

Lieberson, Stanley, and Mary C. Waters. *From Many Strands: Ethnic and Racial Groups in Contemporary America.* New York: Russell Sage Foundation, 1988.

Lovell-Troy, Lawrence A. "Clan Structure and Economic Activity: The Case of Greeks in Small Business Enterprise." In *Self Help in Urban America: Patterns of Minority Economic Development*, edited by Scott Cummings, 58–85. Port Washington, NY: National University Publications, Kennikat Press, 1980.

Massey, Douglas. "The New Immigration and Ethnicity in the United States." *Population and Development Review* 21, no. 3 (1995): 631–52.

Mulcahy, Maria. "The Portuguese of the U.S. from 1880 to 1990: Distinctiveness in Work Patterns across Gender, Nativity and Place." PhD diss., Brown University, 2003.

Nee, Victor, and Jimy M. Sanders. "The Road to Parity: Determinants of the Socioeconomic Achievements of Asian Americans." *Ethnic and Racial Studies* 8 (1985): 75–93.

Pap, Leo. *The Portuguese Americans.* Boston: Twayne Publishers, 1981.

Pereira, Maria G. "The Socioeconomic Achievement of Portuguese Males in Massachusetts and Rhode Island." MA thesis, Brown University, Providence, RI, 1985.

Perlmann, Joel, and Roger Waldinger. "Second Generation Decline? Immigrant Children Past and Present—A Reconsideration." *International Migration Review* 31, no. 4 (1997): 893–922.

Portes, Alejandro. "Gaining the Upper Hand: Economic Mobility among Immigrant and Domestic Minorities." *Ethnic and Racial Studies* 15 (1992): 491–522.

Portes, Alejandro, and Min Zhou. "The New Second Generation: Segmented Assimilation and Its Variants among Post-1965 Immigrant Youth." *Annals of the American Academy of Political and Social Science* 530 (November 1993): 74–98.

Ross, Edward A. *The Old World in the New: The Significance of Past and Present Immigration to the American People.* New York: Century, 1914.

Ruggles, Steven, Matthew Sobek, Trent Alexander, Catherine A. Fitch, Ronald Goeken, Patricia Kelly Hall, Miriam King, and Chad Ronnander. *Integrated Public Use Microdata Series: Version 3.0.* Minneapolis: Minnesota Population Center, 2004.

Silvia, Philip T. "The Position of 'New' Immigrants in the Fall River Textile Industry." *International Migration Review* 10, no. 2 (1976): 221–32.

Taft, Donald R. *Two Portuguese Communities in New England.* New York: AMS Press, 1969. First published in 1923.

Waldinger, Roger. *Still the Promised City? African-Americans and New Immigrants in Post-Industrial New York.* Cambridge, MA: Harvard University Press, 1996.

Williams, Jerry R. *In Pursuit of Their Dreams: A History of Azorean Immigration to the United States.* North Dartmouth, MA: Center for Portuguese Studies and Culture, University of Massachusetts Dartmouth, 2005.

Notes

1. Stanley Lieberson and Mary C. Waters, *From Many Strands: Ethnic and Racial Groups in Contemporary America* (New York: Russell Sage Foundation, 1988), 32.

2. Joel Perlmann and Roger Waldinger, "Second Generation Decline? Immigrant Children Past and Present—A Reconsideration," *International Migration Review* 31, no. 4 (1997): 893–922.

3. Richard D. Alba, *Italian Americans into the Twilight of Ethnicity* (Englewood Cliffs, NJ: Prentice Hall, 1985), 164.

4. See Cristiana Bastos, this volume.

5. Donald R. Taft, *Two Portuguese Communities in New England* (New York: AMS Press, Inc, 1969), 18.

6. Taft, *Two Portuguese Communities in New England*, 346–50.

7. John Bessner Huber, *Consumption, Its Relation to Man and His Civilization; Its Prevention and Cure, by John Bessner Huber* (Philadelphia and London: Lippincott, 1906), 104.

8. Douglas Massey, "The New Immigration and Ethnicity in the United States," *Population and Development Review* 21, no. 3 (1995): 631–52

9. Perlmann and Waldinger, "Second Generation Decline?," 903.

10. Andrew Greeley, "The Ethnic Miracle," *Public Interest* 45 (Fall 1976): 20–36.

11. Edward A. Ross, *The Old World in the New: The Significance of Past and Present Immigration to the American People* (New York: Century, 1914), 285–86.

12. Lieberson and Waters, *From Many Strands*, 1.

13. Lieberson and Waters, *From Many Strands*, 248.

14. Richard Alba and Victor Nee, "Rethinking Assimilation Theory for a New Era of Immigration," in *The Handbook of International Migration: The American Experience*, ed. Charles Hirschman, Philip Kasnitz, and Josh DeWind, 137–60 (New York: Russell Sage Foundation, 1999).

15. Nathan Glazer and Daniel Patrick Moynihan, *Beyond the Melting Pot: the Negros, Puerto Ricans, Jews, Italians and Irish of New York City* (Cambridge, MA: Harvard University Press, 1970), 207.

16. Alba, *Italian Americans into the Twilight of Ethnicity*, 159–60.

17. Madison Grant, *The Passing of a Great Race: The Racial Basis of European History*. New ed. (New York: Charles Scribner's Sons, 1918), 148.

18. Leo Pap, *The Portuguese Americans* (Boston: Twayne Publishers, 1981); Taft, *Two Portuguese Communities in New England.*

19. Cited in Pap, *The Portuguese Americans*, 110.

20. Taft, *Two Portuguese Communities in New England*, 177.

21. Pap, *The Portuguese Americans*, 99–100.

22. Taft, *Two Portuguese Communities in New England*, 345,

23. Maria Mulcahy, "The Portuguese of the U.S. from 1880 to 1990: Distinctiveness in Work Patterns Across Gender, Nativity and Place" (PhD diss., Brown University, 2003).

24. Dorothy A. Gilbert. *Recent Portuguese Immigrants to Fall River, Massachusetts: An Analysis of Relative Economic Success* (New York: AMS Press, 1989).

25. Maria Glória de Sá and David Borges, "Context or Culture: Portuguese-Americans and Social Mobility," in *Building Ethnic Communities: Portuguese-Americans along the Eastern Seaboard*, ed. Kim Holton and Andrea Klimt, 265–90 (North Dartmouth, MA: Center for Portuguese Studies and Culture, University of Massachusetts Dartmouth, 2009).

26. Gilbert, *Recent Portuguese Immigrants to Fall River, Massachusetts.*

27. Philip T. Silvia, "The Position of 'New' Immigrants in the Fall River Textile Industry," *International Migration Review* 10, no. 2 (1976): 221–32.

28. Maria Glória de Sá, "Mobility Ladder or Economic Lifeboat? Self-Employment among Portuguese Immigrant Women in the U.S. from 1970–2006," in *A Mulher e o Trabalho nos Açores e nas Comunidades/Women and Work in the Azores and the Immigrant Communities*, vol. 5, ed Rosa Neves Simas, 1271–88 (Ponta Delgada: UMAR-Açores, 2008).

29. P. Bourdieu, "The Forms of Capital," in *Handbook of Theory and Research for the Sociology of Education*, ed. J. Richardson, 46–58 (New York: Greenwood, 1986).

30. Charles Hirschman, "America's Melting Pot Reconsidered," *Annual Review of Sociology* 9 (1983): 474.

31. George Borjas, "Assimilation, Changes in Cohort Quality and the Earnings of Immigrants," *Journal of Labor Economics* 3 (1985): 463–89.

32. Victor Nee and Jimy M. Sanders, "The Road to Parity: Determinants of the Socioeconomic Achievements of Asian Americans," *Ethnic and Racial Studies* 8 (1985): 75–93.

33. Borjas, "Assimilation."

34. Bourdieu, "The Forms of Capital"; Nee and Sanders, "The Road to Parity."

35. Lawrence A. Lovell-Troy, "Clan Structure and Economic Activity: The Case of Greeks in Small Business Enterprise," *Self Help in Urban America: Patterns of Minority Economic Development*, ed. Scott Cummings, 58–85 (Port Washington, NY: National University Publications, Kennikat Press, 1980).

36. Pap, *The Portuguese Americans*, 155.

37. de Sá and Borges, "Context or Culture."

38. Pap, *The Portuguese Americans*; Silvia, "The Position of 'New' Immigrants"; Maria I. Baganha, "The Social Mobility of Portuguese Immigrants at the Turn of the Nineteenth Century," *International Migration Review* 25 (1991): 277–302; Jerry R. Williams. *In Pursuit of Their Dreams: A History of Azorean Immigration to the United States* (North Dartmouth, MA: Center for Portuguese Studies and Culture, University of Massachusetts Dartmouth, 2005).

39. Taft, *Two Portuguese Communities in New England*, 349.

40. Silvia, "The Position of 'New' Immigrants."

41. Edna Bonacich, "A Theory of Ethnic Antagonism: The Split Labor Market," *American Sociological Review* 37, no. 5 (1972): 547–59.

42. See Penn Reeve, Daniel Georgiana, and Camilo Viveiros, this volume.

43. Taft, *Two Portuguese Communities in New England*, 231–32.

44. Gilbert, *Recent Portuguese Immigrants to Fall River, Massachusetts*, 133.

45. Maria G. Pereira. "The Socioeconomic Achievement of Portuguese Males in Massachusetts and Rhode Island" (MA thesis, Brown University, Providence, RI, 1985).

46. Maria Mulcahy, "The Portuguese of the U.S. from 1880 to 1990."

47. de Sá and Borges, "Context or Culture."

Fall River Portraits: People
Andrea Klimt

Since 2014, over 180 amateur photographers have worked to create a collaborative portrait of the people, culture, and neighborhoods of Fall River, Massachusetts. They have explored and documented the everyday life and landscapes of this small New England city and found hope, beauty, and vitality in unexpected places. Their images foster an appreciation of what the city has to offer as well as a deeper understanding of the challenges it currently faces. Curated by anthropologist Andrea Klimt, this selection of Fall River portraits documents contemporary men and women working in the spaces of the mills that once hosted the textile industry.

Figure 1. Vanson Leathers specializes in creating one-of-a kind handmade leather jackets and suits for motorcycle racing. Mike Van Der Sleesen started the company in 1974. They have created leather outfits for famous names such as The Dark Knight Rises and X-Men and partnered up with well-known companies such as Supreme. Even in the face of stiff competition from overseas, at Vanson every bit of the work, from the letters to the inner lining passes through a pair of real human hands who put time and effort into every cut and stitch. So, when you buy a product from Vanson, you're not only buying a product of leather and cloth but one of effort and soul. *The company has had to downsize to about 40 employees, down from a height of about 145, due to competition from overseas plants. Many of the employees are immigrants from many different parts of the world. However, the recent restrictions on immigration to the US have made it increasingly difficult to find employees interested in doing this type of work.*

Photographer: Alexandra Marceau, University of Massachusetts Dartmouth

Figure 2. Louie has been working at New England Shirt Company since he came from the Azores, Portugal in 1978. He is one of the company's managers and is very proud of their commitment to quality. *The New England Shirt Company, founded in 1933, endured many of the repercussions of outsourcing to offshore production sites. Operating in the niche of high-end men's shirts allowed the company to employ many Fall River workers until 2017 when it was forced to close and lay off its remaining 50 workers. At its height, the company employed about 1,200 workers and produced shirts for the likes of Ralph Lauren, UNIONMADE, Thom Browne, Woolrich, and L.L. Bean.*

Photographer: Rodney Chanax, University of Massachusetts Dartmouth

Figure 3. Lina, the woman in front, is the floor manager at BC&J. She came to the U.S. from the Azores over thirty years ago and has been working at BC&J for about three years. Isabel, pictured in the back, has been working at BC&J since September and is an immigrant from El Salvador. When there is a lapse in orders, the workers are laid off until new contracts come in. *These cyclical lay-offs are typical of smaller companies such as BC&J, which are dependent upon time-limited contracts from a wide range of businesses.*

Photographer: Sophie Von Maluski, University of Massachusetts Dartmouth

Figure 4. Joyce is one of the hardest working employees at Hague Textiles – and is the mother of the company's owner, Tim Couto. Each day before going to work, she gets up at 5 to feed all forty-one of the goats on her farm in Westport. *Hague Textiles, a family-owned business founded about 100 years ago, makes leather items such as tool belts, gun holsters, and phone cases on contract to other companies. Competition from overseas has made it increasingly difficult to stay in business and the current owner is struggling to keep his remaining employees on the payroll. Consequently, many of the factory's work stations are currently empty.*

Photographer: Elijah Pontes, University of Massachusetts Dartmouth

Figure 5. In a largely automated and mechanized world, it's reassuring to see there are still craftsmen who hand pour, measure, cut, press, and sand items to exacting specifications. Gabe is forming a hat with one of the pressing machines and an aluminum mold that he crafted himself. He has been working at Korber for fourteen years and has been making hats nearly his whole life. *Korber Hats, founded in 1919, makes 5,000 to 10,000 hats a month of all types of straw and felt for companies such as L.L. Bean, Orvis, Stetson, Goorin Brothers, & Tommy Bahama.*

Photographer: Erica Hammond, University of Massachusetts Dartmouth

Figure 6. João is glad the factory floor is air conditioned. *He and other members of his family came to Fall River from the Azores and have worked many years at Anchor Uniforms Company. The 50-year old company makes uniforms for police and first-responders all around the U.S. The company's current Vice President, Joe Pinto, came as a teenager from mainland Portugal in the 1960s. Given the requirement that all government employees wear "made in the US" uniforms, the company is doing extremely well. This is in stark contrast to many other apparel companies that are struggling to compete with lower production costs in other parts of the world.*

Photographer: Nick Simbro, Diman Regional Vocational High School

Figure 7. Jesus at work. *A scene from the factory floor of Anchor Uniforms. The company employs primarily Portuguese immigrants. Catholic religious symbolism and other visual evidence of Portuguese culture can be found throughout the factory floor and Portuguese is the primary language amongst many of the employees.*

Photographer: Nick Simbro, Diman Regional Vocational High School

Figure 8. Joe Araujo at Anchor Uniforms cuts the layered fabric along the precise lines of the paper pattern. The chain-linked glove protects his fingers from the blade. The patterns are hand-drawn, then computerized versions are pinned on top of the fabric to be cut. Joe has been working in apparel manufacturing for forty years, and came to the U.S. from Portugal almost sixty years ago.

Photographer: Tristin Flood, University of Massachusetts Dartmouth

Figure 9. Isabel is originally from the Azores and has been working at New England Shirt Company for many years.

Photographer: Rodney Chanax, University of Massachusetts Dartmouth

Figure 10. At Vanson Leathers, most people have decorated their work stations to remind them of home.

Photographer: Alexandra Marceau, University of Massachusetts Dartmouth

Figure 11. Born in the Dominican Republic, Miguel was raised in New York City. He is now a minister with a wife of over 40 years and three sons, two of whom serve as officers in the United States Coast Guard. *The work force at Korber Hats is extremely diverse with employees who are native to Fall River as well as immigrants from Portugal, the Caribbean, and Central America. Many have been working at Korber for decades.*

Photographer: Nicole Snyder, University of Massachusetts Dartmouth

Figure 12. Ester is sewing on colorful bands around the outside of each hat. Behind her you can see the stacks and stacks awaiting her quick talented fingers. She works just across from her sister, Hermi. They emigrated to Fall River from Portugal and have been working at Korber Hats for almost 40 years.

Photographer: Erica Hammond, University of Massachusetts Dartmouth

Figure 13. Mili and Tania are both from Bangladesh. This was their first job upon coming the U.S. and they have been at Commonwealth ever since. *Commonwealth Soap Company is a very successful company that continues to see significant growth. It employs about 100 workers who hail from many different countries including Cambodia, Thailand, Bangladesh, Vietnam, Portugal, Puerto Rico, and various Central American countries. The workforce is very stable and many have been working at the company for decades.*

Photographer: Kylie Cooper, Diman Regional Vocational High School

Figure 14. Laura Kuy, originally from Cambodia, has worked at Commonwealth Soap Company for almost 20 years.

Photographer: Kylie Cooper, Diman Regional Vocational High School

CHAPTER 17

Race, Gender, and Class in the Makings of Portuguese Otherness in a New England Town (1920s-2010s)[1]

BELA FELDMAN-BIANCO

My involvement with the study of transnational migrations began in 1987, when I was hired as University Professor of Portuguese Studies at Southeastern Massachusetts University (SMU, now University of Massachusetts Dartmouth). The chair was created in response to demands from Portuguese American leaders for the university to encourage its faculty and students to carry out research on the Portuguese and their descendants based in the small towns surrounding SMU, such as Fall River, New Bedford, and Taunton. These requests had intensified in the face of escalating discrimination and xenophobia triggered by a notorious gang rape case that took place in 1983 on the pool table of a barroom of ill repute known as Big Dan's Tavern in a Portuguese working-class neighborhood of New Bedford. The victim was a young, third-generation Portuguese American woman, and the alleged rapists were a handful of unemployed Portuguese immigrants from the Azores. Exacerbated by intense media coverage and a televised trial, this dramatic event exposed different cultural codes about gender, bringing to the fore, on the one hand, increasing xenophobia and discrimination against the "Portugee" and, on the other, a heightened politicization of Portuguese (collective) ethnic identity. New Bedford itself, a city portrayed by Melville in *Moby-Dick* and known as the Portuguese capital of America, was redubbed after the incident the "Portuguese gang rape capital of America." Permeated by cultural misunderstandings, this social drama turned into a field of struggles in the historical conjuncture of the 1980s, when multiculturalism (in its cultural pluralism phase) was the hegemonic discourse in the United States and the politics based on class relations was being replaced by the politics of identity with an emphasis on difference. Because of these combined ingredients, the *Massachusetts Lawyers Weekly* cited the Big Dan's gang rape among the thirty most memorable cases of the last thirty years. In addition to the extensive examinations of its legal aspects,[2] the case was also among those examined for the roles mass media have played in constructing rape[3] and covering sex crimes.[4] The media's responsibility in overplaying the events and heightening the tensions and divisions in New Bedford and the surrounding region has invariably been highlighted by Portuguese transmigrants as well as local feminists.[5] This incident formed the basis for *The Accused,* a Hollywood movie starring Jodie Foster, whose performance in the film won her an Oscar. The movie was purposely silent about the national origins and ethnicity of the main protagonists, and this concealing of the ethnic features of the rape and its occurrence in New Bedford was the outcome of negotiations between the movie producers and both local public officers and the Portuguese Continental Union.

Somewhat fortuitously, after I arrived in New Bedford, new demonstrations on the Big Dan's case took place. Portuguese immigrants were feeling discriminated against because the convicted Azoreans had received longer sentences than those given to a gang of doctors who had been accused of raping nurses in the Boston area. In that ethnographic present, the open telephone lines of American broadcasters in the region transmitted xenophobic calls regarding the Portuguese. At the same time, the anchor of a call-in show on the local Portuguese radio station compared the Big Dan's victim to the biblical figure Magdalena. I even witnessed a public event in defense of the alleged rapists in a local park, during which the demonstrators, carrying "Save the Big Dan's Five" posters, made plans to visit the "boys" in prison. At the same time, during my first walks through the city's Portuguese neighborhoods, I was faced with multiple and contradictory images of Portuguese temporalities and spatialities—such as the Feast of the Divine Holy Spirit procession on an American highway—that imposed on and contrasted drastically with the American industrial landscape. These metaphors of Portugueseness seemed to delimit symbolic boundaries around the ethnic enclaves spread across New England's cities. They drove me to reveal the meanings of the multiple temporalities and geographies in the everyday lives of Portuguese immigrants and their descendants in New Bedford as well as in the construction of their social fields and long-distance nationalism.[6]

This research further engaged me in attempts to elucidate the apparently paradoxical and bizarre Big Dan's rape case against the background of New Bedford's social history, and the ensuing chapter focuses on this internationally ill-famed social drama and its aftermath as a way of unveiling the conjuncture between gender, race, and class in the processes of transnational migrants' unequal incorporation in New Bedford. Toward this end, I critically examine the relations between multiculturalism and the reconstruction of identities and their symbolic productions during the rescaling of this gateway city in the light of changing structures of capitalism in the last four decades. By adopting a global perspective on migration[7] and viewing migration as part of the dynamics of capital formation, which is simultaneously global, national, and specifically local, I concentrate on both the global processes restructuring the locality and migrants' political mobilization and their local and transnational practices through time. From this standpoint, I further attempt to underscore the changing positioning of the Portuguese in the city since that dramatic episode in 1983, with their history, gastronomy, and folklore having been incorporated into a "Taste of Portugal" in the marketing of the local historical heritage in today's neoliberal times.

As I indicate throughout this chapter, the global perspective of migration allows me to highlight the dynamics of unequal power as they have been shaped and are contested at the local level at specific times. It also enables me to discern how the global, national, regional, and local have been constructed on the ground through networks of unequal social relations. It has further led me to study migrants not as discrete ethnic or transnational communities but as actors whose life trajectories and identities are shaped by and shape the locality. By engaging with place, political economy, and time, I aim to critically examine the tensions of multiculturalism, the ongoing multiplicities and reconstruction of identities, and the related symbolic productions of locality, region, and nation in the context of transnational migration.

It is important to remember that multiculturalism emerged in the context of the social movements of so-called minorities as an attempt to challenge the cultural hegemony of the dominant groups.[8] Yet, in the current conjuncture of global capitalism, the relations between neoliberal policies and multicultural ideologies rest upon "the formulation of a *rule of exclusion, of visible or invisible borders,* materialized in laws and practices."[9] This perspective stresses the distinction between nationals and foreigners, reinforcing the notion of exclusion or at least unequal preferential access to goods and rights—a fundamental element in specific national projects. Consequently, there are a variety of multiculturalisms aimed at different segments of the population.

In the United States, multiculturalism is an offspring of cultural pluralism. Formulated in the 1960s by the U.S. government and powerful charity institutions to control and depoliticize the black movement,[10] the focus of cultural pluralism was expanded to incorporate the urban poor through the channeling of resources along ethnic lines.[11] Whether in its pluralistic version or as today's multiculturalism, this ideology rests on a "divide to control logic" that is often revealed through grants given to celebrate ethnic identities. Currently, neoliberal governance is based upon flexible labor and the criminalization of immigrants, while the interrelationship of investment politics and politics of culture has further stimulated the marketing of culturalism. Thus, we see ethnic identities being celebrated with the purpose of attracting tourism and subsidies for urban development.

I emphasize the importance of examining the relations between multicultural ideologies as part of national projects and the political and transnational practices of transmigrants in specific localities and situations. From this angle, I locate the Big Dan's gang rape and its consequences in the social history of New Bedford, delineating the processes of the incorporation and exclusion of immigrants and their local and transnational mobilizations and practices.

Transnational Migrants and the Downscaling of New Bedford

Any analysis of New Bedford's history and political economy must consider its position as a gateway city. This frame of reference allows us to understand the transformations and mobilizations of migrants in the Big Dan's case, as well as the active role played by immigrant men and women and their social networks in shaping these processes. This narrative begins with the Azorean and Cape Verdean crew members whose labor on the whaling expeditions of the eighteenth and nineteenth centuries created the capital that was invested in New Bedford's early textiles mills. Both the whaling industry and textile production meant that the formation of capital in the ports and streets of New Bedford reflected a process that was regional, national, and global. Many of the whalers, as well as many of those that labored in the mills and made New

Bedford the preeminent city in textile production in the nineteenth century, came from the Azores, continental Portugal, Madeira, and Cape Verde. The Portuguese workforce, whose labor contributed to the global wealth and power of the city, was racialized and disempowered within the leadership of both labor movements and the city.

It was only when the international position of New Bedford's mills was lost at the beginning of the twentieth century that attempts to compensate for falling profits with more intensive exploitation of labor were met by fierce labor struggles on the part of Portuguese migrants. This included a six-month strike against wage reductions in 1928—a period of economic rescaling in the city when local textile producers were progressively scaling down their activities and/or moving to the American South, where workers' wages were lower.[12] The workers' struggles and the destruction of the local textile mills' international status during the first quarter of the twentieth century of that period marked the full incorporation of Portuguese migrants into the local class structure. At that turning point, return migration expanded and strengthened the transnational social fields that connected New Bedford to the Azores, continental Portugal, Madeira, and Cape Verde.

Like other textile cities, New Bedford never recovered its position of prominence in the United States and globally, but the textile mills, while reduced in size and significance, still attracted immigrant workers. The gates were closed in the mid-1920s and reopened in 1958 to provide relief for Azoreans escaping the aftermath of the eruption of the volcano of Capelinhos on the island of Fayal, and New Bedford continued to receive Portuguese immigrants, who were invariably related to the earlier contingents.[13] These new arrivals were confronted with a new regime of intensive factory work developed in the partially abandoned industrial area. About three decades later, in a period noted for the retraction of Portuguese immigration and closing of the borders, undocumented migrants from Guatemala, Mexico, Nicaragua, and Brazil came to New Bedford and replaced the Portuguese as unskilled workers in the remaining labor-intensive and fish-processing industries. Meanwhile, Portuguese migrants and their descendants became central actors in the efforts of New Bedford and neighboring towns to reposition themselves regionally as the south coast of Massachusetts and, at the same time, as a location for investment, commerce, and tourism.

In the present conjuncture of capitalism, the processes that led to the transformation of Portuguese migrants from racialized others to central actors in urban regeneration efforts cannot be understood without reference to the ways in which the city of New Bedford and its workforce have been constantly repositioned and rescaled within larger networks of economic and political power. Within this story, immigrant workers have had to constantly struggle to find ways to maintain senses of self and family economies that often stretch transnationally. These struggles have often been part of a broader-ranging social movement for rights and cultural representation.

The need to position the representation of particular nationalities of immigrants as aspects of urban restructuring, which is a reconstitution of global processes of capital accumulation, first became clear to me when I started fieldwork in New Bedford in the late 1980s. I refer to representations of culture as "an aspect of urban restructuring" rather than to "representations within the context of this restructuring" in order to emphasize that identity constructions and cultural representations, including ideologies of multiculturalism, are central aspects in the constitution of political economies.

The Big Dan Social Drama and the Politicization of Identities

Public politicization of identity and the politics of identity happen in specific historical situations. The internationally infamous Big Dan's rape case occurred in a period that saw a renewal of Portuguese immigration in New Bedford that was associated with a new cycle of factory closures and capital relocation to countries where labor was cheaper that had resulted in an increase in unemployment in the locality. It also coincided with the opening of a special unit directed at aiding victims of sexual abuse and promoted by the local woman's center.

The chronology of events indicates that when the first news of the 1983 gang rape came out, local communitarian groups formed a coalition against sexual violence and organized a candlelight vigil against sexual abuse at which three thousand people marched silently. The night vigil attracted notorious feminists such as Gloria Steinem to the town and quickly reached the national and international media. Almost at the same time, xenophobic callers to a local radio station's phone-in began to denounce the Portuguese background of the alleged rapists. When they became aware that the media was covering the rape as an ethnic crime, Portuguese leaders formed the Committee for Justice and a Portuguese American Defense League to fight discrimination against the Portuguese. Later, the decision of a Portuguese American judge to broadcast the trial heightened the schisms even more and made way for growing cultural misunderstandings. After four of the six accused were found guilty, more than fifteen thousand Portuguese and descendants took to the streets in two public demonstrations. Described by perplexed non-Portuguese observers as a "bizarre protest,"[14] the public confrontations challenged the prevalent characterization of the Portuguese as an "invisible minority" and a "case of ethnic disappearance."[15] Interpreting the sentences as a judgment on all in the community, the demonstrators transformed the accused into symbols of their own oppression and lack of power in the locality. At the same time, the victim was penalized for attracting attention and bringing visibility to the problems of the "Portuguese Community."

It is important to remember that in the 1980s, in a context of the renewal of migrant flows and increasing vigor within the feminist and black liberation movements, feminists and African American struggles were set at odds. Furthermore, from the 1970s, having been "whitened" in part by accepting the U.S. racial order that placed African Americans at the bottom, older immigrant groups in aging industrial cities began to reject their previous claims to having assimilated and began to openly defend their ethnically based voting blocs with an ideology of cultural pluralism, an early form of multiculturalism. Spike Lee in *Do the Right Thing,* a movie that came out in 1989, portrayed these tensions of race, gender, class, and ethnicity as they were manifested in New York City at that time.

In New Bedford, the split between gender and ethnicity around the Big Dan's case exposed subjacent class and race discrimination and brought to light existing divisions in different spheres of social life, including the workplace and labor unions. Male and female feminists, including some of Portuguese descent, who were then becoming increasingly involved with "body politics," tended to perceive the Portuguese protests as expressions of male chauvinism.[16] Meanwhile, significant numbers of Portuguese and Portuguese Americans felt they were enacting, through public demonstrations, their painful emotional reactions to recurrent experiences of discrimination, racism, and second-class citizenship in everyday life.[17]

In the context of the prevailing U.S. ideology, which dichotomously separated whites from nonwhites, the Portuguese and descendants, like others of various origins, were considered nonwhite.[18] They were stigmatized as "Black Portuguee," along with the Cape Verdean immigrants who were part of the New Bedford's Portuguese community until Cape Verde gained independence from Portugal in 1975.[19] While earlier generations of Portuguese Americans had been forced to disguise their Portuguese ancestry to get upward social mobility and avoid racialization, the newer contingent of immigrants and their children, stigmatized as "(ignorant) greenhorn(s)," were exposed to discrimination in everyday life. Furthermore, the Big Dan's drama revealed how women of Portuguese descent, in particular, positioned themselves differently in the face of the exacerbated Portuguese cultural codes on gender, positioning themselves either as members of the Portuguese ethnic group or as feminist activists against sexual violence, or even articulating their Portuguese ancestry with feminism.

By and large, the Big Dan's social drama and its polarizations revealed the complexity of identity politics, showing that underneath the schisms between gender and ethnicity were different cultural codes and perceptions of gender. It must be remembered that, in everyday life in New Bedford and the surrounding region, Portuguese cultural constructions of gender and gender roles, marking difference and otherness, have often paved the way for conflicts between older and younger generations of Portuguese men and women. Yet misinterpretations of these discrepant gender codes became politicized and highly publicized in the aftermath of the rape. The politicization further exposed the entanglements between gender and ethnicity in the ongoing clashes between generations and the ambiguities, negotiations, and radicalization of younger Portuguese and Portuguese American females.

Varieties of Transmigrant Experiences in Everyday Life in New Bedford

In a historical period marked by the continuous renewal of immigration from continental Portugal and the Azorean Islands, the deciphering of the apparently bizarre demonstrations of the Portuguese requires an understanding of the ways in which the emotional and painful reactions were embedded in their varied everyday experiences of discrimination and second-class citizenship in the locality. As I have shown elsewhere,[20] successive flows of male and female immigrants from rural backgrounds who entered industrial work recurrently tended to reconstruct their memories and the social practices of their homeland's past in their everyday lives in reaction to the time discipline imposed by industrial capitalism in New Bedford. The reinvention of their immediate past of nonindustrial labor reflected their experiences with and perceptions of different rhythms and different meanings of time, work, and life: from more natural rhythms in the homeland to the time discipline of industrial capitalism in New Bedford.[21] The symbolic representations and social practices of their past of nonindustrial labor provided the basis on which these migrants reconstituted themselves as Azoreans, Madeirans, and mainlanders, thus demarcating, in the context of renewed migration, their strong regional identities. This (re)elaboration of regional and national identities was accompanied by exacerbated reconstructions of cultural gender codes. In this scenario, for many Portuguese women and men, the concerns with body politics voiced by feminists at the outbreak of the Big Dan social drama did not make sense at all.

Different perceptions of gender roles and gender relations represented different forms of resistance and negotiation of female identity in the context of immigration. Above all, these perceptions expressed how women's condition and the reconstruction of Portuguese regional and national identities were distinctively entwined in the subjectivities of female immigrants. With reference to this topic, my research indicated that women who emigrated as adults and whose history of immigration encompassed the transition from preindustrial task-oriented activities in the homeland to industrial work in the United States tended to reconstruct their "selves," fragmented by migration, through the recreation of imageries and social practices of their pasts of nonindustrial labor. Since childhood, they had been subjected to an apprenticeship in domestic chores, and this was associated with the construction of the "virtuous woman" and a rigid demarcation between (unequal) female and male roles. These women learned to accept, or to simulate that they accepted, their submission to a male authority and to distinguish themselves from the "biblical Magdalene" type of sinner. Faced with the dramatic changes in their conditions of existence caused by immigration, these women reterritorialized themselves to the ways of life of their regions and villages of origin. Thereby, they tended to mask the actual transformations of power relations between the sexes and generations caused by women's entrance into the American labor market and (because they tended not to speak English) by their constant dependence on the cultural brokerage of bilingual offspring. At the same time, along with their husbands, they tried to indoctrinate the same values in their daughters as a form of social control.

In particular, older immigrant religious women tended to act as the extreme arbiters of the moral values that the traditional Catholic Church and Salazar's national ideologies, prior to the 1974 Carnation

Revolution, constantly reinforced. In their everyday lives in New Bedford and its surrounding region, they faced discrimination and confrontation with new structures of domination. Therefore, these women tended to (re) interpret the moral values related to gender roles and gender relations and act as the bastions of Portugueseness in the diaspora. While their local and transnational spatial temporalities tended to be stronger in their everyday social practice,[22] in situations of discrimination, such as at the outbreak of the Big Dan's social drama, their traditional moral values related to gender and gender roles became equated with Portuguese nationalism and ethnicity.

Yet, the defense of equal rights for women and men among younger bicultural women represented a response to the repression, prohibitions, and social control imposed on them by their parents as well as in their differing social locations among different cultural codes. Young women who experienced the social changes caused by the Carnation Revolution in Portugal and who, while still in the homeland, challenged the prevailing (traditional) gender roles confronted with (double) perplexity the reconfiguration of these very values in the Portuguese enclaves in New England. Women who were in their teens or even younger when they came to the United States after the 1974 revolution reacted to these traditional female roles from the background of their experiences of lives fragmented by simultaneous exposure to Portuguese and American values. While their parents tended to reinvent Portuguese times and spaces in their everyday lives in America, these women tended to construct dual identities that revealed the subjectivity of experiences lived on the borders of dissonant worlds, as well as diverse Portuguese nationalist projects.

This political entanglement of distinctive gender constructions was inculcated in the painful emotional decisions that led women and men of Portuguese descent to mobilize either as members of an ethnic group or against sexual violence at the time of the Big Dan's social drama. While criticizing the prevalent male chauvinism, many of the women who acted as brokers for their families and community chose to align themselves with members of the Portuguese ethnic group. Other women, reacting to the exacerbated reconstructions of Portuguese cultural codes related to gender and generation, repudiated their Portuguese identity, positioning themselves as feminists fighting against sexual violence. Still others allied themselves in favor of the ethnic group but, articulating their Portugueseness and feminism, subsequently also became active in the local women's center.

The outcome of this political entanglement ultimately heightened the rape victim's personal drama. Caught between contested domains, she managed to disguise herself throughout the televised trial by covering her face with a black veil, until one of the prosecutors inadvertently disclosed her identity. Accused of exposing the "Portuguese community," she was unable to remain in New Bedford, and, after the trial was over, she moved to Florida with her two children, only to die in a car accident just four years after being gang raped.

The Big Dan's Case: New Bedford's and Portugal's Upscaling and the Changing Positions of the Portuguese in New England

The city of New Bedford was pejoratively portrayed as the "Portuguese gang rape capital of America" by the local, national, and even international media. It was not by chance that, independent of their opposing position regarding the polarization between "gender" and "ethnicity" issues, different protagonists systematically associated the explosive outfall of the Big Dan's social drama with the "hard times the city had suffered since the 1928 six months' strike" over wage reductions. In an interview with the *New York Times* entitled "Barroom Rape Shaves Town of Proud Heritage," then mayor John Bullard, whose ancestors had helped to build the city's whaling industry, summed up the situation by claiming that the "city has had hard times since the textile strike of 1928. It's been economically depressed for two generations. Expectations have been lowered." Reflecting his interests as a leader of the project to restore New Bedford's waterfront for tourism purposes, he continued, "People have become sincerely negative about themselves and about the city," asserting that the barroom rape "hurts us more than it would a lot of other cities. . . . Then we just have to try that much harder to get back up to zero."[23]

In effect, the textile industry in New Bedford drastically diminished in 1940. Most of the tools and dyeing operations left the area in the 1970s. In that decade, labor-intensive factories based on piecework began to replace the former textile mills. Ongoing American policies accelerated migration flows in the early 1960s, enabling these shops to hire a cheap immigrant labor force related by kinship to the older contingent of Portuguese already settled in the region. In the 1980s, local factories had already begun moving to other countries or were being forced out of business due to increased exposure to global competition. In this context, the gang rape case symbolically turned the once celebrated "whaling city" into a "city of bizarre immigrants,"[24] marking the beginning of a new economic rescaling in yet another historical juncture, when flexible capital and progressive outsourcing paved the way for a new cycle of local factories closing and/or their dislocations to other countries where labor was cheaper.

Since the 1980s, Portuguese laborers, along with workers elsewhere, have become exposed to even greater economic vulnerability, many forced into flexible labor employment that offers neither job stability nor social benefits. However, in a visible paradox, they have advanced their position within the local working class. The ensuing decrease in immigration from the Azores and continental Portugal to New England has been followed by a new flow of immigrants from Latin America and the Caribbean, who have settled in the city and taken the unskilled jobs in the remaining factories and fish-processing plants. Since most of these new arrivals—from Guatemala, Mexico, Nicaragua, and, to a lesser degree, Brazil—are undocumented migrants, they have become the local underclass, exploited by their employers and exposed to the draconian post-9/11 immigration policies that have made them victims of increasingly frequent Homeland Security and workplace raids.

Within the framework of New Bedford's downscaling, the Portuguese seem to have enhanced their structural position in the locality and region, including within the realm of local politics. While most members of the contingents of immigrants from the Azores and continental Portugal that settled in the city and surrounding regions from the late 1950s began their lives as factory workers or fishermen, they have experienced a gradual process of differential social mobility and unequal incorporation. Many have managed to attain retirement in the United States and thus access to the American structure of social benefits. Moreover, their sons and daughters have been able, at least since the 1970s, to pursue an education. Some offspring who have earned college degrees have served as cultural brokers between immigrants and American institutions. They have benefited from the prevailing ideologies of multiculturalism and from their bilingual and bicultural skills by entering occupations within the local government structure, the bilingual educational system, and local and regional Portuguese institutions created in the 1970s with the aid of federal grants.[25] Others have managed to open businesses or become professionals in various fields. And a few immigrants and descendants have even become millionaires.[26]

Above all, the improved position of Portuguese immigrants and descendants in the city has been the result of an interplay of complex factors, including the drastic reduction of their immigration to New England in the last decades, the gradual process of their incorporation and the corollary process of upward mobility and suburbanization, and the fact that, for the first time in over a century, the recent flow of immigrants settling in the locality have not been Portuguese. In this context, it is important to consider the shifting position of the Portuguese postcolonial state in the global economy as well as its changing relations with the Portuguese "diaspora," including the increasing role played by long-distance capitalism nationalism, activated by bilingual and bicultural brokers to change the image of Portugal and the Portuguese in the south coast of Massachusetts. This process began in 1985 when Portugal signed the Agreement Treaty to join the European Communitarian Space in June 1985, just a couple of years after the Big Dan affair.[27]

The changing relations between the Portuguese state and its deterritorialized citizens was reinforced by new nationality legislation prioritizing the jus sanguine and thus the "rights to blood" in 1981. Formulated after decolonization and in preparation for Portugal's future membership of the European Community, this new law recognized Portuguese transnational migrant populations' continuing ties with the homeland and, from this viewpoint, acknowledged their rights to dual nationality and citizenship.[28] Thus, unlike in the past, the new law allowed Portugal's emigrants to become citizens in the countries in which they resided without losing their Portuguese nationality.

After the Portuguese state recognized the diaspora as part of the nation, dual nationality and citizenship rights became valuable resources in localities such as New Bedford. At the same time, Portuguese governmental authorities intensified their relations with those citizens of the diaspora who have been able to gain positions of power in the localities and countries of residence and who play a brokerage role in favor of the Portuguese politics of culture and investments. This long-distance nationalism has helped these transnational brokers to increase their political power as an ethnic group in U.S. politics.

As we have seen, in the past, Portuguese immigrants and their descendants were confronted with a choice to either continue to be part of Portuguese immigrant communities or to assimilate to elude the issue of race and gain upward mobility, even though in many cases they retained the Portuguese language and traditions.[29] In the 1970s, as part of continued efforts to establish themselves as part of the majority, some affluent and influential Portuguese Americans decided not to make use of affirmative action[30] and distance themselves from a racially defined minority status—a path chosen by immigrants from the newly independent Cape Verde. In the next twenty-five years, newer generations of upwardly mobile immigrants and descendants thus joined an established stratum of Portuguese Americans, some of whom had reasserted their Portuguese American identities after the shift from assimilation to ideologies of multiculturalism in the United States. Members of this stratum have also revived the historical memory of the Portuguese discoveries and promoted Portugal's politics of high culture to enhance their own position as representatives of a "modern" Portugal at the local level. These strategies were further aimed at erasing memories of the Big Dan's social drama.

Portuguese and Portuguese American professional and business people used their transnational social fields and practices to become involved in "the concerted efforts by local governance in partnership with state and federal governments, citizens and business organizations, non-profit agencies and institutions of higher education regarding the implementation of economic development policy" to meet "the twenty-first century challenges."[31] By 1997, efforts to fund local urban reinvention initiatives by attracting international investment bore fruit. Facilitated by leading Azoreans from New Bedford, Portugal's Ministry of Foreign Affairs (then headed by an Azorean) gave the local Whaling Museum a $500,000 grant for the construction of a special wing to portray the cultural heritage of the Azorean whalers of the city. This donation enabled the Azorean whalers to be finally incorporated into the city's historical heritage.[32]

Before Portugal's 2008–9 debt crisis, attempts were also made by the New Bedford Economic Council to attract Portuguese enterprises to the city's business park and free-trade zone. These resulted in, for example, the opening of Portuguese banks in the city, one of which was subsequently closed. Directors of the council have visited Portugal in search of investment, and, in 2008, a delegation of government, education, and business leaders went to the Azores on a trade mission designed to strengthen the archipelago's educational, cultural, and economic ties with the south coast of Massachusetts. It is important to note that access to the Azores also meant access to European markets.[33]

Promoting New Bedford as a tourist destination—with multicultural and multiethnic attractions—proved another cornerstone of the city's economic revitalization efforts. Moreover, the Portuguese identity, which was previously racialized and then linked to the moniker of "Rape Capital of America," became a component of the cultural heritage of the city. As part of the Office of Marketing and Tourism's strategy for attracting tourists, Portuguese restaurants, bakeries, and summer festivals were promoted as "A Taste of Portugal" and, as such, became a constitutive part of the city's intangible yet highly marketable cultural diversity. This more public identification of New Bedford with Portuguese immigration and Portugal became an asset in the city's struggle to become more competitive regionally and globally. Migrants proved to be able to play a crucial role in securing the transnational reach of the city. The entrance of Portugal into the European community was crucial to the new positioning of Portuguese migrants in New Bedford as social, economic, and political actors within both their place of settlement and vis-à-vis Portugal and the Portuguese state.

With the aim of counteracting America's restrictive immigration laws, bicultural community leaders started an extensive "naturalization" campaign in 1997 as a way of ensuring that immigrants living in the United States had access to social benefits and a political voice. The naturalization campaign resonated with the politics of dual citizenship rights promoted by the postcolonial Portuguese state. These politics emphasized the incorporation of the Portuguese abroad in the localities of settlement while they continued to act as representatives of Portugal. Accordingly, the motto "to be a good Portuguese, it is necessary to be a good American," which had been employed during the Americanization campaign of the 1930s to persuade immigrants to assimilate into American society, was redefined still in the 1980s by then-president Mario Soares to stimulate biculturalism.[34]

The naturalization campaign was also supported by the Luso-American Development Foundation (FLAD), a Portuguese, financially autonomous, private institution created in 1985 as a counterpart to the agreement to let Americans stay at the Lajes military base until 1991. This foundation has aimed to contribute "to national development, through the promotion of scientific, technical, cultural, educational, commercial, and business cooperation between Portugal and the United States."[35] In 1999, it launched the Portuguese-American Citizenship Project to promote citizenship and civic involvement in Portuguese American communities across the United States.

The historic and contemporary deterioration of the regional and global positioning of New Bedford meant that the transnational reach of Portuguese migrants and especially their reach into the European Union were especially significant for both the migrants and the city. Their connections positioned them more centrally in the political and economic landscape of the south coast because they facilitated educational and economic partnerships in their homeland, particularly in the Azores. Portuguese migrants were also brokers who channeled much-desired Portuguese funds to New Bedford and the region. They became part of the repositioning efforts of both New Bedford and the Portuguese state within the neoliberal global order.

However, the gain in social position and cultural capital of these migrants in New Bedford and in their homelands came with significant losses to the quality of life and future aspirations of those who labor and must migrate to seek work. The neoliberal regime of flexible capital and labor, together with stringent immigration policies, which criminalize undocumented migrants and approach immigrants from the perspective of national security, means not only the end of the safe and secure working conditions won by the labor mobilizations of the early twentieth century but also an increase in exploitation and economic vulnerability.

The interplay between the politics of culture and the politics of investment seems to have masked the rigorous American immigration policies and the continuing immigration raids by Homeland Security officers against undocumented workers. In 2004 and 2007, New Bedford attracted national news coverage because of Homeland Security raids. Thirteen undocumented immigrants working at a fish-processing plant were detained in 2004, and Homeland Security agents arrested three hundred women and men, mostly from Guatemala, Nicaragua, and Mexico, in 2007. Although in smaller numbers, Brazilians and Azoreans were also among the detained. Yet, since the "Mayans" had become the new scapegoats, the media largely ignored the Azoreans arrested. As a considerable number of mothers were separated from their small children when they were arrested, their drama caught the attention and sympathy of local and state authorities. This incident, which brought attention once again to gender issues, mobilized (this time without schisms) the citizens of New Bedford, including the leaders of labor unions and other community leaders. This local and state support also acknowledged the significant role of unskilled female and male labor in maintaining the economic base of even the reinvented and restructured city of New Bedford. It also made apparent that among the New Bedford residents who were subject to these raids and were deported there were people who had permanently settled in the area and were contributing to the revitalization of neighborhoods and commerce in the city. However, despite the considerable social solidarity displayed and the reliance of the city on its immigrants, the tough federal immigration laws did not leave room for appeal.[36]

The social solidarity on display called attention to the mobilization of different segments of civil society (including labor unions, feminists, NGOs, churches, and intellectuals) in favor of the citizenship rights of these immigrants and their struggle for a world without borders—not just in New Bedford but also in other localities. Therefore, hand in hand with the marketing and consumption of identities that have reinforced ethnic groups and provided strategies for access to political and social resources, there have emerged mobilizations that involve different segments of civil society in support of undocumented immigrants who have been systematically criminalized and excluded from the neoliberal policies and their multiculturalism ideologies. From the point of view of transnational migration, the emergence of these movements seems to signal a new type of social mobilization in contemporary globalization.

Conclusions

Since transnational migrants have been both protagonists in and a constitutive part of the social fabric in both their localities of origin and localities of residence, I included the Big Dan's gang rape case into the social history of New Bedford and focused on the processes of inclusion and exclusion of immigrants at work in their local and transnational mobilizations and practices. In so doing, I outlined the geographies of inclusion, unequal access, and participation of immigrants through time, which allowed me to discern the changing positioning of the Portuguese in the city, as well as the roles they have played throughout the processes of local and global restructuring.

I emphasized the importance of examining the relations between multicultural ideologies as constitutive of specific national projects in neoliberal times and the political and transnational practices of transmigrants in specific localities and situations. However, while multiculturalist ideologies emphasize belonging to only one nation-state, transnational migrants are part of at least two countries and develop transnational social fields. It thus became necessary to consider the new conceptions of nations that emerged in the mid-1980s, by which, by way of either legislation or rhetoric, both the former imperial metropolis and former colonies have incorporated their emigrant populations. These new conceptions of nation, based on long-distance nationalisms, have stimulated and reinforced the connections and transnational practices of their transmigrants with their localities and countries of origin and particularly the role of transmigrant leaders as transnational brokers for both locality and region of origin and those of residence.[37]

Opening my analysis by focusing on the Big Dan's rape case and its aftermath in New Bedford, I argued that public politicizations of identity and the politics of identity happen in specific historical situations and conjunctures that are molded by the continuing global repositioning of cities and their populations. I have demonstrated that this infamous gang rape was such a conjuncture, occurring in a period noted for the renewal of Portuguese immigration and a new downscaling of this gateway city, a period when class-based politics was being replaced by identity politics that emphasized cultural difference.

Since then, concurrently with the continuing economic downscaling of the city, local laborers have confronted the increasing institutionalization of neoliberal agendas worldwide. Furthermore, I have discerned the multiple factors that led, in this historical conjuncture, people of Portuguese descent to become central actors in the efforts of New Bedford and neighboring towns to reposition themselves regionally as the south coast of Massachusetts and become a location for investment, commerce, and tourism. Among the main factors was the increasing role played by a long-distance nationalism, activated by bilingual and bicultural brokers, in both changing the image of Portugal and the Portuguese in the region and, at the same time, providing investments and access to the European Union to local officers.

I further unveiled how multiculturalism in neoliberal times has stimulated the marketing and consumption of identities that have reinforced ethnic groups and provided strategies for access to political and social resources. At the same time, in the context of draconian immigrant policies, mobilizations have emerged that gather different segments of civil society in favor of undocumented immigrants who have been systematically criminalized and excluded from the neoliberal policies and their multiculturalism ideologies. I argue that these mobilizations of displacement flag a new type of social movement in contemporary globalization.

Works Cited

Almeida, Onésimo T. "Media-Made Events: Revising the Case of Big Dan's." In *Community, Culture and the Making of Identity: Portuguese-Americans along the Eastern Seaboard,* edited by Kimberly da Costa and Andrea Klimt, 247–64. North Dartmouth, MA: University of Massachusetts, 2009.

Balibar, Étienne. *We, the People of Europe? Reflections on Transnational Citizenship.* Princeton, NJ: Princeton University Press, 2004.

Barrow, Clyde, and David R. Borges. "Greater New Bedford Economic Base Analysis: Critical and Emerging Industries and Work Force Development Target." Economic Research Series 29. North Dartmouth, MA: Center for Policy Analysis, University of Massachusetts Dartmouth, 2001.

Bash, Linda, Nina Glick-Schiller, and Christina Szanton, eds. *Nations Unbound: Transnational Projects, Postcolonial Predicaments, and Deterritorialized Nation-States.* Amsterdam: Gordon and Breach, 1994.

Benedict, Helen. *Virgin or Vamp.* Oxford: Oxford University Press, 1992.

Bennet, Liz. "New Bedford: Bigotry Misnamed." *Inside Aegis* 39 (1985): 10–16.

Brodkin, Karen. *How Jews Became White Folks and What That Says about Race in America.* New Brunswick, NJ: Rutgers University Press, 1998.

Bumiller, Kristin. "Fallen Angels: The Representations of Violence against Women in Legal Culture." *International Journal of Law* 18 (May 1990): 125–42.

Cabral, Stephen. "Big Dan: A Bad Case of Victimization." Unpublished manuscript, 1985.

Clendinen, Dudley. "Barroom Rape Shames Town of Proud Heritage." *New York Times,* March 17, 1983.

Cuklanz, Lisa M. *Rape on Trial: How the Mass Media Construct Legal Reform and Social Change.* Philadelphia: University of Pennsylvania Press, 1996.

Feldman-Bianco, Bela. "The Aftermath of a Rape Case: The Politics of Migrants' Unequal Incorporation in Neoliberal Times." In *Migration in the 21st Century: Political Economy and Ethnography,* edited by Pauline Gardiner Barber and Winnie Lem, 213–34. New York: Routledge, 2012.

———. "Brazilians in Portugal, Portuguese in Brazil: Cultural Constructions of Sameness and Difference." *Identities: Global Studies in Culture and Power* 8, no. 4 (December 2001): 607–50.

———. "Multiple Layers of Time and Space: The Construction of Class, Ethnicity and Nationalism among Portuguese Immigrants." *Annals of the New York Academy of Sciences* 645 (December 2006): 145–74.

———. "Remaking Locality: Uneven Globalization and Unequal Incorporation of Transmigrants." In *Locating Migration: Migrants and Cities,* edited by Nina Glick-Schiller and Ayse Çaglar, 213–34. Ithaca, NY: Cornell University Press, 2011.

Georgianna, Daniel, and Roberta Hazen Aaronson. *The Strike of '28.* New Bedford, MA. Spinner Publications, 1993.

Glick-Schiller, Nina. "A Global Perspective on Transnational Migration: Theorizing Migration without Methodological Nationalism." In *Diaspora and Transnationalism: Concepts, Theories and Methods,* edited by Rainer Bauböck and Thomas Faist, 109–30. Amsterdam: University of Amsterdam/IMISCOE, 2010.

———. "Locality, Globality and the Popularization of a Diasporic Consciousness: Learning from the Haitian Case." In *Geographies of the Haitian Diaspora,* edited by Regine Jackson, xxi–xxix. London: Routledge, 2011.

Glick-Schiller, Nina, and Ayse Çaglar. "Beyond Methodological Ethnicity and towards the City Scale: An Alternative Approach to Local and Transnational Pathways of Migrant Incorporation. In *Rethinking Transnationalism: The Mesolinks of Organizations,* edited by Ludger Pries, 40–61. New York: Routledge, 2008

Glick-Schiller, Nina, and Georges, Fouron. *Georges Woke Up Laughing: Long-Distance Nationalism and the Search for Home.* Durham: Duke University Press, 2001.

Goulart, Tony, ed. *Capelinhos: A Volcano of Synergies: Azorean Emigration to America.* San José: Portuguese Heritage Publications of California, 2008.

Haltern, Marilyn. *Between Race and Ethnicity: Cape Verdeans Americans Immigrants (1860–1965).* Urbana: University of Illinois Press, 1993.

Knappman, Edward W., ed. *Great American Trials.* Detroit: Visible Ink Press, 1994.

Lang, Scott W. "State of the City Address." City of New Bedford. https://www.newbedford-ma.gov/, March 1, 2008.

Moniz, Miguel. "The Shadow Minority: An Ethnohistory of Portuguese and Lusophone Racial and Ethnic Identity in New England." In *Community, Culture and the Makings of Identity: Portuguese-Americans along the Eastern Seaboard,* edited by Kimberly da Costa Holton and Andrea Klimt, 409–530. North Dartmouth, MA: University of Massachusetts Dartmouth, Center for Portuguese Studies, 2009.

Ramos, Rui Manoel Moura. "Continuidade e Mudança no Direito da Nacionalidade em Portugal" *Revista de Informação Legislativa* 37, no. 145 (January–March 2000): 87–94.

Rosen, Ellen I. "Rape Trial in New Bedford. New Thoughts on an Old Problem." *Dissent* (Spring 1985): 207–12.

Sá, Maria Gloria de. "The Azorean Community on the East Coast." In *Capelinhos: A Volcano of Synergies—Azorean Emigration to America,* edited by Tony Goulart, 159–70. San Jose: Portuguese Heritage Publications of California, 2008.

Sá, Maria Gloria de, and Borges, D. "Context or Culture: Portuguese-Americans and Social Mobility." In *Community,* Culture *and the Makings of Identity: Portuguese-Americans along the Eastern Seaboard,* edited by Kimberley Costa and Andrea Klimt, 265–90. North Dartmouth, MA: University of Massachusetts Dartmouth, Center for Portuguese Studies and Culture, 2009.

Santos, Boaventura de Sousa. "Modernidade, Identidade e a Cultura de Fronteira." *Revista Crítica de Ciências Sociais* 38 (1993): 11–42.

Smith, Estellie M. "Portuguese Enclaves: The Invisible Minority." In *Social and Cultural Identity: Problems of Persistence and Change,* edited by Thomas K. Fitzgerald, 81–91. Athens, GA: University of Georgia Press, 1974.

Thompson, E. P. "Time, Work-Discipline and Industrial Capitalism." *Past and Present* 38 (December 1967): 56–97.

Turner, Terry." Anthropology and Multiculturalism. What Is Anthropology That Multiculturalism Should Be Mindful of It? *Cultural Anthropology* 8, no. 4 (2008): 411–29.

Notes

1. This chapter is essentially a revised and summarized version of my "The Aftermath of a Rape Case: The Politics of Migrants' Unequal Incorporation in Neoliberal Times," first published in *Migration in the 21st Century: Political Economy and Ethnography,* ed. Pauline Gardiner Barber and Winnie Lem (New York, London: Routledge, 2012).

2. Edward W. Knappman, ed., *Great American Trials* (Detroit: Visible Ink Press, 1994).

3. Lisa M. Cuklanz, *Rape on Trial: How the Mass Media Construct Legal Reform and Social Change* (Philadelphia: University of Pennsylvania Press, 1996).

4. Helen Benedict, *Virgin or Vamp* (New York: Oxford University Press, 1992); Kristin Bumiller, "Fallen Angels: The Representation of Violence against Women in Legal Culture," *International Journal of Law* 18 (May 1990): 125–42.

5. For an analysis of the role of the media in covering the Big Dan's rape from the perspective of the Portuguese, see Onésimo T. Almeida, "Media-Made Events": Revising the Case of Big Dan's," in *Community, Culture and the Making of Identity: Portuguese-Americans along the Eastern Seaboard,* ed. Kimberly da Costa and Andrea Klimt (North Dartmouth, MA: Center for Portuguese Studies, University of Massachusetts Dartmouth, 2009), 247–64. For an analysis from the perspective of local feminists, see Liz Bennet, "New Bedford: Bigotry Misnamed," *Inside Aegis* 39 (1985): 10–16.

6. Onésimo Teotónio de Almeida of Brown University introduced me to the Portuguese in New England just after my arrival in southern Massachusetts. My colleagues Dona Huse and Penn Reeve of the Anthropology and Sociology Department and Fred Giffun of the History Department helped me to establish a Portuguese Oral History Project at the university. Subsequently, an invitation from Frank Sousa, then director of the Center for Portuguese Studies and Culture, to occupy the Hélio and Amélia Pedrosa Chair in spring term 2008 allowed me to update the research data that I had continued to gather over the years.

7. Linda Bash, Nina Glick-Schiller, and Christina Szanton, eds., *Nations Unbound: Transnational Projects, Postcolonial Predicaments, and Deterritorialized Nation-States* (Amsterdam: Gordon and Breach, 1994). Nina Glick-Schiller and Ayse Çaglar, "Beyond Methodological

Ethnicity and Towards the City Scale: An Alternative Approach to Local and Transnational Pathways of Migrant Incorporation," in *Rethinking Transnationalism: The Mesolinks of Organizations*, ed. Ludger Pries, 40–61 (New York: Routledge, 2008).

8. Terry Turner, "Anthropology and Multiculturalism. What Is Anthropology That Multiculturalism Should Be Mindful of It?," *Cultural Anthropology* 8, no. 4 (2008).

9. Étienne Balibar, *We, the People of Europe? Reflections on Transnational Citizenship* (Princeton, NJ: Princeton University Press, 2004), 23. Emphasis in the original.

10. Bash, Glick-Schiller, and Szanton, *Nations Unbound*.

11. Nina Glick-Schiller, "A Global Perspective on Transnational Migration: Theorizing Migration without Methodological Nationalism," in *Diaspora and Transnationalism: Concepts, Theories, and Methods*, ed. Rainer Bauböck, Thomas Faist, 109–30 (Amsterdam: University of Amsterdam/IMISCOE, 2010).

12. On the 1928 strike, see Daniel Georgianna and Roberta Aaronson, *The Strike of '28* (New Bedford, MA: Spinner Publications, 1993) and Georgianna's chapter in this volume.

13. In this regard, see Tony Goulart, ed., *Capelinhos: A Volcano of Synergies—Azorean Emigration to America* (San Jose: Portuguese Heritage Publications of California, 2008), especially Maria Gloria de Sá's chapter on "The Azorean Community on the East Coast."

14. Ellen I. Rosen, "Rape Trial in New Bedford. New Thoughts on an Old Problem," *Dissent* (Spring 1985): 210.

15. Estellie M. Smith, "Portuguese Enclaves: The Invisible Minority," in *Social and Cultural Identity: Problems of Persistence and Change*, ed. Thomas K. Fitzgerald (Athens: University of Georgia, 1974), 82.

16. Liz Bennet, "New Bedford: Bigotry Misnamed."

17. This polarization between gender and ethnicity was still strong at the time I arrived in New Bedford in 1997. Stephen Cabral, "Big Dan: A Bad Case of Victimization" (unpublished manuscript, 1985).

18. On the whitening of the Jews, see Karen Brodkin, *How Jews Became White Folks and What That Says about Race in America* (New Brunswick, NJ: Rutgers University Press, 1998).

19. Until 1975, the Portuguese community of New Bedford was composed of Azoreans, Madeirans, continental Portuguese, and Cape Verdeans. For a comprehensive analysis of issues related to race and ethnicity among Cape Verdeans, see Marilyn Haltern, *Between Race and Ethnicity: Cape Verdeans American Immigrants (1860–1965)* (Urbana: University of Illinois Press 1993).

20. Bela Feldman-Bianco, "Multiple Layers of Time and Space: The Construction of Class, Ethnicity and Nationalism among Portuguese Immigrants," *Annals of the New York Academy of Sciences*, 645 (1992): 145–74. Feldman-Bianco, "Brazilians in Portugal, Portuguese in Brazil: Cultural Constructions of Sameness and Difference," *Identities: Global Studies in Culture and Power* 8, no. 4 (December 2001): 607–50; Feldman-Bianco, "Remaking Locality: Uneven Globalization and Unequal incorporation of Transmigrants," in

Locating Migration: Migrants and Cities, ed. Nina Glick-Schiller and Ayse Çaglar (Ithaca, NY: Cornell University Press, 2011).

21. This analysis is based on E. P. Thompson's distinction between "natural time" and the "time-discipline of industrial capitalism" in "Time, Work-Discipline, and Industrial Capitalism," *Past and Present* 38 (December 1967): 56–97.

22. Feldman-Bianco, "Multiple Layers." Boaventura de Sousa Santos, "Modernidade, Identidade e a Cultura de Fronteira," *Revista Crítica de Ciências Sociais* 38 (1993): 11–42.

23. Dudley Clendinen, "Barroom Rape Shames Town of Proud Heritage," *New York Times*, March 17, 1983.

24. Rosen, "Rape Trial in New Bedford," 210.

25. Feldman-Bianco, "Multiple Layers."

26. Maria Gloria de Sá and D. Borges, "Context or Culture: Portuguese-Americans and Social Mobility," in *Community,* Culture *and the Makings of Identity: Portuguese-Americans Along the Eastern Seaboard,* edited by Kimberley Costa and Andrea Klimt (North Dartmouth, MA: Center for Portuguese Studies and Culture, University of Massachusetts Dartmouth, 2009).

27. Feldman-Bianco, "Multiple Layers."

28. On these changing Portuguese nationality laws, see Rui Manoel Moura Ramos, "Continuidade e Mudança no Direito de Nacionalidade em Portugal," *Revista de Informação Legislativa* 37, no. 145 (January–March 2000).

29. Feldman-Bianco, "Multiple Layers."

30. Miguel Moniz, "The Shadow Minority: An Ethnohistory of Portuguese and Lusophone Racial and Ethnic Identity in New England," in *Community, Culture and the Makings of Identity: Portuguese-Americans along the Eastern Seaboard,* ed. Kimberly da Costa Holton and Andrea Klimt (North Dartmouth, MA: Center for Portuguese Studies, University of Massachusetts Dartmouth, 2009).

31. Scott W. Lang, "State of the City Address," City of New Bedford, https://www.newbedford-ma.gov/, March 1, 2008.

32. Feldman-Bianco, "Remaking Locality."

33. Feldman-Bianco, "Remaking Locality."

34. Feldman-Bianco, "Remaking Locality."

35. See the Luso-American Foundation webpage https://www.flad.pt/sobre-a-flad/.

36. Feldman-Bianco, "Remaking Locality."

37. Feldman-Bianco, Remaking Locality"; Nina Glick-Schiller, "Locality, Globality and the Popularization of a Diasporic Consciousness: Learning from the Haitian Case," in *Geographies of the Haitian Diaspora*, ed. Regine Jackson, xxi–xxix (London: Routledge, 2011).

Contributors

CRISTIANA BASTOS

Cristiana Bastos (PhD, CUNY 1996) is an anthropologist and research professor at the Institute of Social Sciences, University of Lisbon. Her research addresses population dynamics, health and medicine, colonial biopolitics, transnational mobility, plantation societies, racialization processes, memory, and heritage. Since 2016 she has led the ERC-funded project The Colour of Labour: The Racialized Lives of Migrants (AdG 695573), with field and archival research in Guyana, Hawaii, New England, Angola, and elsewhere. She has been a visiting researcher at the University of Hawaii at Manoa, East West Center, and Harvard University and a visiting professor at Brown, UNICAMP, UERJ, UMass Dartmouth, and UMass Lowell.

BELA FELDMAN-BIANCO

Bela Feldman-Bianco, PhD in anthropology (Columbia) with postdoctoral studies in history (Yale), is a senior professor of anthropology at the State University of Campinas (UNICAMP) and a senior research fellow at the (Brazilian) National Council of Scientific and Technological Development. Among other distinctions, she was past president of the Brazilian Association of Anthropology (2011–12) and received the Gilberto Velho Academic Excellence Award (2017), the Roquete Pinto Award for her contributions to anthropology (ABA 2014), and the Zeferino Vaz Award for Academic Excellence (UNICAMP 2001). Her research and publications focus on issues related to culture and power with an emphasis on migration and displacements in comparative perspectives. She is currently a counselor at the (Brazilian) National Council on Immigration, where she represents the Society for the Advancement of Science (SBPC), and an elected member of the World Council of Anthropological Associations Board.

FILIPE LEAL DE FARIA

Filipe Leal de Faria was born in Lisbon, 1976; as an architect he has worked in Aveiro, Lyon, Paris, and Ryadh and is now settled in Lisbon. He is a founding member of the Urban Sketchers movement in Portugal. He draws to remain alert in the universes he inhabits.

ROSE RODRIGUES

Rose P. Rodrigues (PhD, New School for Social Research) is a professor of sociology in the Department of Sociology and Anthropology at Fairfield University. Her teaching focuses on intersectionality theory as it applies to law, criminal behavior, and social class. Her research has explored both historical and contemporary communities, alternative incarceration programs, and gender identity within the sports world. Her recent scholarship relies on geographical information systems for analyzing and visualizing social data. She is a founding member of the Women, Gender, and Sexuality Studies Program at Fairfield University and has served as chair of the Department of Sociology and Anthropology.

GRAÇA INDIAS CORDEIRO

Graça Índias Cordeiro (PhD, ISCTE, 1996) is professor of urban anthropology and ethnographic fieldwork at the ISCTE-University Institute of Lisbon and is affiliated with CIES-IUL. Author and coauthor of several national and international publications and visiting professor at universities in Catalonia, Brazil, and Massachusetts, she is involved with graduate education in the social sciences and urban studies, namely within the PhD Program of Urban Studies at FCSH-UNL and ISCTE-IUL. Lisbon has been her main field site, but currently she is carrying out ethnographic and historical research on Portuguese Azorean heritage in Greater Boston.

PAULA NOVERSA

Paula C. G. Noversa is a native of Fall River, Massachusetts, and a professor of history at the University of Massachusetts Dartmouth. Her areas of research include Luso-American diplomatic relations and Portuguese immigration to the United States. Her dissertation (University of New Hampshire, 2012), "Shifting Alliances and Fairweather Friends: Luso-American Relations, 1941–1951," analyzed the diplomatic relations between Portugal and the United States. This study asserted that Portuguese Prime Minister António Salazar permanently altered Portuguese-American relations in order to supplant the assurances found in the flagging Anglo-Portuguese alliance with a series of American initiatives—the European Recovery Program, the North Atlantic Treaty Organization, and the Mutual Defense Assistance Program. Noversa is the current director of the Center for Portuguese Studies and Culture, as well as the faculty director of the Ferreira-Mendes Portuguese American Archives at the University of Massachusetts Dartmouth.

PHILIP SILVIA

Philip Silvia, PhD, is emeritus professor of Bridgewater University. A lifelong resident of Fall River, he is a specialist in the city's social history.

DANIEL GEORGIANNA

Daniel Georgianna is chancellor professor emeritus in economics at the University of Massachusetts Dartmouth, where he taught for thirty-five years. He is the author of over thirty journal articles and chapters in books, over thirty-five monographs, and over 150 newspaper and magazine articles and has successfully completed over twenty government research grants. He is the coauthor with Roberta Aaronson of *The Strike of '28*, a book that focuses on the role of immigrants, especially from Portugal, in the strike. He is also the coauthor with his grandson Sebastian Georgianna of the article on Portuguese Americans in the *Encyclopedia of the American Left*, revised in press.

PENN REEVE

Penn Reeve is professor emeritus of sociology and anthropology at the University of Massachusetts Dartmouth. He specializes in social inequality, ethnicity, and labor issues and has conducted research in Brazil, the Azores, and the Alentejo, Portugal, and among Portuguese Americans in southeastern Massachusetts.

MIGUEL MONIZ

Miguel Moniz (Instituto de Ciências Sociais, Universidade de Lisboa) received the PhD in Anthropology from Brown University. His research and publications focus on mobilities of Portuguese-speaking migrants in North America examining racialization processes, ethnic group formation, labor practices, and civic associativism. Moniz scholarship has been supported by projects funded through the Fulbright Foundation, Fundação para a Ciência e Tecnologia (FCT), Fundação Luso Americana (FLAD), European Research Council (ERC), and the National Endowment for the Humanities, among other grant institutions. Additionally, he creates programs linking academic research to community social justice issues, including through the Migrant Communities Project, a 501(c)(3) non-profit where he is Executive Director. Working on the ERC *Colour of Labour* project (2016-2018) Moniz examined racialization processes through the law, unionization, associativism, and political community building.

NELSON H. VIEIRA

Nelson H. Vieira, emeritus professor of Portuguese and Brazilian studies and Judaic studies at Brown University, is American founding editor of the journal *Brasil/Brazil*, and former president of Latin American Jewish Studies Association (1995–2002). His current research focuses upon fiction by Brazilian Jewish voices as well as narratives by contemporary Brazilian authors. Among his major publications are *Contemporary Jewish Writing from Brazil* (ed. and trans., 2009); *The Prophet and Other Stories* by Samuel Rawet (intro. and trans., 1998); *Jewish Voices in Brazilian Literature: A Prophetic Discourse of Alterity* (1995); and *Brazil and Portugal: The Reciprocal Image* (1991).

CARMEN RAMOS VILLAR

Carmen Ramos Villar is a senior lecturer in Hispanic studies in the School of Languages and Cultures at the University of Sheffield. Her doctoral thesis (2004) examined the theme of emigration in Portuguese literature, concentrating on the works produced by writers from the Azores Islands and from the Azorean American community. Since then, her research interests have centered on Azorean and Portuguese American literature. She is currently looking at autobiographical writings and biographical studies of the Portuguese migrant community in the United States.

KADY PHELPS-EL MERNISSI

Kady Phelps is the development and communications manager at Bread & Roses Housing, Inc., in Lawrence, Massachusetts. She spearheads fundraising and communication efforts to create and preserve affordable housing opportunities for low-income families using a community land trust model. Kady's research emphasizes how immigration, gender, and social activism impact community structures. She coauthored exhibits such as Continuity and Change in the Mill City's Portuguese Community and Remembering St. Joseph's Hospital. Previously, she served as an advisor for immigrant youth in Lowell, Massachusetts, managing academic and support services for them. Kady earned a BA and MA in history from UMass Lowell.

CAMILO VIVEIROS

Camilo Viveiros is a labor educator at the UMass Dartmouth Labor Education Center conducting trainings on organizing, direct action, base building, and social movement strategy for grassroots efforts of students, workers, tenants, youth, immigrants, people of faith, LGBTQ+ groups, seniors, housing and welfare rights organizations, racial justice activists, and environmental justice activists. He uses history, theater, and the arts to educate people about social and labor movements. Viveiros facilitates community-based research, including participatory action research, and fosters intergenerational oral histories focused on gathering organizing lessons. Camilo grew up in a working-class immigrant family from the Azores, learning firsthand from an early age the need for immigrant, racial, and economic justice.

ONÉSIMO TEOTÓNIO ALMEIDA

Professor of Portuguese and Brazilian Studies at Brown University, Onésimo Teotónio Almeida holds a PhD in philosophy from Brown. He teaches Portuguese cultural and intellectual history, and he was department chair for twelve years. He also teaches in the Center for the Study of the Early Modern World, as well as a university course on values and worldviews for the Wayland Collegium, also at Brown. Author and editor of numerous books, his most recent was *O Século dos Prodígios. A Ciência no Portugal da Expansão*, the winner of four prizes. He was elected to the Academia da Marinha (Lisbon), to the Academia Internacional de Cultura Portuguesa (Lisbon), and to the Portuguese Academy of Sciences. He received honorary degrees from the University of Aveiro and Universidade Lusófona, Lisbon, Portugal.

FRANK SOUSA

Frank F. Sousa is Professor of Portuguese, Portuguese Program Coordinator, and Director of the Saab Center for Portuguese Studies at the University of Massachusetts Lowell. He is the author of the often-cited *O Segredo de Eça: ideologia e ambiguidade em A cidade e as serras.* From 2003 to 2013, he was general editor of the first 23 volumes in the Portuguese in the Americas Series, published by Tagus Press at UMass Dartmouth, which he founded. He has twice been a Fulbright Scholar at the National Library in Lisbon, Portugal. He is the supervisor of the Portuguese American Digital Archive at UMass Lowell, developed with consecutive $300K grant awards (2020, 2023) from the William M. Wood Foundation. At UMass Dartmouth, he proposed and led the efforts to establish the Summer Program in Portuguese (1994), the

Center for Portuguese Studies and Culture (1996), the Department of Portuguese (2000), the Hélio and Amélia/FLAD Visiting Professor in Portuguese Studies Endowment (2001), the Ferreira Mendes Portuguese-American Archives Endowment (2005), the Ferreira-Mendes Portuguese-American Archives in 2009, and the Portuguese American Digital Newspaper Collections (2009). He is a Comendador da Ordem do Infante D. Henrique, an honor bestowed upon him by the President of Portugal in 1997. He received the President's Public Service Award from the University of Massachusetts in 2000 and the Medalha de Mérito from the Government of the Autonomous Region of the Azores in 2010.

M. GLÓRIA DE SÁ

M. Glória de Sá is a retired sociologist who taught in the Department of Sociology and Anthropology at the University of Massachusetts Dartmouth, where she also was the faculty director of the Ferreira-Mendes Portuguese-American Archives and a member of the Center for Portuguese Studies and Culture. A Portuguese immigrant herself, she devoted most of her academic career to studying and writing about the process of socioeconomic adjustment of the Portuguese in the United States. She received a PhD in sociology from Brown University and has been involved with many Portuguese American organizations.

ANDREA KLIMT

Andrea Klimt is an anthropologist at the University of Massachusetts Dartmouth. Her research interests include the formation of class, identity, and community across the Portuguese diaspora, especially in Germany and southeastern New England. Most recently, she founded the Fall River Portraits project, which brings together students and Fall River residents in a collaborative effort to photograph the people and diverse neighborhoods of Fall River, Massachusetts.